D0475951

REAL FRENCH COOKING

REAL FRENCH COOKING

With a Selection of Outstanding Recipes from Other Countries

by

SAVARIN

Translated by E. M. HATT

FABER AND FABER LIMITED

24 Russell Square

London

A good cookery book is a worthwhile literary offering. It has the considerable advantage of being comprehensible to everybody, of flattering the readers' taste, of arousing in them an interest that is reborn two or three times daily. Is there any poem, any drama, any academic discourse that could ever merit such glowing praise?

HOFFMANN

First published in England in mcmlvi
by Faber and Faber Limited
24 Russell Square, London W.C.1
Printed in Great Britain by
William Clowes and Sons Limited
London and Beccles

First published as
LA VRAIE CUISINE FRANÇAISE

DEDICATION

To Maurice Saillant-Curnonsky,
Prince-elect of Gastronomes, without whom the pleasures of the palate would not be what they are.
To my Peers in the Principality of Gastronomy:
Dr. Edouard de Pomiane,
Prof. J. R. Roger,
Dr. Paul Ramain,
Dr. Bécart.
(with apologies for omitting some of these).
To my wife.
To Madeleine Decure, editor of the *Cuisine et Vins de France*.
And to all housewives who know how to make 'kitchen stove' and 'love' rhyme; and finally,
To the great chefs and the *cordons-bleus*, thanks to whom France is still the land of good living,
I respectfully dedicate this work.

SAVARIN

CHEVALIER DU TASTEVIN
COMMANDEUR DES CORDONS-BLEUS DE DIJON
COMPAGNON DU BEAUJOLAIS
CHEVALIER DE LA CHANTEPLEURE
CHEVALIER DES SACAVINS D'ANJOU
ECUYER DE LA CHAÎNE DES RÔTISSEURS
CHEVALIER DE L'ORDRE DE LA MÉDUSE
CHEVALIER DU CEP.

PRANDIAL PROVERBS

A ditherer at table is everywhere unstable.
Gascon proverb.

Your bidden guest is one whose well-being is your responsibility for every minute he spends under your roof-tree.
Brillat-Savarin.

Clever catering is not unlike love in requiring both tact and variety.
J. Berjane.

A man who has eaten liberally of garlic should confine himself, for several hours, to third-person observations.
Curnonsky.

Where the food's no good, there's no good medicine.
Dr. de Pomiane.

A fish may be born in water, but it surely must die in oil.
Provençal proverb.

CONTENTS

Contents

Preface

concerning simple cookery and Savarin

As a champion of simplicity in cookery, of the type of dish in which 'things taste of what they are', and of France's incomparable regional recipes, I am delighted to introduce this book of my young colleague and friend Savarin, who shares my view that in cookery, as in the arts, simplicity is the badge of perfection, and that from a fine dish an appreciative eater can derive as exalted a pleasure as that which a discriminating man of letters gleans from a La Fontaine fable or a passage of Voltaire.

Any man worth his salt writes well on a subject close to his heart and clear to his understanding. Almost from boyhood Savarin (the pseudonym has no mystery for those who know the Paris journalistic world) has been guided by the notions that France's cuisine is one of her noblest adornments and that France is the gastronome's heaven on earth. This book of his seems to me to have singular originality, with its skilful blending of tasteful anecdote and tasty meal. And to my mind there is no reason at all to suppose that a subtle gastronome must also be a first-rate cook. After all, one can worship great music without being anything of a performer. One can relish to the full the pleasures of eating without being a superb chef.

Gastronomy's masterpiece, a book unmatched elsewhere in the world, is the great Brillat-Savarin's *La Physiologie du Goût*, which gave a scientific basis to the cult of good eating. This work contains only a few recipes. Moreover, we know that these were contributed by his sister, 'la Belle Aurore'. Indeed, this is the work of a scholarly man, of an epicurean philosopher, rather than of a dab hand with the oven. For Brillat-Savarin, food and its preparation were just agreeable pretexts for learned discourses, for little stories and anecdotes in well-turned prose, for unexpected ruminations that are often profound.

It is only rarely that a gastronome of the first flight is also a good cook. Both Charles Robine and Gustave Pignot (who succeeded him as president of the Club des Purs Cent) illustrate this point, not to mention other members of the Académie des Gastronomes which will one day, I have no doubt of it, enrol the young Savarin.

Our author knows what is what at table. He makes a fair enough showing at oven or kitchen-range. He realizes that you do not invent a new dish by pouring fish soup over a sirloin nor yet by smothering a jugged hare in peppermint. He is aware that a superfine dish is the master achievement of many generations.

Savarin never tires of repeating Escoffier's precept—'Above all, no complications!' He has collected his recipes, which are accompanied by most apt quotations, from the famous chefs and from competent cooks here, there, and everywhere; from distinguished trenchermen and from unassuming provincial 'plain cooks'. All these recipes are simple, practical and workable, and have been adapted to the exigencies which the high cost of living upon this ever-less-habitable planet imposes on all of us.

But never mind this. As he himself says, 'It costs something to eat well. But health is priceless, and doctoring is even costlier.' By virtue of this alone, his book deserves to become every bride's Guide-book to Impeccable Cooking.

Sailland Curnonsky

Wherever in the civilized world men take their places at table with other aspirations than the mere satisfaction of hunger, the word 'France' is synonymous with 'perfection' in culinary matters. This universal respect for *la cuisine française* is respect for centuries of connoisseurship in cooking, eating and drinking; a connoisseurship blessed with every encouragement, so vast and varied are the country's regional riches which have, in the realms of gastronomy, served to transform the results of patient experiment into a kind of popular poetry.

And the culinary art (the good citizen Thomas, in his exordium to a *Manuel de la Friandise*—a 'Guide to Dainties', called it 'the first among the arts, since it nourishes mortal men')—this art, I say, old as the world and of which both Greeks and Romans were masters in their turn, has found in France more poets to sing its praises, more geniuses to formulate its laws, than in any nation of the modern world.

It is none too easy, is it, to enjoy your dinner in company with a person against whom you may be plotting, a person whose downfall would suit your book? For a true gourmet, it is next door to impossible. Not so many years ago we heard a good deal about 'guns instead of butter', so it is not too fanciful, if one accepts guns as a symbol of strife, to maintain that butter is a lubricant of peaceful relations, a liaison between civilized peoples. True gourmets sometimes go so far as to wonder whether an exchange at various levels of cooking lore might not offer as sure a means to union and world peace as any other. Often, indeed, it is a conviction with them. And it is obviously a notion having all the support of those who, in the Eastern as well as the Western world, urge the cooks and chefs of France (adding golden to verbal inducement) to go and cook for them; to create with loving devotion and flawless skill such dishes as those to which Lucullus was wont to invite himself, saying that such chefs d'œuvre were worthy of the formality.

Foreword

Monselet has staked ambitious claims for gastronomy. 'It makes,' he said, 'for beauty and wit; for holy meekness allied with dashing courage.' My own aphorisms maintain that 'To know how to eat is essential to knowing how to live', and 'To know *how* to cook is to love cooking'. But for all that, this book is not a recipe book only. That is why (except in the pastry-making instructions, which must either be precise or useless) I have not always given exact and minute specifications regarding weights and proportions of ingredients. In the first place, few housewives work with scales when adding salt, pepper, butter, and so on. They work by rule-of-thumb methods, by tasting, by intuitive assessment, and these seem to me the right ways. It seems logical to me (but readers may scent a paradox) that the first effort at a new dish (whether from this book or any other) should not be strictly successful. The housewife who is a truly imaginative cook adapts and rectifies, consulting her own and her family's tastes and those of frequent guests.

My second reason for an unusual approach is this: there are far too many recipes in the world. Especially in the highest levels of *cuisine*. A creamed sole à la *This* becomes a creamed sole à la *That* simply by virtue of the addition of a pinch of saffron; and the suppression of a nothing-at-all-of-nutmeg converts it into a creamed sole à la *Those*. The woman cooking for her family scorns such niceties. Her interest is to acquire a sound knowledge of how to cream soles; the trivial differences between one and another will be dictated by her mood, her means (saffron, nutmeg or anything else) and the occasion. I think most readers will agree.

Rather than compile thousands of recipes, I have tried to present a guide, an aide-mémoire. All among the verses and anecdotes are practical hints, and recipes in abundance—but the kinds of recipe, I hope, that will serve as a series of themes for enterprising cooks to vary and elaborate. 'Well, *that's* a thought,' I like to imagine them saying, 'I hadn't realized that a sole would go well with a sorrel purée. We'll try that, for a change.'

And change matters. Appetite is bred by variety as contempt is bred by familiarity, kitchen-lore thus resembling love. And the woman at home, mistress of many arts, must know that table-ties are powerful ones, perhaps, in the long run, the strongest of all. Good tables are indeed the centres of happy homes, the lure and the sustainer of loving hearts.

SAVARIN

Soups and Broths

The queen of soups is 'Leek and Potato'. Next come 'Watercress and Potato', 'Lettuce and Potato'—thin, semi-transparent, cleansing, inducing just sufficient thirst to enable one to follow on with unwatered wine. DR. BESANÇON

Soup is, to dinner, what a peristyle is to a building. GRIMOD DE LA REYNIERE

It is like the few handfuls of good soil cast on the surface to receive the sown seed. To soup you owe your first impression of being well looked after at table.

MARQUIS DE CUSSY

Soup is a habit—a truly French one. Creamy-textured, savoury of smell, soup is a comforter. It allays the most acute pangs of hunger, alleviates end-of-the-day weariness, and immediately after it has done its work it allows one to take a good long draught of wine, tonic and wholesome. Soup is one of the mainstays of the rural kitchen, being in itself alone a complete food; its composition has been empirically studied, and the time and care involved in its preparation have not been stinted.

Let us give honour where honour is due, and begin with that boiled-beef-and-carrots broth which is the base of so many soups: as it were, the national soup of France. Then let us go on to acknowledge that it is the Osmazome which makes good soups what they are.

Osmazome is the 'sapid' constituent of meat which is soluble in cold water, unlike the 'extractive' constituent which yields up its flavour only in boiling water. The moral is that if you are making a broth, it will be better if your meat is started in cold water; if the meat is put into boiling water it will retain its savour within itself at the expense of the broth or stock.

Meat Broth

Use silverside, shoulder, top-ribs, shin of beef or top-round (this last will be tougher meat). Put the meat into cold water and bring to boil on a fairly low flame. But before boiling point is reached, remove all the scum that rises to the top of the stew-pan. Do this skimming as thoroughly as you can. Now add salt (not before), carrots, turnips, parsnips, leeks, celery, parsley, a bay-leaf, a clove, a little garlic, a browned onion, pepper to taste. A good broth will require six to seven hours' cooking. It is served piping hot (after straining) poured over thin slices of toast.

A few potatoes may be added an hour before serving.

Meat being so dear, the nutritive value of broth with less meat may be enhanced by adding two or three bones (as well as the ritual marrowbone) and a piece of milt.

Veal broth is for invalids.

Auvergne Soup

Put into a braising pan some potatoes cut up finely, a handful of lentils, some onions, a clove of garlic, thyme, salt, pepper, and plenty of water. Cook slowly for two or three hours. Pass the soup through a vegetable masher and then return a little of the cooking stock to the paste to obtain a mellow texture. Add a knob of butter or dripping and serve with small fried bread cubes and a sprinkling of chervil (cut this with scissors).

'Berry' Soup

Of the Berry region. Same as preceding recipe but lentils to be replaced by dry white haricot beans.

Flanders Soup

Same procedure again, but beans (or lentils) replaced by celeriac (a quarter of the weight of the potatoes used) and concentrated tomato purée added.

Provence Soup

Begin in the same way but omitting lentils and the previous replacements, adding instead fresh tomatoes to equal the weight of potatoes. Before straining add some small white onions, previously parboiled. And instead of fried bread cubes serve slices of toasted bread rubbed over with garlic.

(*N.B.*—These four soups come to me from M. GUSTAVE PIGNOT, President of the 'Club des Purs-Cent'.)

Cabbage Soup

In your stew-pot: water, a white cabbage cut into four, potatoes, a pound of belly of pork, pickled, from which most of the salt has been soaked away. Put on lid, allow to simmer for an hour and a half, and the soup is ready. Add salt if necessary, and pepper. Mash the vegetables into the broth before serving.

N.B.—Obviously a simple little soup. Gourmets would include, with the belly of pork, some lean bacon and two savaloys (highly seasoned dry sausages), also carrots, onions, cloves, turnips, parsnips, and, in season, a handful of garden peas (or small green beans). It is also possible to pre-cook, or partly cook, the cabbage; especially if those with a poor digestion are to participate.

GARBURE is a cabbage soup enlivened with haricot beans previously softened by soaking.

ELTZEKARIA is a garbure to which small pieces of pumpkin have been added—also, if desired, a piece of rib beef with the fat. Needs three hours' cooking.

Onion Soup

Chop onion finely and brown in butter. Sprinkle flour over the fried onion and let the flour brown too. Moisten with water. Add salt, pepper, boil for twenty minutes. Pour over bread slices.

This is a 'democratic' onion soup, and here, in contrast, is a richer one. Instead of water, use meat stock or broth. Place in a soup tureen alternating layers of bread fried in butter (use stale bread) and of grated gruyère in generous quantity. Pour over the pile two small glasses of brandy, finally the soup over this.

Other variations:

(1) Add grated cheese and put tureen in oven for cheese to brown.

(2) Bind the soup, at the last moment, with two egg yolks and one teardrop of brandy.

(3) Replace brandy by a dash of vinegar.

(4) Use parmesan instead of gruyère.

(5) Use milk instead of either water or stock, but if you do so, leave out the cheese.

Sorrel Soup

Chop coarsely a good big handful of sorrel and put it to 'sweat' in a thick pan over a low flame. Add a nut of butter (more would be an improvement), and when butter and sorrel have melted together add two and a half pints of water, a little salt and pepper. If necessary thicken with an egg yolk, previously blended with some of the liquid, cold of course.

Leek and Potato Soup

Two walnuts of butter, six leeks diced, are cooked together until golden-brown. Two and a half pints of water are added (salted) and five or six potatoes cut up small. Cooked for one hour. Before serving, mash the potatoes into the liquid. Serve with fried bread pieces and a sprinkling of chervil.

Garlic Soup (Aigo Boulido)

Put two soupspoonsful of olive oil into a pan, add a few crushed cloves of garlic, salt, pepper, a bayleaf, one and three-quarter pints of water. Boil, with the lid on, for five minutes. Meanwhile put two egg yolks into a warmed tureen, and pour soup over these, stirring constantly and thoroughly. Add slices of bread (crust removed) that have been dried in a slow oven, and which have had egg *whites* spread over them.

Grated Bread Soup

To a pan of strained vegetable stock add enough grated bread crumbs to make a smooth paste. Stir in a gill or so of cream and one egg yolk just before serving.

Black Bread Soup

Cut thin slices of rye bread and brown them in butter in a saucepan. Add water, salt, pepper, grated nutmeg, a large onion stuck with a clove or two. Put lid on, simmer for an hour or more. Pass through sieve to obtain a flavoured bread purée. Put back over heat, and thin down with red or white wine. When boiling hot transfer to soup tureen in which an egg yolk, beaten into two tablespoonsful of thick cream, awaits it.

BECAUSE THEY GAVE A DISH THEIR NAME THEY ALL STAYED (OR BECAME!) FAMOUS

ROSSINI *was a composer: but he created Tournedos soup.*

SOUBISE *was a general: but he invented Soubise Soup.*

CONDE (*the Great Condé*) *was architect of many a victory: but he also gave his name to a soup.*

GRAMMONT (*Duke de*) *would be unknown if it were not for his Omelette à la Grammont.*

CHATEAUBRIAND, *from beyond the grave, is unforgettable because of his method of steak-preparation.*

STANISLAS LECZINSKI—*is that Square at Nancy named after him because he was the first to suggest the royal Pheasant à la Leczinski?*

THE DUBARRY *had a favourite—and it was certainly her turn to have one—a cauliflower soup.*

MELBA *was a singer who is applauded nowadays for her peach Melba.*

PARMENTIER *was an innovator—of potatoes, a certain soup, and a certain omelette.*

MARGUERY *was a restaurant-keeper and now he is a fillet of sole.*

REJANE *never played with more subtlety than when she presented her 'Oyster Medallion'.*

BRILLAT-SAVARIN *was of course bound to give his name to a poultry dish.*

AND *there are still* VORONOFF *soufflé eggs,* STRAWINSKI *Soup,* COLETTE *crayfish ragoût,* ANDRE THEURIET *mushrooms,* JOSEPHINE BAKER *flan . . . and a host of forgotten ones.*

Normandy Soup

Slice a quarter of a pound each of turnips, carrots and white part of leeks, put in a pan with an ounce of butter. Cook very gently, not allowing butter or vegetables to colour. Pour over these a bare pint of stock (or water with meat extract) and add a quarter of a pound of sliced potatoes. Cook gently and when almost ready to serve add two tablespoonsful of boiling milk, the same of thick cream, a walnut of butter and a pinch of chervil. Serve boiling hot (if you like, on oven-crisped bread, but not toast).

Broad Bean Soup

Shell new, tender broad beans. Place one pound of the beans in a pan with a little goose dripping. Cook gently for ten minutes. Add a gallon of water, a *bouquet garni*[1] and two good-sized slices of potted goose. Cook for two hours. The soup and some of the beans are served on dried sliced white bread, the rest of the beans with the goose meat.

Esterel Soup

Lightly fried, medium-sized onion (done in olive oil) with about a quart of stock (or water), half a pound of fresh (not dried) beans and the same quantity of diced pumpkin, all boiled together until beans are tender. Strain, add salt and pepper. Thin with some of the strained-away liquid, eking out, if necessary, with a little milk. Cook about an ounce and a half of coarse vermicelli in this final liquor.

Woodsman's Wife's Soup

Cook in three and a half pints water, three-quarters of a pound of fresh French beans (shelled), or, failing these, of haricot beans previously softened by soaking. Add a fair-sized carrot slit into quarters, an onion stuck with cloves, and a bouquet garni. Cook until beans are tender.

In a separate pan melt a quarter of a pound of fat bacon chopped in small pieces, and when it is transparent add less than a quarter of a pound of kohl-rabi, and the same amount of turnip and potato in thin slices. Cook together for five minutes, stirring with a wooden spoon over a good strong flame. Then place lid on pan, lower heat, allow to cook gently for twenty minutes longer. Now pour over these ingredients the water in which the beans, etc., were cooked. Add salt and white pepper.

Discard carrot, clove-stuck onion, and the herbs, drain the flavoured beans and add them to the soup. Now allow the soup to simmer for half an hour. Place slices of bread in a slow oven to turn golden-brown, cover these with a little grated cheese, replace in oven for cheese to brown as well, and pour soup over these just before serving.

[1] A bouquet garni is usually thyme, marjoram, parsley, bay-leaf, tied together.

Pelou Soup

Boil together the 'tops' of a bunch of radishes and five or six potatoes. Strain, then thin down with a little of the cooking liquor. Season with salt, pepper, nutmeg. Serve boiling hot over oven-toasted *buttered* bread thinly covered with garlic-sausage slices.

Arabic Soup (Cherbah)

Cut several onions into large pieces and par-cook these in olive oil. Add halved tomatoes, a handful of coarsely-chopped wild mint, some red pimentos, salt, pepper. When all are tender add a quart of stock and bind with an egg yolk.

It is permissible to add two or three cloves of garlic crushed in a mortar, and the juice of a lemon. Bread slices covered with grated cheese are floated in the soup.

Russian Soup (Bortsch)

The essentials: a large stew-pot, plenty of water, a lavish julienne of vegetables (carrots, turnips, cabbage and so on) and two pounds beef, cooked all together for three hours. Cooked beetroot, chopped up finely, is then added, and the soup is cooked for three more minutes. A tablespoonful of vinegar is the last addition. Each soup-plate receives a tablespoonful of thick cream before the soup is ladled in.

Smoked bacon may replace the beef, tomato may replace beetroot, as in the Ukraine—in this case with the merest dash of vinegar.

Egg Soup

To two and a half pints of cold water add several onions, chopped white portion of a few leeks, some crushed garlic cloves, fennel, thyme, pepper and salt. Boil for twenty minutes with lid on pan. Then add saffron (to taste) and a tablespoonful of olive oil. Continue cooking for five minutes. In this soup poach one egg for each person. Serve in deep plates, the poached eggs standing on slices of bread fried in olive oil, the soup poured over.

Wine Soup

'To *Chabrot*' (or *Chabrol*) is to pour a glass of (red) wine into one's plateful of boiling-hot soup. Perhaps it's not very inviting in appearance, but wine-in-broth is a powerful pick-me-up and an influenza chaser. CHAUDEAU is a light-weight veal and chicken soup to which a glass of wine (preferably a full-bodied white wine) has been added, together with egg yolks, cinnamon and other spices. It must be sweetened with sugar.

Here (according to Curnonsky) is KING ALPHONSE XII's WINE SOUP: broth, milk, wine lightly blended with two egg yolks, sugar, cinnamon, clove, nutmeg. Bread crusts may be added.

Fish Soups

There are many of these, but generally speaking they differ only in the kinds of fish included and the kinds available on the sea-coast concerned. The difference between Bouillabaisse and Cotriade is, in a sense, the difference between the Mediterranean and the Atlantic.

Bouillabaisse contains such fish as red gurnet, hog-fish, hake, weever, gilt-head, perch, dace, soles. Six and a half pounds of fish will serve eight. Add a score of mussels, a small lobster cut in portions, six onions cut in quarters, two crushed tomatoes, bay-leaf, lemon juice, zest of a dried orange, cloves, pepper and salt, parsley, saffron, a bare pint of white wine. (The fish must be cleaned and sliced, then covered with the wine first, followed by the same quantity of olive oil, topped with water.) These ingredients are boiled over a lively heat for forty minutes, then the fish is removed and the rest poured over slices of bread.

Loire Fish Soup. Demands two separate procedures. A 'fumet' or fish stock is made by boiling first and then simmering for some time, in a half-and-half mixture of water and dry Vouvray, the heads of these fish: roach, pike, carp, tench (or eel). In another vessel melt butter and olive oil and cook in them a mixture of chopped onion and white of leeks. Then add the fish 'bodies' cut into small pieces, the strained fish stock (discarding the heads) some potatoes, and cook together—with a few minutes' boiling for the fish that require it. Add salt and pepper, serve on slices of bread fried in olive oil.

Bordelaise Fish Soup (of Bordeaux). Put pieces of any fish you happen to have in a pan with a small glass of olive oil, four shallots, some garlic, thyme, bay-leaf, parsley, leek, chopped onion. Cover with dry Graves (for preference). Add salt and pepper and cook over a slow heat for half an hour. Serve on fried bread dice. It is allowable to add saffron and to bind with egg yolks and lemon juice.

Rochelaise Fish Soup (of La Rochelle). Cook over a good heat, in olive oil, a large onion and the white part of two leeks. Add four chopped tomatoes and two cloves of garlic. Add two quarts of water (at least), salt, pepper. When liquid boils throw in a bouquet garni and a couple of pounds of small fish (such as whiting, red gurnet, weevers, a few baby crabs, a dozen and a half mussels). Cook for twenty minutes, then pass through sieve, squeezing fish (but not too hard). Drop into this broth 12 oz of vermicelli, and 'poach' for twenty-five minutes.

Another Fish Soup (Henri Duvernois' recipe). Take whiting, dabs, soles, even soft roes, and remove the fillets of fish, leaving bones and heads to cook with water, white wine (court bouillon), carrots, onions, bouquet garni, peppercorns. When this has been cooking for an hour, pass through sieve and then poach the fish fillets in the liquor. Add some good consommé (clear soup) to reinforce, sieve again (using a fine mesh), bind with cream, and add finally a little saffron.

Baby-Crab Soup

Make a court bouillon (i.e. a wine-stock for boiling fish) of half water, half dry white wine, with thyme, bay-leaf, rosemary, garlic and cloves. Add baby crabs, tomatoes, cleaned mussels, various fish heads, and cook for two hours at least over gentle heat. Then force the mixture through a sieve, strain the liquor, blend, bind with egg yolks. Add the egg whites stiffly beaten, and serve on small toasted bread squares.

(Recipe supplied by the actor ROBERT MURZEAU)

Mussel Soup

Clean about two pints of mussels then 'open' them in water in a saucepan set over a low flame. Discard shells. In another pan containing two tablespoonsful of olive oil cook (for five minutes) two peeled tomatoes, two bruised cloves of garlic, adding (when cooked) pepper and salt to taste. Increase the mussel water to two and a half pints by adding boiling water. Pour into the second pan, boil contents for ten minutes. Then add the mussels, and serve with fried sippets.

Clam Soup

Open several dozen clams. Put the 'kernels' on their own in a pan and the beards, together with the liquid that will collect in aforementioned pan, into a fine strainer. Add to liquid thus collected three-quarters of a pint of plain water, boil for ten minutes, then poach the clams. Add a generous pint of cream, brought to boiling point, salt, pepper, nutmeg. Blend, remove from heat, stir in two ounces of good butter.

Variant: CLAM CHOWDER

Proceed as for clam soup. Then cut into small cubes half a pound of lean salt ham (unsmoked) and four ounces of onion. Boil these in a quart of good clear stock, adding twelve ounces diced potatoes, six ounces of tomatoes (skin removed), six ounces of green beans cut into lozenge shapes. When cooked, add the clams and a bouquet garni, boil again for twenty minutes, season, add cream and butter.

Oyster Soup

As clam soup, using oysters instead of clams.

Meat Soup Variants

Using the meat-stock or meat-broth (pot-au-feu) basis described on page 18 the following additions and variations, to your own choice, are possible:

(*a*) a few handfuls of rice (first washed in warm water). Cook for fifteen minutes;

(*b*) a few handfuls of vermicelli. Drop it in a 'shower', stirring soup all the time with a wooden spoon. Same cooking time. Skim before serving;

(*c*) various freshly-mixed 'paste' or dumpling shapes. Cooking time depends on their size and thickness;

(*d*) four tablespoonsful of semolina for every quart of soup;

(*e*) or, three of tapioca. In both cases 'rain down' the cereal into the soup, stirring constantly;

(*f*) a tablespoonful and a half of flour-based 'thickener' previously blended into a smooth paste with a little cold stock. Boil, while stirring, for two minutes.

Meatless Soups

Same elements as for above 'variants' but instead of meat stock use onion-water (onion browned in butter, with flour added, then water) or use milk. Such soups may later be either salted or sweetened with sugar, as you prefer.

Purée Soups

Cook (for example) half a pint of peas in enough cold water to cover them. When done (this takes about an hour and a half with dried peas) pound and sieve them, then add salt, pepper, and a nut of butter. Thin down in any way or to any extent that suits you, and serve piping hot on bread cubes fried in butter.

VARIATIONS:

Conti: from lentil purée.
Parmentier: from potato purée.
Condé: from red bean purée.
Savarin: from white bean purée.

These may also be made with milk instead of water, and will be much more velvety-textured, of course. It is especially desirable to use milk for a pumpkin-purée soup (which may have sugar rather than salt).

FAMOUS GOURMETS AND COOKS

APICIUS. *There were three Apiciuses, all equally gluttonous, but all equally discriminating as well. The one attribute excuses the other. The first has not proved memorable, but the second, having spent money like water, having also invented several cakes and stews mentioned in Pliny's writings, found that all he had left to live on was an income of a mere £250,000. Fearing that he could never live on such a sum, he poisoned himself.*

The third Apicius discovered a way of keeping oysters fresh and was able to send some in admirable condition to the Emperor Trajan who was campaigning against the Parthians many leagues away.

But this secret died with him.

BEAUVILLIERS. *At one time looked after all the food and drink worries of the Comte de Provence, then founded a restaurant (date not precisely known, but it lay between 1782 and 1786) at 26 Rue de Richelieu. In 1824 he issued his* Art of the Cook, *which had a brilliant reception. He had an exceptional memory and never forgot a client, not even the most casual birds of passage.*

LOUIS DE BECHAMEL *was a prosperous financier who became major-domo to Louis XIV. A courtier-cook dedicated to him the sauce known as 'Béchamel' which must, however, have existed in more or less the same form long before this episode. Or so we are bound to believe, for the Duc d'Escars exclaimed, 'He's a lucky chap, this Béchamel fellow. I myself was slicing up the white meat of yesterday's chicken and serving it with a thick cream sauce twenty years or more before he came into the world! And there it is, I've never had the joy of giving my name to even the most insignificant little sauce!'*

CAMBACERES. *He was Second Consul and subsequently Grand Chancellor during the Empire and kept the best table in France after that of Talleyrand. He said, one day, to Napoleon: 'How on earth can one make friends unless one can offer them choice dishes? Government is a matter of keeping a good table.'*

Julienne Soup

This is the prototype of all vegetable soups but is not by any means the simplest. The least complicated of vegetable soup recipes is the one compiled by Marcel Dorin, whose well-known restaurants are at Paris and Rouen. His advice is:

Put your vegetables (no matter which, but as far as possible those in season at the moment) into unsalted water, having cut them into tiny pieces. Cook them only as long as is necessary to have them just nicely done as the meal is about to begin. Pour into tureen and add cream or butter. Serve at once and have on the table a little salt-mill with coarse sea-salt so that each diner may take as much or as little as suits him.

Here, however, is a Julienne Soup for four people: Cut into small strips four ounces carrot, four ounces turnip, slightly less of leek (white part only) and of onions. Melt an ounce of fat in a saucepan, add vegetables, salt, pepper, and a lump of sugar. Cook gently without browning. While it is cooking chop up finely a small green cabbage heart, add to the pan, then pour in a bare quart of stock or of water reinforced with yeast extract or similar. Cook for an hour at least.

Take a lettuce heart, cut it across into thin ribbons, add a handful of sorrel and 'sweat' these in butter over a low heat. Add to cooked soup, together with four tablespoonsful each of garden peas and lozenge-cut runner beans cooked in salted water.

Taste and season. Pour into a tureen already containing plenty of stripped-off chervil leaf. Add an ounce of butter and three tablespoonsful of fresh cream.

N.B.—It is also permissible to strain away the liquid to obtain a vegetable purée which is served with fried bread cubes.

Spring Soup

Add to a little oil in your saucepan as many vegetables as you wish (or can find) chopped small, with skinned and quartered tomatoes, rounds of marrow or eggplant, green salad leaves, garlic, a bouquet garni. Add potatoes later, as they cook more rapidly. Use water, but if you have any, stock is preferable. A handful of rice. You may sieve this soup to make it more presentable, but maybe this robs it of some of its flavour.

Crecy Soup

Has a carrot base, and is so named because the carrot which is most suitable for its confection comes from Crecy-sur-Morin, county-town of the Meaux district.

A classic carrot purée has a rice base, which makes for smoothness. If you are in a hurry, use cream of rice.

Melt an ounce of butter in a saucepan. Add a large onion chopped finely, a pound and a half of young carrots, sliced, then salt, a little sugar, a bouquet garni. Set lid on pan and cook gently, stirring and shaking frequently. Pass through a hair-sieve. Dilute two ounces cream of rice with cold stock and when the sieved soup comes to boil again, add it, stirring all the time. Boil for five minutes, skimming from time to time. If the soup is too liquid add cooked rice or tapioca.

Villagers' Soup

Make a julienne of finely sliced leek white and cook gently in an ounce of butter for ten minutes. Add a quarter of a small but closely-leaved cabbage cut into tiny scraps, and cook for a further twenty minutes. Now put in half a pound of potato dice and a pint of water or stock. Ten minutes' cooking, and as it seethes you boil a couple of ounces of spaghetti in salted water. When done, stretch the spaghetti on a cotton or linen cloth and cut into pieces about an inch long. Put them in the soup with a pint of milk and a walnut of butter. Boil up once more, season, serve with a dish of grated cheese.

Minestra

Stew-pot, water, a julienne of vegetables, tomatoes. Cooking time: one hour. Add noodles or rice, not lavishly, salt and pepper. Before serving, put a few drops of olive oil in each plate.

Languedoc Julienne

An ordinary julienne, but (as is obvious from its name), olive oil is used instead of butter. Pea purée is added, and the cooking must be long and slow.

Mushroom Julienne

Another 'ordinary julienne' but half an hour before serving add prepared, sliced mushrooms.

Watercress Soup

Cut off bottom stems of a bunch of watercress and boil it with six or seven medium-sized potatoes. Ninety minutes' cooking. Pass through a fine strainer and bind with butter or cream in the soup-tureen.

Celery Soup

Blanch and then boil small pieces of celery, adding salt and nutmeg. Make into a purée and moisten with stock.

Herb Soup

Wash and chop coarsely the following herbs, etc.—sorrel, lettuce, chervil, purslane, borage, white beet, red beet, chives, one onion. Cook in a small quantity of water with salt and a little knob of butter. Mash all together when soft, cook for a few more minutes then add two beaten egg yolks.

Cucumber Soup

Remove skin and seeds of small cucumbers and slice them, put in a pan with a little salt to draw out the juice. Drain the cucumber slices then sauté them in butter, adding a handful of sorrel, some chervil, a little pepper. Pour in stock, or water, and boil for fifteen minutes. Bind it (if you wish, and can afford such a dish) with egg yolks.

Quick Soup (no buttering required)

Very good, though easy. Line your tureen with thin slices of bread and line these with finely chopped chervil in a thick layer. Add salt, pepper, three generous tablespoonsful of heated cream. Soak all this with boiling water.

Giblet Soup

To a pint of water add chicken giblets, a carrot, an onion stuck with a clove or two, a bouquet garni, a bay-leaf, two leeks. Cook for an hour and a half, then add chicken livers.

Cook separately a good half ounce of butter with a little less flour, blending them by constant stirring to a pale gold paste. When this is cooler, thin it down with the giblet liquid. Boil the lot for about twenty minutes, keeping it in motion with a whisk and skimming at the end of this.

Put the giblets (discarding legs and claws) into the serving tureen, with a dash of Madeira and a teaspoonful of chopped parsley. Over these pour the soup, boiling hot.

Creamed Soup

A 'white roux' (although strictly speaking a *roux* is a 'brown sauce') is the basis of most creamed soups. At the last moment they are improved with a little fresh cream. A roux may be taken to be a mixture of fat and flour cooked briefly or less briefly, according to the purpose for which it is required. Thick rich gravy soups are based on roux.

Cream of Lettuce Soup

Blanch a pound of lettuce in boiling water (salted) leaving it in for a few minutes, cooling it in cold water afterwards. Squeeze out liquid, chop coarsely. Make a white roux with butter and cream of rice (better than flour), adding a quart of milk or clear stock. Add lettuce, blend all together, cook very gently for an hour. Every now and then scoop off the 'skin' that will form on the surface. Strain, add cream on serving.

Cream of Asparagus Soup

Same as cream of lettuce, but using asparagus tips instead of lettuce.

Cream of Salsify Soup

Same procedure. The cooked salsify must be mashed (it has been cut up before cooking) and tapioca or pearl barley may be added.

Andalusian Creamed Soup

Take onions, tomatoes, thyme, a stick of celery, salt, a little sugar. Boil in stock for two hours, then strain. Thicken with a roux (as for giblet soup), serve, having added two skinned, sliced, grilled sweet peppers.

Oran Creamed Soup

Cook half a pound sliced onions and four ounces white of leek in butter. Add three pounds chick peas (soaked previously for twenty-four hours in cold water) three quarters of a pound of lean bacon, one ounce of roasted groundnuts, five pints of water. Cook for three hours then remove the bacon and 'tammy' the remainder before putting back over the heat. Put in eight ounces of butter. Chop the bacon you removed into dice and add to the soup in the tureen. Serve with slices of dry toast.

(These two recipes come from M. LEON ISNARD, author of *African Gastronomy*.)

Cauliflower Velouté

In well-salted water place a whole small cauliflower weighing about a pound, and let it cook until tender. Make a roux, using something less than a pint of the cauliflower cooking water, while still hot. Season the roux with salt and pepper. Bring to boil over a good heat, stirring constantly to prevent curdling. During the subsequent half hour of cooking, skim off the 'skin' from time to time. If necessary, bind with egg yolks. The cauliflower may be used as a separate vegetable.

Crayfish Bisque

Brown lightly in butter a mirepoix of half a carrot, half an onion, some parsley, thyme and a bay-leaf. Add four or five (according to size) cleaned crayfish for each person and cook the whole in the butter over a good steady heat, with a moistening of Cognac that has been 'flamed', of white wine and of concentrated fish stock. Salt and pepper to taste. Cover and simmer for ten minutes at least.

Boil in a separate pan four ounces rice. Remove the crayfish husks, keeping tails separate and draining the rest of liquid. Pound the crayfish bits and the mirepoix, add the cooked rice, sift the whole. Thin down if necessary with stock, and at moment of serving add cream, butter and a dash of Cognac. The crayfish tails may be served separately or added in tiny cubes to the bisque.

Shrimp Bisque

Same procedure. About one and a half pounds shrimps to three pints of soup.

DO NOT FORGET . . .

- An intelligent housewife turns all her scraps to good use. For instance, her soups and broths will be all the better if she adds the leg of mutton bone, or other bones, and trimmed-off meat bits.

- She will also use up left-over vegetables. A cupful of cooked noodles, a few cooked beans or fried potatoes, sieved or pounded together, will give creaminess to soups and good, if unforeseen, flavours which will please the family by introducing variety.

- One common-or-garden tomato, a sprig or two of parsley, a stem of fennel, a dash of spice, will make the customary vegetable soup a little more piquant, stimulate appetite, come as a pleasant surprise, and give an impression of 'something different' at small trouble.

- Good cooking, they say, costs a lot of money; and that is true. But even the simplest food may be much improved at slight cost if the cook uses imagination and 'shows willing'. This applies not only to soup-making, and we shall revert to the notion more than once in the course of this little book, which aims at being the skilful housewife's *vade-mecum.*

Hors d'œuvres

Hors d'œuvre, in all their variety, are extremely useful. Besides being decorative in themselves they keep your guests happily employed until the main dishes come to table. They 'titivate' the palate, whence their designations as 'amusettes' or 'amuse-gueules'. Moreover, it cannot be gainsaid that while passing themselves off merely as appetizers, they are actually quite satisfying, and permit the housewife to save a few shillings on the meat bill.

Hors d'œuvre fall into three classes:

(1) Simple hors d'œuvre.

(2) Various pork-based hors d'œuvre.

(3) Hors d'œuvre that require cooking processes.

SIMPLE HORS D'ŒUVRE

Radishes: You need only the tiniest scrap of leaf, and keep the rest of it for soup (see page 23, Pelou Soup).

Black (Spanish) Radish: Must be sprinkled with salt and left to 'sweat'.

Horseradish: Grated, then sprinkled with vinegar.

Cucumber: Also 'sweated' with a sprinkling of salt.

Tomatoes.

Celery: Dressed with a sharp (remoulade) sauce, or in small sticks.

Artichokes: In vinegar. Or, better, just the artichoke bottoms alone.

Olives: Black or green. If green, keep the round ones for kitchen use and use the elongated ones for hors d'œuvre.

Mushrooms: Cooked whole. Choose the very smallest you can find and dress with olive oil.

Sardines, Tunny, Mackerel, Potted Anchovies.

Hard-boiled Eggs.

Potatoes, Green (or even Haricot) Beans, Lentils: All as salad.

Caviar, Cavial (salmon-caviar), Shrimps, Cockles and Mussels: All with a vinegar sauce.

And so forth. It goes almost without saying that the more you vary your selection of hors d'œuvre, the better your meal will be at its opening stages, the more successfully will appetite be stimulated, and the more easily will it be gratified . . . since it is usual to eat plenty of bread with hors d'œuvre.

HORS D'ŒUVRE OF PORK BASE

These are numerous, and it is correct practice to serve many of them either as hors d'œuvre or as principal dish. We should be deeply aware of our obligation to the pig, monarch among animals, for such delicacies. As Charles Monselet informed him in a well-known sonnet, he is:

> '*All solid worth, flesh, fat, outside and in,*
> *Splendid as brawn, superb in sausage-skin,*
> *Whose trotter, sanctified in kitchen lore,*
> *Fragrant with earthy tang of Périgord,*
> *Might well have re-established harmony*
> Chez *Socrates and shrewish Xantippe.*
> *Whose loin, with sportive gherkin dressed, affords*
> *The favourite noonday feast at humble boards.*'
> . . . and so forth.

We shall confine ourselves to a list, by no means complete, of geographically or regionally arranged specialities, taking a little trip from one dressed-pork dish to another. Here is our:

French Tour . . . From Pork Speciality to Pork Speciality

ALSACE	Choucroûte de Strasbourg.	Sauerkraut (pickled cabbage).
ANJOU	Rilloux de Segré, fressure de Cholet, lard de Baugé.	Remember that rillettes are a kind of potted minced pork. Fressure is the 'pluck' and lard is bacon 'flare' or 'fleed'.
ARDENNES	Boudin blanc de Rethel.	Or white pudding.
ARTOIS	Andouillettes d'Arras.	Andouillettes are small sausages of chitterlings base.
AUVERGNE	Andouillette de la Franchette, jambon à l'Auvergnate.	Regional 'ham' treatments are many and various. The 'Charcuterie' family comprises all the known ways of serving pig meat.
BEARN	Jambon de Bayonne.	
BERRY	Charcuterie de Châteauroux.	
BOURBONNAIS	Andouillettes de Moulins.	
BOURGOGNE	Sauçisson fumé de Dijon, chaud de Mâcon, jambon d'Autun.	Smoked sausage (of the large dry kind) Chaud is 'spiced heavily'.

BRETAGNE	Pâté de Courrée, andouillettes d'Auray, jambon de Morlaix.	Pâté is a pie or pasty.
CHAMPAGNE	Pieds de porc de Sainte-Ménéhould, andouillettes de Troyes.	The 'Sainte-Ménéhould' is the best-known trotter treatment (the one referred to in Monselet's verse).
CORSE	Lelonzo, la copa, le prisuto, les figatellis.	Note the 'local' flavour of names which are not translatable.
DAUPHINE	les fricassés.	
FLANDRE	Tripes et andouillettes de Cambrai.	
FRANCHE-COMTE	Jambon de Luxeuil.	
GASCOGNE	Saucisses de Masseube, jambon des Landes, cambajou et confit.	Confit—found in many regional designations of 'potted' or otherwise preserved foods.
GUYENNE	Jambons de Tonneins.	
LANGUEDOC	Foie de porc salé d'Albi, saucisson de Limoux.	Salted liver, and another sliceable sausage.
LIMOUSIN	Clafondis d'Ussel.	Clafondis—not to be confused with the sweet 'Clafoutis', see p. 312.
LYONNAIS	Saucisson de Lyon, andouille de Roanne, grattons et chines.	Grattons, Chines.—See note above, on local names.
MAINE	Andouillettes de Gorron, rillettes du Mans, charcuterie de Laval.	
NIVERNAIS	Saupiquet du Morvan, porcs de Château-Chinon	Saupiquet—*see* p. 236.
NORMANDIE	Andouillettes de Rouen, courraye de Valogne, andouille de Vire.	Andouille—Chitterlings.
ORLEANAIS	Rillons du Blésois, andouillettes de Vendôme et d'Orleans.	Rillons—'greaves', shins.

A FEW FAMOUS GOURMETS AND CHEFS

PARMENTIER. *This pharmacist attached to the Army was a prisoner in Germany, and from that country he brought back to France a few potato tubers, trying thereafter to popularize the vegetable. He wrote a great number of books dealing with nutrition and has given his name to a variety of dishes having potatoes as one of the ingredients . . . soup, omelette, fowl, tournedos, etc.*

MONSELET. 1825–88. *Charles Monselet was a writer of light verse, a witty author and an eminent gastronome. He is known especially for his* Gourmand's Almanac, *his* Letters of a Gourmand *and his* Poetic-Cook. *He too lent his name to quite a number of dishes, especially those including artichoke bottoms and truffles, of which he was passionately fond.*

VATEL. *He was in the service of M. le Prince before he became Fouquet's major-domo. As we all know, and as one of Madame de Sévigné's letters testifies, he killed himself because one morning the fresh-caught sea-fish failed to arrive. The fraternity of great chefs does not acknowledge him as being one of themselves, since it is part of a chef's business to be able to improvise. An epicurean poet, Berchoux, has devoted this couplet to him:*

'All you who cope with banquet or collation
Spare him a tear . . . but please, no emulation.'

TALLEYRAND. 1754–1838. *No details needed concerning this statesman with his niche in history. But he was also a gourmet and a remarkable host. A diplomat, as he was about to take his leave for the Congress of Vienna, he said to King Louis XVIII: 'Sire, I need saucepans far more urgently than I need written instructions'. Carême was his chef during the Second Empire.*

ROUERGUE	Saucisses et jambons fumés.	
SAVOIE	Saucissons chauds du Bugey.	
TOURAINE	Rillettes de Tours	
VIVARAIS	Jambonnets de Saint-Agrève, charcuterie de Vals.	Jambonnets—*see* note on 'Hams' on p. 35.

(The above list has been taken from that first-rate little book *Vieux Pots, Saulces et Rosts Mémorables*, by Charles Gay (winner of Prosper Montagné[1] prize for 1951).

COOKED HORS D'ŒUVRE

Quiche Lorraine

Add a little salt and pepper to seven gills, or a little under a quart, of milk that has just reached boiling point. Break sixteen eggs into an earthenware dish and add the 'boiling' milk, beating vigorously all the time. You will already have lined a pie-dish with short pastry (the making of which is described on p. 308), and have spread over the pastry lining first a layer of fine breadcrumbs and on top of that, a layer of fat bacon, ham and garlic sausage all chopped into very small pieces. Pour over this the egg and milk mixture and place the quiche in a moderately hot oven for a quarter of an hour.

N.B.—The 'Quiche Tourangelle' (that is to say, of the Touraine persuasion) requires a bed of 'rillettes et de rillons désossés' on the dough lining, and a sprinkling of fresh chopped parsley.

Pies and Savoury Tarts

(*a*) ONION PIE . . . known as PISSALLADIERE PIE.
(*b*) RUSTIC PIE . . . known as DE CAMPAGNE.
(*c*) VOSGES PIE . . . or VOSGIENNE.
(*d*) LORRAINE PIE.
(*e*) CEVENNES PIE . . . or CEVENOLE.
It is important to use the specified crust in each case.

(*a*) ONION PIE (called 'PISSALLADIERE'). Prepare a yeast dough, described on p. 309. It is the type of dough used for milk-bread. Brown lightly in olive oil, over low heat, some finely minced onion. When

[1] The Prosper Montagné Club holds periodical meetings at which chefs prepare a given dish, or dress a given food item, each in his own original fashion. Distinguished judges assess the merits of finalists' creations, and the Prosper Montagné prize goes to the best. Montagné was a literary man and a gourmet of acknowledged pre-eminence who flourished between the two World Wars, and the club bearing his name was founded in his memory. He was chef of the Grand Hotel, Monte Carlo, and author of *Le Grand Livre de Cuisine* and *Le Larousse Gastronomique*.

cold, add finely chopped anchovies. With this mixture fill your pie case, in its dish, dot over with a few black olives, and bake in a brisk oven.

(*b*) Rustic Pie. Flaky pastry this time. Spread upon it a good mixture of well-chopped meat left-overs, whatever you may have by you, with sausage meat, shallots and parsley. If necessary, bind with egg. Add a glass of brandy. Put on a top crust and cook in a moderate oven.

(*c*) Vosges Pie. Use either short or flaky pastry. Spread over it pieces of pork chine that have been put to marinade the previous day in Madeira and Cognac, together with onions, shallots, parsley, salt, pepper and grated nutmeg. Fill the pie-dish and when you put on the top crust, leave a small hole about half an inch in diameter. Brush over with egg yolk and bake in a moderate oven.

A few minutes before pie is completely cooked, use a funnel to pour through the central hole in the piecrust two eggs beaten into a tablespoonful of cream.

(*d*) Lorraine Pie. Same general scheme as for previous recipe, but add veal to the pork in the marinade. And ten minutes before completion of cooking, pour through the central hole, using funnel as before, the remainder of the marinade combined with cream and one egg.

(*e*) Cevennes Pie. The pastry is made from half a pound of flour to a quarter pound of butter and two eggs. The filling consists of:

one-third chopped raw pork,
one-third rennet (dessert) apples,
one-third chestnuts boiled in water,
with one raw egg, salt and pepper to your liking.

Cover with pastry, seal edges very firmly, and bake for up to forty minutes in a moderate oven.

Vol-au-vent

If you make your own vol-au-vent, bear in mind that the pastry must be a light flaky pastry (see p. 308), but it is possible to buy unfilled vol-au-vent cases at pastrycooks' shops. For the filling you have the following choices: poultry in white sauce (blanquette), fish in Béchamel, veal scallops cut into cubes, forcemeat balls (quenelles) and mushrooms, the brains and sweetbread of lamb or, less suitably, of veal, crayfish tails (à l'Américaine), oysters poached in white wine, chicken or other poultry liver, or poultry left-overs.

It is also possible to fill with spaghetti cut into short lengths and blended with tomato sauce and diced Parma ham.

Cheese Tartlets

Enough short pastry for a dozen tartlets, using a bare half-pound each of flour and butter, with one egg yolk. Make a well in centre of flour pile, add the butter, egg yolk and a very little water. Mix the dough thoroughly and leave in a cool spot for twenty minutes. Roll it out eight times without using too much pressure.

Reduce half a pound of cream cheese (milk curds) to a smooth purée. Separately beat two whole eggs stiffly, mix with the cheese purée, adding two tablespoonsful of fresh cream, and a little salt, pepper, and grated nutmeg. Fill tartlets with mixture and cook in a moderate oven.

Brain Loaf

Calves' or pigs' brains, cleaned carefully and cooked in a court bouillon (that is, a wine-and-spice-flavoured stock), are reduced to a gruel-like consistency. Then two tablespoonsful of cream, some chopped parsley, and three egg-yolks are stirred in and blended thoroughly. The three egg-whites are whipped to a stiff snow in a separate vessel and added to the mixture last of all. This is then put at once into a well-buttered mould and cooked for an hour and a quarter in a bain-marie.

Tomato sauce makes a good accompaniment.

Summer Garden

You will need one tomato for each person. Choose large and evenly matched tomatoes, slice off a 'lid' from each, remove contents with a spoon.

Cut some hard-boiled eggs (half as many eggs as tomatoes) in two lengthwise, and take out the yellow. Use these yolks with soft bread-crumbs soaked in milk, chopped chervil, chopped black olives, to make a forcemeat. Stuff the hollows of the egg-whites with this.

Either buy or prepare a macédoine (medley) of vegetables and add to it some diminutive dice of Bayonne ham, also some peeled shrimps. Fill the tomatoes with this and place one of the stuffed egg pieces on each filled tomato (the tomato 'lids' will not be needed).

Chop into long ribbons the leaves of a very fresh, crisp lettuce and the flesh of a few green peppers. Form these into a kind of nest, and put the tomatoes on top. Garnish each with a criss-cross pattern of anchovy strips.

Good Housewife's Savoury Cake

Whatever the nature of the leftovers of meat, it is a good idea to see the last of them in the following simple and inexpensive fashion.

Cut all the pieces into very small scraps, adding sausage meat in the proportion which the 'dryness' or otherwise of the rest of the meat dictates. Soak some soft bread in milk and mix it into as much chopped shallot, onion, parsley, chervil as you like, omitting any ingredient which you prefer not to use. Use salt and pepper liberally if possible, combine one egg-yolk. Put the paste into a greased mould and bake in the oven. This is to be eaten cold, with gherkins, or served hot with a garlic-flavoured tomato sauce.

AND DO NOT FORGET . . .

- That your potato salad will be better if you add seasoning while the potatoes are still hot, and use white wine rather than vinegar.
- That some people (and they're not far wrong) like their sausage (i.e. luncheon sausages) cut in thick slices. So don't slice it up before serving. I speak here of the 'large, dry' types of sausage of the cut-and-come-again variety (Lyon sausage, peasant speciality sausages). Salami and the Arles regional-speciality sausages are better cut in thin slices.
- That raw salads and raw vegetables may be seasoned and dressed with either cream or vinegar, refreshing to the palate. Grated raw carrots or chopped radishes thus treated are both palatable and digestible.
- That the butter should be served in little 'shells' and pats only if you are hoping to encourage people to eat less of it. If not, don't hesitate to place a bowl full of butter on the table.
- That not everybody cares for olive oil, but that it is highly digestible, nutritive and well flavoured. So try to adopt it.
- That the meat left in the stockpot, diced and added to a salad, furnishes an excellent hors d'œuvre item if you are lavish with spices, parsley, shallot and similar flavour-imparters. And failing an ounce of fresh cream, add a little melted butter.
- That with herring fillets you may serve plain boiled potatoes—piping hot, of course.
- That if you have some potato purée left over, you can make some small croquettes, brown them nicely, and serve with a vinegarless tomato salad.

Eggs

Eggs are a complete food; an egg gives you eighty calories (sixty-two supplied from the yolk alone). It is rich in albumen, contains iron, calcium, phosphorus, fat, a little sugar, and several of the vitamins. But it should be borne in mind that it may also cause certain toxic conditions, which Dr. Pomiane classifies thus:

(1) An egg, even quite a fresh one, may be infected with pathogenic organisms if, during its formation inside the hen, the white or the yolk (as yet unprotected by shell) should be polluted by paratyphoidal bacteria. This is a comparatively rare occurrence and is most often associated with ducks' eggs.
Moral: Avoid boiled ducks' eggs.

(2) An egg laid some time before use may develop certain anaerobic bacteria (not dangerous in small numbers) which could produce toxins.
Moral: Eat only fresh eggs.

(3) Some people with liver disorders cannot digest eggs.
Moral: They should eschew them.

(4) There are folk who have an allergy to eggs, just as others are allergic to strawberries, shellfish, or other fish, which may bring them out in a rash. Egg allergy, known as 'egg anaphylaxis', is rare.
Moral: Consult your doctor.

I do not recommend the use of preserved eggs. It may, however, be useful to bear in mind that French regulations insist, at present, on the following markings:

(*a*) 'CONSERVÉ' on liquid preserved eggs, also on their packing label. The letters of egg-markings to be at least 2 mm deep.

(*b*) Refrigerated eggs to have word 'RÉFRIGÉRÉ' in the same way, same size.

(*c*) Stabilized eggs to have word 'STABILISÉ'.

(*a*), (*b*) and (*c*) may be replaced by (respectively) a circle, a triangle, a diamond-shape, each one centimetre at least in height or diameter.

The English egg markings,[1] at the time of going to press, are as follows (as will be seen, mainly a classification by weight):

[1] Eggs (Amendment No 4) Order, 1953, coming into operation 31/1/54.

1. 'First-Quality'

(*a*) Eggs not less than $2\frac{3}{16}$ oz=LARGE (a) (*b*) Eggs less than above, but not less than $1\frac{7}{8}$ oz=STANDARD (a) (*c*) Eggs less than above, but not less than $1\frac{5}{8}$ oz=MEDIUM (a) (*d*) Eggs less than above, but not less than $1\frac{1}{2}$ oz=SMALL (a) (*e*) Eggs less than $1\frac{1}{2}$ oz=EXTRA SMALL	All such marks in a circle of not less than $\frac{1}{2}$ in. diameter. Letters to be not less than $\frac{1}{16}$in. high.

2. 'Second-Quality' (but subject to stringent requirements as to translucency of white, freedom from rot, mould, blood-ring, etc.) any weight=(a) SECOND.

(a) in each case is replaced by licensed packer's specified registration number.

Omelettes

These must have three qualities above all others: they must be of melting consistency; piping hot; and golden-brown. The secret of how to make a good omelette is confided by Dr. Bécart of the Academy of Gastronomes:

'One of the essentials of success is the employment of a really good pan—that means a thick one with a really flat and level base, not dented, not concave, not convex: this is so that the butter shall flow evenly and prevent the omelette from sticking, when it's just about cooked through, to the raised portions of pan from which the melted butter has slipped away.

If it can be done, purchase your pan from a restaurant supplier, a specialist in such things. And if it costs a little more than a chain-store pan, it will, on the other hand, last you a lifetime if you look after it properly. This entails:

(*a*) using it for omelettes only,
(*b*) never washing it.

It is quite enough to rub it round, while still hot, with crumpled paper. You could, if necessary, use a little coarse salt to remove any egg adhering to the surface; then grease the pan to avoid rusting or other deterioration and wrap it in a sheet of paper.

As a general rule, do not attempt an omelette of more than three or four eggs. Buy your pan with this in mind. It is easier to make two omelettes of three eggs each than one omelette containing six. For a three-egg one take half an ounce to three-quarters of an ounce butter (no need to be over-parsimonious with it, however), a small pinch of refined salt, a pinch of freshly ground pepper. Put butter in pan on electric hot-plate, or whatever you use (electricity is better than gas in this case because the heat is more evenly spread), and let heat be lively to melt butter. When it is smoking just faintly, pour in the eggs, lightly beaten only that very moment, and seasoned at the last second before turning into pan. Allow mixture to set but only just. And now . . . you must watch carefully. Move the egg slowly, using a steel fork and drawing it from one side of the pan to the other—rather as if you were scrambling the eggs, but much less vigorously. This is to ensure uniform setting of the mass, a homogeneous texture and a mellow blending.

Turn over without respite, and when the mixture is solidifying to desired consistency, deliquescent and nicely moist to suit your own inclination, draw the pan away from the hottest area and slip your fork under the edges of the omelette all round. Now shake the pan to detach the rest of it.

The next stage is the folding. If we simply fold in halves the runny, bubbling part will escape. It is a good wrinkle to fold as you would a table-napkin, thus sealing in the liquid. With your fork fold in a quarter of the omelette farthest away from the handle, then fold over a half of the side nearest to the handle. This closes it and you leave it on the side of the hot-plate, and just before taking it to table gloss over its surface with a little butter.'

Thank you, DR. BECART.

You can make your omelettes:

— quite plain, eggs and seasoning only
— with herbs (chopped parsley, chives, spring onions)
— with mushrooms (previously cooked gently in butter for a few minutes)
— with morels (sauté in butter in frying-pan, together with chopped shallot)
— with truffles (in thin flakes)
— with cheese (parmesan or grated gruyère)
— with bread (an egg-sized piece of the middle of a loaf soaked in milk and stirred in with beaten eggs)
— with kidney (veal, beef or mutton, previously cooked and diced. You may use kidney fat to replace butter)
— with macaroni (cut small and cooked of course. Add grated cheese)
— with bacon, ham or chipolatas
— with onion (previously fried in butter)
— with asparagus tips
— Italian style, that is, stuffed with a paste consisting of pounded garlic cloves (cooked in water), two anchovies, capers, olive oil to soften. Add tomato sauce.

FAMOUS COOKS AND GOURMETS

CAREME *was born in Paris on the 8th June 1774 and died on 12th July 1833.*

He was one of twenty-five children. His first job was in a humble eating-house, then he became kitchen-boy in a small restaurant: next, a pastry-cook at Bailly's, rue Vivienne, then a fashionable establishment; and in the course of time was appointed chef to Talleyrand, staying twelve years with him. François-Antoine Carême (he signed himself Antoine Carême) published the following:

The French Major-Domo
The Royal Pastry-cook of Paris
The Parisian Chef
The Culinary Art in the XIXth Century
The Picturesque Pastrycook.

These works are still held to be masterpieces of exposition of cooking on a grand scale.

GRIMOD DE LA REYNIERE (1758–1838) *was a barrister, but being the grandson of a pork-butcher he abandoned the law for gastronomy and wrote a* Handbook for Hosts, *then a series of* Gourmands' year-books *that sparkle with wit.*

LA VARENNE *was a cook to the sister of Henry IV. The latter used him as go-between in his love affairs, whereupon his employer said to Varenne: 'You have earned yourself as much credit, as carrier of my brother's chickens,*[1] *as you have as baster of mine'. He was, however, a superb chef, and wrote some of the best of the early culinary treatises—such as* The French Pastrycook, The French Cook, *and* Stewmakers' School.

LAGUIPIERE. *Died in 1812. He was an outstanding inventor of sauces, and, according to his pupil, Varenne, he put all his genius into his sauces. He accompanied Murat to Naples and even to Russia, where he died during the Retreat from Moscow. Unfortunately, Laguipière left no published work.*

[1] A 'chicken' (poulet) means also a witty or amorous letter to one's love of the moment.

— with cream: adding a dessertspoonful for each egg before beating.
— with tomato, using half a pound of tomatoes to three ounces of onions, with chopped garlic, tarragon, parsley, basil all cooked in olive oil and added at first stage of cooking
— with shellfish (oysters, mussels, cockles, blanched scallops)—cooked in a wine-stock and added to beaten eggs
— with chicken livers (which may be garnished with mushroom (diced), sliced truffles, or fresh cream)
— Viroflay (that is, with ham and spinach)
— Jardinière (with mixed vegetables cooked in salted water, then tossed in butter)
— with hog's pudding (yolks mixed with grilled skinned pudding, then cream and the beaten egg-whites added)

According to Austin de Croze this last omelette may be partly cooked only, then put in the oven with a layer of potato purée on top; left until nicely browned.
— with acacia (a few clusters of acacia flowers, chopped). If required, add a few drops of kirsch.

Finally, Brillat-Savarin esteemed above all other omelettes the
— Parish-priest's (or fresh tunny) omelette. It is stuffed with carp roes (well cleaned and blanched), and a slice of fresh tunny-fish sauté in butter. Also parsley and young green onion. The dish is kept very hot (over live charcoal, he says), and the omelette is sprinkled with lemon juice.

Extra-Nourishing Omelette (for convalescents or children)

Two tablespoonsful oatmeal, three of milk, with sugar *or* salt to taste, are blended in a basin, then beaten into two whole eggs. This omelette may be served as a dessert with rum or jam.

Coq Eggs (not à la coque)

The 'Coq' here comes from the Latin word for 'cook', and 'coque' means 'shell'. This is more like the English 'coddled' egg. The egg is placed in boiling water and left there for three minutes at the outside. Use only just enough water to cover the egg (but make certain that it *is* covered). It is taken to table inside the folds of a napkin, to keep the heat.

Eggs Grilled in Butter (on menus, 'sur le plat')

Nicer in a china dish than any other. Must be done in fresh butter (oil, even olive oil, makes a totally different dish). Do not allow the yolk to set completely, even less the white—I had forgotten to say that they must cook under the grill, all the heat coming from above. Sometimes a dash of vinegar is added.

The Same (Jeanne Granier Style)

Spread over bottom of china dish a layer of very lightly cooked chopped onions (unbrowned), season with curry, place eggs on top and cook as before. Garnish with little scallops of sauté brains (done in butter) and a rim of curry sauce and slices of mushroom.

Echelle Egg Scramble

Combine with eggs diced ham browned in butter. Place the cooked scramble in layers separated by layers of sorrel and lettuce *en chiffonnade.*[1] Sprinkle with parmesan and brown the top before serving.

N.B.—This and the previous recipe are by Prosper Montagné. The second derives its name from that of his restaurant in the Rue de l'Echelle.

Scrambled Eggs

Two eggs at a time. Beat in small basin with a fork, add salt. Melt in frying-pan a good-sized walnut of butter, pour in the eggs. When the bottom layer has set, lift it off the pan surface with your fork and stir and blend the eggs over a low flame. The eggs may be served just as they are, or with chopped ham, diced savaloy, asparagus tips, truffles, cooked mussels, cleaned shrimps, green peas, and so on.

Fried Eggs

Place one by one in smoking-hot oil. Put a pinch of salt on each yolk and fold in the white, as it sets, with a spoon. Brown lightly, drain away fat. May be served on fried bread, with sorrel, cooked salad, beet leaves, etc., or fried in olive oil and served on a bed of tomatoes and aubergines, with garlic, in a fine purée.

Eggs and Bacon

Do not add the eggs to the pan until the thin rashers of bacon are sufficiently cooked for the fat edge to be transparent. If liked, sauce may be added to the cooked dish.

Eggs with Ham, Savaloy, Sausage, etc.

As above.

Soft-boiled Shelled Eggs

In boiling water, boiled for five minutes, then plunged forthwith into cold water. Shells to be removed carefully. Served with various sauces

[1] *Chiffonnade*=A pile of shredded ingredients.

(white ones, green ones, spicy ones, shallot-flavoured ones; with gravy, with sorrel).

Crecy Eggs (soft)

Shelled soft-boiled eggs, as in previous recipe. Place on a bed of cooked carrot rings, mask with a sauce made with butter, flour, salt, pepper, nutmeg, grated cheese and milk. Sprinkle with grated cheese and gratinate in oven for a quarter of an hour.

Brittany Eggs

Soft-boiled and shelled, as before. A good way of using up left-over haricot beans. Make these into a purée, if possible adding meat gravy. Place in a dish, cover with parsley chopped very fine, place eggs on top.

Egg Bouillabaisse

Into a quart of cold water, seasoned with salt and pepper, put sliced onions and white of leeks, bruised garlic cloves, fennel and thyme, cover, boil for twenty minutes. Add saffron and a tablespoonful of olive oil, and boil for a further five minutes. Poach your eggs in this savoury brew. Serve them in soup plates, the broth poured over slices of bread fried in olive oil, and a poached egg surmounting.

Matelote of Eggs

(A matelote is some form of wine-and-onion-stock-based stew.) Melt one and a half ounces butter in a saucepan, add two grated carrots, some onion, parsley, six shallots, half a garlic clove, quarter of a pound of mushrooms, a bouquet garni. Fry all together very gently. Add a pint and three-quarters of a sound red cooking wine and cook on until volume is reduced by a half.

While this is happening, blend in a bowl, one and a half ounces of butter and half that quantity of flour. When smooth add to the reduced *matelote* and whisk vigorously as it all boils together. (If you have used a somewhat acid wine, add now a tablespoonful of caster sugar.)

Pour the liquor over the eggs (either soft or hard cooked) in serving dish. Garnish with fried bread cubes and chopped parsley.

Stuffed Eggs (Meatless)

Cut in halves (longitudinally) hard-boiled eggs, and remove yolks. Mix these yolks with milk-soaked bread (or broth-soaked), chopped herbs and finely minced shallots, adding salt and pepper and a little nutmeg. Cook this forcemeat slowly in butter, adding a little milk, stock or water to achieve a creamy consistency. Fill the egg whites with the forcemeat and replace into egg-shapes. Arrange the stuffed eggs on serving dish, thin down the remaining forcemeat to a sauce, and pour this over; reheat in oven before serving.

Poached Eggs

The knack is to have your hands as close as possible to the boiling water when you drop the egg into it, so that its fall is brief and its chances of staying whole are good. Poach few at a time, so that they may stay separate. Withdraw with a pierced ladle after five minutes' poaching, and drain away the water. Poached eggs may be served:

Sévigné style: on pieces of bread (crust removed) fried in butter, hollowed in the middle to receive a purée of chicken (left-over portions).

Créole style: on saffron-flavoured rice, with curry sauce.

Béarn style: in a sauce made by reducing wine, *fine*-champagne, adding shallot and ham; butter liaison.

Parmentier style: baked potatoes are hollowed out, poached egg inserted, perhaps on a thin slice of ham. Covered with a Béchamel and reheated in oven.

Jellied Eggs

Use hard-boiled, shelled soft-boiled, or poached eggs. Boil half a pound of good purchased meat jelly with a tarragon-bouquet infusion, adding a wineglassful of port wine or Madeira. Turn off the heat, remove the tarragon, and when the cooling jelly is of syrupy texture pour it over the eggs. Garnish with leaf tarragon and then cover with a bed of thinner jelly.

Monster Eggs

Their principal purpose is to amuse and astonish the young. Separate the yolks from the whites of a dozen eggs. Put the yolks inside a well-washed lard bladder and fasten with thread, plunge into boiling water. When it cools down you will have a yolk of unusual size! Take an even bigger bladder, put in the whites and also your huge yolk (its weight will keep it in the middle). Fasten up, harden it, as though it were a hard-boiled egg, in boiling water.

Dieter's Eggs

Place in a pan with a nut of butter a handful of young lettuce leaves. Break two eggs over these and cook as 'sur le plat' eggs above, using a fork to stir. Serve with a slice of lean ham.

Sauces

The sauce is better than the fish,” the accessory better than the principal.

We'll blend together cumin, marjoram, sesame, thyme, with wild thyme too, and a thousand other herbs.

BERCHOUX (*Gastronomy, Canto I*)

It's the sauce that makes the fish swallowable (an old proverb that just isn't true).

A sauce must enhance the flavour of a dish but must never disguise it or change its nature.

FERNAND JOBERT

England has three sauces and three hundred and sixty religions, whereas France has three religions and three hundred and sixty sauces.

TALLEYRAND

Truth to tell, this estimate of Talleyrand's is modest. Count Austin de Croze drew up a catalogue of more than three thousand different sauces. The word 'sauce' is taken to mean, generally speaking, any liquid seasoning for made dishes.

The most important element of any sauce is the LIAISON, or thickening (both the *process* and the *means*) and its success depends upon the individual cook's 'knack' and the school of thought to which he or she belongs. And if the *liaison* is all it should be the sauce becomes, at will of its maker, thicker, thinner, more unctuous, more velvety.

The ideal liaison ingredient is an egg yolk beaten into a little cold stock and then added, with constant stirring, to the rest of the stock as it heats up; the sauce must not be allowed to come to the boil after this addition.

It is possible, but less desirable, to use flour for liaison. But in order to avoid curdling and lumpiness, first blend the flour in cold liquid, then stir into the hot with a wooden spoon, the hot sauce being already 'on the simmer' at the moment of addition. This may boil for ten minutes (to cook the flour).

Starchy products should never be used as sauce thickeners.

Carême, and other great writers on culinary matters, have usually divided sauces into four groups, with four 'mother sauces' from which all others spring. These 'mother sauces' are:

ESPAGNOLE: basically, a piquant brown sauce.

VELOUTE: basically, a thick gravy sauce.

ALLEMANDE: basically of flour, butter, eggs, white meal.

BECHAMEL: basically a white cream sauce.

Another classification recognizes 'Brown sauces' and 'White sauces'. And now to our sauce-making.

A Simple Roux

Melt butter in a saucepan and add flour (variable quantity dictated by thickness of sauce aimed at). When both have browned (real brown, not pale gold), water and/or stock are added, with salt and pepper.

If a 'white' roux (something of a contradiction in terms) is required, the flour and butter must still be of pale colour when the liquor is added. Stir with a wooden spoon.

White Sauce

The secret of making a first-class white sauce *is to use only best-quality butter*. Roux: 'brown sauce', 'browning'. The frequent instruction 'Faites un roux'='Brown some butter'. Melt a fair-sized piece of good butter in a thick pan, but do not let it brown. Add very slowly to the liquid butter a level tablespoonful of flour, with a little salt and pepper. Stir slowly while adding slowly (almost drop by drop) a tumblerful of boiling water. When all is smooth and well-blended withdraw pan from heat and add one beaten egg yolk and a dash of vinegar.

If you do not wish to use an egg yolk it is just as feasible to use a nut of butter instead.

Variation (for fish). Neither egg nor vinegar, but either capers or chopped gherkins.

Cream Sauce

Early stages of preparation as for white sauce, but replace the glassful of boiling water by the same quantity of cream. Add salt, pepper, chopped young green onion and parsley. Stir until the desired thickness. (Usually served with potatoes, hard-boiled eggs, fish.)

Blanquette Sauce

This is, so to speak, a cream sauce made without cream, and in it you may cook pieces of meat or chicken, also, if you wish, small onions, artichoke bottoms, mushrooms.

Béchamel Sauce

Is the white sauce again, with a glassful of milk replacing the water.
(It is not known whether this sauce was actually the invention of Louis de Béchamel, Marquis of Nointec, a famous gourmet of the seventeenth century, or whether it was dedicated to him by a chef of that time.)

Béchamel Variations

If, on completion of the above sauce, you add crayfish butter, the result will be Nantua Sauce.

Or the addition of hard-boiled egg, sliced, gives a sauce to accompany poached cod.

Add chopped parsley and lemon juice to obtain a general-purpose fish sauce.

Mornay Sauce

This is a Béchamel reduced by one-third and then, with the addition of a little cream and some grated parmesan or gruyère cheese, used with vegetables; with stock from white meat of poultry, used with eggs, poultry.

With fish-stock-concentrate, for fish and shellfish.

Poulette Sauce

This is a somewhat liquid white sauce (thinned down, for instance with white stock) which is reduced and mingled with egg yolks, lemon juice and chopped parsley. Useful for a fish dish (in which case the stock should be a fish stock), and for offal dishes (notably, sheep's trotters).

Vinaigrette Sauce

One spoonful of vinegar to two of olive oil (or other oil), with salt, pepper, chopped chervil and chives. Blend and stir well together then add a thoroughly hard-cooked egg yolk, creaming it into the liquid.

This *vinaigrette* is good not only with salads but also with sheep's trotters, fish, or slices of boiled beef.

Gribiche Sauce

Consists of the yolks of hard-boiled eggs pounded to a paste and dressed with oil and vinegar, stirring constantly as for a mayonnaise. Salt and pepper added, also chopped gherkins and parsley, capers, any green herbs. The whites of the hard-boiled eggs, chopped into tiny pieces, are sprinkled over the finished sauce.

Used with cold fish, calf's head, tongues, etc.

Remoulade Sauce

Mix into a paste two hard-boiled egg yolks and one uncooked yolk. Add a tablespoonful of mustard and 'work' the paste, as for a mayonnaise, with olive oil, added gradually. Blend and 'work' for as long as possible. Before finishing, add a tablespoonful of vinegar.

Mustard Sauce

Stew gently some finely-chopped onions, in good butter with salt and pepper. Add white wine, then reduce and stir in a little mustard mixed to a smooth paste with vinegar, and the juice of a lemon. Add a tablespoonful of butter at the last moment.

Hollandaise Sauce

Put half a pound of butter and two egg yolks in a basin with a little table salt, and a dessertspoonful of vinegar. Now place bowl in a pan of boiling water and stir its contents together as the butter melts, but without letting them cook. Add the juice of one lemon. If the sauce gets too thick, add a very little hot water. This sauce is superb with fish cooked in a wine-and-spices-stock (court-bouillon)—e.g. turbot, brill.

Piquant Sauce

Put vinegar, pepper, chopped shallots, chopped parsley, in a saucepan with a nut of butter. Melt all together and combine with a brown roux. Add chopped-up gherkin at last moment. Good with, for example, beef or cold pork.

Mousseline Sauce

Is like Hollandaise, above, but at the last moment thick cream (whipped to stiffness) is mixed in with the egg-whisk. Its principal role is to accompany asparagus.

Madeira Sauce

Make a brown roux but using stock instead of water to thin it down. Infuse in it, for half an hour over a slow heat, a bouquet of parsley, thyme and bay-leaf. When on the point of serving, add two tablespoonsful of Madeira.

Good with kidneys, or even with a simple beef-steak.

Tomato Sauce

Whenever you can manage it, do make your own tomato sauce, instead of relying on the bottled ones. Cut seven or eight tomatoes into small pieces and put into saucepan with bay, thyme, sliced onion (cut in rings, that is), a clove of garlic. Cook all gently together, adding no water at all. Shake from time to time so that the tomatoes do not stick to the pan. Pound in a mortar, put the pounded purée into another pan with a walnut of butter and work all together slowly and thoroughly.

Robert Sauce

Also called CHARCUTIERE. Fry some shredded onion golden brown in good-quality butter. Add a tablespoonful of flour and half a pint of stock, also salt and pepper. Cook gently. At moment of serving, add a tablespoonful of vinegar and a little made mustard.

This sauce may be used as a medium in which to warm up meat left-overs, especially pork, goose, turkey. A garnish of gherkin strips is arranged on top.

Black Butter Sauce

Melt, and cook to a very dark brown, some butter (using the frying-pan). It must be dark, but not burned. Now add some sprigs of parsley which will fry very quickly. Perhaps a spot of vinegar. Pour at once over your fish (e.g. skate).

Wine Sauce

As a general rule, when making wine sauces, use in the preparation and reduction only half of the total amount of wine you intend to employ. The rest will be added at a later stage, and thus none will be sacrificed unduly in the process of reduction, now over and done with. This ensures that the wine retains its aroma more abundantly.

But here is a recipe with a difference for wine sauce—a bit of an oddity. Mix in a quart of wine a number of egg yolks—if possible twelve; also a quarter of a pound of sugar, the zest of one lemon, some cinnamon. Heat up to, but not beyond, boiling point, stirring constantly.

Green Sauce

Blanch for a few minutes in boiling water some watercress, spinach, chervil, chives and tarragon, about four ounces in all. Drain away water, twist all the greenstuff in a clean, dry cloth, pound it in a mortar, pass through hair sieve, and add a mayonnaise sauce.

Mayonnaise Sauce

This was once spelt 'Mahonnaise', having been invented by the Marshal de Richelieu when at the gates of Port Mahon. Carême, in his works, spells it 'Magnonnaise'. 'Mayonnaise' is a distortion, and the sauce itself has the reputation of being somewhat prone to distortion, proving all too easily a disappointment.

Mademoiselle Alice Cocéa, basing her method on the principle that the larger the beating surface, the greater are the chances of success, makes her mayonnaise by rubbing a flat disc against a flat plate containing the ingredients. It is simpler still to use a clamped-down whisk, a mechanical beater.

Mayonnaise does not like cold. And heat is only slightly less unfavourable. The oil should be used at kitchen temperature. The proportions are: in your salad bowl, eight egg yolks, a tablespoonful of mustard; salt, pepper, dash of vinegar. Add oil drop by drop, beating all the time, until you have achieved the desired consistency. If too thick, add a few drops of vinegar to 'loosen' the texture.

Variations on Mayonnaise

(1) Add some 'reduced' tomato purée and a little crushed pimento (or allspice) and you have a NICOISE SAUCE.

(2) Add an infusion of mint leaves (in a mixture of two tablespoonsful of vinegar and one of water). This is perfect with, for example, cold leg of lamb.

(3) Add, in very small instalments at a time, a gill or two of reduced

(aspic) jelly, melted and cooled, and you have a 'jellied mayonnaise' that's excellent with cold meats.

(4) Add the creamy portion of a lobster's interior, also some caviar if you are a millionaire. Stir in a little mustard for piquancy, and the result is a RUSSIAN SAUCE.

White Butter Sauce (Nantes Fashion)

Shallots are boiled down completely in white wine vinegar and allowed to cool. Add a little at a time some creamed, slightly salt butter, whisking all together over low heat. Put in salt, butter, a little vinegar. This admirable sauce is none too easy. It is good with fish of all kinds. But in Nantes they serve it with pike, particularly, and use a muscatel wine instead of vinegar.

Aioli

This is, to all intents and purposes, a mayonnaise with which bruised garlic has been incorporated—that is, in day-to-day kitchen practice. But the real aioli experts pound the garlic to a very fine paste with pestle and mortar, in the proportion of eight cloves (not bulbs) to one egg yolk and half a pint of oil for every four people—olive oil of course.

Maître d'Hôtel Sauce

Butter is worked with chopped parsley, salt, pepper, nutmeg, a little finely chopped spring onion, a dash of vinegar, for a good long time, until smooth.

Indian Sauce

First melt together in a saucepan two ounces of butter, a coffeespoonful of curry powder, a little saffron, one ounce of flour. Moisten with stock, allow to reduce for a quarter of an hour. Strain through a sieve. A good curry powder, obtainable from dealers in exotics, contains coriander, cumin, black pepper, ginger, Cayenne pepper, cardamom and dry mustard.

Béarn Sauce

Chop up some shallots and some tarragon and put in saucepan with a half-and-half mixture of white wine and vinegar. Boil over a brisk heat until reduced to three-quarters of original volume. Beat two egg yolks, season with salt, pepper, a pounded red pepper and add a little butter. This mixture goes drop by drop into the reduced stock. You must stir unceasingly, as though you were making mayonnaise sauce. But do not allow sauce to boil. Just before serving add a few drops of lemon juice.

Especially associated with red meat.

Duxelles Sauce

Serves as garnish to numerous meat dishes: or, in its thicker consistency, as gratin sauce. A gill of white wine is mixed with a gill of strong, concentrated mushroom stock and a little chopped shallot. Reduce to three-quarters of volume, add quarter-pint brown sauce and a tablespoonful of tomato purée, and boil for a minute or two.

Mirepoix Sauce

As well as being a sauce in its own right, it serves as basis for others. Fry lightly a quarter-pound of lean bacon, cut into small cubes, together with two medium carrots and an onion (all sliced), a bay leaf, a little thyme. Cook gently for half an hour, stirring frequently. Press through sieve.

'Rabid Black Sauce'

Allow to drip into a small glass of vinegar the blood of two ducks. Make a roux with ten cloves of garlic. Chop up an egg-weight of bacon with the duck livers and six more garlic cloves. Add to the roux. Pour a little stock over, add salt and pepper. When sauce is half cooked, add the blood. Place lid on pan, cook for two hours, then pound well in mortar and serve with the roasted ducks.

(Recipe supplied by Simon Arbellot of the Gastronomes' Academy.)

AND DO NOT FORGET . . .

- Sauce and gravy are two quite different things. Gravy is a natural product of cooking processes, brought about by exudation. Sauce may consist either of this 'spontaneous' gravy reinforced in some way or of an entirely different set of ingredients.

- The sauce-maker's art is reputed to be one of the most subtle. Carême, speaking of Laguipière (a master in this sphere), said (as I have reported elsewhere) that 'he put genius into his sauces'.

- Without aspiring to such levels the housewife should bear in mind that a sauce of savoury aroma and delicate 'bouquet' is a pleasant stimulant—first of the sense of smell, and then of the taste-buds. She must not be afraid of using condiments.

- A meat gravy, and a sauce, lose quality if they are too fatty.

- The incorporation in a sauce of a high-quality wine is a controversial procedure. If, for example, you use an exquisite Chambertin of a vintage year in a 'Coq au Vin', will you reap all the benefits that the label promises? Some say yes, some say no. Whatever the truth of the matter, it is not only preferable, but essential, always to use a wine of solid worth and reliability.

Spices and Seasonings

I love to pull the spice-drawer open, freeing
The Orient. Not a penny changes hands,
Yet, joy undreamed-of, I am in magical lands,
Ceylon . . . Colombo . . . savouring, though
unseeing.

ROGER LECUYER

It seemed logical to include at this point the chapter devoted to condiments, spices and aromatics—for surely they are the complements of sauces?

I am aware that many of them, unfortunately, are pretty costly, but nevertheless they will prove indispensable to the housewife who wishes to vary the flavours of her dishes, even if the dishes themselves are not all that varied. This diversity of flavour is by no means easy or cheap to achieve.

Many spices have health-giving properties, even curative value. They must always be used knowledgeably, never casually. Remember, above all, that you are better off with no spices whatsoever than with the 'near-spices' and other ersatz products of second-rate packers.

GARLIC: Curnonsky wrote, 'A garlic caress is stimulating, a garlic excess soporific'. Once cooked it loses much of its virulence. It is credited with many virtues—as antiseptic, vermifuge, and reliever of rheumatism.

ONION: and his sister SHALLOT, need no introduction from me.

CHIVES: large and small varieties: are also bulbous plants, but we eat the leaves in this case. Finely chopped, they have no rival—say in an omelette, or mixed into cream cheese.

CHERVIL, PARSLEY, TARRAGON: well-known herbs of slightly different flavours, that should replace one another from time to time. Medicinal properties.

CHERVIL (bulb-rooted): is a variant of ordinary chervil, and the bulb only is used. Eaten just with salt, or in a salad, or sauté (with butter, as potatoes are), it must always be newly gathered. It is alleged (for example, by Boni de Castellane) to have roborative value.

HORSERADISH: is a root of salsify stature, yellow-white colour, and of a pronounced mustard-like taste. It may be grated, salted, or in direct contrast it may have its pungency diminished by the addition of fresh cream. It is served with boiled beef, *charcutaille*, and meat stews.

GHERKINS: these are the young fruits of a variety of cucumber; they are picked while green and set in vinegar—usually purchased bottled, but here is a recipe for home use:

SPICE AMONG THE ANCIENTS

The Ancients were far more lavish than we are in their use of spices and aromatics. Many which they favoured are no longer in use. In his charming book entitled La Table et L'Amour, *Curnonsky supplies several titbits of information concerning* AMBERGRIS, *a product of the sperm whale, which was one of the ingredients of almost all the dishes of classical antiquity. He speaks also of* CERNEAUX *or the interiors of green walnuts used for making Verjuice; of* GARUM, *which, according to the Elder Pliny, was obtained from fish intestines macerated in brine; of* MUSK, *of animal origin, which the folk of Iran and Tibet still use in cookery (our forebears incorporated it in aphrodisiac lozenges); of* SATYRION, *an orchid which amatory authors of golden times extolled with vast enthusiasm.*

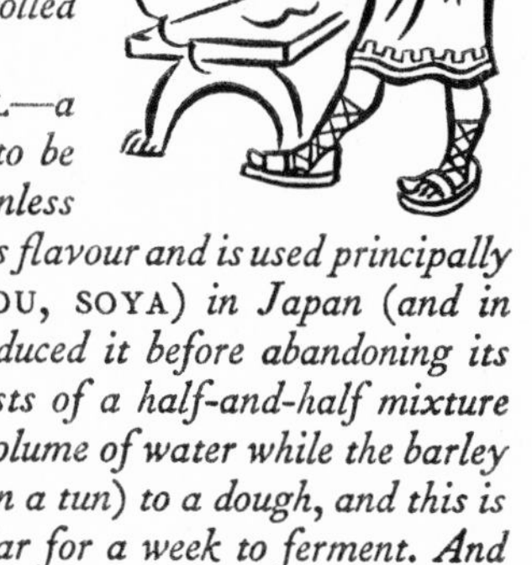

I was almost forgetting the PINE-KERNEL*—a small, smooth, practically oblong seed that is to be found concealed in the heart of pine cones (unless squirrels get there first). It has a faintly resinous flavour and is used principally in oriental dishes—as also is* SOY (SHO-YOU, SOYA) *in Japan (and in America, to which country the English introduced it before abandoning its use for themselves).* SHO-YOU *actually consists of a half-and-half mixture of soya and barley. Soya is cooked in its own volume of water while the barley is grilled. The two products are then blended (in a tun) to a dough, and this is formed into loaves which are left in a sealed jar for a week to ferment. And that's the lot, save that these loaves must now be put into double their total volume of salted water and left for a period of one to three years. The juice which then runs out under pressure is the* SHO-YOU, *sold in bottles and flasks.*

AT THE RESTAURANT

'Good heavens, waiter . . . ! Wiping the plates with a handkerchief?'
'Oh, don't worry, sir. It's my own.'

* * *

'And now . . . if the ladies and gentlemen are connoisseurs . . . I'm going to let them sample something out of this world . . . a 1772 *Napoleon* fine!*'*

Rub them vigorously with a clean cloth and cover with coarse salt in an earthenware pan, where they must stay for twenty-four hours. Then drain, wash in water slightly acidulated with vinegar. Drain again and dry thoroughly in a clean cloth. Pack them into a glass or stoneware jar adding, according to your own particular fancy, tiny silver onions, pimentos (red and green), sprigs of tarragon, cloves, etc., cover with wine-vinegar and seal hermetically. Keep in a cool place and bring to table about five weeks after sealing.

PIMENTOS, PEPPERS are of several kinds:

(1) Pimentos, peppers, 'berries' which turn red as they ripen (or perhaps yellow). They are dried, pulverized, and used as a condiment. Berries picked at 'pepper-corn' size.

(2) Cayenne pepper, sun-dried and ground capsicum, which is very strong: not unlike paprika, also called 'Hungarian pepper'.

(3) 'Sweet pepper' or 'Jamaica pepper'—large, grown beyond the stage of greatest pungency, and used as a vegetable or salad. Comes from Spain, Italy, French S.E. Africa.

MUSTARD: this is the seed of a cruciferous plant extensively cultivated in France. 'Black' mustard is the domestic variety. The seed is first decorticated, then crushed, and mixed with grape 'must', verjuice or vinegar. Aromatic herbs and a small quantity of oil are added finally.

Mustard was used in earliest times. In later days the mustard makers of Dijon and of Orleans were at strife to settle which had the remotest historical origins and could boast most royal testimonials. Louis XI, among others, never moved far without his pot of mustard.

SALT: the experts will tell you that the normal need of the human body is 13 grains of salt every day, but that the average daily food supply furnishes all but 4 or 5 grains of this. Do not forget that too much salt is prejudicial to health.

PEPPER: the seed of the true pepper (see above) and it is black in its natural state. White pepper, of milder flavour, is produced by soaking decorticated black pepper seeds in salted water. It is almost essential to good cooking that you should buy your pepper unground and use your own pepper-mill As suggested above, Cayenne pepper is not true pepper (and neither is Hungarian pepper or paprika), these being forms of pulverized red pimento.

CUMIN: is a seed of strong aromatic properties and distinctive flavour. It's not much used in French cookery, save in Alsace (where it may also be used to accompany Munster Cheese). It also gives its aromatic qualities to Kummel.

GINGER: is a rhizome of Indian origin, cultivated in Africa as well. It is used in preserves, marmalades, etc., and (in England) for ginger beer, ginger brandy, gingerbreads, etc., and with cream and its own syrup as a dessert.

CINNAMON: is the bark of the cinnamon tree, coming from Ceylon and China (this latter being a coarser variety). It is used mostly in cakes and pastry making, in stewed fruit dishes and in mulled wine. Spaniards love it in hot chocolate, to which it imparts, it must be admitted, a magnificent 'bouquet'.

NUTMEG: is the fruit of a shrub grown in Brazil, the West Indies, Guiana and the Indies generally. A little at a time is grated into sauces (Béchamel), vegetables, certain hors d'œuvre, etc., and it is one of the ingredients of punches.

CLOVES: these are stuck into onions and added to the family hot-pot (or even stuck into garlic for the same end). They are likewise used to flavour and add strength to pickling liquids, and are added to pies and potted savouries. Essential in English bread-sauce.

SAFFRON: Indispensable to bouillabaisse and fish soups. Colours rice, flour mixtures, even butter, in the South-of-France cuisine. It is a powder made from stigmas of a flower of the Iris family (autumn crocus). It takes nearly three thousand flowers to produce less than an ounce of saffron, and so it is all too often adulterated with worthless additions. A saffron essence is also obtainable.

BAY, THYME, LAUREL: are all too well known for detailed description. But the SARRIETTE of the South of France ('Savory' of English gardens) is a pleasant herb of the mint family with a flavour less pronounced than that of thyme. It goes into many a German Sauerkraut.

SAGE: has its own legend, which was set to music. It also has a faintly bitter taste. But if you like it, it's all right in sauces. Sage and onion stuffing is far more English than French.

MINT: is an improvement to vinegar dressing and sauces, but it is advisable to be sparing with it for the sake of keeping rival flavours intact.

VANILLA: much used in pastries, creamy desserts, milk and rice puddings, egg desserts, etc. It is sold in pod form. But there is, alas, a manufactured vanilla—that is, 'vanilline', in pastels. The vanilla plant, of the orchid family, is well equipped to deceive. Its flowers are of insignificant size and are practically colourless—of a pale green that's almost white—and with only the most fugitive scent. The vanilla plant kept its mystery and its treasure concealed for a very long time. It is only during the last two hundred years at the most that it has been used in kitchen and confectioner's. Pepper and spices are of far more ancient usage.

In Mexico, which seems to have been its birthplace, and from whence it spread all over the globe, pollination by insects induced fruit formation, the insects creeping right inside the flowers to that end. Among these insects the most accomplished was a variety of Mexican bee, which brushed against the stamens and then the stigma to complete its delicate work.

The shape of the flowers is such that without such outside intervention, pollination could not occur. This is yet another peculiarity of this capricious plant. But as it happens, this is an advantageous circumstance (difficult as it is for us, with our mania for devoting industrial processes to over-production, to admit). For this method of fertilization results in high-quality fruit of a good size. All the energy of the plant seems to be concentrated on the best possible presentation of these fertilized fruits. However, in the great vanilla plantations of Mexico the intervention of human beings is necessary, and hand-pollination is carried out on a considerable scale. Mexico, its chosen location, is no longer the only vanilla-growing region; it has known the joys and sorrows of expatriation, and has adapted itself perfectly, and with no modifications or difficulties, in fresh soils to which explorers have transplanted it.

It has gone as far as Réunion, taking in France *en route*. A traveller monk, inheritor of the enquiring mind and practical outlook of the conquistadores, brought to Paris a stalk of vanilla which was ceremonially planted in the Botanical Gardens; it took root and flourished. It might well have lived and died at last in the sole charge of a conscientious staff naturalist, had not a high official of the colony of Réunion, some time in 1822, asked the Botanical Gardens officials to let him have one or two slips of the plant. Then off he went to St Denis, Réunion, and at once planted his slips. The climate suited them admirably and the plants made spectacular growth.

But its presence there was more or less pointless; it made no particular headway until a negro, Edmund Albins, keen on botanical experiments, noticed that his master was adept in 'marrying' certain flower-species, so tried his hand with the vanilla. He succeeded so well that little by little the original plant spread over ten thousand acres. As a result this island became the largest vanilla-producing area in the world.

Vanilla is cultivated nowadays in the Congo, Madagascar, Réunion, Tahiti, the Comoro Islands, and at Nossi-Bé as well as in the Seychelles, in Martinique, Guadeloupe, Guiana, Ceylon and Java.

CURRY is a composite paste, prepared in India. The most usual mixture is as follows (see also 'Indian Sauce', page 59):

¼ lb onions (or saffron bulbs)
a bare ½ oz (each) of ginger, cinnamon
1 oz tamarind pulp
1 oz of the fruit of the true anise tree
a few cloves
a well-flavoured pimento.

All these ingredients are crushed and pounded in a mortar. In a separate pan an onion-and-butter roux is cooked, and in this the pieces of meat or fish—or else rice—are cooked. When the cooking process is half completed the curry from the mortar is added (one tablespoonful for five people).

Sea-food

'The lobster . . . cardinal of the deep.'

CHARLES MONSELET

'How do *they cook the things?' She meditates,*
Uncertain, this young housewife from the States.
'Now look,' the lobster tells the meditator,
'Drop the whole thing. We'll talk about it later.'

ANON.

Oysters

First of all, their secret—as revealed by Dr. Louis Lambert, Chief Inspector of the Shellfish Sanitary Control:

Oysters may be, in France at any rate, of two kinds. First the indigenous oyster, which the naturalists style *Ostrea edulis*, and the commercial name of which is the 'flat oyster'. Second, the Portuguese oyster (*Gryphoea angulata*), a very different species, which has been imported for sixty years or so, and now appears to have acquired 'citizen rights', as it has taken the place, on the south-west coasts, of the vanished native oyster.

For many long years, for centuries in fact, it was the custom to procure oysters from their natural beds only and to put on the market those which had attained a respectable size. The most which was done, apart from this straightforward fishing, was to allow them to sojourn for a short period in a special oyster-bed in which they improved in condition a little.

These oyster 'measures' or 'banks' seemed at one time to be so numerous and so rich in yield that it was tempting to think of them—in fact they *were* thought of—as being inexhaustible.

But this illusion could not last. Heedless exploitation grew more and more feverish and this circumstance, allied with the fact that natural conditions were unfavourable, led to a gradual deterioration of the oyster beds. Some even vanished completely. A crisis had arisen. And, as always occurs in moments of crisis, government action was called for, and an immediate inquiry into the steps that should be taken was demanded.

The government was that of Napoleon III, and it inaugurated various kinds of safety measures. Some could have no possible effects until a date in the far-distant future. But study and experimentation began at once, De Bon and Coste being names still memorable in that connection. The latter, with the collaboration of one or two enterprising people professionally interested, founded an entirely new technique and this, later perfected, became the practice of oyster-culture as known in our own times.

Oyster-culture may, for simplicity's sake, be divided into three principal phases:

(1) The production, or the obtaining from natural sources, of the 'oyster-spat'.

(2) The actual breeding or culture (or, more usually, semi-culture).

(3) The refining and 'plumping'.

The flat, or shallow, oyster is a hermaphrodite. But even though the characteristic organs of both sexes are present, they do not function simultaneously; and therefore in order for the species to continue, there must be the necessary male-female co-operation. The female lays eggs which she keeps safe in, as it were, a fold of her mantle, and there they are fertilized. At this point the oyster is 'milky', and not good eating—not palatable, that is, for although some say it is actually harmful, this probably holds good only for people with a high degree of intolerance, who might thereby suffer from a not very serious gastro-intestinal upset.

A few days later, the oyster-mother changes character. 'Milky' no longer, she becomes 'slatey' (bluish grey), and at that stage hatches the eggs, which release embryonic, larval individuals, of microscopic size, each wearing a little crown of vibrating filaments by means of which it will be able to swim.

Another few days elapse and the mother oyster decides that it is high time she got rid of her offspring. So she expels them into the water, and there they thrive and develop. They are for a time one of the elements of marine plankton, the food of countless creatures, including the parent oysters.

So much for the first type. The Portuguese oyster has things much more simply arranged, being unisexual. Both males and females cast into the water their ovules and their fertilizing elements, and confide to pure hazard the responsibility for the union. A 'flat' oyster lays, on an average, two million eggs, a Portuguese still more.

The life of liberty which the larval forms can expect is brief indeed; its duration is not definitely known, and it certainly varies in accordance with biological environment; but in most oyster-culture waters it is probably of something like ten days. At a certain stage the crown of filaments begins to atrophy and mobility decreases. The creature has grown, it is now no less than two or three tenths of a millimetre, and it is a matter of pressing urgency for it to find something to cling to.

Now it is one of the first duties of an oyster-spat breeder to furnish, at the spot where the emission of the larvæ took place (that is to say, near a natural bank or bed known to be well supplied with oysters), the necessary supports to which they will anchor themselves. Almost any material will do, provided it is wholesome and of sound consistency. Some such items are pieces of stone or slate, sea-shells, tree boughs.

But in two of the principal breeding zones, Morbihan and the Arcachon basin, preference is given to limed tiles. These are arranged in clusters, planted in the earth by means of a stake (Morbihan) or in 'hives'—large cages, as it were, raised above ground level (Arcachon). The 'spat' will attach itself well and truly to either, with firm grip. Thanks to the chalky deposit it is comparatively easy to detach them when the time comes.

A few figures will give some idea of the magnitude of this industry. In the oyster-bearing streams of Morbihan (Auray and the Bono Saint-Philibert, Crach) they lay down, in good seasons and bad, some ten million tiles; and almost as many in the Arcachon basin.

* * *

Oysters, as a food, are rich in phosphorus, calcium and vitamin A. It is not so much the actual oyster that fattens for our consumption as its liver, which swells with a hydrocarbonic substance chemically related to starch and sugar. This substance is supplied by diatomic entities on which it gorges itself avidly, and these same entities give it its special coloration: green, in the case of Marennes or Portuguese oysters; brown, in the case of Belons; red, in the case of Côte Rouge oysters.

It is usual to eat the oyster living and unadorned. It is permissible to add a spot of lemon juice, but this is not essential. The practice dates back to the days when transport was long and uncertain, and the drop of lemon showed whether the oyster was still alive and therefore fit to be eaten without undue risk. Some prefer a shallot and vinegar sauce, a bottled sauce or ketchup, but this is not a good idea. Brown bread, or toasted bread with butter, should accompany oysters.

Oysters—and most sea-fruit, for that matter—call for a very dry and not over-fruity white wine. To my mind it is not desirable to choose an Alsatian wine. Champagne, Meursault, Chablis—but, better than any, a Muscadet.

Here are a few recipes for 'cooked' oysters:

Oysters au Gratin

Remove oysters from shells and put in a basin. Save and strain the sea-water escaping from them. Wash the hollow shells. In a plate beat together 4 oz butter with white breadcrumbs, pepper, parsley, chopped shallots, then mix with the juice of two lemons and the strained oyster-water. Put a little of this stuffing in the bottom of each shell, then the oyster, then a top layer of stuffing. Sprinkle with grated parmesan or gruyère cheese, bake for five minutes. Serve cold.

François Villon Oysters

Take out the oysters and poach in nearly-boiling water. Remove, firm them up in cold water, dry them on a cloth.

In a small pan melt some butter and cook in it, to a light brown, two dessertspoonsful of flour. Now add two glasses of white wine and a little stock, also salt, Cayenne pepper and nutmeg. When your sauce is smooth and creamy, put in the oysters, and let them reheat without boiling.

Other Procedures

As above, but instead of the sauce described use a Mornay sauce, American sauce, Béchamel, or Curry sauce.

Skewered Oysters

Affix half a dozen oysters (raw, and each enveloped in a thin slice of bacon) on a skewer, and grill. Serve on toast with plenty of Cayenne pepper.

Bordeaux Oysters

Take a dozen 'flat' oysters, very, very cold, a small sausage very strongly garlic-flavoured, very heavily pimentoed, very hot to the tongue. You then take a bite of scorching-hot sausage, followed by a cooling mouthful of oyster. This is the only oyster preparation with which one could, at a pinch, drink red wine (Bordeaux).

Sea Urchins

These are also called 'sea-chestnuts'. They are found, at low tide, in cracks in the rocks. The best are the green and the black urchins. Opening them on their flat side you remove the 'mouth' portion and then, using scissors, cut away the flat part and discard it. Pour away the water that is inside and you are left with a star-like 'shell' whose orange-coloured rays represent the only edible portion. The over-fastidious cook this orange portion 'in the shell' as though boiling an egg. It is really a cream extremely rich in iodine and it may be used (oddly enough) to give aroma to a soup, to line an omelette, to flavour a mayonnaise sauce.

Sea-Violets

These are a 'soft' sea-denizen which the true Marseillais seems to prize, and not without reason. Once you get used to them you will sprinkle them with lemon juice and engulf them as though they were a lowly oyster.

Various Lesser Shellfish

This description embraces Clams and Cockles (with menu mentions as *Palourde*, *Coque*, *Bucarde*, *Clovisse*) and even mussels, of which more will be said shortly. They may, of course, be eaten raw, especially at the sea-side, newly harvested and fresh: or the following simple and practical recipes are useful for most of them:

(*a*) A LA MARINIERE (for mussels and cockles particularly): Scrape and wash thoroughly. Put into a saucepan with a little white wine, sliced onions and chopped shallots, pepper, some parsley heads (no salt, obviously). When the shells open, over gentle heat, add a piece of butter, the size of a large egg. Serve only half the shellfish (the rest have of course served to flavour the brew) and pour away the liquor, which is almost sure to be sandy.

(*b*) A LA POULETTE: Same procedure, but bind the sauce with one or two egg yolks, some cream, and lemon juice. Sprinkle chopped parsley over them before serving.

(*c*) AU GRATIN: Open shellfish while still raw and arrange in a heat-proof dish, then cover with a sauce made thus: chop finely 4 or 5 oz of mushrooms, half an onion, two shallots. Squeeze all these together in a cloth to get rid of superfluous moisture. Cook lightly in a couple of tablespoonsful of olive oil, and add the water that came from the shells, also a glass of white wine. Pour in some creamed butter and a small handful of white breadcrumbs, for binding. Season. Add cream if desired. Sprinkle with chopped parsley. Serve very hot.

(*d*) A LA BONNE FEMME: Open shells in a small quantity of white wine, heated gently. Add then a chopped shallot, some chopped celery white, chopped mushrooms, pepper. Remove shells, take out the fish and keep them hot in a vegetable-dish. Reduce the cooking liquor and add butter and flour creamed together. Pour sauce over the shellfish.

(*e*) A LA VAPEUR: Open shells in smallest possible quantity of water, unseasoned except for a little pepper. Put the unshelled shellfish into an oven-dish and bake for one minute. Serve with a sauceboat of melted butter.

(*f*) VARIATIONS: Proceed as for 'à la Poulette' above, then add either a pinch of curry powder or of saffron, whichever you prefer.

(*g*) SHELLFISH PILAF: In your first vessel open the shellfish over a low flame, using white wine, chopped parsley, thyme, bay, and a good assortment of shellfish (the more varied, the better the dish). When shells are open, remove them and take out the meat.

In your second saucepan put two tablespoonsful of olive oil, some chopped onion and shallot, and cook very gently indeed, stirring frequently. Then add 6 oz of rice and cook on, stirring constantly. Add three times present bulk of liquid, this to be half cooking liquor (first pan) and half water. Salt and pepper. Two tablespoonsful tomato purée. A bouquet garni. Cook in oven for 20 minutes without any more stirring. As it leaves the oven, add a walnut of butter.

In your third pan put the remaining half of the first cooking liquor and the same quantity of water-plus-white-wine, fifty-fifty. Add a couple of tablespoonsful of tomato purée, then make a brown roux with butter and an ounce of flour. When roux has cooled, add it to the liquid and bring to boil, whisking it well at the start. Allow to cook for an hour, skimming from time to time, if necessary. When this sauce is well reduced, taste and season appropriately (with pepper, bruised garlic, Cayenne pepper).

Butter a dish and put in two-thirds of your cooked and flavoured rice, leaving a hollow in the centre. Fill this with the shellfish and some of the sauce. Add the rest of the rice and reverse the dish on a larger one that has been warmed over the bain-marie. Pour the rest of the sauce (re-heated) over the pilaf and sprinkle with chopped parsley.

Mussels

These have their letters patent of nobility. The Romans doted on them, Louis XVIII adored them. And here is Curnonsky's account of the beginnings of myticulture in France:

In 1235 a boat laden with sheep was wrecked in Aiguillon Bay, a few miles from Escande (Maurice Straits). Of the three members of the crew only the owner, an Irishman named Walton, survived. Completely ruined, he decided to settle down where he was, and to become a hunter in order to keep body and soul together.

He had often noticed that at night time certain birds flew very slowly along the shore. So he drove stakes into the ground, attaching an enormous net to these. After some time had passed, he observed that mussels had attached themselves in large numbers to these stakes. It was later remarked that the mussels on the posts fattened more speedily than those in natural banks, and the first myticultural station was therefore established in 1246.

The devoted collectors of mussels are known as *Bouchots* (bouchot= mussel-farm, usually).

* * *

Besides the general recipes for shellfish (given above) which include mussels, the following are particularly suitable:

(1) Mussel Pilaf: See (*g*) above, and use mussels only.

(2) Fried Mussels: Removed from shells, bearded, dried, then rolled in breadcrumbs and fried. Served with vinaigrette sauce in individual saucers.

(3) Mussels in Mayonnaise: Cooked in a marinading liquor, unshelled, dried, mixed with a mayonnaise sauce sharpened with garlic and shallot.

(4) Skewered Mussels: as for oysters (p. 75). When the mussels have been poached, dried and rolled in breadcrumbs, each is wrapped in

a small piece of smoked bacon of transparent thinness. They are cooked in the oven. Serve a tomato sauce separately.

(5) Mussels with Sorrel: Poach unshelled, put in frying-pan with small bacon strips and pour all, when cooked, on to a bed of cooked sorrel. Serve fried breadcrumbs with these.

Crabs

There are numerous crab species and the commonest is vulgarly named 'Sea Tortoise' or 'Sea Spider'. Other, smaller ones are known as *Etrilles* (Curry-comb Crabs). In the kitchen they may be used to replace lobsters and crayfish in almost all recipes for these. Unfortunately there is not a great deal of meat on them, and it is seldom as good as lobster meat. But its liver is large and of creamy texture and is therefore used in bisques and for gelatinous sauces.

Scallops (Coquilles Saint-Jacques)

This is undoubtedly one of the choicest shellfish. The best way of opening it is first to scrape and wash it thoroughly and then stand it on hot-plate or enamel stove plate, when the flat portion of the shell will rise. Remove the 'meat' and discard all but the white 'kernel' and the 'coral', which is red with yellowish base, and is often scimitar-shaped.

It is usual to poach these edible portions as a preliminary, but some say that this is not necessary as cooking can be straightforwardly done without initial poaching. You must judge from your own experience.

Some people serve them up in the scallop shell, three or four in each one, but I do not see much point in this. However, the hollow shells should be kept as they are useful for serving fish left-overs, cold with mayonnaise (and salad accompaniment) or baked with a Béchamel sauce and served hot. The following are all good Scallop preparations:

Scallop Treatments

(1) Fried: Poach and drain, marinade for half an hour in oil, lemon juice and chopped parsley. Soak in thin batter and fry in boiling fat. Drain. Serve with parsley.

(2) Colbert: Again, poach first. Roll in egg and breadcrumbs and fry in clarified butter. They may then be served either piled up and sprinkled over with chopped parsley or served with melted butter, or Tartare sauce, Béarnaise sauce, etc.

(3) Au Gratin: On a thick Duxelles (see p. 60) of chopped mushrooms, onions and tomatoes, place the poached scallops, and cover over with a layer of Duxelles. Sprinkle with fresh breadcrumbs, dot with butter, and place in the oven to brown all over the top.

(4) Dieppe fashion: As preceding recipe, but shrimps and mussels included with the scallops.

(5) In Mayonnaise: In oil and vinegar with plenty of parsley, shredded lettuce, capers, anchovy fillets, all drowned in mayonnaise.

(6) Brittany fashion: Place scallops on a layer of finely chopped shallots. Add salt and pepper and the merest trace of nutmeg. Cover with good grated gruyère cheese and white soft breadcrumbs. Dot butter over the top and place in the oven to brown. If scallops have not been poached, fifteen minutes will not be too long.

(7) On Grid-iron: Put raw scallops on grid (a light one) and turn when half-done. Serve with lemon juice and chopped parsley.

Winkles (Bigorneaux)

This little 'sea-snail' is usually eaten raw, withdrawn from its shell with a pin. It's a trifle to keep you occupied while waiting for a guest, or your wife, perhaps.

Prawns (Bouquet Shrimps)

Grey shrimps are smaller than pink or 'rosy' shrimps (called 'Bouquet shrimps', or, more usually, prawns).

If you buy them alive, cook by plunging into boiling, strongly salted water (or, preferably, sea-water). Eat as hors d'œuvre, with fresh butter, or use as a garnish. They are also a good bisque ingredient. If added to a salad, only the peeled tail portions are used. May also appear in mayonnaise, fried, or in shells. Here is a Creole recipe: Take some very fresh prawns and peel them, pound with pimento, lemon juice, salt, a little olive oil. Work all together into a kind of velvety mayonnaise.

Lobsters, Rock Lobsters, Norway Lobsters

Some French people assume that the 'Homard' is the 'Langouste's' husband.[1] But these crustaceans, although very similar in appearance, are distinct, and each has its males and females. The chief visible difference between spiny lobster and lobster is the larger size of the latter's fore-claws. The 'spiny' or 'rock' lobster has no specialized 'great claws'. Gastronomes find the flesh of the lobster (*homard*) more delicate in flavour, but also tougher and less digestible than that of the rock lobster

[1] The Lobster (*Homarus*) has the last segment of the thorax fixed; in the Crayfish (*Astacus*, French 'écrevisse') it is free. Crayfish is also styled, unfortunately, 'Homard épineux', or 'Spiny lobster' (French 'langouste') and in English sometimes 'Rock Lobster', 'écrevisse' being reserved for fresh-water Crayfish. Langoustine= Norway lobster. The Norway lobster (*Nephrops norvegicus*) is common in the North Sea, and has slender claws and kidney-shaped eyes. The most useful reminders are that *Homard*=lobster as we usually know it; *Langouste*=rock lobster; *Langoustine*=Norway lobster, or Dublin Bay Prawn. Ordinary Prawn=*Bouquet*.

(*langouste*). Generally speaking, recipes suitable for one kind serve equally well for the others.

Langoustines (Norway crabs) are smaller than the other two lobsters. They may be prepared in the same ways, as well as serving as hors d'œuvre, like shrimps and crayfish (of these, more will be said later).

N.B.—Lobsters should be cooked in a court-bouillon in a copper or enamel pan, as the flesh of crustaceans is apt to turn black in iron vessels. This advice comes from M. Wernert, rich in years but forever young, President of 'Les Cuisiniers de Paris'.

LOBSTERS IN COURT-BOUILLON: This is, of course, the simplest treatment. The court-bouillon, or stock, consists of water, salt, pepper, a carrot cut in rings, an onion, a bouquet garni, some parsley, all boiled together. When it is boiling the living lobster (previously washed in cold water) is plunged in. When cooked it is drained and allowed to cool. The flesh is mixed with mayonnaise or Tartare sauce. The best way of serving it, if you can spare the time, is to halve the large 'shell' and empty the contents. Empty the claws as well. Chop up the tail flesh and arrange it on the 'shell' with thin strips of truffle and some jelly. Surround with raw tomatoes with pulp removed and with artichoke bottoms filled with Russian salad in which the broken bits of claw meat have been incorporated. To be decorated with hard-boiled egg rings à l'Américaine (and not, as we shall prove in a minute, A L'ARMORICAINE).

Charles Monselet has left a rhymed recipe, the prologue of which runs:

'Take a firm lobster; on his crusty shell
  Clamp a firm hand, and let him vainly leap;
Dismember, though he struggle and rebel,
  His living flesh . . . cardinal of the deep. . . .'

And the recipe follows. But before you can compare the lobster with a cardinal, you must cook it, and this lack of accuracy on the poet-gourmet's part makes us a little anxious about recommending his recipe. That is why we prefer to give this one, supplied by a practising chef:

Cut up the living lobster and place the pieces in a sauté dish over a good heat, adding a little fresh butter. Then 'flame' it with some good brandy. Pour over it a glass of dry white wine and three tablespoonsful of tomato sauce. Add shallot, chervil, tarragon, all well chopped, and some Cayenne pepper. Cook for twenty minutes. Take out lobster, arrange on serving dish, bind the sauce with the interior of the lobster which you have set aside earlier, and also thicken it with butter and flavour with lemon juice. Pour sauce over dish.

N.B.—Whisky may be lit on the lobster instead of brandy (which will make it all the more 'American' but of not quite such subtle bouquet).

A L'AMERICAINE OR A L'ARMORICAINE?

I think I can tell you the name of the actual inventor of this dish. As you so rightly observe, 'Homard à l'Américaine' was created in France, and, naturally, by a Frenchman, Peters, born at Sète. His real name was Fraisse.

I knew him round about 1900. He was then between 78 and 80 years old, I'd say, and lived quite modestly with his wife in the Rue Germain-Pilon. One evening, in expansive mood, he spoke to me of the famous lobster. On his return from America, where he held a chef's post for some time in Chicago, he opened his own restaurant—the Restaurant Peters—in Paris. If I am not mistaken, this was a little before 1860.

Now one evening, long after most of the diners had left, eight or ten people turned up just as Peters was about to shut up shop for that night, and they demanded dinner most insistently, alleging moreover that they had only an hour in which to eat it. Peters was the soul of good nature and he consented to get back to his ovens for their sake. But for all that, he was rather worried, not quite knowing what he could find for them. 'While they get on with the soup and hors d'oeuvre,' he reflected, 'I'll have time to knock up some sort of a fish course.'

But he had no fish, he soon discovered. Nothing but live lobsters in reserve for next day's luncheons. And there was no time for the usual preliminary cooking in court-bouillon. . . .

And it was at that point that Peters was struck with inspiration. He cast some butter into a pan with tomatoes, pounded garlic, shallot . . . then white wine, a little oil, and last of all a good soaking of cognac (which at that time cost something like 1400 or 1500 francs a quart). When all was bubbling together, Peters said to himself, 'There's only one way to get these lobsters to cook quickly: they must be cut up small and left to simmer in the sauce.'

And that is what he did. The result was superb. The guests, enraptured, asked this remarkable restaurateur *to tell them all about the exquisite dish. What, they enquired, was its name? And Peters, still under the influence of his recent sojourn in the States, replied with no hesitation, 'It's called "Homard à l'Américaine".'*

I have the recipe as Peters himself gave it to me, and it is the one I always use. As for the story behind it, that I take to be utterly authentic, for Peters was a man of great probity and frankness, as well as good nature.

(Letter from M. GAERTIGUE to Curnonsky)

It is also possible to proceed as above, but removing all the flesh from the shell and putting it in a *timbale* (pie-dish).

Also, when the meat is thus free of the members, it may be sauté with two tablespoonsful of cream, a glass of port wine and some paprika, then covered with the Américaine sauce reinforced with butter.

There are a thousand other possible variations and you yourself will no doubt invent some new ones. It is a matter of taste, time at one's disposal, and ingredients available.

GRILLED LOBSTER: Cut lobster in two (you need a good pound to serve two people) and put on a quick grill, with melted butter to taste. Serve very hot and slightly browned, pouring a teaspoonful of cognac over it. (You naturally remove the unwanted portions before grilling.)

N.B.—This may have as accompaniment a Béarnaise sauce mixed with the cooked 'coral' and 'flamed' with a little brandy.

Another possibility—especially if it's a good-sized lobster in the two-pounds-or-more class—is to poach it gently before grilling it, and to use as poaching medium a mixture of vinegar and white wine with onion quarters, shallots, a clove or two, a piece of garlic, a bouquet garni. This is served with a sauce consisting of fresh cream containing chopped parsley, chervil, tarragon, after a brief sojourn on the salamander-stove (hot-plate for browning quickly).

Yet another idea is to serve with a sauce made by reducing shallots (finely chopped) in a glass of Madeira, then blending with about the same quantity of thick clotted cream reinforced with two egg yolks.

CREAMED LOBSTER: The same principle as for 'à l'Américaine', but no tomato sauce. At the end of the cooking period thick cream seasoned with a little grated gruyère cheese is added to the sauce, then it is cooked just sufficiently to restore the heat, and served at once.

NEWBURY LOBSTER (a classical, *Haute Cuisine* recipe): Dismember the living crab and brown in butter (smoking hot) in a sauté pan. Pour in enough Madeira or sherry to cover the meat and leave to cook for twenty minutes. Then remove flesh from the pieces and leave in a warm place while you thicken the cooking liquor with a basinful of cream reinforced with four egg yolks. Be very careful not to let this sauce boil. Then add the hot lobster meat and a little butter 'worked' with the coral, which you remove at the start. Serve with Creole rice.

(A recipe from M. WERNERT, already mentioned.)

A LA NAGE: also known as 'Swimming maidens of Cherbourg'. This method is for small ones of about half a pound each. They are put into a court bouillon of onion and carrot rings, a bouquet garni, peppercorns, dry white wine, a touch of Cayenne pepper. (This stock must boil for twenty minutes at least before the lobsters go in.) Cook them for about twelve minutes. Serve in cooking liquor with a dash of cognac and a sprinkling of chopped parsley.

May also be eaten cold with a Tartare sauce.

STUFFED LOBSTERS: Cook in a court bouillon, allow to cool, then cut in two and remove meat. Cut in rings as far as possible. Chop the interior together with some mushrooms, green olives, and mixed herbs. Make a Béchamel sauce. Use some of it to bind the stuffing, fill with this one half of the carapace, place over the stuffing some rounds of meat, moisten with Armagnac, now pour on the rest of the Béchamel, add grated gruyère and some breadcrumbs, a knob of fresh butter. Heat up again in the oven.

CROUSTADE OF LOBSTER (Lobster Pie or Patty): Fill a pastry case of good butter-based light dough that has just emerged from the oven with dice of lobster meat (cooked in court bouillon and then mixed with a Béchamel made with cream, and mushroom and truffle slices). Then serve very hot.

LOBSTER PILAF=Same procedure as for Shellfish Pilaf (p. 76).

Freshwater
Food

CRAYFISH

Do not forget to geld these, as it were, by removing the central strip of the caudal fin, for this is attached to a little gut-portion of extreme bitterness.

Crayfish are cooked in a court bouillon, à la nage (see p. 83) in a cream sauce or in pasties (see lobster recipes). There is also the famous Gratin.

Take two dozen live crayfish, wash and 'geld' (as above) and put in a pan with an egg-sized piece of butter, a little salt and pepper. Sauté until a beautiful cardinal red. Add a glass of high-quality champagne and set this alight. Now pour in a quarter of fresh cream and cook for five minutes.

Crayfish Gratin à la Royale (or Crayfish-tail Gratin)

Take out the crayfish, remove the tails. Crush the rest in a mortar with a piece of butter the size of three walnuts. Add this purée to your sauce, heat it again, taste for correct seasoning. Arrange the stripped tails on serving dish and cover with the sauce. Sprinkle liberally with parmesan cheese and gratinate in the oven.

(Recipe of M. LERCH, 'best workman in France', 1936.)

Crayfish Ragoût Colette

Take a dozen good crayfish and cook them in a lightly-flavoured court bouillon made with carrots, thyme, bay, pepper, salt, garlic, onions in a liquor that's one-quarter water and three-quarters white wine.

In an oven dish put two ounces butter and when it melts add some well-washed and dried mushrooms. In another pan make a thick tomato sauce (tomatoes cooked in a glassful of the stock) and force it through a sieve. Bind with a small pinch of flour. Mix this sauce with the mushrooms and add the crayfish. Before eating pour a glass of Armagnac over and set light to it.

(This recipe was dedicated by PIERRE VARILLON, author, to Madame Colette, of the Académie Goncourt.)

Frogs

If you do not buy them already prepared, this is how to set about the job. Skin the animal and cut away the forepart so as to retain the thighs only. Thread these on a small stick and soak in cold water, renewing it every two hours (this must go on for about twelve hours at least). When the flesh is white and spongy take out of water and dry on a cloth.

In America they have numerous recipes for Bullfrog (regional recipes which could often be used for our own native frogs). But the classical French frog recipes are:

FROGS IN BUTTER: Put butter in sauté pan, add frogs, season, cook very gently. A minute before serving, sprinkle with ginger, pepper and chopped parsley.

FROG FRICASSEE: A good heat, sauté pan containing a good lump of butter and a little flour. Stir constantly with a wooden spoon. Put in the frogs, add a little white wine and ordinary seasoning plus a little red pepper. Bind the sauce with cream or with egg yolks.

FROGS WITH SAVOURY HERBS: Soak frogs in cold milk during their last two hours of soaking, instead of cold water. Roll in flour, sauté in butter heated to very high temperature. When done, sprinkle with chopped garlic, shallot and parsley.

FROGS IN SAUCE: Frogs sauté in butter are served with any one of the following sauces: Tomato and garlic; Béchamel and parmesan; Mornay, Mirepoix; Poulette; Curry.

American Frog Recipes

FRIED FROGS: Macerate in lemon juice with salt and pimento. Roll in a fritter batter just before frying in boiling oil.

DIANAH FROGS: Soak in boiling white wine, with large mushrooms as well, for five minutes. Then let the frog legs cool down while the mushrooms go on cooking in the reduced sauce, to which curry should be added. Replace the frogs and heat through again.

N.B.—The great chef Escoffier first made use of the expression 'Nymphs' to replace 'Frogs' Thighs', shocking to some Anglo-Saxons.

Snails

The Burgundy snail, or vine-snail, is the best, but there is also the 'small grey' kind from the south (although fairly common everywhere else). In order to avoid poisoning yourself by absorbing certain plants which the snail can support and you cannot, you must compel the snails to fast for a spell. While this is going on a calcareous film grows over the shell entrance. This is removed and the creature is 'sweated' for two hours in a solution of coarse salt, vinegar and a pinch of flour. The snails are then washed in plenty of changes of water used without stint. Finally, they are blanched for five minutes in boiling water.

They are then drained and washed again in cold water. It is time to remove them from their shells and take off the black extremities. The snails are now ready for one or the other following treatments:

SNAILS IN BUTTER: Cook the snails in a bouillon made from carrots, onions, thyme, salt, pepper. When cooked, replace in shells, which have been carefully washed (if necessary boil them in water with a few soda crystals added, then rinse thoroughly). Make separately a paste of fresh butter, crushed garlic, chopped parsley and pepper. Seal the snail in with this paste and warm up in the oven.

ARLES SNAILS: Cook the prepared snails gently with a little bacon (diced and sprinkled with flour, then moistened with dry white wine). Add tomato, garlic, chopped parsley.

CHABLIS SNAILS: Put a few drops of Chablis-and-shallot-reduced-together in the bottom of each shell.

POULETTE SNAILS: as Poulette Mussels (see p. 76).

CORSOISE: Cook the snails in red wine seasoned with garlic, onions, wild thyme, bay, cloves. Serve in the cooking liquor.

SNAIL FRITTERS: Put the cooked snails in a marinade of oil, lemon juice and chopped parsley. Dip them in batter and put in boiling fat. If you like, serve with tomato sauce.

And, to conclude these notes on gasteropods, this recipe on the grand scale is from Austin Croze (see p. 95).

Li Cagaraulo

'Throw your snails into a saucepan of boiling water containing thyme, bay-leaves, basil, a strip of orange peel, a piece of bacon rind. When they are almost done take them out and replace in their shells. Warm them up in olive oil surrounded with finely chopped bacon, pounded walnuts, anchovy fillets. Add salt and pepper, three bruised garlic cloves. Bind with a minute quantity of flour and serve on a dish of spinach.

N.B.—'Li Cagaraulo' is a very near relation of the 'Cagaroulade' of Montpellier, a dish which gave rise to the proverb: 'To every snail its own sauce'. In Charente snails are called 'cagouilles'. They are prepared in very much the same way, but instead of oil pork fat is used, with a glass of white wine to moisten, and a 'little enlivener of cognac'.

In Alsace the local wines are used, naturally, in the court bouillon, and a little aniseed or anisette cordial is added to the butter paste that seals the shells.

Fish

Govern the Empire as you would cook a little fish. LAO-TSE.

In the hands of a clever cook fish can become an inexhaustible source of endless enjoyment.

The smelt is the beccafico of the world of waters: same diminutive stature, same bouquet, same superlativeness.

BRILLAT-SAVARIN

Let Bacchus join the party, to extol
Sweet Amphitrite and this crisp-fried sole.

TRISTAN DEREME.

Great men pride themselves on knowing how to prepare a fish for table.

MONTAIGNE.

So now the nobs, who've realized
How high this wholesome fish should rate,
Cry up and rehabilitate
The cod we've overlong despised. . . .
If any should her neighbour slate
With 'Fishwife!', the apostrophized
Takes no offence. How out-of-date
The notion that she's been misprized
In street-boy's slang, when all that's meant
Is plaudit, homage, compliment!

HUGUES DELORME.

Fish has high nutritive value. Chemical analysis shows that the albuminoid substance in the flesh of fish has a composition similar to that of butcher's meat. It is, however, richer in phosphorus and potassium salts. The flesh of river eels, for example, contains (according to Dr. Pomiane) a thousand times more Vitamin A than beef does. Tunny fish, forty times more. If it is true to say that there are costly fish which might even be called 'luxury fish', there are many others that will give the housewife brilliant opportunities for providing first-class dishes. And it is as well to bear in mind that the high price of certain fish is due not so much to excellence of flavour as to a kind of formal elegance permitting such fish (e.g. mullet, turbot, salmon, trout) to be served up spectacularly for special displays. France is not a great fish-eating country, more's the pity.

Fish may be divided into two main categories: sea-fish and fresh-water (lake and river) fish. Another valid classification is into 'oily-fleshed' and 'lean-fleshed' (the former being a heavier tax on the digestion). Examples of 'oily-fleshed' fish are: shad, eel, bream, conger-eel, herring, lamprey, mackerel, marine eel, sardine, salmon, tunny, turbot.

Examples of 'lean-fleshed' fish are bass, pike, fresh cod, dorado, dab, whiting, skate, sole, tench, trout.

Fish needs to be very fresh. Freshness is perceptible: look for firmness of flesh, brilliance of scales, clearness of eye. Make certain especially that the gills are of a good, clear red colour. There must be no ammoniacal smell arising from the fish-slab.

A general rule of fish preparation is that the larger kinds (skate, pike, salmon, turbot, etc.) are cleaned by slitting the belly, while smaller ones (trout, herring, whiting, etc.) may be emptied through the gill orifices. The brill, exceptionally, has a transversal gash made behind the head, on its dark side, and the innards are removed through this. If braising is contemplated large fish are cut along the back, or the 'spine' is severed longitudinally.

It is usual to leave the roe, the eggs, inside (e.g. in the herring).

Fish cookery recognizes five principal and classic procedures:

(1) Cooking in court bouillon; (2) grilling; (3) baking; (4) frying; (5) matelotes of fish (fish stews).

(1) COOKING IN COURT BOUILLON: this being a stock or 'infusion,' and vegetables. Sometimes a tablespoonful of oil is added, frequently white or red wine, or vinegar (see for example, Trout 'au Bleu').

(2) GRILLING: the fish should be dried in a cloth lined with oil, and the grilling or boiling plate used should be very hot and also oiled.

(3) BAKING: more or less same effect as 'au gratin' or braising procedures. The fish is placed in a good large dish on a bed of sliced onions, well spiced (also with an addition of mushrooms, if you like), moistened with wine (preferably white) dotted with butter. A good hot oven.

N.B.—(*a*) To avoid scorching or overcooking the exterior too soon, cover fish, if necessary, with oiled paper.

(*b*) You must be guided by the oiliness or otherwise of the fish and either increase or diminish the addition of butter, cream, or oil.

(*c*) Different stuffings are permissible.

(4) Frying: mainly for small fish. They must be dried and rolled in dry flour (or batter) and put in boiling fat (oil for choice).

(5) 'Matelotes' or Stews (see, for instance, recipes for bouillabaisse, stewed eel, 'pauchouse'). Left-over fish cooked according to the four preceding methods may be used as a good recooked dish (matelote) or served cold, say in scallop shells or shell-shaped crisp lettuce leaves, with mayonnaise or a vinegar-dressing, accompanied by hard-boiled eggs or a potato salad. The fish pieces may also be mixed with vegetables of various kinds, blended with a Béchamel sauce, and reheated in an oven-dish.

SEA FISH

These are listed alphabetically under their French names, or menu names, the English equivalent being added. As only *English* fish-names are indexed, you will find the fish of your immediate concern in the index on pages 381 seqq.

Alose (Shad)

The shad is a migratory fish of the *Clupea* genus (same as herring) and is anadromous (i.e. goes up rivers for spawning). The Thwaite shad is quite common around the coasts of Britain, the common shad chiefly in lower parts of larger rivers. The flesh is fine but rather full of small bones, and it taints easily. It should not be left soaking too long but should be gutted, washed, and dried in a cloth as soon as possible. It lends itself to the same preparations as perch, wolf-fish (blenny type), fresh cod, herring and mackerel, of which more later.

Alose (Shad) (Cocherel style)

Stuff a 3 lb shad with the following stuffing: pound whiting or pollack (coal-fish cod) with salt, pepper, grated nutmeg, a white of egg (raw), then pass through hair-sieve. Work into this, with a spatula, half a pint of fresh cream. Add two tablespoonsful of chopped chives (blanched) and one of parsley. The stuffed shad is then wrapped in thin bacon 'rasherettes', fixed on short skewers, and cooked in a brisk oven for forty-five minutes. A few minutes before serving, remove the bacon pieces so that the outside surface may be browned over.

Potato halves, boiled then browned in boiling fat, accompanied by artichoke bottoms, are a good garnish. Dilute the cooking liquor with dry white wine and a little cream. Serve separately in its own receptacle.

(A recipe by PROSPER MONTAGNE)

Alose (Shad, Mayfish)

The shad is stuffed with a chopped sorrel stuffing, and cooked in the oven with seasoning, bouquet garni, sliced onions and carrots, and a half-bottle of dry white wine.

N.B.—Another method is to finish the cooking in the oven after five minutes' 'grilling'. It bakes on a bed of sorrel for thirty minutes. The acidity of the sorrel breaks down the nasty little sharp bones of the shad.

Alose (Provence style)

The shad is cut in pieces which are lightly cooked in olive oil. Then a layer of sorrel and small onions is topped with a layer of the fish, and these layers are made alternately. The dish is then covered with a hermetically sealing lid and cooking should go on for six or seven hours in a slow oven. The sorrel may then be thrown away, for it will have 'imbibed' the troublesome bones.

Anchois (Anchovies)

Atlantic or Mediterranean. These are preserved in brine or oil and are most often used as hors d'œuvre. They may also be pounded into a paste for sandwiches or a toast spread. Fresh anchovies may be cooked in the same way as smelts.

Bar (Sea-Perch) (Bass)

The vulgar name of the Labrax. Also called sea-dace, sea-wolf. Simply 'wolf' in the Mediterranean basin (see p. 105) where it is as abundant as it is rare in the Channel.

It may be boiled, soused, braised, cooked in sauce (gratinated), and cooked in butter (*meunière*), served cold with various sauces, or à la Dugléré (Dugléré is a fish velouté sauce of shallot, tomato, butter, white wine, flour, parsley).

Grilled Bass, Perch with Fennel

This is best in winter, when the fennel is fresh. If you have to use dried fennel, push it into the gill-apertures and lay it inside the fish. If you are, however, doing it in winter, cut a fresh head of fennel and arrange strips of it on a dish, adding salt, pepper, olive oil. Grill the fish separately, and when about half cooked put it on the bed of oil, fennel, etc., and bake, basting frequently with the cooking liquor.

Bass with Lemon

Cut a good heavy bass into cutlets. Heat some olive or other cooking oil to a high temperature and add a clove of garlic, then the cutlets. Then cover with the juice of five lemons and water to make up bulk required. Add salt to taste then either pepper or curry powder. Simmer for twenty minutes.

This is also a pleasant way of cooking pollack and mullet. It is an Egyptian recipe, and in that country they eat it cold, for the sauce congeals into an agreeable jelly.

Fisherman's Bass

Cut some carrots in flute-like strips and line bottom of fish-kettle with these. Make a finely-chopped mixture of 2 cloves of garlic, 2 cloves, mixed herbs, white pepper. Add to 1¾ pints good fish stock (*fumet*) or white stock. Put fish on carrots, add flavoured liquor, seethe for about twelve minutes after boiling point is reached. Strain half the liquid through fine muslin, remove grease, bind with worked butter, adding a fair quantity of tomato purée and a few drops of anchovy essence. This sauce is to be served separately.

VARIATION—Put fish on bed of herbs and cook in oven, basting with butter. For sauce, add a bare pint of Chablis to most of the cooking liquid.

Barbue (Brill)

This is a flat fish with flesh very like the turbot's. It abounds particularly on Atlantic coasts and may reach a length of twenty inches or more.

Preparations: boiling, poaching, sousing, braising, au gratin, grilled (fillets), baked, eaten cold, with different sauces, a la Dugléré.

American Brill

Season inside and outside and put the fish in a buttered dish with sliced onion and a bouquet garni. Pour a little white wine over it, then some fish stock, and cover with lid. Cook in slow oven. Drain away liquor, put on long narrow serving dish and garnish with slices of lobster (à l'Américaine) or crayfish and cover with an Américaine Sauce made from the cooking liquor reduced.

Brill in Wine

As above, but let the 'sauce' be either a red or a white wine, as you choose.

VARIATIONS:

With Burgundy: small onions, small mushrooms, a half-pint of red burgundy.

With Chambertin: use Chambertin as above.

With Champagne: bone the fish and stuff with creamed pike. Moisten with dry Champagne.

ANCHOIADE OF CROZE

Count Austin de Croze was a grand seigneur *and a gourmet, author of a long series of works on the cuisine of France, which he never tired of extolling. Notable among these was his* Psychology of the Table. *He was very fond of quoting his Anchoiade recipe:*

'I dedicate my Anchoiade Croze *to the musicians and gourmets among Crozes dead and gone, as well as to their successors of today. It is quintessentially Provençal and will be eaten from Les Ambiers to the Lofotens, from Martigues to the Kuril Islands, and at Papæiti, but not in the U.S.A., for there they blaspheme against wine. Here, then, is the recipe for the anchoiade which I composed in Corsica in 1888, improved upon in London in 1913, and brought to perfection in Paris in 1925, in honour of a double quartet of gourmets.*

Take, for six persons:

12 Collioures anchovies in oil, 12 in brine,

12 high-quality almonds (fresh), skinned; or, failing these, six walnuts,

9 fine dried figs. The acme of refinement is to get figs partly browned by the sun,

2 cloves of garlic and a medium onion (barely an ounce),

½ lemon (Bergamot for choice),

1½ ounces of seasoning herbs, including southern wild thyme, and 3 sprigs of fresh tarragon, a few fennel sprigs, a small red pepper. Some good olive oil, a fruity quality, and a coffeespoonful of orange-flower water, also of good quality,

12 small rolls of bread, unsweetened, with thin crust.

Here is the method:

(1) On a chopping-board cut up very finely the onion, garlic and herbs, so that you have a good tablespoonful of the mixture. Tail the figs and mix them in too.

(2) Take a mortar, either of marble or of well-polished stone, and pound the pimento to a powder, then the almonds (or walnuts), then the anchovies in oil (previously well drained), and remember to remove all the bones from the anchovies first. Now add the fillets of anchovy in brine, previously rinsed, but

not over-soaked, also 'cleaned' and drained of liquid. Use the pestle vigorously and happily and without pausing for a rest until you have achieved a very smooth paste. Now moisten this with two tablespoonsful of olive oil, added a few drops at a time.

(3) When this paste is of the consistency of a good thick mayonnaise, add the chopped herbs. Mix and turn in the mortar, adding the half-lemon juice drop by drop. After ten minutes of this blending, add the orange-flower water, also in drops.

(4) Cut up the rolls, longwise and on the under-halves spread the paste (a quarter-inch layer). On the soft part of the upper halves, place six or eight drops of good, fruit-rich olive oil, and spread this with the back of a spoon. Put the dressed rolls into a very hot oven—into which you have previously cast a few twigs of pine, lavender and rosemary—for about five minutes.

(5) Pile on a dish, setting off the saffron-gold of the crusts with the tender green of very young fennel shoots, crowning the whole with fine black olives, velvety, moist, rich-hued, like shot silk.

And the drink to go with this dish?

From spring to autumn, good and genuine Saint-Péray, very cool. From Michaelmas to Easter, a true Clos Bodin de Cassis. And let the wine be not over-glacial, but of a noticeable coolness. Ice is suitable only in American bars.

BRANDADE

Lest this sweet flesh should only half reveal
Its store of virtues, pound it hot and strong
While standing like a pilot at the wheel
Toiling, if needs must be, the whole day long.

To your bland paste add oil, the best in town,
Heat it and stir. Grate garlic—not too much.
Add it, with fine-chopped parsley. Crowning touch,
Serve bread squares fried, in butter, golden-brown.

Such unctuous richness waits you gourmands then
As duck, or golden pheasant rich and rare,
Or lark ragoût, or savoury guinea-hen,
Or truffle tucked in turkey flesh, or hare,
Can never promise. Nothing can compare
With cod brandade—nothing of mortal ken.

RAYMOND FEVRIER

With Macon: use red Macon wine.

With Cider: use one or two bottles of cider and thicken the cooking liquid with butter and cream.

Brill with Shellfish

Cook as brill in white wine, then take out and drain thoroughly. In the cooking liquor poach some cleaned shelled mussels and cockles, picked shrimps, one or two oysters. Put these all round the brill on a serving dish and cover with a sauce made from the cooking liquor reinforced with cream. Powder with grated nutmeg.

VARIATIONS:

Cancale: garnish with poached oysters only, and cover with Normande sauce.

Shrimp: shrimps only as garnish, shrimp sauce.

Dieppe: mussel garnish, white wine sauce.

Nantua: crayfish tails and Nantua sauce.

Cardinal: lobster scallops and white sauce.

Suprêmes of Brill (Saint-Germain)

Cut brill fillets, trim them, dress them in breadcrumbs and cook in butter (or grill). Serve with grilled small fresh tomatoes and Béarnaise sauce.

Carrelet (Plaice)

A flat fish not unlike the dab but of less esteem for quality of flesh. Preparation, according to size of fish, follows Bass or Dab instructions.

Plaice Dugléré

Cut the fish across into seven or eight cutlets and place these in a well-buttered sauté dish. Sprinkle over the butter, before fish is added, a tablespoonful of chopped onion, some thyme, parsley, bay, a *grated* clove of garlic; also some skinned tomatoes. Moisten with white wine. Begin with good brisk heat, then lower flame. Bake for ten minutes. Then drain the pieces and reconstitute the fish.

Add to cooking liquor two tablespoonsful of a thin velouté and three oz of butter. Pour over fish and sprinkle with grated parsley.

N.B.—Dugléré was chef at the Café Anglais, a well-known restaurant during the Second Empire. He it is who invented this recipe, and legend has it that he originally used a plaice; but it is an equally good treatment for turbot, bass, shad, etc.

Cabillaud (Fresh Cod)

According to Larousse, 'Cabillaud' is the vulgar name for 'Morue' (fresh cod). But other authorities have it that 'Cabillaud' or 'Cabliaud' is the correct name for cod which does not become 'Morue' until it is dried. All recipes which may result in dishes appearing on the menu as either 'Cabillaud' or 'Morue' are given later, under 'Morue'.

Colin (Pollack)

Also called 'White salmon' and being of the 'Merlin' class was at one time salted, like salt cod. Almost all cod recipes are suitable. But when the fish are exceptionally large, it is better to cut them into thick slices and fry in the ordinary way. Or they may be sauté, or boiled, eaten cold, etc. (with mayonnaise). It is particularly important with this fish to be sure that it is quite fresh. It taints very easily, especially in stormy weather.

Colin à l'Italienne (Pollack in wine and tomato sauce)

Cut fish in thick slices and fry golden in oil to which a sliced onion has been added. Remove fish, add to oil a few tomatoes which have been freed of pips and passed through sieve. Bind this oil and tomato mixture with a little flour, dilute with white wine, and put the fish back to cook for twenty or thirty minutes without boiling. Put on dish and mask with the sauce (sieved to remove solids).

Stewed Pollack and Rice

In a court bouillon (tomatoes, bouquet garni)—just enough to cover, cook fish slowly for a quarter of an hour (the fish cut in biggish pieces). Prepare at the same time a dish of steamed rice, and place fish on this. Serve the cooking liquor separately as sauce (strained) and flavoured with a few spoonsful of curry.

Congre (Conger Eel)

Also called Sea-eel. A common fish of Southern Europe it may attain a length of over ten feet. The black kind is more highly esteemed than the white as the latter is inclined to be flabby and over-oily. Generally speaking, recipes suitable for river eels will serve for congers. They are also a very valuable ingredient of fish stews; if cut in slices or cutlets they may be prepared as Colin à l'Italienne (above).

Stewed Conger Eel with Peas

Cut up a conger fillet, discarding tail piece, as it is full of little bones. Cook in a little butter with onions, garlic, a bouquet garni, shallots. When the fish is nicely browned, add as little liquor as possible (stock water). Then add a few drops of brandy and some fresh green peas. Cover and cook slowly.

(Recipe of BREST railway station buffet.)

Daurade
(Gilthead, Chrysophrys, Bullhead and related species)

This is one of the acanthopterygious fishes, and Daurades are commoner in the Mediterranean than elsewhere. Its maximum length is about 20 inches. It is silvery blue, glaucous-bellied, and with a golden crescent between the eyes. The ancients called it 'Golden Eyebrow'. See 'Bar' and 'Mulet' for the most satisfactory treatments. May be boiled, braised, grilled, gratinated (i.e. cooked in oven sauce until sauce is well reduced and top crisp), done à la meunière (i.e. slowly in butter) or à la Dugléré (see pages 93 and 97).

TUNISIAN FASHION: remove scales and clean out the inside of a fish weighing about a pound (for 3 people). In a mortar pound a clove of garlic with parsley, half a red pimento (strong). Add pepper, salt, now blend in two walnuts of butter. Put the smooth paste inside the fish, place it in a heat-proof dish, dot with more butter, and bake for thirty-five minutes.

STUFFED: take four ounces of dried cod, 2 oz soft white 'milky' breadcrumbs, 2 ox button mushrooms, 2 oz chopped onions, 2 oz chopped parsley. Combine these with an egg yolk, and stuff the fish with this. Place on a buttered oven-dish with some chopped shallots, cover with white wine (slightly diluted with water, if you like). Leave a good hour in the oven, but cover the fish with a well-greased paper. As it cooks, baste over the paper with liquid. Serve with reduced cooking liquor, reinforced with melted butter, a tablespoonful of flour and a beaten egg yolk.

IMPERIAL: same procedure as above, but the basis of the stuffing may be pike, and red wine may replace white. Serve with fried herring roes and mussels cooked in the sauce. If you like, add as well a few oysters cooked in their own water.

Eglefin (Haddock)

Eglefin=Aiglefin. A smaller fish than cod, but closely related. White flesh of good quality. When 'fresh' it is adaptable to all the Colin and Cabillaud treatments. Frequently, however, it is split open and smoked, and it appears to be the most usual form in which it is bought nowadays: poached and served with melted butter and plain-boiled potatoes, it may have a leaf-spinach accompaniment. A simple but nourishing dish is provided by serving egg (*sur le plat*, see p. 48) on each helping of haddock. Used cold, it may be cut into small pieces and added to a salad as hors d'œuvre.

Espadon (Swordfish)

Another of the acanthopterygious fishes, the swordfish is found around

Sicily, and in the Baltic and North Seas. It can attain a length of some twelve to fifteen feet, thanks to its prolonged upper jaw which juts out like a spur. The flesh is delicate and white. It is used in the same way as tunny-fish which it resembles.

Esturgeon (Sturgeon)

This migratory fish goes up river for spawning. Its eggs are then taken to serve as caviar, its bladder makes excellent fish-glue. The sturgeon is common in Russia (Volga sterlets) but is rare around north European coasts. It does, however, appear more abundantly in Gironde, where there are French caviar fishing-establishments (e.g. Maison Prunier). Three tons annually is the total production for France.

At one time sturgeon was a royal preserve. It is still customary to offer fine sturgeon to the reigning monarch. The flesh is firm and a little difficult to digest. Whole sturgeon may be served braised, in champagne, with garnish of truffles, braised cucumber, mushrooms, etc. But the housewife is more likely to be dealing with a fillet or cutlet of about one or two pounds weight. This she will cover with small scraps of bacon fat (lardons) to keep it basted, and cook as though she were making a Veal Fricandeau (see p. 205). Like a fricandeau, it is served with gravy, with sorrel, etc.

Grondin (Red Gurnard)

(Often sold also as gurnard or red mullet, although the red colour marks the chief resemblance).

Preparations: fried, grilled, meunière (slowly in butter), lightly boiled, and soused, in white wine. Very good when newly smoked. It is also a bouillabaisse ingredient.

Gurnet in Butter, with Herbs

For each person you require a fish of about 6 oz. Remove scales, empty fish, wash thoroughly. Take out the bones, wipe dry, sprinkle salt and pepper inside the fish. Roll balls of butter in chopped parsley, and put one in each fish. Butter an oven-dish, spread over the butter two finely chopped shallots. Lay the fish back to back over the shallots and pour a little white wine over them.

In another pan melt about half an ounce of butter and cook in it (without browning) a large chopped onion. Add a bare half pound of sliced mushrooms, a little salt and pepper. When the mushrooms are done, add contents of pan to the gurnets and cook all together in the oven until fish are done. Then put them on a plate and reduce the cooking liquor in a small pan. If necessary thicken with some worked butter or white breadcrumbs. Pour sauce over fish, and sprinkle top with chopped herbs (parsley, chervil, chives, in equal quantities).

N.B.—All mullet recipes may be applied to gurnet.

Harengs (Herrings)

Fish of our Northern Seas and found in great abundance: they arrive in vast shoals around our coasts in the month of March, millions at a time. May be eaten as fresh, salt or smoked herrings.

(a) Fresh Herrings

May be fried, grilled, served meunière-fashion, maître d'hôtel. Pickled, they make a good hors d'œuvre, and the treatment is:

Soused Fresh Herrings

First of all soak the cleaned herrings for twelve hours in brine, then place in an earthenware dish on a bed of sliced onions and carrots with chopped parsley, thyme, bay, peppercorns, a few cloves. Add enough liquid to cover, a mixture of half white wine, half vinegar. Cover with another layer of carrots and onions, then a greased sheet of paper. Bring to boiling point, then put lid on and simmer for a quarter of an hour. Let herrings get cold in cooking dish.

Mustard Herrings

Before grilling, cover with a thick layer of made mustard, then baste with oil.

Fécamp Herrings

Put cleaned herrings on a base of sliced onions and carrots in an oven dish. Add a clove of crushed garlic and some parsley, a few slices of lemon (with peel). Pour over a pint of boiling vinegar and go on boiling over gentle heat for twenty minutes, basting frequently.

Boulangère Herrings

Surround them with thin slices of potato and onions. Season lavishly and dot generously with butter. Bring to boiling point then keep hot in the cooking dish. Bring this to table, with a sprinkling of chopped parsley and shallot.

(b) Smoked and Salted Herrings

There are two smoking procedures, the 'hot' and the 'cold' methods. The actual salting is done either on the herring boats or at the landing ports. Smoked herrings, Kippers, Bloaters, etc., are usually purchased in their 'finished' state. Kippers are heavily smoked, but the degree of saltiness varies, as do size and plumpness.

Lamprey

The lamprey, also a sea fish that goes to the estuaries and rivers for spawning, has certain species which remain in fresh water all their lives. The skin is slimy but the flesh delicate, although very fatty. All eel recipes are suitable, but as the Gironde lamprey is the best obtainable, the most successful recipe for lampreys is obviously:

Bordeaux Lampreys

Cut off the end of the tail of a live lamprey and hang it up for the blood (which will be needed) to drip into a vessel. Scald and scrape skin to remove slime. Slowly and with every precaution make a circular cut around the head. A large nerve or muscle will be revealed. You must pull hard on this and withdraw it without breaking.

Cut fish into small pieces, cook gently in oil and remove all unwanted scraps. Put in separate dish, and mix a roux into the cooking oil, adding twice as much red wine as there was oil, also a bouquet garni.

Fry lightly some slices of white of large leeks, some small onions, diced ham, and pour the wine sauce over them. Cook for one hour. Then add the pieces of lamprey and a few mushrooms, and cook over gentle heat for another half-hour. Before serving, use the blood as sauce liaison. Butter slightly and serve surrounded with fried bread cubes.

(Recipe of the DUBERN restaurant, Bordeaux)

Limande (Dab)

One of the Pleuronectidæ—a flat fish of Atlantic regions. Flesh soft but of good digestive quality, thus useful for invalids and convalescents. All plaice recipes applicable.

Lemon-Sole

Like dabs or sole, but more oval and elongated. Flesh more fibrous and insipid than that of sole. Prepare as sole or plaice. If very large, treat as 'Barbue'.

Lotte (Eel-Pout, Burbot)

There are sea and river varieties. The sea 'lotte' is also called 'sea-devil' and is principally used as a bouillabaisse ingredient or in other fish stews. It is not very tasty but has no troublesome bone (to make up for this):

Preparations: fillets braised in white wine; steamed; baked; fricandeau; fried; matelote; in hot or cold pies (like eel pies). All eel and lamprey treatments are suitable for burbot or eel-pout.

Mackerel

Another acanthopterygious, migratory fish. It is of a handsome steely blue with greenish reflections, and silvery-white underside. The flesh is oily and full of flavour. It is at its best for table in April.

Preparations: fried, grilled, cooked in a court bouillon, or meunière fashion, plain boiled, gratinated, fillets cooked separately, and so on.

Mackerel Fillet Papillotes

Remove heads, gut and wash well, then trim fillets and season with salt and pepper. Pour a little oil over the seasoned fillets. Oil a hot griddle and grill these fillets.

Cut some strong white paper into large heart-shapes and oil them thoroughly. Mix chopped parsley with butter, salt, pepper. Dress half of each 'heart' with this, put a fillet on top, fold over the rest of the paper and close by folding in the edges. Put on an oiled oven sheet and leave in hot oven for two minutes. As soon as the papers have begun to puff and swell, serve the papillotes at once.

Fried Mackerel, American Method

Open the fish into two sections and fry these. Then on your serving dish place alternately a piece of fish and a fried rasher of bacon.

Stuffed Mackerel

Empty at gills and stuff through these same apertures with any chosen stuffing. For example: stale breadcrumbs, chopped herbs, yellow of egg, seasoning all blended together. Grill, with melted butter and lemon-juice.

Another stuffing: a 'mousse' of whiting and mushrooms.

Mustard Mackerel

Daub inside and outside with made mustard (strong) and grill or bake.

N.B.—It is also a good idea to sauté in frying pan some large green gooseberries and pour these over the finished mackerel.

Mackerels with Sorrel

Split longitudinally, clean, grill, serve with a purée of sorrel or spinach.

VARIATION: or with strongly spiced tomato purée.

Soused Mackerel

Same principles as for Soused Herrings, but substitute rings of lemon for the carrot rings, and be lavish with the chopped shallot, using ten of these as well as three cloves of garlic. Leave twenty minutes in slow oven. Allow to get cold in cooking dish. If you do not touch it with your hands, this fish and pickling liquor will keep for a week. If you use vinegar instead of wine and leave the fish, etc., in an earthenware vessel it will keep longer still. But you must not let your hands come in contact with it.

Merlan (Whiting)

Fine texture, easily digestible. Quite abundant in northern waters, Baltic, English Channel, etc.

Preparations: boiled, fried, gratinated, grilled, meunière, fillets, etc.

Whiting and Mustard Sauce

Six small whiting, cleaned, washed and drained, in pan with water half-way up the fish. Add salt, pepper, and then a gill of wine-vinegar. Cook very gently over low heat until water bubbles, then put in oven for a quarter of an hour. Prepare this sauce meanwhile: ½ oz flour, just over ½ oz butter, a quarter of the boiling cooking liquor. Whisk well. Remove from heat when smooth and well-whisked and add a tablespoonful of white mustard. Pour over fish and serve at once.

Whiting and Spinach Pomiane

A doctor's recipe. Remove heads and interiors of some medium whiting, wash, remove spine. Line each with chopped and seasoned spinach. Close up the fish, arrange on oven dish, butter, pour over white wine. Bake in oven. Add a thread of tomato purée before serving.

Catalan Whiting

Cook in sauté pan in half butter, half olive oil. Put them on serving platter and garnish with a julienne of sweet peppers, also tomatoes and aubergines. Sauté in olive oil, and sprinkle with lemon juice; serve very hot.

Paupiettes of White Fillets

Trim the fillets and on one side set a thin layer of fish forcemeat. Then roll them 'en paupiettes' (coiled in on themselves) and poach in fish stock. Serve in any of these ways:

BERCY: red wine sauce.

DIEPPOISE: mussel sauce.

NORMANDE or NANTUA: au gratin, herbs, etc., or with creamy crayfish sauce.

Morue (Cod)

See earlier note on cod, p. 97. The flesh of this fish is particularly rich in assimilable phosphates and iodine, the latter facilitating the digestion of rich elements and contributing towards the balance and good

THE TWO TURBOTS

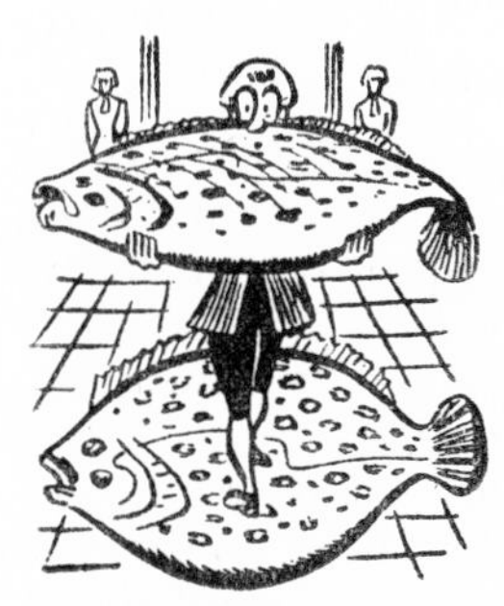

Talleyrand, as is well known, was a diplomat, as well as being a gourmet and a wit. One day Chevet, purveyor of high-class foodstuffs in the Palais-Royal quarter, made him a present of two simply gigantic turbots, the like of which had never been seen in Paris. Talleyrand summoned his kitchen staff to a conference. What was to be done? For he would be giving, next day, a dinner for twelve guests, people of sufficient discrimination to appreciate the exquisite flesh of these fish, not to mention their unusual girth. But to serve both turbots would smack of nouveau-riche *vulgarity. And yet . . . and yet, it flattered his vanity to be able to put both on display.*

After some thought, he smiled into his lace ruffle. Inspiration had come. Next evening, the soup plates removed, the butler-in-chief threw open the double doors to the dining-room and revealed two footmen carrying, on an immense serving-dish, the most colossal turbot that any of the diners had ever seen. There were admiring cries, exclamations of wonder, glowing compliments . . . then suddenly, a gasp of horror. One of the footmen had slipped on the polished floor and the turbot had fallen to the ground. All present were sorely vexed.

And then: 'Have the second turbot brought in', ordered Talleyrand, without turning a hair. And two more members of his staff bore in, to the applause of the enchanted visitors, the second turbot.

A STORY FROM MARSEILLE

'Waiter, what on earth is this fish?'

'Golly, sir, I'd 'a thought everyone knew him—he's a sea-wolf. Mediterranean speciality.'

'Fair enough. But he certainly tastes a bit muddy, your Mediterranean sea-wolf.'

'There now, I'll bet he's been traipsing all over the oceans then, sir.'

functioning of the thyroid glandular system. It is therefore a most useful dish for convalescents, those with thyroid deficiencies, overworked people with poor appetites, growing boys and girls. Moral: unless your doctor forbids it, eat plenty of cod.

It may be braised, boiled, boulangère (see herrings, p. 101). All brill recipes are suitable.

Cod, Bonne Femme Preparation

Empty and clean the fish, dry after washing and mop off water patches with a cloth. Season with table salt, white pepper, four chopped shallots and a clove of garlic, also chopped up finely, a sprig or two of thyme, bay-leaf, ten onion rings. Pour a gill of white wine (dry) over it, and two tablespoonsful of olive oil. From time to time baste the fish with this cooking liquor as it marinates before the actual cooking.

Put fish in baking dish, strain the liquor through a fine strainer, put the 'grounds' with the fish and put all in the oven. Baste occasionally and after half an hour turn the fish. Cook separately in salted water, small potatoes cut in quarters. Ten minutes before probable end of cooking time cover with fine dry breadcrumbs mixed with chopped parsley. Take out and discard the bouquet garni. Put a walnut of butter on top to brown the breadcrumbs lightly. Serve potatoes separately.

If you use salted cod it should always be de-salted before cooking, either by leaving under running water or by soaking for twenty-four hours to thirty-six hours, with several changes of water. After this it is usual to poach the fish by putting it in clean unsalted water over a low flame, skimming directly it begins to bubble, then placing lid on pan and leaving it to simmer at the side of your hot-plate or range for a quarter of an hour. It is drained before any further cooking process begins.

USUAL PREPARATIONS:

(1) Exceptionally, do not 'poach' as above. Fry pieces of cod previously soaked in milk (or grill them).

(2) After 'poaching'. Further boiling in stock – with black butter – with Béchamel – au gratin – with tomato – with cream (creamed cod) – with spinach or sorrel – boiled and served with any of the sauces listed in sauce chapter excepting those of meat base – maître d'hôtel – meunière – in salad – Parmentier (i.e. with potatoes) – in omelettes. These are only a few of many possibilities.

Cod and Beans

In a very little salted water cook some haricot beans. Boil the cod separately in as little water as possible and cut into very small pieces.

In another pan put an egg of butter and four tablespoonsful of olive oil. Bring to boil and add two chopped onions and four bruised garlic cloves. Add a few tablespoonsful of the water in which the beans were cooked, taking this out before it has coloured. Press two tablespoonsful of the beans through a sieve and use the bean paste to thicken the sauce. Add salt and pepper if required. Now place the fish pieces in the sauce and boil together with the beans for a quarter of an hour. Serve with bread fried in olive oil.

(This recipe was supplied by MONSIEUR HENRY ROUJON of the Académie Française.)

Gourmets' Cod

Empty six large ripe tomatoes, season them and fill with the following salad: cubes of cold poached cod, cucumber dice, chopped hard-boiled eggs, sliced raw mushrooms, pepper, mayonnaise, lemon juice.

N.B.—To supply a touch of elegance, a pink shrimp could surmount each.

Cod Croquettes

Cut your poached cod into very small pieces, and make into croquettes, with mushrooms if necessary, or even truffles. An alternative is to mix the cod with potato purée. Roll the croquettes in flour, fry in good hot fat and serve, if you like, with tomato sauce.

Cod Ramekins

Make some ordinary choux pastry (4 oz flour, 3½ oz butter, 4 eggs, salt, ½ pint water). Add to this dough two tablespoonsful of poached cod, cut up very small, a tablespoonful of grated cheese, and a pinch of nutmeg. Make with this mixture some shallow round cakes a little larger than half-crowns, and bake in a hot oven.

N.B.—These ramekins make an excellent hors d'œuvre, especially when served with cream cheese to which you have added either chives or parsley chopped very small.

Nice Fish Cakes (Cod)

With 6 oz flour and 3 oz butter make some short pastry (small glass of water to moisten). Set it aside for a spell, then roll it out to a thin cake of pancake type. Place in greased flan dish or tart tin, rolling and pinching up the edges to form a crest. Prick the dough here and there to prevent its puffing-up, and dot with butter.

Cut some anchovy fillets into very small strips (use de-salted ones). Flake some poached cod and mix with the anchovy. Spread over the uncooked pastry and arrange stoned black olives on the surface.

Make in another dish a fairly 'runny' tomato sauce, incorporating three whole eggs, well whisked. Cover the tart with this sauce (you will need about half a pint). Bake for half an hour and serve warm, not hot.

Cod in Puff Pastry

Prepare two pieces of rolled out pastry (puff) about ten inches by four and a half. Put one on a greased baking tin and spread upon it a mixture of 4 oz flaked poached cod, a beaten egg, a tablespoonful of plain boiled rice, some melted butter, chopped parsley, a little garlic, some cooked onion (also plain boiled). Wet the edges and cover with the second piece of pastry, crimping the edges together to seal. Gild with beaten egg yolk and bake in a hot oven.

Serve separately melted butter with parsley and lemon juice.

Cod Vol-au-vent

Puff pastry cases filled with creamed cod, or brandade of cod (ragoût), or even a mixture of cod and cooked mushrooms.

Brandade (Ragoût of Cod)

This is the renowned Brandade, of Provence in general and Nîmes in particular—a jealously guarded secret, and that is as good a reason as any for giving this recipe, supplied by the Nîmes Station buffet authority:

Use cod not over-soaked but with all scales removed. Poach, drain, remove all bones. But leave the skin for it is necessary to the success of the recipe. Keep the pieces of cod warm (but not drying up) in the oven. Have two small pans in a moderately warm place, one with oil and one with milk (in equal quantity). First put a tablespoon of oil over the cod, and work at the fish vigorously with a wooden spoon, crushing it against the sides of the pan. Next add a spoonful of milk and then one of oil, alternating them but not forgetting to 'brandish' your wooden spoon with great decision (whence the name, 'brandade'). When you have a creamy mixture the brandade is ready. You may add, if you like, pounded garlic and a few slices of truffle.

N.B.—It may be a good idea to begin by pounding garlic and truffles in a mortar.

Brandade is served hot or cold. If hot, with small pieces of puff pastry fried in oil as croûtons, or soft white bread cubes similarly fried.

NANTUA BRANDADE: is a variation. Fresh raw cream replaces milk, and the brandade is put in timbales with alternating layers of crayfish-tail ragoût.

Mulet (Mullet)

Another acanthopterygian (spiny-finned) fish. There are several varieties, and the flesh is highly esteemed. All recipes given for Bass are suitable. Mullets' roes are used in the confection of Poutargue, an oriental hors d'œuvre also much favoured in the Mediterranean Basin.

Pagel, Pagre (Gilthead, Becker)

Often sold as DAURADE (gilthead). Of inferior flavour and texture, but the same recipes apply.

Raie (Ray, Skate)

There are many varieties. Scale-less and flat. In most places, but not France, is sold without the black and sticky skin which must be removed, anyhow. It has one advantage—when it has been wiped off the fish it will re-form as long as ten hours after death. There are some gastronomes who maintain that this is the only fish which is worth eating when a little 'gamy'.

COOKING: If very large cut in thick cross-cut slices. If of medium size divide into two 'wings'. Cook in salted court bouillon (a quart of water and a third-pint of vinegar), with a bouquet garni. Bring to boil, skim, then leave on side of hot-plate to complete cooking. Drain and remove all traces of skin. It is now ready for one of the following treatments:

—*with black butter* (do not forget to add a tablespoonful of vinegar). Serve with potatoes boiled in the fish-cooking water.
—*with vinegar dressing* (preferably served cold).
—*boiled* with fish-based sauces.
—*meunière* (with butter).
—*au gratin.*
—*fried.* In which case the preliminaries are omitted, and the skinned pieces are first soaked in milk then dusted with flour, to be fried in boiling oil, drained, and served with parsley and lemon.

Skate with Cheese

Make a white roux, moisten with the fish-cooking water, add chopped parsley, broken mushrooms, and cook for ten minutes, stirring all the time. Put the skinned pieces of fish in oven dish, pour over the sauce, sprinkle with grated cheese and breadcrumbs, dot with butter, bake in a hot oven.

Skate Fritters

Make a fritter 'batter' thick enough to roll out like pastry. Flatten it, cut into squares, place on each a piece of fillet with a sprinkling of lemon juice on top. Fold over to enclose fillet and fry golden-brown in very hot fat. Serve with tomato sauce.

Skate Liver

This is deemed a great delicacy. It is cooked, with the skate, in court bouillon, and served with it. But here are:

Skate Liver Crusties

Hollow out some slices of white bread (crusts removed) and fry these 'boats'. Then fill with the cooked skate liver cut into rounds, cover with Mornay sauce, sprinkle with grated cheese and then baste with melted butter. Put in hot oven to brown and crisp.

Rascasse (Hogfish)

A tough-skinned Mediterranean fish, its sole use is as bouillabaisse or other fish-soup ingredient. But it is only in the Midi that it is said to be utterly indispensable thereto.

Rouget (Red Gurnet, Surmullet)

Another mullet relation, also called red gurnard, etc. Very common in the Mediterranean. Exquisite flesh. Gourmets style it 'the woodcock of the sea' and eat it grilled and with nothing removed.

CLASSIC PREPARATIONS FOR SURMULLET, ETC.: Frying, grilling, au gratin, en papillote (see p. 103), meunière, boiled (fillets), with fennel, etc.

Surmullet with Capers

Cook a large fish in court bouillon, just enough to cover it. Serve surrounded with steamed potatoes and hand separately this sauce:

In the same saucepan mix a bare ounce of butter with the same quantity of flour. Pour on (in one splash) 1½ gills boiling water. Add salt. Whisk while mixture boils. Beat two egg yolks with four tablespoonsful of milk, and add this liaison to the sauce, whisking without a moment's pause. Boil for a few minutes, remove from heat, and add 2 oz butter and three tablespoonsful of capers.

Surmullet, Greek Fashion

In olive oil cook lightly some skinned tomatoes, small onions, shallots, garlic, finely chopped parsley, a bouquet garni. Season with salt and Cayenne pepper, adding a little saffron as well. Cook gently, with a very little water if needed, and a pinch or two of flour. Part-grill the fish and add to sauce to complete cooking. Eat cold for choice, as the olive oil will not congeal.

Bordeaux Surmullet

Cook fish in buttered sauté pan, very gently, moistening with white wine. Add finely chopped shallots. When cooked put to drain while you use the cooking liquid to make a brown roux. When this is of creamy texture add tomato sauce to it and pass through a hair-sieve. Add a little butter. Put fish in sauce and scatter chopped tarragon over the dish.

Surmullet with Button Mushrooms

Cook button mushrooms in white wine with herbs and butter. Meanwhile cook the fish slowly in butter, and when nearly cooked pour the mushrooms and liquor over them. Put in oven to reduce, serve hot.

Roussette (Dogfish)

Has many odd names—sea-dog, musky-flesh, etc., and is not much prized; but third-rate restaurants in France sometimes use it in what passes for Matelote of eels. Obviously a money-saving device.

Sainte-Pierre (John Dory)

An oval, flattened fish with a large bristling head. Sometimes called 'Jean-Doré' in France, sometimes Poisson de Saint-Pierre. Another ingredient of Mediterranean bouillabaisses, but as its flesh is of such good quality it may be treated as turbot—grilled, braised, poached, in fillets.

Sardine (Pilchard, Sardine)

A migratory fish, abundant in Sardinia, whence its name, but found almost everywhere. They are usually preserved in oil (olive oil is best), in tomato sauce, white wine or just brine, and make a good hors d'œuvre that is also nourishing. Sardine butter (3 parts sardine to four parts butter) is a useful spread for toasts, canapés, croustades (see 'Crusties', p. 110) and pasties.

Fresh Pilchards may be prepared in these ways:

Fried (like smelts).

Grilled (first daubed with oil and served with maître d'hôtel butter).

Stuffed (various stuffings, then braised in white wine).

En papillotes (in well-greased paper. See Mackerel en papillote, p. 103).

Provence Pilchards

Cook in oil and serve on a layer of skinned tomatoes stewed gently in oil. Add garlic, parsley, pepper.

Pilchards and Spinach

Blanch some spinach then soak it in milk and spread over oven dish base. Clean some pilchards, wash, dry and flatten them, then cover the spinach with them. Add breadcrumbs, salt, pepper, a good splash of olive oil. Bake in moderate oven.

Saumon (Salmon)

Pink and oily flesh. A sea fish which goes to the rivers for spawning. Some may reach 60 lb or thereabouts, but the average weight is 11 to 16 pounds. Whether whole, cut into various pieces, or in cutlets (or 'darnes') it is usually cooked in a court bouillon. It is best served cold, with cold sauces—mayonnaise, sauce tartare, green, remoulade, etc. Some connoisseurs like it cooked on spit or griddle.

Salmon on Skewers

Cut salmon in cubes and thread these on skewers, alternating with halves of buttered mushrooms. Finish each with a tomato in which a strip of bacon fat has been inserted. Damp all over with melted butter, sprinkle with breadcrumbs and cook on gridiron. Serve with parsley and lemon juice.

VARIATIONS: If you like you can butter, egg and breadcrumb the salmon cubes before skewering.

Salmon Coulibiac

Prepare some brioche pastry (see p. 309) and put it in a cool place to harden a little.

Chop 2 oz onions, cook gently in melted butter. Lay this mixture over some very thin strips of salmon in an oven dish, and bake in slow oven for twenty minutes. Remove from oven, spread chopped parsley over the dish.

Boil a pint of salted water. Stirring constantly, throw in 5 oz semolina in a 'rain' of grains. Add one tablespoonful butter, boil without failing to stir for a moment. Then cover and leave over very low heat for a good half hour; and when the water is completely absorbed add another tablespoonful of butter and spread this paste (called 'kache' in Russia) with a fork to cover the bottom of a serving-dish.

Chop coarsely two hard-boiled eggs. Roll out the brioche paste on a floured board. Make a long oval a quarter of an inch thick. The next ingredient will have been purchased from a shop specializing in out-of-the-way provisions—it is some 'vesiga' (dorsal sinew of sturgeon). It is a kind of gelatinous band and about two ounces will do, since it absorbs four times its own weight. You will have had it soaking for ten hours or so, with two or three changes of water. Then you have boiled it for five hours in plenty of salted water, drained it, chopped it coarsely.

To go back to your oval of pastry. In the middle put a layer of 'kache' (same depth as pastry), then a layer of chopped egg, then one of vesiga. Top this with half the cooked salmon strips in their onion and parsley flavouring. Next chopped egg again, then vesiga, the rest of the salmon,

THE RECIPE FOR BOUILLABAISSE

(1) BY JOSEPH MERY. 1798–1865. Born at Aygalades, Bouches-du-Rhône.

Before your epic starts, turn to and cook
A savant stock, the Preface to your book.
And what a stock! To baby fish and 'fry'
Of scores of kinds . . . that morning's catch . . . apply
The slow, distilling heat of embers clear
And precious, spicy gravy will appear.
Steep in this sauce, with fine discrimination,
The this-and-that designed for titillation,
Manilla pepper, saffron, and bouquet
Of fennel, with a crackling leaf of bay,
Salt, friend of man, and urchins from their bed
In warm Arenc, well-flavoured and well-fed.
When this great brew blows bubbles, sheds its skins,
And all is nicely done, your ode begins.

One thing is sure . . . this fine Phocaean dish
Is not the same without one master fish,
The vulgar hogfish, scorpion of the seas,
Which, lonely on its grill, could never please
The crudest tastes. Yet in a bouillabaisse
It has no peer, and nothing can replace
Its subtle odours. If, indeed, they fail,
No other art or cunning will prevail;
Hogfish alone, from chinks in shifting sand
Where bays and myrtles fringe the tenuous land,
Or from some shadowed shelf of thymy cliff,
Provide such wafts for avid guests to sniff.

Next come such fish as choose a deeper stream
And hug the reefs: fine mullet, gilthead, bream,
Saint Peter's fish, embalmers of the stew
(Such game, in fact, as greedy perch pursue).
And last, the gurnard, with Boöptic eyes,

And some the ichthyologists despise,
Grand fish which Neptune, under flaming sky,
Chooses with table-forks, lays trident by.

You heedless trippers, do not judge the case
From any one-and-tuppenny bouillabaisse.
Go to the Château-Vert. Say: 'Something nice.
I'm not a haggler . . . never mind the price.
Dispatch your diver, let him burrow well
Around those rocks of heady ocean smell,
From Greece and Rome "thys" and "parangry" borrow,
And skip the cost. We'll talk of that tomorrow.'

(2) JACQUES NORMAND on the same theme.

Garlic? A little. Only just enough
To keep the faith,
The smallest scrap. A souvenir. A puff.
A fading wraith.
Saffron . . . a fair amount, but understand,
Strictly controlled.
Enough, let's say, to leave upon your hand
A splash of gold.

Fish? Well, of course. But fish of style and class,
Of recent haul.
Crayfish and whiting, Dory and 'rascasse',
This above all.

Oil? That as well. The fruitiest ever pressed.
Provence's choicest vintage yields the best,
Superbly fresh.

Rosemary, fennel, thyme and parsley green,
You next enclose
In tightly-knotted muslin, fresh and clean,
Sweet as a rose.

Now boil. On thick-sliced bread, new-baked, pour out
The fragrant mess
And maybe you've achieved (or just about)
A bouillabaisse.
But if you want a dish beyond compare,
Gem of pure ray,
Take fish, herbs, saffron, garlic, and . . . some air
Breathed in Marseille.

egg again, then vesiga, and on top the remainder of the 'kache'. Raise one side of pastry, then the other side, so that they overlap at the join. Seal the pastry cover by moistening with water. Roll out the other ends as well, forming as it were a long pillow. Put it into a symmetrical shape with your hands. Leave this for two hours in a fairly cool spot, then place it, joins on the underside, on a buttered dish. Brush over with melted butter, making a central opening in pastry to release steam, making also a little 'chimney' of rolled-up greased paper, and bake in a moderate oven. When done, pour through this paper tube two tablespoonsful of melted butter. Serve either hot or just warm.

(If sturgeon is used instead of salmon, this is a subtler dish.)

Sole (Sole)

A fish dwelling in the sandy depths of almost all the seas of Europe and having particularly fine and delicately flavoured flesh.

Preparations: frying, boiling, poaching, braising, grilling, cooking in butter. Sole fillets are dressed in hundreds of ways and with every imaginable sauce. Generally speaking, the presentation of sole fillets, an important branch of restaurant catering and quite in order for special dinners and banquets, is not to be recommended for family cookery; and there is nothing to beat a fine specimen of a sole cooked whole, either grilled or with butter in the oven. I give, however, a few typical sole treatments (for whole sole and fillets).

BURGUNDY: cooked in red wine with small onions and mushrooms.

BERCY: red wine, shallots.

PROVENCE: cooked in fish stock, garnished with fresh tomatoes, artichoke bottoms and, of course, garlic.

DIEPPE: mussels, shrimps and white wine sauce.

NORMANDY: cream sauce.

AMERICAN: American sauce.

And of course, as many variations as you yourself care to invent, the basic principles never changing much. So it is quite in order to serve either whole fish or fillets (poached) on a bed of spinach (Florentine Sole); on rice, aubergine purée, etc.

Fillets of Sole with Cucumber

Season fillets with salt and pepper, coat with flour and cook gently in butter in the frying-pan. In a separate pan cook (also in butter), a sliced medium-sized cucumber, previously blanched. Put fillets on oval dish and surround with cucumber, sprinkle with chopped parsley. Add a few drops of lemon juice. Reheat butter in which fillets were cooked, and pour this over the dish.

Sole Fillets Max

The fillets are cooked in just enough fish stock to cover, then are served in pairs at once in plates almost too hot to touch, the first fillet masked with white sauce or Mornay sauce, the second with American sauce.

Sole Fillets 'Basque Coast'

Cook in butter with white wine added, a finely sliced julienne of mushrooms, shallots, pimento (Spanish). Roll your poached fillets into turban shapes surrounding tiny new potatoes no bigger than filberts (you may have to 'manufacture' these from larger potatoes). These will have been boiled in salted water and rolled in parsleyed butter and slightly flavoured with garlic. Put the 'turbans' in an oven dish with the julienne and cook until liquid is reduced and the surface browned. Mask, before taking to table, with a thick tomato purée.

Alsace Sole Fillets

Poach fillets. Make a base of sauerkraut, lay fish on this, cover with Béchamel. Add a second layer of sauerkraut, fillets, sauce, and continue until you have enough to serve the family. Gratinate in the oven.

(M. Maurice Vaucaire, who introduced this recipe, said of it on one occasion: 'If the host's resources allowed, this dish could attain incredible heights, but let us be satisfied with three stories skilfully disposed'.)

Farmstead Paupiettes of Sole

Roll your poached fillets around large, stone-free, black olives which have purée of anchovy replacing the stone. Brush all over with a sauce made from olive oil, egg yolk and mustard. Bake in oven, inspecting dish from time to time to make sure that it is not drying up. Serve with a garlic-flavoured tomato sauce.

(Recipe supplied by MAX REVOL, comedian.)

Sole Fillet Vol-au-vent

If you are not serving individual pasties use a timbale (pie dish). But if you have purchased vol-au-vent cases or made them yourself, put the poached, rolled fillets inside with (to your choice) mushrooms, mussels, forcemeat balls, shrimps (any of these with a white sauce) or mushrooms, small onions, even little shreds of bacon (these with a wine sauce, Chambertin).

Thon (Tunny Fish)

Another spiny-finned fish of temperate seas, especially the Mediterranean. Some weighing over 1800 lb have been captured, about 18 feet long. This fish is usually tinned or preserved in other ways.

Provence-style Tunny Fish

Buy a good-sized piece of tunny and insert here and there on its surface anchovy fillets, then marinate for an hour in olive oil, with salt, pepper, bouquet garni, lemon juice. Now brown an onion (chopped) and the tunny in a pan together and add a small clove of garlic, some tomatoes from which seeds have been removed, a fresh bouquet garni. Cook with lid on for a quarter of an hour, then moisten with white wine and complete cooking in oven, basting frequently.

Tunnyfish Loaf

Use a tin of tunnyfish in oil. Mash it with a fork, adding a fair amount of the middle of a loaf, previously soaked in milk. Add also two egg whites beaten to a snow. Then mix in some chopped parsley or tarragon. Butter a mould and cook in bain-marie for thirty minutes.

N.B.—May be served with tomato or Béchamel sauce.

VARIATIONS: instead of the soaked bread, use a purée of haricot beans. Then put in an oven dish, powder with gruyère cheese, and bake golden-brown. Germon=white tunny.

Turbot (Turbot)

A large flat fish of Atlantic waters, Mediterranean too. Not unlike the brill, but its flesh is superior.

Preparation: All brill recipes are suitable for turbot (or for the young turbot appearing on the menu-card as 'turbotin'). Likewise use turbot recipes for Brill (see pp. 94, 97). Here are a few more recipes applicable to both.

Turbot and Rice

Cook some onion lightly in butter and add some pieces of turbot already cooked in court bouillon. Allow them just to brown. In a separate vessel cook some rice in fish stock. Now put a bed of the cooked rice in an oven dish, turbot on top, then another layer of rice. Grated cheese, dotted with butter. Bake in oven.

Turbot and Almonds

Braise a young turbot, using dry white wine or champagne. Pound some almonds (peeled and salted). When the turbot is cooked through, brush it over with yolk of egg and stick almonds over this. Heat again in the oven and serve with a jug of melted butter.

Gentry Turbot

Plain boiled turbot served with plain boiled potatoes and mint sauce.

N.B.—There is a receptacle called a turbot-kettle, irregularly shaped but four-sided, specially designed for the easy cooking of turbot and other flat fishes.

Bouillabaisse

This has already been mentioned in the chapter on Soups. It is essentially a Southern dish—almost, one might say, a speciality of Marseille. Some have attributed paternity to a native of Bordeaux named Baysse. Whatever its variations (and they are numerous) bouillabaisse is the Mediterranean version of a mixed netful of fish cooked as soon as they are caught.

'As with women,' a connoisseur writes, 'there are preferences. One likes blonde, one brunette, one russet-red . . . and as women are, so this is; always the same, yet always different.' Paul Reboux, however, in an unguarded moment, dared to remark that a bouillabaisse most resembles the contents of a rubbish bin. I suppose he must be forgiven.

The origin of the word remains uncertain. One of Méry's well-known poems begins thus:

> 'Pour le vendredi maigre, un jour, certaine abbesse
> D'un couvent marseillais crea la bouillabaisse'.[1]

Others say that the name comes from the fact that the fishermen boil it (bouillir) very much 'abaissé' (low down) as it is in a cooking-pot standing on three pebbles or pieces of shingle. Another derivation is from the Provençal 'bouilla-pesca' (broth of fish).

We need not worry too much about the Marseille people's contention that a bouillabaisse is not a bouillabaisse without hog-fish, weever, John Dory, parrot-fish and a dozen other varieties of sea-fish. The housewife is aware that the savouriness of the dish is due to the variety of fish used, and will realize that these must number six at the very least.

In a saucepan (better still, a pipkin both wide and flat-based) heat some olive oil and parcook some chopped onions, peeled tomatoes, bruised garlic, parsley, pinch of fennel, bay-leaf, a scrap of orange peel, a pinch of saffron. Cut up a quantity of firm-fleshed fish, also mussels and crayfish (or a spiny lobster cut in two would be better still), and add to the mixture. Cover with boiling water and bring quickly to the boil. A little

[1] 'An abbess of Marseille, for Friday (frugal day of fixed abstemiousness) invented bouillabaisse.'

THE EEL OF MELUN

A Melun speciality is its far-famed eel-pie. And there's a saying that's pretty general in this town—'like the Melun eel that began to yell before it was skinned'. It all began with an apprentice of bygone days named LANGUILLE *(he'd have been* EALES *if Melun had been Melton Mowbray) who was entrusted with the role of Saint Bartholomew in a 'mystery-play'. At the moment when, as the Saint, he was about to suffer martyrdom, another actor moved towards him, a cutlass in his hand. Languille, taking fright, escaped from restraining hands and dashed, half-naked, through the city streets.*

Whence the proverbial comparison. It is also alleged that Languille had very good reason to be on his guard, since he was known to be somewhat over-affectionately inclined toward the wife of the worthy merchant playing the role of executioner.

FUNERAL ORATION

Fish was much esteemed at the court of Louis XIV, and Lent was awaited with impatience. If we can believe Madame de Sévigné, the courtiers even went so far as to stake so much fish on the run of the cards. She says in one of her letters, 'The Abbot of Verteuil lost eight louis' worth of fish at play'. This same Abbot ended his days in a manner befitting a gourmet. We read in the memoirs of Saint-Simon: 'The Abbot of Verteuil died almost as soon as I arrived. They charged me with having killed him, since he did indeed die at my place following indigestion caused by eating sturgeon. I shall miss him, for he made an excellent guest.'

later add some fish with less firm flesh (such as red gurnet or surmullet, whiting, bass).

When done, take out the fish, thicken the liquid with flour blended with oil, and pour over slices of toast rubbed well with garlic. Replace fish, serve very hot.

VARIATION: In Toulon, they add potatoes.

In Hyères I was told by a fisherman that you must use one glass of sea water to every quart of plain water in your bouillabaisse.

At Sète they make a 'bourride' by adding to the broth part of their fish soup two egg yolks and some aioli.

FRESH WATER FISH

Anguilles (Eels)

Fish with a slimy skin found in spring-water or ponds or pools (in ponds its skin is darker and the flesh has a muddy tang).

N.B.—Whatever the source of your eel supply, you should keep it alive as long as possible; in order to dispel the brackishness, proceed as follows:

If the eel is kept alive, keep it for two or three days before you need it in capacious tub or bucket of clean water. But if you wish to use it soon after it has left the water you must put into its mouth, whether it is alive or dead, a teaspoonful of vinegar sauce—a soupspoonful for a large specimen—at the same time closing the gills so that the liquid may penetrate thoroughly. The fish must at once be scaled and cleaned out in the ordinary way.

This is the method to employ for all fresh-water fish likely to have a brackish or muddy taste.

Stewed Eels

This is the principal eel recipe.

Melt a large walnut of butter in a sauté pan, add 6 oz. sliced onion, a little garlic (be guided by the family's tastes), and cook gently. Add the slices of eel with a good rich bouquet garni. Pour over these a quart of dry white wine and bring to boil. Add a dash of spirit (optional) and ignite it. Place lid on pan for rest of the cooking time. Drain the fish pieces and put in another dish with some tiny onions and mushrooms (both cut up and cooked separately beforehand). Reduce cooking liquor by one third and thicken it with kneaded butter. Then pour over the fish, etc. Bring again to simmering point before serving.

VARIATIONS: Cider instead of white wine (Normandy version). Or a good red wine (Burgundy). Tench may be mixed with eel. May be served with fried bread cubes. If red wine is used, add cubes of fat bacon. If white wine or cider, add mussels and fresh cream.

Roast Eels

Soak prepared eel for a few hours in oil with a drop or so of vinegar added, also savoury herbs and an onion. Then insert thin basting strips (lardons) here and there, run a skewer through it, roast in oven, turning it fairly often and basting with good butter.

N.B.—If eel is very large, proceed as above but use portions of the fish.

Olden-days Eel

Salt some Frontignan wine and put the live eel in it. When eel is dead take the blood and add to the wine. Clean out inside of eel, scald it, then place in a circle in an earthenware dish. Cover with oil, salt, pepper, nutmeg, clove mixture, put on lid, cook for half an hour in a slow oven.

With the wine and blood mixture make a sauce which will include roasted almonds (pounded) and currants. Pour sauce over the eel and cook for a further half-hour, adding the juice of a lemon.

Paprika Eel

Use small eels of 12 oz to 1 lb and cut in rings a quarter of an inch through. Put in a saucepan 4 oz sliced onions, some chopped garlic, a bouquet garni. Arrange eel slices over these, just cover with dry white wine. Add a dozen peppercorns and a generous pinch of paprika.

Bring to boil over moderate heat, with lid on pan (about 25 minutes). Drain the fish, put in an earthenware dish, pour over enough cooking liquor to fill dish and set aside to cool and jellify. Serve cold with quarters of lemons.

Simon Arbellot Dressed Eel

Roll a medium-sized eel into a ring and fry in very hot olive oil until nicely browned. Remove from oil and allow fish to get cold, then cover with anchovy butter first and then bread raspings. Set under grill for a few minutes. Serve with a sauce made from

—a green pepper,
—a quarter of a red pepper,
—three cloves of garlic,
all chopped and pounded with pestle and mortar, then blended with a mustard and vinegar dressing.

Barbeau, Barbillon (Barbel)

A fish of insipid flavour and abundant bones. The 'small fry' may be grilled, fried, cooked in butter (see Bass recipes). Larger ones are cooked in court bouillon, stewed, braised (see Brill and Tench recipes).

Brème (Bream)

River or lake fish not unlike Carp and for which the same recipes will serve. Most often stewed.

Brochet (Pike)

Fish of white, firm flesh. Roe, eggs, considered to be poisonous at spawning season (February to April). Choose river pike in preference to lake pike—the latter are dark-bellied.

Preparation: In court bouillon with 'white butter' (see Sauces, p. 59), or au Bleu (see Truite au Bleu, p. 130). Also baked.

Fillets of pike may be prepared in the same ways (and served with the same sauces) as Brill, Turbot, Sole.

Roast Pike in Chablis

Season interior of pike with salt and pepper, gash the outside every half-inch diagonally, and season the exposed flesh in the gashes. Grease a long dish, sprinkle chopped shallot and parsley over it, add the fish, cover with two parts Chablis and one of water. Place in hot oven for forty minutes, during which period it must be basted eight, nine, or ten times. Then add a good-sized lump of butter, put back in oven, and go on basting for a further twenty minutes.

Put fish on serving dish. If the sauce is by now too thick, dilute it with Chablis and water (in equal quantities). Stir and strain sauce. Serve hot.

Pike Boulangère

As above. But make a stuffing of

2 oz breadcrumbs soaked in milk or stock
1 boiled, chopped onion
2 shallots and some parsley, chopped together.
Thyme and bay-leaf.

Mix all together over gentle heat and blend with a whole egg. Stuff pike through gills and through an incision which must be sewn up afterwards. Then proceed as in previous recipe, but add mushrooms before putting in the oven. At end of cooking sprinkle with breadcrumbs and dot with butter; garnish, in their season, with small new potatoes.

Polish Pike

Slit back of pike to remove bones. Stuff with a forcemeat of breadcrumbs, boiled rice, chopped onion and mushrooms, a hard-boiled egg, all cooked gently together with cream and seasoned to your liking.

LUCULLUS PIKE

Let's go back to 1900, the Golden Days, when ALBERT GUILLAUME, humorous artist, gave this reply in the course of a 'gastronomic quiz':

'As you have honoured me with a request for a dish of my own invention, I think the best I can do is to describe a really remarkable creation: 'Lucullus Pike'. Actually I was given the recipe by one of the descendants of the great Vatel. This man was a grave-digger, at Courbevoie, whom I met a few years ago at a little private dinner given by my friend Alfred Picard: that great and justly famous man to whom an appreciative country is, and always should be, grateful for his abolition of Great Exhibitions.

But to get back to the pike.

Just as you must have a hare before you can make a jugged hare, even so you must, in order to make a Lucullus pike, have a pike. But he must be alive, and therein resides the originality of this recipe. The trick is to make the creature himself eat all the ingredients, condiments, and so on, that are to aromatize his flesh and render it utterly delicious. You therefore place him in a vivarium containing about two gallons of distilled water, and purge him, on three consecutive days, with Epsom salts, one coffeespoonful night and morning. It is hardly necessary to say that you change the water as often as seems advisable. Once this preliminary treatment is accomplished, you put the pike (still living, of course), into a fish-kettle that will take about a quart of water (for choice, a good mineral water like Vittel), and add a nice bunch of parsley, two handfuls of salt, three pinches of red pepper, two large onions cut into slices, a carrot, two dozen mushrooms, three or four tomatoes, and a half bottle of really good white wine. The pike, by now ravenously hungry, will lose no time in making a meal of the savoury items. Do not give him time to digest them. Put your kettle over gentle heat, jam on the lid, and allow contents to boil for an hour at least.

Making sure that the pike is as dead as he can be, remove pan from flame, allow to cool, and serve your pike on a long, narrow dish, a fish-server in fact, garnished with little pastry-boats filled with wine-soaked 'lights'—and topped with Roquefort cubes sprinkled with cinnamon. The small bones are usually served separately in mayonnaise, but as a decoration for the main dish it is the custom to thread five or six fresh garden peas on the larger bone 'needles' and stick these in a circle all round uncooked artichoke bottoms

dusted over with caster sugar. The pike's head is dressed in a ruff in Henry IV style, and two garlic cloves serve as the whites of the eyes. On the centre of each of these you will affix, with a blob of sterilized seccotine, a small round of black cloth—or of truffle, if you happen to have any by you; these serving quite satisfactorily to represent pupils.

N.B.—It is possible to vary the facial expression by altering the location of these artificial eye-pupils.

IN THE RESTAURANT

'Listen, waiter, is this stuff really pork?'
'At which end of the fork, sir?'

* * *

'Waiter . . . a calf's head, please, but no ears!'
'Sorry, sir. We don't serve freaks.'

* * *

'Funny taste, this soup has.'
'Yes. Probably the waiter's thumb.'

* * *

'A cup of tea, sir?'
'No tea, thanks.'
'Cup of coffee, sir?'
'No coffee, thanks.'
'Whisky and soda, sir?'
'No soda, thanks.'

Put the pike on a dish and splash with cream and dots of butter. Cook in a slow oven. As soon as the butter begins to brown, add a little white wine. When fish is tender, thicken sauce with cream.

(Another of DR. POMIANE's recipes.)

Grilled Pike Cutlets

Cut these quite thin and marinate for a few hours in a mixture of olive oil, lemon juice, parsley, shallot. Drain away the liquid from fish and cover the cutlets with beaten egg and a coating of breadcrumbs. Put a small knob of butter on each side as you grill them.

N.B.—May be served with lemon juice squeezed over, or Tartare Sauce, even with spinach purée.

Pike Quenelles
(Quenelles are forcemeat balls)

Pike quenelles are a well-known and frequently encountered item of *la grande cuisine*. They are poached and covered with a cream sauce or a simple Béchamel. Or perhaps served on spinach with a masking of Mornay sauce. Or, 'à la lyonnaise', with a Nantua sauce.

To make the quenelles, cook a flour panada in a small pan (half-pint water, salt, 2 oz butter). Bring to boil, add 5 oz flour, mix with wooden spoon, cook until it leaves pan sides clean. Allow to dry off.

In a mortar pound 16 oz pike flesh, with salt, pepper, grated nutmeg. In a separate vessel grind the panada and crush it to powder. In another, break up the fish with half a pound of butter. Mix the contents of these three receptacles. Add, one after the other, three whole eggs. Then three yolks. Pass the resulting paste through a hair sieve.

Now work it with wooden spoon for a few minutes, and it is ready to form into quenelles, either with a small round-bowled spoon or a piece of apparatus made for the purpose. The quenelles are poached and dressed in any of the ways described above.

Carpe (Carp)

River or lake or pond fish which may weigh as much as twenty pounds and live to a great age—not, however, for a hundred years, as legend assures us. Legend says, too, that this fish comes from China and made its first appearance in Europe round about 1600 (in England, Holland, Scandinavia). There are several kinds, the 'mirror carp' being the most generally esteemed (and, in Belgium, the Kollar carp).

Preparations: in court bouillon, with various sauces as used for other fish, au bleu (with Hollandaise sauce if served hot, Ravigote if cold). Fried, grilled, maître d'hôtel, baked. Fillets may be treated as sole fillets.

Girondine Carp

(We include this exceptionally complicated and lavish recipe as a curiosity. It is the work of Mme Jane Catulle-Mendès, and the poetic spirit of this writer is reflected throughout its narration:

The first thing to do is to make a stuffing of white meat of chicken, mushrooms, a very fresh young pig's trotter, some quenelles. This must then soak in old sauternes to which you have added thyme, bay, tarragon, peppercorns, cloves, ginger, nutmeg, juniper, onion, carrots. It must soak, completely covered, for three days.

In another vessel put eight or ten good-quality truffles to soak in cognac or port wine, also for three days. At the end of this period, put all excepting two or three of these truffles into the stuffing. Fill the carp and sew up the insertion, also bind the fish carefully with twine into a good shape.

You will have had in reserve for cooking the carp a strongly flavoured chicken stock. Add to this two tablespoonsful of the cognac (or port) marinading liquor and four of the sauternes marinade. The carp must only just be covered with liquor. Cook gently until one third of the stock has evaporated.

Remove carp and place on its serving dish, removing strings and threads. Decorate with cleaned shrimps and the few truffles you reserved cut into rings. Pour the cooking stock over it gently, with additions of red and green peppers. The whole dish is then put into refrigerator, ice-box or ice-house for two hours, and will emerge with a coating of succulent jelly.

At table it must be sliced as though it were foie-gras, with a knife dipped in boiling water. It may be accompanied by a salad (of potatoes, celery, walnuts, beetroot, extra celery macerated for a few hours in oil and a little lemon juice. (Above all, no vinegar.)

Canapés of Carp

Clean carp, place on buttered and parsley-besprinkled dish. Put a little sliver of shallot in the head, plenty of salt and pepper inside and outside, a little thyme here and there. Plenty of butter (in balls) all over the surface, a coating of bread raspings. Bake for a few minutes in a brisk oven, then pour in sufficient white wine to come halfway up the fish. Make one canapé (slice of bread fried in butter) for each person, and slip these under the fish as soon as it is cooked. Pour a basinful of cream over all, replace in the oven to get really hot again. Serve at once.

(This recipe was furnished by the historian GEORGES LENOTRE, who added this coda: 'Give your guests the fleshy portions from the back of the carp. First they are the correct portions with which to do the honours.

Second, they are full of bones. Keep for yourself the flesh near the tail. It is far more delicately flavoured, but this fact is little known.)

Provence Carp

Cut the carp into equal segments and put in pan with a little butter previously 'worked' free of water, also some good savoury herbs, garlic, chopped spring onions and mushrooms, salt and pepper. For cooking liquor mix olive oil and red wine in equal quantities and cook rapidly. Serve when the liquor is well reduced.

Carp in Beer

A medium-sized carp is added to the following: onions and chopped celery lightly cooked in butter, bouquet garni, two ounces of crumbled gingerbread. Cover with light beer and bake in the oven. Strain the reduced liquor and pour over fish in serving dish.

Stuffed Carp

Carp are all the better for being stuffed before poaching in white or red wine, or even beer; or, in the case of smaller carp, grilled or baked. One possibility is a creamed fish stuffing. Another is a mixture of onion, shallot, chopped parsley, milk-soaked breadcrumbs. Another is left-over potato purée with bacon scraps, well seasoned with pepper and pimentos.

Jewish Recipe for Carp

Cut into even-sized segments a medium carp, if possible a live one. Collect the blood. Salt the pieces and leave on a dish for several hours. Cut up three large onions and, in a separate pile, five or six shallots. Make a third pile of chopped garlic and parsley.

Heat to smoking point four tablespoonsful of olive oil in a saucepan, cook lightly the onion, then add the shallot and cook that too. Add a tablespoonful of flour and stir until all is light brown in colour. Add the fish pieces, then either water or fish stock or white wine (but this is out of tradition) and when boiling point is reached and passed put in the chopped parsley and garlic, also some ginger and pepper (both in powder form). Leave lid off and cook on briskly for a good half hour.

N.B.—Jewish cooks of Asia Minor add currants (or Smyrna or Malaga raisins), with a tablespoonful of sweetened vinegar, to the cooking liquor when reduced.

Carp Roes

Many gourmets prefer fish roes to the fish itself. And carp roes are perhaps the most recherché of all. They are, indeed, very often used as garnish for many dishes featuring large braised fish of other kinds. If you leave them with your carp, they should be poached rapidly in a court bouillon or, better still, cooked with the strict minimum of liquid—a dash of lemon juice and a walnut of butter—in a covered pan. They are then added to the main dish or the stuffing.

Eaten on their own the roes of carp (or of herring, mackerel, etc.) may be presented in several ways when cooked:

A L'ANGLAISE: that is, dried, rolled in egg and breadcrumbs, cooked in butter.

IN FRITTERS.

IN SCALLOP SHELLS: with Béchamel, Mornay and similar sauces.

IN MAYONNAISE: with quarters of hard-boiled eggs in shell-shaped lettuce leaves.

WITH BLACK BUTTER: and adorned with a caper or two.

Chevaine, Chevesne (Chub)

A cyprine fish of fresh water habitat. Fairly common. Sometimes called 'Cabot' or 'Chabot' in France, as well as two names given above. It is often used in fish stews and is also prepared in the same ways as Trout.

Gardon (Roach)

A red-finned river fish with a good many bones. It is used as fried basis in fish cookery.

Goujon (Gudgeon)

Delicate-fleshed fish living on the sandy beds of rivers. Good 'small fry'.

Gremille (Ruffe, Pope)

Common in rivers of North France—also called gudgeon-perch. Cooked as perch, or in fish stews.

Loche (Loach)

The river loach is a small slender fish, of tough texture, another 'small fry' subject.

Ombre Commun (Grayling)

A comparatively rare river-fish, and one not to be confused with the 'ombre chevalier' that is found in the deep lakes of Switzerland and Savoy. Both have fine-textured, delicate flesh and may be prepared as trout. But this fish travels badly and it is not often found at any distance from the place where it was caught. Before the war the royal kitchens of England were served by a specially equipped aeroplane with vivarium that brought live char (ombre chevalier) from Lake Leman to London.

Perche (Perch)

Extremely voracious acanthopterygious fish of very well-flavoured flesh. There are numerous varieties, e.g., common perch, black-perch, perch-trout (the last two trans-Atlantic) sun-perch, rainbow-perch (Japanese perch), tough-skinned, and so on. When very small the perch is a good 'friture' ingredient. Medium or large (they may weigh up to four pounds) they are prepared meunière fashion, stuffed, au bleu, and especially in accordance with prescription for Shad.

Racouchot Perch

Cut in halves some half-pound perch. Now cook lightly in oil some onions, sliced leeks, skinned tomatoes, a bouquet garni, a little garlic, a stick of celery. When all is tender add $\frac{3}{4}$ pint of white (dry) wine, a glassful of burgundy. Thin out with white stock, add salt, pepper, a pinch of curry powder, two of saffron. Cook for twenty minutes.

Into the thick mixture put your fish pieces with just about their weight of raw potato in 'olive shapes'. Cook together for twenty-five minutes, and serve in the cooking liquor.

Tanche (Tench)

Another of the Cyprinidae (small toothless mouths and naked heads). A thickset fish that prefers the muddy depths. Eliminate the muddiness of flavour by the process described for eels. However, the tench's chief employment is in fish stews. When very small it is quite good prepared with white or red local wines, meunière or braised.

Lorraine Tench

Put prepared fish on a bed of parsley, sliced onions, chopped shallots, a bouquet garni, salt, peppercorns. Pour on a half-bottle of Lorraine 'grey wine', cook gently without stirring, and when the stock has reduced by half its volume, add some fresh cream and bind with two egg yolks. Put fish on serving dish and cover with sauce. Put in a very hot oven for five minutes to brown.

Truite (Trout) (Salmon Trout)

Of the salmon family. The flesh is white, pink or orange-tinted, according to habitat, and to small creatures serving as nourishment. Lives in lakes or swift-running streams, the lake fish being the most recherché. It goes almost without saying that artificially bred trout—the fish in its natural state being king among freshwater fish—are, to quote Curnonsky, as dull and dry as lengths of bandaging gauze. The many ways of preparing trout include frying, grilling, braising (white or red wine), stewing, boiling, stuffed, filleted (use Sole fillet recipes).

Trout 'au Bleu'

The trout should be live ones. Remove from water, stun with a blow on the head, remove inside promptly, sprinkle well with vinegar and put in a court bouillon with plenty of vinegar in it. Cook as rapidly as possible, drain, serve on a linen cloth, with melted butter or a hollandaise sauce.

N.B.—It is also permissible to leave the fish to cool in the cooking stock, then serve cold with Ravigote sauce, a mayonnaise or a green sauce.

Stuffed Trout

Empty and stuff through the gills instead of making an incision. But if you cut, do it along the backbone and remove this before stuffing.

Suggested stuffings: roe purée; shallots–breadcrumb–beaten eggs–chopped chervil; mushroom purée; mousse of truffles and foie-gras; fish and vegetable mirepoix; creamed pike: shrimp-butter; and so on.

Trout with Rice

Take fish out of the cooking stock just before this comes to the boil. Drain fish, remove skin carefully, place on a bed of saffron-flavoured cooked rice, nice and dry. Cover with a white wine sauce, strongly spiced, and put a peeled shrimp at each of the four corners.

Jellied Trout

Poach the fish in a court bouillon that has been highly seasoned with mixed spices. Drain the trout and put in a fairly deep dish, garnish with a stem of tarragon, and mask with a thin jelly. If you like, add as further adornment some thin strips of truffle.

N.B.—It is also a good plan to braise in thin jelly of white wine base —or base of Chambertin or champagne.

Marcel Grancher Trout

Cut a large salmon trout in slices and set them in clear vinegar for a quarter of an hour. In another pan mix sliced carrots, onions in larger slices, thyme, bay, parsley, Cayenne pepper. Dry the fish cutlets in a cloth and add the vegetables. Add two glasses of very dry white wine. Seal hermetically and cook over brisk heat for a quarter of an hour. Then put fish in an oven dish. Strain the cooking liquor, dilute with white wine, add a few black olives from which the stones have been removed, a glass

A 'CARP AU BLEU'

By GUSTAVE GUICHES

It could have happened only in France, where the blue skies of Paradise and the bouillon in which fish are sometimes cooked are covered by the same word.

I knew Doctor Boujade well. He was very old and I a mere child. My memories of him are embittered by the fact that it was he who wished on me my first taste of cod-liver oil and my first dose of rhubarb. He had an untidy mop of white hair, cheeks a fiery red, a large nose patterned with capillaries, and cherry lips. 'As fond of food as Boujade' was quite a current expression. He knew all kinds of out-of-the-way recipes, restored some that had been only half-remembered, and elaborated others said to be for simple fare.

One dish was especially dear to his heart: carp in wine, or carpe au bleu. He had embellished the usual procedure by adding a stuffing: one which 'an egg white ran through like a Milky Way', according to his own description, and which was enlivened with a dash of brandy. But there was one prerequisite: the carp must weigh exactly three pounds.

One day Bernard, our angler, caught one, presented it to Boujade, and was invited to share it when cooked. There it was on the table before them, this carp au bleu, like a ship in sunlight. The river tang rose to the nostrils, and the doctor had just gripped his knife when a villager came in and said:

'Quick, Doctor Boujade, t'old lady up at Rigal's, she'll be dyin' if 'e don't come.'

It was a grisly moment. However, duty triumphed, and crumpling his table napkin, the good doctor, his voice choking with words unsaid, replied, 'All right, I'm coming.'

True enough the old body was dying. He could not hope to do much beyond making her last hours on earth as easy as possible. With the carp still in the forefront of all his meditations, he said, 'The poultices, now. Boil up some linseed, make it into a nice forcemeat, enliven it with a dash of . . . um, a dash of laudanum.'

'And when do I apply them?'

'Well, you begin of course, by removing her whole inside . . .' General stupefaction ensued. But Boujade was aloof from the puzzlement of the old woman's attendants, for his heart and mind were at home with the waiting carp. So that when the nurse opened the door of the sickroom and announced, in hushed tones, 'It's all over. She's just passed away . . .'

'Au bleu,' the doctor sighed.

of cream and a tablespoonful of Armagnac. Cover the fish and brown in the oven for a few minutes.

Vairon (Minnow)

Will serve in 'friture' if you have no gudgeon.

Pauchouse (or Pochouse)

This is a soup made from freshwater fish and is so highly acclaimed in Verdun-sur-le-Doubs that a 'Pauchouse Brotherhood' has been founded. Following the publication of an article on the subject in the periodical *Cuisine et Vins de France*, a women reader, actually from Verdun-sur-le-Doubs, sent the editor a letter containing 'the authentic' pauchouse recipe, which we are pleased to have the opportunity of reproducing:

'My parents used to have an old friend born in Verdun-sur-le-Doubs, and who also spent her early days and youth there. She died, nearly ninety years old, in 1926. At her house I have eaten pauchouses with which the dishes now passing under that name have very little in common.

She gave me her recipe, which has nothing mysterious about it, and also explained to me at some length that since the phylloxera invasion it has not been possible to make a pauchouse worthy of the name. And indeed, before this trouble afflicted vineyards the peasants of the Verdun region used to cultivate the grape on inconsiderable undulations facing the East which one could hardly call 'hills'. In the Ecuelles district they harvested a minor white wine of extreme dryness and so acid that it was barely drinkable. It was with this product that pauchouses were made.

After the phylloxera scare the peasants uprooted their vines, and those who replanted put in plants already grown, notably 'Noah' stock—yielding a wine equally undrinkable but without the saving grace of being a good pauchouse ingredient, or of serving in the confection of any kind of sauce. My old friend lamented at having to use an Aligote, the harshest she could find. I am quite certain that it would never have occurred to her to use a Meersault or any other vintage product, whose alcoholic content and bouquet would have spoiled the dish entirely. Here, then, is her recipe:

Take pike, eel, tench, perch, and perhaps an eel-pout or blenny (once quite common, but fairly rare nowadays—perhaps he, too, has been smitten with phylloxera!). All plump, large fish of their kind. In a copper bowl put several bulbs of garlic divided into cloves, but with their tough skin left on. Spread the cloves all round the bowl, put the fish heads in the bottom and a large and well-furnished bouquet garni, salt, plenty of pepper. Pack in as tightly as possible the rest of the fish, cut in thick slices. Cover completely with white wine and start cooking over a brisk heat. Boil hard for twenty minutes. Take out slices of fish and put on a serving dish. Take out garlic and bouquet garni and strain liquor. Thicken it with fresh butter, but do not let it boil again.

Above all: no onions, no bacon, no cream. To add these is to be guilty, it would seem, of heresy. Garnish with fried bread cubes previously rubbed with garlic.

We used to drink with this highly-coloured dish a sound little white wine—Macon of that same year (Vire type) or, failing that, a Montagny —that, too, of the same year.'

Poultry
and
Feathered
Game

'June offers tender young fowls and pigeons, youthful fat pullets, the turkey-poult just trying his wings for the first time; and Caen ducklings, so delicate when taken at the exact moment: the cockerel, bachelor of the poultry-yard, who cannot be confused with that fine, mature fellow (his uncle of course) the capon, so exclusive are the bouquet, the flavour of the latter, the fruit and flower of a blameless life.'

MAURICE GERMA

'A good roast chicken served with nothing but the gravy in the dripping pan is a treat to be eaten either at one's own table or that of the perfect host.'

ANDRE ROBINE

Over there a capon lies
In its platter—could be fatter,
Never mind, it's plump enough,
And, I'm certain, far from tough.
Is it fresh? Let nose apprise,
Questing round its end—the latter.

F. COLLETET
Les Tracas de Paris

'Sire, if your Majesty so wishes and permits, I should feel myself privileged to have served up to him every single day a chicken in some new guise.'

MARQUIS DE CUSSY. *Chamberlain to Napoleon I.*

POULTRY

The word is used to cover fowls, chickens, fat pullets, capons, cocks, hens and their nearest relations, also geese, turkeys, turkey-cocks, farmyard ducks, guineahens, guinea-chickens, pigeons.

High quality poultry is light fleshed and of fine texture. The birds should be plucked as soon as they are killed, and care must be taken not to break the skin. They are 'drawn' through an incision under the body, and the bitter contents of the sac next to the liver must not be allowed to escape. If you do break this bladder, wash the interior at once in hot water. Run a lighted taper over the outside (to burn off feather stumps) and over the feet, so that the wrinkled skin may be pulled off.

Duck

This palmiped, originally a wild bird, is now represented by several domestic varieties. The best French ones are the Barbary, Nantes, Rouen (especially Duclair) and the best English, Aylesbury. It is best eaten young (duckling) and the test for age is flexibility of beak. In the young bird it yields and bends to a mere touch of the fingers. Ducks are at their best, for table, from September to February.

Braised Duck

Prepare and truss the duck. In a saucepan, braising pan or any suitable broad-based vessel put a few scraps of bacon fat or pork fat, some onion rings previously fried lightly in butter, a bouquet garni. Add the duck and cook all together gently for a quarter of an hour, with lid on pan. When it is brown all over, pour in a glass of white wine. Allow to reduce, then pour in a good basinful of stock, or of brown veal or poultry broth if you have any. Put in the oven, having removed the lid, and leave to cook fifty minutes (medium-sized duck). The bird may be served with vegetables braised separately or cooked in water then sauté in butter.

Suitable ones are garden peas, small onions, young turnips and carrots, tomatoes. Or a macédoine of spring vegetables. Or a Provençal macédoine—tomatoes, baby marrows, etc. Or cucumbers, chestnuts, stoned and stuffed olives added a quarter of an hour before the end of the cooking time, or fennel branches.

ALSACE FASHION: placed on a layer of sauerkraut and surrounded with poached Strasbourg sausage or similar charcuteries.

Duck on the Spit

'The more holes in the duck the quicker the loss of his juices', wrote Alexandre Dumas, and his pronouncement applies to all birds cooked on the jack or spit. When the duckling is trussed fix a piece of fat bacon over its breast to baste it as it turns. Let the fire be a good glowing one.

Dr. Bécart's Duck Recipe

Peel half a dozen handsome dessert apples (rennets), remove pips, etc., cut into quarters and gild them in clarified butter, but do not cook through. Put on a dish and sprinkle, as they cool, with Grand Marnier.

Stuff a good plump duck, carefully drawn and 'run over' with a flame, with the apples, keeping in reserve a few pieces for garnishing. Put duck on spit and roast, with plenty of basting, at moderate heat. A few minutes before it is quite done, pour off the contents of the dripping-pan and baste the duck with a mixture of equal quantities of orange juice, *fine* champagne and Grand Marnier. In a saucepan put five lumps of sugar and five tablespoonsful of vinegar, and caramelize the sugar to a light brown. Add a glass of orange juice and the blanched zest of the orange. Reduce and cook for a quarter of an hour. Add the dripping-pan contents, first removing the extra fat therefrom, put salt and pepper to taste. Set the duck on a narrow dish, surround it with thin slices of orange alternating with the buttered apple pieces. Cover with several tablespoonsful of the sauce (kept very hot) and serve the rest of it in a jug.

(Compiled by DR. BECART, of the Académie des Gastronomes.)

APPROXIMATE COOKING TIMES FOR POULTRY AND GAME

TABLE FOWL	For a bird weighing about 3 lb net, from 55–60 minutes, medium heat to begin with, then low heat.
PLUMP PULLET	Weighing about 1¾ lb. Thirty to forty minutes in medium-hot oven 2½ lb, 40–50 minutes.
GUINEA-FOWL	1¾–2 lb, 40–50 minutes.
YOUNG TURKEY	Net weight 7–8 lb. Two and a quarter hours in medium heat.
DUCK	About 3 lb, 45–50 minutes, very hot oven.
AYLESBURY DUCKLINGS (or ROUEN DUCKLINGS)	About 3 lb net. 35 minutes at brisk heat (in its own juices). See 'Tour d'Argent' duck.
GOOSE	Medium size, 1½ hours in hot oven.

(From the periodical *Cuisine et vins de France*).

Rouen, or Aylesbury, Duck

Pluck and draw, trying not to lose any of the blood in the process. Roast for a quarter of an hour, then cut off the legs and wings, which

TOUR D'ARGENT DUCK

Everybody knows that the speciality of the Tour d'Argent restaurant in Paris is a Canard au Sang *(or a 'duck in duck-juice')—the recipe for which assumes that two extra ducks are available to supplement the principal one. The best practitioner was Frederick, an outstanding nineteenth-century chef: and the Tour d'Argent recipe inspired the Marquis Lauzères de Thémines to comment thus:*

'That's where they take the carcase of a duck,
Enclose it, crush and grind it to a paste,
Pound it with some crude engine that can suck
Its juices out, those saps of heavenly taste.
They've sliced what's sliceable, dark meat and light,
Served leg, wing, skin: so surely it's all right
To toss the dogs the frame, and let them scoff it?
Oh, no. . . . The "Silver Tower" turns bones *to profit.'*

* * *

Every duck served in this restaurant has its own special number. Here are a few historic examples:

No. 6,043 *was eaten by the Grand-Duke Vladimir* (1900)
No. 40,362 *by Alphonse XIII* (1914)
No. 71,676 *by Pierpont Morgan* (1924)
No. 112,151 *by Franklin Roosevelt* (1929)
No. 147,883 *by the Duke of Windsor* (1935).

And during her sojourn in Paris Queen Elizabeth the Queen Mother and her guests had Nos. 185,197 *and* 185,198. *Eight months later, No.* 203,728 *went to Marlene Dietrich.*

* * *

PRESENCE OF MIND

A canon, invited to dine at the establishment of a lady with extremely rigid notions of etiquette, offered to carve the two partridges. But instead of performing his autopsy on the serving dish, he casually transferred the first bird to his own plate. 'And who, canon,' the dowager drily enquired, 'is to be the recipient of your leavings?' 'Madam', he replied, 'I am not expecting to leave anything.'

will be grilled separately, and cut all the white meat in narrow strips. Put these on a warmed dish and add pepper and salt. Then ignite with brandy. Crush the carcase and liver in a meat-press and pour over this juice a glass of good burgundy. The juice should be increased by the addition of a dash of brandy and a little port. Pour this over the fillets of white meat. Serve very hot, but do not allow juice to boil as you reheat.

Mounet-Sully Duck

Two days before required for eating, prepare duck as for 'Duck on the Spit' and put it to soak in white wine in an earthenware vessel. Add onions cut into very thin slices and a little pepper and salt. Next day take out a few of the onion slices and chop together with duck livers. Add some truffled foie-gras and stuff the duck with this. Now cook on spit *for a quarter of an hour and no longer.*

In a saucepan brown some large onions in fat over a very low flame, and add a tablespoonful of flour. Stir around for three minutes and add some strained juice of veal, tomatoes cooked together (only a little of each required). Add next a glass of any kind of poultry blood mingled with vinegar. When the sauce is done, strain it, set aside.

The duck (already cooked for fifteen minutes) must now be cooked for a further two hours in a saucepan, just covered with white wine diluted with half a glass of water. At the end of this time, put it in the sauce which you set aside and leave over a very low flame for one hour. Let it get cold.

On the second day, take the duck from the sauce an hour before serving, and serve it just as it is. Strain the sauce again and add a glass of Malaga and a tablespoonful of old brandy.

(The great tragedian whose name is associated with this recipe lived, as is obvious, in days when there were both leisure and money to command.)

Duck in a Bladder

A plump duck is put into a cleaned pork bladder and cooked in veal stock until tender. It is served with a Béarnaise sauce (without tarragon, but finished with butter and zest of orange).

May be served with chestnuts.

Stuffed Duck

Cook in a fish-kettle or similar vessel; or braise it; or roast it. There are many possible stuffings, all based on the liver of the duck crushed with very finely-chopped bacon and with breadcrumbs soaked in milk. Any of the following may be added to this basic mixture: raw ham; anchovy fillets; mushroom stems or button mushrooms; poached oysters combined with chopped shallots and egg yolk to bind; also olives. In each case add salt, pepper, nutmeg, bay, thyme, savoury, to your choice and liking.

Duck with Fruits

Compare Dr. Bécart's recipe above, using dessert apples and oranges to give a special flavour to the duck meat.

DUCK AND ORANGE. Every restaurant has its own version, but it may be prepared according to Dr Bécart's recipe, leaving out the apples.

DUCK AND PEACHES is almost the same basic recipe, and so is DUCK AND MONTMORENCY CHERRIES. The cherries need to be sourish, as Montmorency cherries are. This is best served cold in its own jelly.

DUCK TUTTI-QUANTI. The duck is surrounded by a macédoine, as it were, of fruits refreshed in some spirituous liquor—peaches, cherries, banana rings, apples, pineapple, etc., but always a preponderance of oranges.

DUCK AND PINEAPPLE is a Chinese speciality.

Duck's Liver

Duck's liver is said to be more delicate and of even better flavour than goose liver. This recipe for Duck Liver 'au Naturel' is taken from Curnonsky's *La Table et l'Amour*.

Take a good fat liver from a duck, such as may be found at its best in the early days of winter when the really cold weather is beginning. Salt lightly, then put in a copper pan with silvered lining previously made to glisten with a few drops of olive oil just warmed. Put over brisk heat and shake pan constantly so that the liver does not stick to it. After twelve or fifteen minutes the liver will have the pale gold colour of a very lightly toasted bread crust, and then it will be done. Serve hot on hot plates. It should be sliced and eaten just as it is, or perhaps with a little lemon juice. Prepared in this fashion, duck liver is a heavenly food. It looks like a rose-coloured jelly, smells exquisite, is highly appetizing: good to look at, to smell, to taste, and its virtues should not remain unlauded.

N.B.—EDOUARD ROUZIER, a very successful *restaurateur* and gourmet who died in February 1952, invented, for his Rôtisserie Périgourdine, a dish called 'Noisettes d'Agneau Brantôme'—that is, lamb *noisettes* garnished with slices of duck liver ('foie-gras') soaking in grape verjuice.

Rochecorbon Duck Pie

Bone a young duckling, take fillets and all the white meat. Chop up together into small pieces 4 oz bacon, a bare half-pound of lean pork, and the liver of the duck. Pack into an earthenware pot, adding salt and pepper on every layer, and setting in the middle a layer of chicken fillets, using whole (not chopped). Add a bay leaf and large glass of Rochecorbon wine (Vouvray) to soak all the layers. Put on lid and cook for two hours in a slow oven.

(Recipe by CHARLES GAY—won Prosper Montagné prize, 1951).

Potted Duck

Collect the blood of the duck in a cup and add to it a glass of red wine (preferably burgundy) and a few drops of brandy. Keep in a cool place. Pluck the duck and draw it, then next day, when it has had time to 'firm', cut off the fillet portions and dice them. Dice the same weight of fat bacon, and the same weight again of ham. (If you have to use salt ham, scald in boiling water, leaving it to soak for five minutes). Take legs and wings of the duck and all the other meat you can find on the carcase. Cut this meat into small pieces and using a mechanical cleaver, if possible, reduce meat and the liver to tiny pieces. The liver must have been previously hardened in frying pan, with a few shallots, over brisk heat. Moisten your meat mixture with a glass of *fine*. If you have them, you may add livers of other poultry, or even some calf's liver.

Now add the blood collected on the previous day, a raw egg, a glass of alcohol and finally mix in the diced fillets, the bacon and the ham. Put in an earthenware pot dotted with pork fat, bay scraps; add a glass of red wine and put lid on tightly. Cook in bain-marie for two hours.

Turkeys and Turkey-Poults

Etymology suggests that these birds came from America (d'Inde) since the continent of America was for a long time known as 'the Western Indies', Brillat-Savarin asserts that the Jesuits introduced the turkey to Europe towards the end of the seventeenth century.

Turkey-hen=*dinde*. Turkey-cock=*dindon*. Young turkey, or poult= *dindonneau*. But *dinde* is the culinary word. And as it should always be eaten young, the 'turkey' is always a 'young turkey'. So strict classification by these various names is not possible.

All recipes which are suitable for chicken, pullets, fowls, are also suitable for turkeys. The principal ways of serving turkey are: with truffles; with chestnuts; stuffed with poultry stuffing with crayfish butter; or with bacon, veal and herb stuffing; roasted; 'en daube' (stew-pot cooked)—a procedure especially useful for an old bird; braised and served with a variety of garnishes as follows:

Alsace style: sauerkraut, lean bacon and sausages.
Burgundy style: mushrooms, glazed onions.
Milan style: macaroni julienne and chopped ham.

Piedmont style: with risotto.

Languedoc style: with tomatoes, aubergines and mushrooms.

Brazil Turkey

Roast turkey served with 'farofa' (cassava roasted and crushed to a flour) and with very thin slices of ham.

Geese

The ordinary goose (*oie*) is known all over Europe, and all poultry recipes will serve for its preparation, especially turkey recipes. 'Toulouse' or 'Strasbourg' geese are larger than the rest and these large geese are usually reserved for 'Confit' (poultry-meat preserved in fat). As is well known the Strasbourg goose is crammed with food so that its liver becomes enlarged, and the immobility that is forced on the bird results in the liver's fatty degeneration being complete and unmistakable.

The best table birds are from five to seven months' old. As with ducks, the age may be assessed by testing the flexibility of the beak.

Goose dripping is extremely useful in vegetable cookery.

Stuffed Goose, German Style

Pluck, draw and singe a young, fat goose. Keep separate the heart, gizzard, lights and liver.

Peel 1½ lb dessert apples (rennets for choice), remove pips, chop up small, cook over slow flame with an onion faintly browned in goose fat. Cook separately 1½ lb chestnuts—which must be still firm when finished, not a pulp.

Chop the 'offals' with parsley and add to the apples. Cook on for a little, stirring the mixture. Add some bread soaked in milk or stock, stir to a good thick consistency, then put in the chestnuts without breaking them.

Rub interior of goose with salt and pepper, then put in the stuffing. Sew up incision, truss, cover with scraps of fat bacon for basting, and roast, allowing fifteen minutes to the pound.

Goodwife's Goose

Pluck, draw and singe a fat goose and cook it for three-quarters of an hour in salted water with vegetables and hot-pot type of seasoning. When it seems to be tender take it out and allow it to get cold. Then cut in pieces of about an inch square, soak these in a whole beaten egg, roll in breadcrumbs, and roast in fresh butter.

In a separate pan brown a tablespoonful of flour in the same quantity of butter. Add a chopped clove of garlic, pepper, salt, a pinch of grated nutmeg. Pour over the mixture half a pint of double cream, and the sauce should be thick and smooth. Put in the roasted goose pieces, very hot, and serve.

(From the singer GABRIELLO)

Jugged Goose

Cut a goose in fairly small pieces and remove as much fat as possible, reserving this for other uses, when melted separately. Put the raw goose pieces into a good red wine sauce to simmer. Cook gently for an hour and a half approximately. If you have been able to save the blood, add after three quarters of an hour's simmering.

N.B.—The pieces may be ignited with brandy, etc., before putting into sauce.

May be served with fried bread cubes, covered with its sauce and sprinkled with finely chopped parsley.

Potted Goose

Cut off the different joints and quarter, also cut the fillets separately; and remove as much fat as you can from these. Put all in brine in an earthenware pot covered with a cloth, and leave for twenty-four hours. Then wipe the pieces and put in a cauldron in which the goose fat has melted. Cook for about three and a half hours. Then drain off fat and put the meat in a large earthenware vessel. Cover with the strained fat. When all this is quite cold, add a half-inch of lard to lengthen the life of the potted goose.

Keep this in a cool, dry place and every time you take out some of the pieces, be careful to re-cover the remainder with fat. In this way you can keep the pot going for a long time. Besides being indispensable for Garbure (see Soups, p. 19), and Cassoulet, this 'confit' or 'conserve' may be served hot or cold with several kinds of accompaniment, as follows:

(*a*) SERVED HOT:

—with mushrooms, sauté in a mixture of olive oil and goose fat;
—with raw potatoes sauté in goose dripping;
—with haricot beans, lentils or split peas;
—with cabbage or sauerkraut;
—with peas, or a macédoine of vegetables.

(*b*) SERVED COLD:

—with a macédoine of vegetables;
—with kidney beans made into a salad;
—with lentils, likewise in salad form;
—with red cabbage.

Goose Liver

May be prepared and used 'au naturel' as with duck liver. The Périgord foie-gras and those of Alsace are the strongest claimants for supremacy, but those of the Landes are also well-supported rivals. Austria, Czechoslovakia and Luxembourg produce foies-gras of fine quality. The finer its texture and the creamier (inclining to pinkness) its colour, the better the liver.

Historians of culinary matters cannot agree as to whether it was Close (chef to Marshal de Contades, governor of Alsace in 1762 to 1768, see p. 269) who created the paté de foie-gras with truffles, or whether it was already well-known in Périgord before his day. There are other quibblers who say that Close's name was not really Close. But what does all this matter when we can, with Curnonsky, do honour to the goose as a 'magnificent and ambulatory foie-gras factory'?

Pigeons (Pigeons)

Specially bred for table (Biset,[1] etc.) or wild ones such as the wood-pigeon (cushat, ringdove) have flesh of good quality. A significant fact—since they belong to the family of doves, symbols of peace—is that there is no gall in their livers.

They are cooked and served, like most other smaller birds, with strips of basting fat in a small pan or casserole, or even on the spit. It is usual to wring their necks as they are not large.

Pigeons in Papillotes

Draw and singe the pigeon, cut off wattles, and truss with the feet inside. Cut the back from the neck to rump and flatten the bird without bruising the flesh unduly. Add salt, pepper and pounded aromatic herbs.

Put in a pan 4 oz finely chopped bacon and a walnut of butter, also four tablespoonsful of olive oil. Cook pigeons slowly for a quarter of an hour, then put birds on a dish. Make a forcemeat with butter, chopped mushrooms, a tablespoonful each of chopped parsley and shallot, and pepper and salt to season. Cover the pigeons with this and let the dish get completely cold. Oil some squares of white paper, enclose the pigeons and fold in the edges. Half an hour before they are to go to table put them to cook gently on griddle or under grill or in the oven.

Creamed Pigeons

Pluck, draw, singe and truss two young, plump pigeons. Cook them gently in a saucepan with a tablespoonful of fresh butter. When they are golden brown, pour in a gill of stock (or water, failing stock) and cook

[1] Biset: blue rock-pigeon, origin of all the domesticated varieties.

for an hour. Ten minutes before serving, stir a gill of fresh cream into the liquor, and sprinkle the dish with chopped chives before serving.

Juniper Pigeons

Make a stuffing with breadcrumbs soaked in milk, the liver, gizzard and heart of two pigeons, and a little fat bacon chopped finely; season it with salt, pepper, nutmeg. Stuff the two pigeons, truss them, and lay over them a few strips of fat for basting. Gild them in a pan containing a little butter, then add a dozen or so juniper berries chopped very small. Moisten with a small glass of brandy, place lid on pan, complete cooking in the oven.

N.B.—If you prefer to do so, add the juniper berries to the stuffing.

Pigeon Compôte

Melt a walnut of butter, brown in it two prepared pigeons. As soon as they are golden, take them out. In the same butter fry, to 'transparency' only, some dice of lean bacon, then make a roux with two tablespoonsful of flour; and when it is nicely browned add two glasses of stock, with salt, pepper, bay leaf, thyme, parsley. Put the pigeons back in the sauce, also a dozen or so tiny onions, and the bacon squares. A quarter of an hour before serving add some mushrooms and some stoned green olives.

Roast Pigeons

The classic accompaniment is new, green peas with small button onions and diced fat bacon. But small roast pigeons may be served with potatoes, watercress, vegetable-stuffed tomatoes, curried rice, lentil or mushroom purée, and so on.

Pigeon Pie

Roast them very lightly so that their juice is still running red. Cut into quarters and skin. Line the bottom of a round pie-dish with half-inch pastry and on this put a layer of forcemeat made up of half pork, half veal soaked in red wine. Now add the pieces of pigeon, mixing them with large cooked mushrooms, strips of lean bacon, cooked very lightly in frying-pan, and shreds of truffle. Top with stuffing and put on the top pie-crust. Bake in a slow oven for about an hour, leaving a hole in the middle of the crust. Before serving, introduce through this 'chimney' a fairly thick wine sauce (hot of course). Serve the pie straight from the oven.

Pintade (Guinea-fowl)

The Romans called them 'Carthaginian fowls'. The guinea-fowl is the game-bird of the poultry-yard but it meets its doom like other

THIS QUEEN OF FRANCE LOVED TURKEY

When, on the 26th of November 1570, King Charles the Ninth married, at Mézières, the princess Elisabeth, daughter of Emperor Maximilian the Second, the wedding breakfast included the first turkeys ever seen in France. The young bride found the meat of these birds so delectable that the Lords of Biron and of Mesmes announced that henceforth turkeys would have to be bred in France. And not long afterwards the Jesuits succeeded in acclimatizing them at Bourges, and from this source they spread all over the country. The following anecdote shows how greatly this innovation delighted gastronomes:

Monseigneur Daviau de Sanzai, Archbishop of Bordeaux, had laid a bet with one of his vicars-general, and had won it—the stake being a roast turkey stuffed with truffles. The loser seemed to be in no hurry to meet his obligations, and as the end of Lent was not far off the archbishop jogged his memory. 'Oh you see, my lord,' said the vicar, 'it's like this. Truffles are simply worthless this year.' 'Rubbish', replied the epicurean Sanzai. 'That's only a rumour that the turkeys are circulating.'

HOST'S DILEMMA

'But surely, sir, you're not helping yourself to both *wings of that fowl?'*
'And why not? If I don't some other uncouth fellow will.'

THE ART OF EATING TURKEY

Morellet, his Reverence that is, used often to assert that it took two to do justice to a roast turkey. Then he would add, 'Whenever I have one to eat, there are two of us—the turkey and myself.'

domestic fowl and does not fall to the guns of sportsmen. There are those who assert that it is the 'pheasant's double', but they are exaggerating its worth—it is much more like the turkey in most respects.

The guinea-fowl should not be bled and must hang for two days. Then, because the flesh is terribly dry, it must not only be basted thoroughly, but it's advisable also to insert very thin strips of fat or fat bacon in leg parts and breast. They are at their best in July. Cook as pheasant or partridge when young (*pintadeaux* or guinea-chickens) and when larger or more mature, treat as fowls.

Roast Guinea-Fowl

Hang just as it is for twenty-four hours in the cellar. Next day pluck, draw and ignite with spirit. Cover well with lardons for basting then place again (in safe) in the cellar, or in your refrigerator, for twenty-four hours. Then roast in oven dish or on the spit.

The best method, perhaps, is to put in the oven in a roasting pan and leave it there for forty minutes, using at least 2 oz of butter for extra basting during that time. Then take away the scraps of fat used for basting and cook for a further ten minutes to brown the outside.

Chop separately some chicken or other poultry livers, also the guinea-fowl's liver and heart, together with a little parsley, and make into a stuffing (seasoned) that you spread on croûtons. Slip these stuffing-covered croûtons into the roasting pan on both sides of the bird, after basting bits have been removed, and make sauce from the pan gravy diluted with water and a little white wine. Strain sauce. This may well have as accompaniment a watercress salad (without vinegar).

Poules, Poulardes, Poulets, etc. (Fowls, Fat Pullets, Chickens)

> *The most delectable portion of a roast fowl is the wing. If it is a boiled fowl, the choicest piece is the top of the drumstick, especially if it is white and fat-fleshed, and meaty. Women have more ambiguous tastes.*
>
> GRIMOD DE LA REYNIERE

Here we must make certain distinctions. In culinary language, POUSSIN is a spring chicken of something between 1 lb and 1¼ lb. POULET DE GRAIN is the young chicken of about 1¼ lb to 2 lb. Then, as summer wears on, we get the POULET, or POULET REINE, the really large chicken which may weigh as much as 3¾ lb. And even heavier is the POULET GRAS, or fat pullet.

The POULARDE, the larger table fowl, is heavier, older and of firmer flesh. The CHAPON is the capon, the emasculated and fattened cock bird. Last comes the COQ VIERGE, the bachelor cock of special flavour, not so delicate as the others.

The race of domestic fowls is numerous everywhere. Favourites in France are the Bresse, Faverolles, Houdan, Le Mans, but every country has its specialized breeds. A good chicken, pullet or fowl must, whatever its breed, have tender and resilient flesh and its feet (varying according to family) should be black, grey or white, but not yellow—yellowness indicating advanced age. The skin should be white and smooth to the touch.

The usual cooking methods are:

FAT FOWLS, CAPONS: roast, pan-cooked, par-boiled, and braised.

PULLETS: casserole, covered-pan grilled, in fricassées, roast.

CHICKENS, SPRING CHICKENS, YOUNG COCKERELS: fried, grilled, roast.

Sauté Chicken

Cut the uncooked bird into its various joints and place in sauté dish with 2 oz butter, to cook golden brown. It is best to make two portions of each leg, two of each wing, pinions, breast meat, neck portion; the carcase in two or three pieces. Cook for ten minutes or so (wings and breast meat to be taken out first as they cook more rapidly). Add a tablespoonful of flour to the cooking fat and add either white wine or stock or water. When sauce boils replace the chicken pieces for a short time.

This is a basic preparation, and many modifications are possible, depending on the garnishing, etc. Some of these are:

Algerian: olive oil replacing the butter. Add crushed tomatoes and aubergines.

Burgundian: use red wine, not white, and add onions and mushrooms.

Parmentier: add well-scraped new potatoes (washed, dried and blanched for a minute in boiling water, then dried again).

en Barboille: add the blood (or some pig's blood) boiled with a glass of water and two glasses of red wine. Add shallots.

Lyon: with onions sauté in butter and chopped parsley.

With Mushrooms: flap mushrooms, chanterelles, morels, button mushrooms, etc. (and truffles may be added).

Creamed: done in butter, and sauce combined with fresh cream.

Indian: add a tablespoonful of curry.

Fine Herbs: with parsley, chervil and tarragon (chopped all together) added to sauce with a dash of lemon.

N.B.—Sauté chicken may be accompanied by almost any vegetable, such as: brussels sprouts with butter; baby marrows; aubergines; tomatoes; noodles or rice; artichoke bottoms; sweet corn.

It is also possible to ignite the chicken pieces with brandy, and to add Cognac, Armagnac, Madeira or whisky to the sauce.

Mithridates Chicken (Sauté)

Sauté as before, but with chopped shallots added. Ignite with liqueur (a small glassful) and moisten with dry white wine. Make a roux with shrimp butter (using cleaned shrimps to make ½ lb weight) and mix with the cooking liquid. Make a ring of cooked rice in which several stoned cherries have been inserted, and pile the chicken pieces in the middle. Cover the whole with the sauce which you will have thickened with cream. Serve with a jar of guava jelly.

(Recipe by SAM, troubadour-cook)

Exotic Sauté Chicken

Sauté the pieces in coconut milk with a little cinnamon, some coriander, saffron, powdered red pimento and Cayenne pepper. Just before serving, thicken sauce with egg yolks.

Hungarian Sauté Chicken

Cut large onion in rings and cook in butter, but do not brown. Add salt, pepper, paprika, and six tablespoonsful of tomato sauce. Put in the chicken pieces, which should have been soaking in water for ten minutes. Cook for one hour. Add to sauce some good thick rich cream and serve with ravioli.

Fowls

Good King Henry wanted everyone to have his boiled fowl on a Sunday. It is cooked in hot-pot fashion. Choose a large bird, and one on the fat side, and put it in cold water. When it boils, skim off the debris from the top and add carrots, turnips, leeks and a stick of celery, with a little salt and pepper. Cook gently for 1½ to 2 hours, according to size of fowl. The boiled fowl may then, having been removed from the pot and cut into various joints, be served in several ways, including:

(1) Covered with a white wine and shallot sauce, with stoned green olives blanched and halved or quartered.

(2) Heated in butter with chopped onions and covered with a white sauce flavoured with savoury herbs (mixed).

(3) Soaked for an hour in a vinegar dressing then covered with mayonnaise, garnished with hard-boiled eggs, green salad, tomatoes, capers, etc.

(4) Soaked for an hour in a lemon juice and oil mixture with salt and pepper, then dipped in batter and fried in boiling-hot oil.

THE CHICKEN COOKED UPRIGHT

Lucien Boyer, the singer, composed this sonnet a few years ago in honour of Dorin Frères' establishment, 'birthplace' of the 'Spitted-Chicken-on-a-String'.

Go hang yourself, Vatel. Your fame's brief light
Has faded at Rouen, where Dorin Frères',
Curnonsky's, Arbellot's, and Labrégère's
Joint arts devised the chicken-cooked-upright.

Pierced through the parson's nose, he stands full height
On shaft of steel: like Turk impaled, he bears
His state alone. No vulgar garnish dares
Disgrace his pure bouquet, no trimmings trite.

Noble and proud, he scorns to writhe and twist
As fragrant juice, from that heraldic breast,
Drips from his rump like lead-drops from crenelle.

So, when they serve him up, all bronzed and browned,
He, still undaunted, and with courage crowned,
Like Cyrano, died standing, and died well.

LUCIEN BOYER

(5) Egged-and-breadcrumbed and fried.

(6) Boned, pounded with egg yolks, chopped ham, salt, pepper, nutmeg—then used as a fresh ravioli garnish.

(7) Au gratin, the meat pounded with ham dice (cooked) and mixed with potato purée, the whole covered with grated parmesan and browned in oven.

(8) With a highly flavoured tomato sauce.

Old-times Boiled Fowl

Chop (together) the liver, heart and gizzard of the fowl, adding half a pound of dry breadcrumbs, a little less than half a pound of ham, some parsley and tarragon, a clove of garlic. Bind with two fresh eggs, add salt, pepper and mixed spice to taste.

Stuff the fowl with this and truss it. Now put it into a large cauldron containing 7 or 8 pints of boiling water. Add cabbage leaves, carrots, turnips, beetroot tops, two potatoes. When it has boiled for an hour add a pound of smoked ham and leave to boil for two hours longer. When it is done serve the soup first and then the fowl.

Fowl and Rice

This is a fowl cooked in a good stock (with parsley, thyme, bay, two garlic cloves, a carrot and an onion cut in rounds). It should cook for four or five hours. Cook your rice in some of the stock.

N.B.—This may be served with a sauce of Béchamel nature, made with egg yolk.

Roast Chicken

Use spit or roast in oven. Serve with watercress, and its cooking liquor in a sauce-boat. It must be cooked fairly fast and when it is giving out a good savoury vapour it should be done.

Marcel Dorin, gastronome and culinary expert, invented the 'vertical spit' and 'chicken-on-a-string'. A clean wood fire is required and the chicken is suspended from a string, its juices falling on a bed of mushrooms, potatoes and artichoke bottoms. Basting must be frequent and a glass of Madeira is added to the gravy just before serving.

Coqs au Vin (Cocks in Wine)

'Coq au vin' is a chicken prepared in wine—any chicken, not necessarily a cockerel or cock.

It is just a sauté bird. Lardons of bacon or similar fat (previously blanched) are lightly cooked with small onions and quartered mushrooms. The chicken pieces are cooked separately in oil, then the contents of both pans are mixed in a saucepan, and the cooking liquor, thinned with spirits and a bottle of red wine added (Mercurey, or Chambertin, in Burgundy) is poured over. When this boils, three chopped garlic cloves are added. Cooking time is then twenty minutes.

The 'Coq au vin' has various designations, these depending on the red wine used. Examples are:

Jurassiene: when an Arbois rosé is employed;

Quercynoise: a Cahors wine;

Nuitonne: a Côte de Nuits (ignited with Burgundy 'marc');

Alsacienne: a Riesling.

In Béarn the wine used in the preparation is an Irouléguy.

In Auvergne, a Chanturgue.

In Pouilly, a white Pouilly (*fumé*).

Coq Vierge (Cockerel)

This young male, the barnyard bachelor, is just right for the table at the moment when he is thinking of changing his state—unhappy age for him. He is cooked on the spit basted with bacon strips.

Coq en Pâte (Chicken Pie)

Unlike the subject of the previous recipe, but as with 'Coq au Vin', the subject is here either a chicken or pullet, etc., as comes to hand. And it may be stuffed with a rich or a simple stuffing, as you prefer. Roll out some brioche paste, not too thin, and wrap the stuffed bird in it, following the shape as well as you can manage. Put on greased baking sheet and cook for at least an hour in a moderate oven.

N.B.—Before you encase it in the pastry you could soak the bird for a few hours in a mixture of oil, port wine, thyme, bay, etc., basting it often.

Stuffed Chickens, Fowls

PIEDMONT: Stuff with a stuffing based on dried bread 'raspings', containing poultry liver and mushrooms. Put the bird to brown in butter with some diced lean ham, and stock poured over. Cook for half an hour and then add 4 oz rice. Serve with the rice in a ring on the serving dish and the chicken in the middle. Moisten the dish with the cooking liquor thickened with tomato sauce. Garnish with chipolatas.

BORDEAUX: Stuffing to consist of 3 oz chopped fat pork mixed with the same weight of calf's liver and the liver of the chicken; these cooked together with chopped onions and scalded bacon strips, also seasoning. Moisten with a little Madeira, ignite with Cognac. Garnish: artichoke quarters, sauté potatoes sprinkled with parsley, fried flavoured onion rings.

MENAGERE ('Good housewife'): A very highly spiced stuffing with base of milk-soaked breadcrumbs, meat left-overs, fat bacon and, if necessary, an egg to bind.

ANDALUSIAN: Stuff the chicken with a rice pilaf mixed with a ham saupiquet (see p. 236). Sprinkle with paprika.

TARRAGON: Make the stuffing of chopped liver and tarragon leaves, mixed with fresh butter. Later, add to the sauce a little more tarragon and two eggs for binding.

Chicken and Cheese

Singe the chicken. Draw it, split it down the back and flatten it out. Cook gently in butter in a saucepan. Pour in half a glassful of stock and the same quantity of white wine. Add parsley, chives (or green of spring onions), garlic, thyme, bay leaf, salt, pepper. Let this simmer over low flame for an hour. Then strain liquid and bind with butter. Put half of this thickened sauce in an oven-dish and sow thickly with grated gruyère cheese. Put chicken on top, pour the rest of the sauce over, add a second layer of grated cheese. Put in oven to turn golden brown.

Italian Chicken

Cut chicken in pieces, salt and pepper these, and put into pan containing smoking-hot oil. When they are browned all over, put them on a dish and add to the hot oil a finely-chopped onion, half a pint of white wine, a bouquet garni. Fill up with stock when you have put the chicken back in the pan. Put lid on pan and cook gently. A quarter of an hour before serving, add to the sauce a fried clove of garlic, two egg yolks and some grilled almonds, all these ingredients worked into a smooth mixture with pestle and mortar. Drain the chicken pieces, strain the sauce and pour over these.

Serve with potato croquettes and tomatoes stuffed with meatless stuffing.

Chicken Stew

In a stewpot place some onions and carrots cut in rings, garlic, a bouquet garni, some fat bacon cut in small pieces, a calf's foot which the butcher will have chopped down the middle for you. Cover with water. Season with salt and bring to the boil.

(As the calf's foot takes longer to cook than the fowl or chicken, the latter is not added to the boiling stock until 20–30 minutes after cooking begins—be guided by the age of the bird.)

Boil for about three hours, and half-way through cooking add a glass of dry white wine. Half an hour before cooking is due to end, add two liqueur glasses of Cognac or Armagnac. At this stage (not before), add pepper to your liking.

When bird is tender, take it (and the calf's foot) from the pan. Strain the cooking liquor through a fine strainer to remove vegetables and bacon. While the stock cools cut bird into pieces suitable for serving and put them in a deep dish. Add, if you like, the pieces of bacon you strained off. Remove fat which will have formed on the stock, and pour enough of it in the dish to cover the pieces. Keep for twenty-four hours in a cool place.

Chaud-Froid of Poultry

This is a quite simple but a lengthy procedure. However, as it needs to be done on the day before it is needed for table, and as it is a really effective creation, the good housewife will not mind mastering the details.

The poultry used must be plump and of high quality. It should be drawn, singed, trussed, and wrapped around with a few larding strips.

Line the bottom of pan with white of leeks, sliced onions, some pieces of pork crackling and a bouquet garni. Put the fowl on top of these and add a pint and a quarter of water or stock. Cook for about an hour, gently. Remove bird, take off the basting strips, set it aside to get cold. Strain the liquor.

In a warmed earthenware dish blend some flour with an ounce of butter, and add slowly the strained stock. Add 8–10 oz fresh cream and reduce to a smooth sauce. When really velvety add an egg yolk, salt and pepper. Put on the side of the cooker to lose heat.

Skin fowl and cut into a dozen pieces. Put these to soak in the cooled sauce—which will be very thick but still liquid—and be sure that all pieces are well blanketed with it. Put these on a wire tray (the kind used for pastries, cakes, etc.) and put it in the refrigerator, freezer, or ice-box.

N.B.—They may be decorated with strips of truffle cut very small. Prepare separately a jelly by soaking in cold water half an ounce of gelatine. Put one egg white in saucepan, add gelatine and chicken stock. Mix, strain, and leave to thicken. Pour it over a dish, to cover it in a quarter-inch layer. On this layer reconstitute the fowl or chicken from the now-frozen pieces. Pour over the remainder of the semi-set jelly and replace to freeze again.

Stuffed Spring Chickens

This is an Egyptian dish with which you might experiment. You need fairly large young chickens—one or two months old. Singe, draw, fill with highly seasoned (spiced) cooked rice, and cook at low temperature in a little oil.

Poached Fowl

Cook in water with carrot slices, or in white stock. When it is done serve surrounded with vegetables plain-boiled in water, blanched dice of fat bacon or belly of pork, celery bouquets, slices of tongue. And it should be accompanied by a Béchamel or a parsley sauce, or a melted butter sauce with capers.

Chicken and Noodles

Roast chicken, but the stuffing is a mixture of noodles with parmesan and black olives.

Chicken and Oysters

Braised chicken, stuffed with oysters poached in their own water. Fry some bread slices (crusts removed) in olive oil, then spread them with anchovy butter. Put the pieces of the bird on these and pour over a sauce made from the cooking liquids to which shallot-flavoured white wine has been added.

FEATHERED GAME (WILD FOWL)

How enchanting life is, how wonderful the conversation, when four are gathered together, and each has just finished his own individual partridge.

SACHA GUITRY

The Phasian bird, the capercailzie too,
The ornaments of twenty rich ragoûts,
Nose, palate, eyes beguiling. . . .

VOLTAIRE

In sportsman's classification there are three types of feathered game:

(1) Highlands, hill or mountain game, such as grouse, hazel-grouse, hazel-hen, mountain partridge, etc.

(2) Land game: bustard, landrail, quail, grey (or common) partridge, red-legged partridge, pheasant, cushat or ringdove or woodpigeon, larks, blackbirds, thrushes, woodcock, beccafico (or blackcap), ortolans, 'larks in season' (mauviettes).[1]

(3) Water fowl: ducks, snipe, moorhens, teal, wild geese, water rails.

[1] It is a little confusing that *mauviette*=field lark, while *alouette des champs*=skylark.

If game is not shot by yourself or someone you know, it is important to know what to look for when you buy. Without insisting on the necessity for freshness, where your nose is always a good guide, there are one or two little helpful dodges. The following were set down by a considerable gourmet, M. PAUL MEGNIN of the Académie des Gastronomes: he is speaking of wildfowl in general:

'With most wildfowl there is an easy test for freshness, and one that gives reliable information. If you are assessing the freshness of partridge, say, or pigeon, or pheasant, take the lower mandible of the beak between thumb and index finger and lift up the bird with no other leverage. If the mandible thus held breaks away at the lip corners, then the bird is *not* an old one.'

But there are other ways:

We need not discuss the quail. The flesh is always tender; the bird should not be hung or allowed to grow gamy, for the lean meat taints and the fat becomes rancid.

With the partridge, have nothing to do with the mean and mangy specimens which the guns should have scorned as the gourmet certainly will. You want only the speckled birds, on which the red is just beginning to cover the head above the eyes, and the grey colour of the plumage is variegated with yellowish and russet patches not unlike links in chain-mail. In October the red between eye and ear has become very pronounced and glows with true vermilion. Also the horseshoe mark has appeared on the breast of the male, and the legs are turning brown. If you want to ascertain whether a partridge is one of the current year, you must examine wings and feet. The first feathers of a this-year's partridge are pointed at the end, and rounded in an older bird. The legs and feet of a young partridge are not so grey, not so scaly, not so rough to the touch as an older bird's.

The young partridge of the current year's hatch, must be eaten fresh—either roasted or spitted (and cooked before a wood fire, best of all before a fire of young woody branches of vine or similar growth). The older bird is cooked with cabbage or sauerkraut, or goes with truffles, into a pie.

If you are inspecting a red-legged partridge, this year's birds have no spurs, the throat white is on the yellow side, and the red circle around the eye is extremely narrow. Its flesh is whiter than that of the grey or common partridge, but flavour and smell are not so good.

With the pheasant you must be prepared to distinguish very precisely between the wild pheasant and the artificially reared. The pheasant has been dubbed the 'king of game birds', but I myself wonder why. From the sportsman's point of view its flight has nothing remarkable about it. From the gastronomic standpoint the pheasant from a game preserve is not in the same street as a good plump chicken (say of Bresse) with red crest, white body and blue feet. As for the wild pheasant, it tastes quite good, and that's all there is to it. The pheasant is remarkable for the beauty of its plumage but not for the delicacy of its flesh. The hen-bird is generally plumper than the male, with finer flesh, but must be young. Test as described above, by holding the bird's lower mandible between thumb and index finger.

Young pheasants are best cooked on the spit. Older ones are cooked with truffles and olives, or in the big pot slowly, or with sauerkraut. Remember that cold pheasant—especially the hen—is better to eat, and of more savoury odour, than the same bird eaten hot.

I shall not describe other wildfowl and feathered game at length, as there would be no end to it. However, as there are, I know, some gourmets who like pigeons, I will add that the young ones are the best. They are known to be young when the 'necklace' is not yet very noticeable and the grey of the plumage has a rusty tinge.

To the question of 'gaminess' we shall return later.

Alouettes (Larks)

Remarkable for its song and the pies named after it.
E. L. BLANCHET

In culinary language the lark (*alouette*) is usually styled *mauviette*. The exception is the renowned *Pâte d'alouettes de Pithiviers*. Larks are, like thrushes, eaten in hot or cold pies, skewered, stuffed, or *en casserole*.

'Minute' Larks

Split down back, flatten slightly. Sprinkle salt and pepper on them. Cook rapidly in butter in a sauté pan and serve on fried bread pieces. Add a little champagne to the sauce.

N.B.—May be served in a 'crown' or a bed of rice pilaf, on cheese polenta, or chestnut purée.

Woodcock

A bird of passage. It flies down at the end of October or in early November, in solitary state, over spinneys, bush-dotted heaths, copses, and around the edges of dense woods. (This information is for the 'guns'.) The consumer needs only to know that this long-beaked bird is first-rate eating, needs to be hung briefly, and that some will eat it only when 'undrawn'.

Roast Woodcock

Pluck, singe and truss, but do not draw the bird, thrusting the beak into the body at top-of-leg level. Put larding-fat pieces on the bird, bind

MAURICE DONNAY SAID IT

Maurice Donnay was having dinner at a little Alpine inn, and the bill of fare promised 'poulets de Bresse'. The author of Lovers, *pleased to see these fine chickens announced, ordered a helping for himself, and was given a bit of dubious poultry, all skin and bone. He eyed it with mistrust and asked to speak to the innkeeper, who came at once.*

'I say, innkeeper, are you sure that your chickens are really from Bresse?'

'Most certainly, sir. They came straight from Bresse', was the answer, delivered with assurance. Donnay shook his head sadly, and murmured, 'Poor wretches. They must have walked all the way.'

PORTLY PAUNCHES

Under the Second Empire a club calling itself the 'Club des Grands Estomacs' used to hold its assemblies in the rue Montorgueil at Philippe's—a restaurant run by Pascal, formerly chef to the Jockey Club. Every Saturday, from six in the evening until noon of Sunday, the twelve members used to eat: eat for eighteen hours at a stretch. In the course of their Pantagruelic banquet these fearless table companions consumed the following: Madeira as so-called appetizer, turbot, beefsteaks, braised leg of lamb, fowls, calves' tongues in gravy, maraschino sorbets, roast chickens, creams, tarts, pastries: each diner washing down his share with six bottles of old burgundy. Then, from midnight until six in the morning, it was: tea, turtle soup, curried chicken, salmon with scallions, venison cutlets with pimentos, fillets of sole with truffle jelly sauce, artichokes with Java pepper, rum sorbets, hazel-hens in whisky, puddings: this consignment washed down with three bottles of burgundy and three of bordeaux for each man. The third instalment, six a.m. to Sunday noon, the third and last act: onion soup, cakes and pastries, champagne, coffee, liqueurs.

Fortunately, they had the rest of the week in which to get over it.

it securely and impale on a skewer. Cook at high temperature for fifteen to twenty minutes. Prepare a canapé of bread fried in butter. Spread on this the chopped intestines of the cooked bird with an equal quantity of foie-gras (if this is not possible, coarsely grated, cooked, unsmoked bacon will do). Add salt, pepper, nutmeg, a dash of spirits.

N.B.—But I advise you to 'draw' your woodcock, especially to take out the gall sac and the gizzard. You can stuff them with olives and put a vine leaf under the larding strips.

Woodcock Salmis

(A salmis is a ragoût of previously roasted game).

Roast or grill the woodcock at brisk heat, and while still 'red' cut into pieces and remove skin from these. Keep hot on a separate dish. In a saucepan reduce some red wine with chopped shallot, add odd woodcock scraps, with pepper and salt. Boil for five minutes. Put sauce through fine sieve then thicken it with chopped innards of woodcock. Serve the pieces you have been keeping hot with a cover of this sauce.

Stuffed Woodcock

Cook in oven, and keep on the 'red' side. Serve with bread fried in oil and spread with the bird's intestines chopped finely.

Adding:

(*a*) anchovy fillets (and lemon, if bird has been stuffed with a few oysters poached in cream;

(*b*) foie-gras (if woodcock has been stuffed with foie-gras);

(*c*) a light mushroom purée (if woodcock has been stuffed with truffles).

The cooking juices should be diluted with spirits, or champagne, or Chambertin, or Madeira, or dry white wine with orange juice added. There are several other possibilities, depending on taste, opportunities, resources.

Bécassine (Snipe)

Migratory birds similar to woodcock, but haunters of damp and marshy spots. They are, naturally enough, cooked in the same ways as woodcock. But this is an opportunity for remarking that feathered game must be basted with nothing but bacon fat, pork fat, and goose fat. Butter and stock should not be used. The exceptions to the rule are water fowl (snipe, teal and widgeon, for instance).

Becfigues (Beccaficos)

This bird is found in the South of France and is also called Béguinette. Brillat-Savarin thought so favourably of it that he claimed he could eat it raw. It is cooked in the same ways as larks and ortolans. Better still, it may be impaled on a stick and grilled, then eaten straight away with salt and pepper.

Cailles (Quail)

From the old Flemish 'kakelen'. They arrive in Europe (from their period of hibernation in Africa) after the swallows. Their fine and rich flesh makes them somewhat difficult to pluck. Their white flesh is a wonderful delicacy. They are eaten quite fresh, and are simply roasted, wrapped in vine leaves.

Other possibilities, however, are:

Vine Grower's Quail

Cover quail with plenty of lardons and colour them in a small pan. Complete cooking in oven. Add a glass of white cooking base, two tablespoonsful of verjuice, and a handful of cleaned *chasselas* (fine white table grapes).

Stuffed Quail

Before cooking in saucepan or casserole quail may be stuffed with foie-gras and truffles, of course. But more simply, with rice, or olives, or any ordinary stuffing with or without meat in it. They may then be served with:

(1) peas—as such, or in purée;

(2) a rich pilaf;

(3) watercress;

(4) polenta with parmesan

(5) sauerkraut, pickled cabbage;

(6) cherries added at three-quarters-through cooking stage.

Also, all partridge recipes will serve for quail.

Canards Sauvages (Wild Duck)

These also are migratory birds. In France the green-necked wild duck is commonest and is 'fair game' from October to March. In England, the mallard abounds, especially where marsh drainage has not driven it away, and it also has splendid emerald, white and chestnut plumage. Recipes given for the barnyard or domestic duck are just as suitable for the wild duck. Roast or pan-cook and serve with Chambertin, orange, port wine, or pressed in a poultry-press.

Salmis of Wild Duck

Save three-quarters of the cooking liquor. Put the cooked duck aside to get cold. When cold cut into pieces suitable for serving, and remove skin. Put these in a buttered sauté dish and reheat, keeping them hot while you make a *mirepoix* of carrots, onions, shallots, thyme, laurel. To this add the neck-piece, the not-very-fleshy wing ends, the skin, the carcase, all rough-chopped. Brown, and pour on some red wine. Cook for three-quarters of an hour. Then strain, reduce and pour sauce over duck. Simmer for a few minutes, then serve.

N.B.—A few heads of mushrooms may be added, and a garnish of fried bread cubes.

Coq de Bruyère (Grouse)
(Wood-grouse, capercailzie)

M. EUGENE BLANCHET writes, in *Queue . . . Tête . . . Pan !*

'The great grouse is the quickest filler-up of the sportsman's game-bag, for it is as big as a turkey. It has a magnificent and forbidding look with its black-striped, slate-blue livery. It is commoner in England than in France. The lesser grouse, black-cock or heath-cock, is more abundant. It is as wary as the red-legged partridge, but is, indeed, even more mistrustful.'

Grouse are cooked as pheasants. In most northerly countries it is usually soaked for two or three days in cream from the milk pans.

Stuffed Grouse

Stuff with a mixture of the chopped grouse liver, fat bacon, ham and spices for seasoning, moistened with one egg yolk and a glass of brandy. Be careful to stitch in all the stuffing, and cook in bain-marie with juniper berries over its surfaces. Serve with myrtleberry jam.

N.B.—If you are not short of money, add foie-gras and truffles.

Roast Pheasant

Pluck, singe the pheasant, and pull out the leg and foot sinews. Remove gall sac and put the liver back inside the drawn bird. Put fat-bacon strips over breast and leg tops, wrap the bird in greased paper, drive a skewer through it, and set to roast, basting constantly. Thicken the cooking juices and serve this sauce separately.

May also be accompanied by fried bread cubes (fried in the pheasant fat) and the following sauce:

Boil half a pint of milk, and when boiling add some soft white breadcrumbs, an onion with a clove or two stuck into it, salt, a nut of butter. cook for twenty minutes, take out the onion, season with a little Cayenne pepper, add one tablespoonful of thick cream. Serve hot. (This is, of course, a quickly made bread sauce.)

Flemish Pheasant

Cover with larding strips and cook gently in pan with a carrot and an onion, both cut in quarters. When slightly cooked, cover and allow to go on cooking very slowly. In another pan melt a nut of butter and put into it some endives, salt and pepper, a glass of water and the juice of a lemon. Cover this pan too and cook in its own steam until almost all the liquid content has evaporated. When the pheasant is nearly done, take it out and finish the cooking with the endives. This should take about fifteen minutes. Serve covered with a liquid from the first of the two pans.

Pheasants with Cabbage

Slice thinly a small, white cabbage. Scald the slices, then rinse in cold water. Cook them in a lidded casserole for half an hour with lard and bacon. Season with salt and pepper.

In another pan 'gild' a pheasant cleaned and trussed, inside which you have placed two tablespoonsful of fresh cream. Add the cabbage, cover with lid, and continue cooking very gently until all is done to a turn.

Normandy Pheasant

Hang pheasant in oven to 'oven spit' it, and brown it evenly all over. In an earthenware casserole lay a bed of finely sliced apples and put the pheasant (freed of its trussing strings) on top. Baste it with the juices that have collected in the dripping-pan, thinned down with a little Calvados. Add a bare half pint of fresh cream, juice of half a lemon, salt and pepper. Put lid on and as additional seal, fix a band of flour-and-water dough all round the pot where lid seam comes. Cook for a good hour in a hot oven.

N.B.—The experts say that the feathers should remain on the pheasant 'until the last possible moment' so as to enhance the flavour. In the four preceding recipes, and in many others—as pheasant recipes may be based on those for chickens, young turkeys, etc.—the bird may be stuffed with foie-gras and cooked with truffles.

Georgian Poached Pheasant

Two pheasants required. Add larding strips, brown in pan with fat, put in the same vessel a quarter bottle of white port and seasoning. Cook in oven with lid on for thirty minutes at the outside. Thicken the liquor with a few tablespoonsful of demi-glaze (semi-jellified) poultry stock. Prepare two dozen miniature potato croquettes (mirabelle-plum size), mix with chopped walnuts, add to the rest.

Skin (and, if you can, remove seeds from) two bunches of high-quality grapes. Fill with these a dozen flaky pastry barquettes (boat-shaped cases).

Put pheasants in the middle of a dish longer than it is broad, put barquettes, alternating with croquettes, all round them: pour over these only a little sauce, serving the rest separately.

Bohemian Pheasant

Prepare pheasant for roasting. Rub the interior with salt and put bird, with a little butter, in an earthenware vessel. When lightly gilded, ignite it with a glass of old brandy, then a glass of Madeira. Cover with lid, cook for an hour, with frequent basting. When done, remove all flesh from the bones and when cold pound with sixteen ounces foie-gras and ten ounces fresh truffles. Force this mixture through a sieve of fine mesh and add to this, working it in with a spatula or a wooden spoon, nearly half a pint of top cream of milk. Season very meagrely. Leave this mixture on ice to harden, then put it in tablespoonsful on a bed of jelly, encrusted with this same jelly. Serve very cold.

(These last two recipes were given me by M. PAUL MEGNIN, of the Académie des Gastronomes.)

Jay

Jays must be eaten very young, or if older birds must be boiled before roasting.

Pigot, in his *Chasse Gourmande*, wrote: 'The Jay's gastronomic and culinary virtues are practically non-existent, and that applies to its nearest relation the magpie, suitable only for the stewpot.' But Paul Megnin, who has a good word to say for Salmis of Jays, also mentions this recipe from Lorraine:

Stuffed Jay

Pluck the bird, singe it, wash and wipe the interior with a cloth dipped in refined spirits of some kind. Chop heart, gizzard and liver of the bird with their total weight in mushrooms—if possible use 'death-trumpets'[1] which have a truffle-like aroma. Bind the stuffing with an egg yolk. Stuff the bird and sew up the incision. Lard it with bacon strips and roast in a brisk oven.

Gelinottes (Hazel-grouse)[2]

These are small grouse of about partridge size. Unlike other grouse (this, again, is a tip for the man out with a gun) it perches only for the sake of bidding defiance. The Vosges and Jura are two of its haunts. It is cooked in the same ways as partridge.

1 This is for French cooks. Our interest is academic.

2 A 'gelinotte' is occasionally a fattened pullet.

TO HANG OR NOT TO HANG?

The French word 'faisandage' (allowing to become 'high' or 'gamy') is connected with 'faisan' (pheasant)–no prizes offered to those who had suspected it. In its fresh state, the flesh of the pheasant is tough and not very tasty. As mortification advances, it becomes softer and more aromatic.

This is so with all other game-birds, and from time immemorial opinion as to the advantages or otherwise of hanging has been divided. Montaigne, speaking of woodcock, extolled the 'tainting of the flavour', Brillat-Savarin's advice was to hang the bird until the abdomen had turned green: and from Grimod de la Reynière we cull the information that a pheasant shot on Shrove Tuesday will be eatable at Easter.

Nowadays we are less strict, and some gourmets even—including Curnonsky—assert that game should be eaten fresh.

It seemed a good idea to ask Dr. de Pomiane for his reasoned views on the question, and he said, in an interview: 'This is a controversy between the gastronome and the sanitarian. Which is right? One or the other. Or perhaps neither. The connoisseur will not eat his woodcock until it falls of its own accord, a disintegrated ruin, from the string on which it hung. He finds it exquisite. But his doctor forbids this kind of thing, and expatiates on the serious risks of intestinal poisoning which the connoisseur incurs. As it happens, they are not necessarily discussing the same phenomenon.

'Suppose that the man out with his gun has bagged a hare or a woodcock. After hanging for a week or more at the kitchen window, the animal or bird has a characteristic smell. Is it 'gamy'? Is it a time for caution? It may be "gamy" or "high". Or it may be "putrefied". In the first case it is eatable, in the second, it is not fit for human consumption. These two kinds of animal-decomposition are effected by different kinds of bacteria and bacterial action.

'If the creature died from the penetration of one or two shots, without

being badly shattered by a whole explosive charge, the corpse will be attacked by microbes of intestinal provenance. These are not toxic. They change the composition and nature, to some extent, of the muscular structure. and give the "high" odour. But if the animal has been much torn, by a blast at too close range, its exposed muscles are infected by microbes causing putrefaction which abound in the game bag, on the sportsmen's fingers, which are bound to be soiled, and so on. These are highly toxic. They too break up the muscular structure, but at the same time impart an unpleasant smell. Game thus infected is a dangerous foodstuff.

'But how, if one is not a bacteriologist, can one ascertain whether the hare in question, which is waiting to be cooked, is "gamy" or rotten? The only safe procedure is to inspect the "bag" as soon as it reaches the kitchen. If the fatal shot has left only slight evidence, hang the item, but if the tissues are torn, dismember immediately and cook the meat before the toxin-producers have had time to do their grim job. Then you'll be eating fresh game, not "high", thus keeping in line with most game-eaters of Europe. For it is mainly in France and Belgium that really gamy game is preferred.

'And what of the really big stuff: venison, boar, etc., cut into joints by the hand of man? Must these inevitably putrefy? Yes, inevitably. But there is a possibility of shielding the flesh from the invasion of toxin-forming bacteria by "marinating" promptly. The joints are steeped in acidulated pickling liquids: these create conditions in which the bacteria causing decay are unable to develop.

'To resume: if you are doubtful about a piece of game, eat it fresh-killed, or at least, after marinating in vinegar and dressing lavishly with spices and aromatics.'

RESTAURANT CHIT-CHAT

'You call this creamed lobster,' he complained to the restaurant proprietor. 'But I can find neither lobster nor cream.'

'Ah, no, sir. That's what makes it our speciality.'

* * *

'And what sort of sole are you serving today, waiter?'

'Oh, your sort, madam. Nicely moulded and with the best kind of mussels.'

Creamed Hazel-grouse

The flesh is white, delicate, and with a pronounced flavour of pine-shoots. This can be diminished by soaking in milk for an hour before cooking.

Start the cooking in butter, then raise the heat of the oven and cook fairly briskly in an uncovered dish. Then remove trussings and baste with fresh cream, continuing the basting until the bird is cooked through.

VARIATION: Mask the cooked bird with a mixture of Béchamel sauce and sour cream. Sprinkle with breadcrumbs and brown in the oven.

Grives (Thrushes)

The flesh of thrushes is delicious, particularly when they have been fed and overfed on juniper berries or else, at harvest-time, have stuffed themselves to the point of intoxication with grapes. Cook as larks or quail.

Roast Thrushes

Remove only the gizzard. Skewer them after larding with bacon both fat and lean. Serve on bread fried in their fat.

Dauphiné Thrushes

Lard, and roast in pan for ten minutes, six good-sized thrushes. Take them out of pan and add to the cooking liquor two egg yolks, if possible a grated truffle, and the insides of the thrushes chopped up small. Beat all this with a fork over a bead of gas. Serve the birds on fried bread with sauce poured over.

Ardennes Thrushes

Line bottom of casserole with bacon dice, put the thrushes in, packed tightly, add salt, pepper, and one sage leaf to every thrush. Cook gently for about an hour and a half.

Liége Thrushes

Remove gizzards only and put into each bird (prepared for roasting) a walnut of butter mixed with crushed juniper berries. Truss the thrushes and seal the juices by turning them in very hot melted butter on top of the stove. Then sprinkle with chopped juniper berries and cook in a covered dish in the oven. Serve with fried bread dice and put a dash of gin over them.

(M. PHILEAS GILBERT'S recipe.)

Thrush Pie

Cook gently in butter half a pound of fat bacon or pork, half a pound of wild rabbit meat, half a pound of poultry and game liver—all chopped to begin with. Add a mixture of truffles and juniper berries, also chopped. Season with salt and pepper, mash all together in the masher or fine-set mincer and then add 4 oz foie-gras and a glass of Madeira, with six egg yolks to bind. Line mould with short pastry, put in half the forcemeat, the six boned thrushes stuffed with truffles. Cover with rest of the forcemeat then the pastry-crust top, leaving a central hole in the pie crust.

Cook in a medium oven for an hour at least, then leave pie to get cold. Jelly to pour into the pie through the aperture is made from the bones and offal.

Ortolans (Ortolans)

They fly from Southern Provence to build their nests in the vines of Burgundy and the cornfields of Lorraine. At the end of the season they are as fat as they should be. But in the Toulouse region they are caught with bird lime and nets and fattened in captivity, kept in dark cellars where ever-burning lamps prevent their distinguishing between day and night. In consequence they eat without stopping and have to be killed before their own fat suffocates them.

They are cooked in the same ways as larks-in-season (*mauviettes*) and beccaficos.

A rule of gastronomy lays it down that *the ortolan must be cooked in nothing but its own fat.*

As mentioned on p. 171 ortolans succumb to the fumes of one or two drops of spirits.

Skewered ortolans, separated by sippets of buttered bread; roasted ones, stuffed with foie-gras; sauté ortolans, braised ortolans, are all exquisite. Here, however, is an original recipe:

Egg-shell Ortolans

With a very sharp knife cut off a piece at the rounder end of a new-laid or fresh egg. Empty it, line with butter, and slip inside it a larded and truffle-stuffed ortolan.

When you have as many as are required put them in the dripping-pan of the grill with sufficient melted butter to come half-way up the shells. Leave in gentle oven for a good hour. If you prefer, remove shells before serving.

Perdreau, Perdrix (Partridges)

'Perdrix' is not, as one might well suppose, the female 'perdreau'. The name 'perdrix' applies to both adult male and female birds, as is testified by the proverb 'A la Saint-Rémi, perdreaux sont perdrix'. The 'perdreau' is the young partridge=poult; 'perdrix' the grown partridge (*grise*=grey, *rouge*=red-legged, *de neige*=ptarmigan, although the word 'ptarmigan' serves as well for the last).

The grey- and the red-legged are the commonest varieties. The red is larger than the grey; and larger than the red, but less common, is the Bartavelle (sometimes weighing a pound or more).

Grilled, roasted, cooked in a covered stewpan, casserole, on the spit, using certain of the pigeon, woodcock and pheasant recipes.

You may come across a dish styled *Chartreuse de Perdreau* on banquet menus or in elegant restaurants. It is really a variation of Partridge with Cabbage. For refined palates the chef first cooks his cabbages with a partridge of some maturity, then, when the dish is about to go to table, replaces the old bird with tender partridge-poults. Also styled, of course, 'Perdrix aux Choux'.

Partridge in 'Shells'

Make a stuffing of their livers, hearts, other offals, a little chopped garlic and parsley, some pepper and salt, truffle strips, a little fat bacon about walnut size, and stuff small partridges with it.

Sew up the gap and wrap each bird in butter muslin. Steam them—if possible over a beef or poultry stock. Serve with a wine and mushroom sauce.

Grilled Partridge

Pluck, draw and singe young, small partridges. Cut off heads at neck level and pinions (terminal segments of wings). Split along the backs, flatten, take out the small bones. Season with salt and pepper. Wash over with oil and leave to soak for an hour.

Heat your griddle and oil it well, grill partridges for five minutes on each side, basting with the oil in which they soaked. You might use a branch of thyme as your basting tool. Put partridges on a dish. Now soak first, and then grill, large heads of mushrooms (stems removed) exactly as was done with the partridges (five minutes each side).

Serve with maître d'hôtel butter very strongly flavoured with lemon.

Catalan Partridge

Sauté partridge, well basted, its gravy blended with concentrated tomato purée. Blanch some garlic cloves and lemon peel, add to sauce. When sauce is well flavoured strain it, add the partridge cut into various pieces, and simmer for a few minutes. Truffle dice may be added to the sauce.

Gypsy-baked Partridge

Draw the bird but do not remove its feathers. Wet some clayey earth with water (better still with wine) and work it into a putty-like mass. Dig out a hollow in the ground and in it light a wood fire. Put the 'egg' of earth (you have enveloped the partridge in the 'putty') on top of the glowing embers, and keep the fire going under it for close on an hour. Then break away the crust of earth—the feathers will come with it—and season this astonishing preparation.

N.B.—Chickens, too, may be cooked in this way.

Suzanne Despres Partridge

Take large red-legged partridges, draw and singe them, fill with a stuffing of the livers, breadcrumbs and fresh truffles (having removed heads and necks to provide entries for the stuffing). Close up, lard with some good bacon in a narrow strip.

Put in stewpan 2 or 3 tablespoonsful of melted butter and lard. Put in the raw partridges and braise very slowly. Keep pan tightly lidded and open it only when it is time to turn the birds or to baste them occasionally. As soon as they begin to brown, pour in a small glass of liqueur brandy (*fine*). Keep liquid content going by adding, in small doses from time to time, some good stock. When cooking is well advanced (half-way) add the salt. The whole cooking time should be about forty-five minutes.

While this proceeds, make a Perigourdine sauce, reducing a glass of dry white wine with spices; when all acidity has left the wine add about the same bulk of brown sauce. Simmer all together, adding a few chopped truffles and, a little later, a few mushroom tops and stoned olives. When sauce is done, pour it into the stewpan to absorb the gravy, then turn it over the partridges in a deep dish. Border with fried bread cubes and serve at once.

(This recipe was dedicated to the celebrity by her husband LUGNE POE)

Ramiers (Woodpigeons, Cushats)

Also called 'Palombes'. Doves in their wild environment. Prepared in same ways as pigeons (domestic) almost invariably. There is, however, this recipe:

Woodpigeons in Armagnac

Pluck the birds, draw them, and in each put 'two walnuts' of this stuffing:

Lard, breadcrumbs, one or two truffles, all chopped extremely finely. A suspicion of garlic, a little grated nutmeg, some chives and parsley. All well blended. Thread the stuffed birds one after another on the spit and roast at a good hot open fire. You will need a piece of apparatus

ON ORTOLANS

The author RENE MAIZEROY *evolved this recipe, which he entitles 'Coffined Ortolans'. You need:*

(1) *An ortolan that is just a feathered ball of fat. It has been properly choked, of course, with a few drops of old Armagnac.*

(2) *A Perigord truffle of reasonable bore. You bone the ortolan, hollow out for him a narrow tomb in the truffle, seal him in with a slice of truffle, and wrap the whole in buttered paper. Cook gently in the oven, and serve with champagne.*

Well, there it is. And may the God of Gluttons preserve us from dyspepsia and gout. But nobody eats just one *ortolan. You need at least three per guest if anyone is to taste anything at all.*

* * *

However, ARTHUR POYDENOT, *a Gascon poet, dedicated this verse to ortolans:*

That crude, fat beast extolled by Monselet,
A sort of walking meal, from boot to bonnet,
Even as a piglet 'nothing-thrown-away',
Inspired the poet to devise a sonnet.

He'd have done better not to linger on it
But praise that sweet, plump bird which gourmets slay
By suffocation—harsh as falcons, they—
Then spit it: and it's smaller than a linnet.

Though not strict etiquette, one must admit,
There's but one way to eat this dainty bit:
Eyes closed, mouth crammed, shut off from fellow-men.

Its wrappings cast, you gently grasp the beak
And gently crunch. It yields, with faintest squeak,
And there's your joy—a Bouchée à la Reine.

known as 'devil's horn'. It is a wrought-iron, cornet-shaped tube with a hole in its pointed end, and its rim is firmly soldered to a long wooden handle. This receptacle you thrust right into the red heart of the fire, and when it is red-hot you drop into it a piece of unsmoked bacon. At once a tremendous flame leaps up as the melted fat drips through the hole in copious gush—a fine roasting flame.

(Recipe of M. GASTON CHERAU of the Goncourt Academy.)

Salmis of Woodpigeons

Pluck, singe and draw two woodpigeons and roast at a high temperature in a buttered pan. Cut into joints and put these to one side. Cut up the carcase that remains and put it back in the pan with butter and chopped shallot. Cook through, then ignite with Armagnac. Add a glass of white wine, with a little pepper and salt. Put lid on and cook for twenty minutes. Add the livers at the last moment and strain liquor through sieve. Mix the strained sauce with the blood of the woodpigeons, the juice of one lemon, and cook the joints in this for twenty minutes. Serve very hot with fried bread cubes.

N.B.—These woodpigeon recipes may be used for turtledoves.

Sarcelles (Teal)

Whether summer teal (known as garganey) or winter teal, these little birds are of fleeter and more animated flight than the mallard, with which they are comparable gastronomically. The recipes are interchangeable. It is most important (in both cases) to lard with fat bacon.

Vanneaux (Lapwing, Pewit)

(The *V. pluvier* is the grey plover. *Œufs de vanneau*=plovers' eggs.) October is the month when, at their maximum plumpness, these birds deserve the tribute of the proverb: 'No plover to eat, then you're missing a treat'. The eggs are, of course, much esteemed, and plovers' eggs omelette is one of the high-lights of the gastronomic picture. The bird is hard to stalk in the open, but is easily tricked. It is cooked as if it were woodcock.

Rabbits and Furred Game

Domestic Rabbit

Should be between four and six months old if the flesh is to be both savoury and tender. Bleed it by making a gash on underpart of neck, between the forefeet. Collect the blood.

To skin rabbit: Make an incision in the skin between the upper hind legs on the belly, widen the gap and turn back the legs so that the wide parts of the legs can be squeezed out through it. Break legs at lowest joint and pull off fur and skin. When the hind quarters are thus skinned, pull back the skin as far as the shoulders and free the forelegs, cutting them at the first joint. Last, free the head by cutting carefully with a pointed and very sharp knife.

To gut a rabbit: Split down the belly in a long gash and pull out the intestines. Remove the gall sac, a little greenish pocket next to the liver, which you must be careful not to break. Wipe the inside, paying particular attention to the anal outlet, and take out the little ball of fat usually found near the tail.

Lapin en Gibelotte (Fricassée of Rabbit)

Cut rabbit into its accepted joints and colour in butter in a saucepan. Sprinkle them with two tablespoonsful of flour, stirring with a wooden spoon. Add half a bottle of white wine. When boiling point is reached put in 4 oz of dice of lean bacon previously browned in a separate pan, also parsley, a bouquet garni, very small onions, salt and pepper. When fricassée is within about a quarter of an hour of being done, add four ounces of mushrooms. Take out the meat when mushrooms are done, strain the sauce, use the blood as liaison, serve all together.

N.B.—If you want potatoes with this, it is best to cook them separately, plain boiled, and add right at the end. If you put them in sooner, they absorb the sauce and over-thicken it.

Marengo Rabbit

Put rabbit pieces in hot oil in a saucepan, season with salt and pepper and cook over a good flame. Half an hour is enough for a young rabbit.

In a little cooking oil, using separate pan, cook some button mushrooms, chopped parsley, some shreds of truffle (if you have any). Add two tablespoonsful of tomato sauce. Serve the pieces in a dish with the sauce over them, and a dash of lemon juice as finish.

Roast Rabbit

It is a good idea for the housewife to use the foreparts of the rabbit as fricassée or Marengo rabbit (preceding recipes) and keep back the rest for roasting. This makes two quite different meals from one rabbit. But since roast rabbit is always inclined to be over-dry, it is essential to soak it well, for two or three days even, in the following 'marinade'—and to spoon the liquid over it fairly often:

Use oil and vinegar in the proportion of two-thirds oil and one-third vinegar, with thyme, bay, parsley, garlic, rings of carrot and onion, salt and pepper to taste. After the third day you may put the 'saddle' or back portions, on the spit, well larded with fat bacon, and cook it fairly slowly. Put the soaking liquor in the dripping pan and baste with it frequently.

Goodwife's Rabbit

Gild the rabbit joints with melted bacon scraps and a little butter in a pan, pour in a glass of white wine and the same amount of stock (or water), together with parsley, chives and chopped shallots, seasoning of salt and pepper. Cover pan or transfer to casserole and cook for an hour. When about to serve, add a piece of butter (filbert size) to the sauce, and a dessertspoonful of some starchy thickening (e.g. potato flour).

Trompette Rabbit

Place inside your rabbit two truffle-stuffed pig's trotters (some delicatessen shops would supply these to order). Sew up the incision and cook on the spit, basting with a little brandy.

(Named after TROMPETTE, Gambetta's chef.)

Rabbits and Prunes

Soak rabbit joints for twenty-four hours in a *marinade*, drain, cook gently in butter. Then pour over them the liquor in which they soaked, cook for a quarter of an hour, add some prunes soaked until soft. Cook on with very low heat.

If you care for it, gooseberry jelly could be added before serving.

Potted Rabbit

If you are using one rabbit, you will need one and a half pounds of veal without bones, the same quantity of boneless pork. Boil veal, pork, and the rabbit's bones for two hours and a half, together with the rabbit meat and onion, bay leaf, salt and pepper. Chop and mix all together, then put a strip or two of bacon in the bottom of an earthenware dish.

Put a layer of the rabbit and meat mixture, then some good-sized truffle rings and some more bacon lardons, then the rest of the rabbit paste, some more bacon, a madeira glass of brandy and some of the bone stock. Cover the top with two bay leaves.

If you want to keep this for any length of time do not add any bone stock or brandy, but seal on the lid with a flour and water dough.

(From the actor BARON FILS.)

ALL THE DOZEN OR SO RECIPES THAT FOLLOW ARE SUITABLE FOR ALL KINDS OF YOUNG RABBIT, WILD RABBIT AND HARE, AS SPECIFIED, AND ALSO FOR TAME RABBITS.

When it is a question of cooking a hare, you must distinguish between the meadow and mountain varieties. There are, of course, the German hare and the Central European, huge, long-bodied, pullulating: they are not graceful to watch in action and their flesh is tough and stringy. The fur of the meadow hare is grey but with a distinct russet tinge: that of higher altitude hares is a black and white mixture that results in a brownish-grey. Its underparts are white and the browny-red effect is more noticeable on feet and breast. The best age at which to make culinary use of them is the 'three-quarters stage' of life: that is to say, when the animal has attained maximum growth and is no longer a leveret.

You can recognize a leveret (young hare) by the little hard 'knuckles' of the forefeet—you can feel them with your fingers.

If the hare is old, or the wild rabbit too, the teeth will be very long and yellow, even blackish, and the bristles around the 'muzzle' will be turning white.

So far as wild rabbits ('warren rabbits') are concerned, says M. P. Megnin, it would be a very fine thing if they could all wear labels around their necks to say whence they came—for there is a very perceptible difference in the qualities of rabbits from different regions. In France, for instance, there are the Seine-et-Oise, the Seine-et-Marne, the Oise, the Sologne, and above all the dune-feeding rabbits, all showing notable variations; for the quality of the flesh depends on the daily fare of the animal, whatever its species; Sologne warrens offer pretty poor feeding, the dunes and sandy downs really execrable stuff.

The young wild rabbit, like the hare, has a tiny bone on the forefeet that feels like a pellet of No. 6 shot. But as an indication of youth it is not completely reliable. Our grandfathers had a surer method of testing for age, and that was to ascertain how tough and resistant the ears were. If they tear fairly easily the rabbit is a young one; if they are tough and untearable, your rabbit has seen many moons.

One advantage of wild rabbits is that one does not easily tire of the taste of their meat, as it lends itself to so many varied treatments.

LIKE FATHER, LIKE SON

Monsieur de la Reynière, senior (it is Curnonsky who tells us the story), farmer-general, and father of the well-known gourmand Grimod de la Reynière, was on a provincial tour of inspection, and he reached the Melun district round about dinner-time one evening. So he went into an inn, and there in the hearth were seven fat turkeys turning on spits, presenting their savoury plumpness to the heat of a fire of twigs and branches. It was a splendid sight. And there was the innkeeper pretending that he had only beans and bacon to offer.

'But the turkeys!' protested the farmer-general, grinding his teeth with irritation.

'All reserved, sir. For one gentleman.'

'One? Just one? Then it must be Gargantua in person. Lead me to him.'

The door of the seven-turkey-man opened, and M. de la Reynière was in the presence of—his son.

'What's all this? You *are the fellow, then, with seven turkeys on the spit, every one for* your *dinner, yours alone?'*

'I do apologize, Father, for falling so low as to eat such tack, but they have neither capon nor fat fowl in this place.'

'I see. When one is travelling one just has to make the best of what offers. Never mind the fact of eating the things. I'm not blaming you for not wanting something choicer, but for demanding no less than seven.'

At which reproach, Grimod de la Reynière, offended, drew himself up. 'Sir,' he said, 'I know what is due to my birth. And in accordance with an opinion which I have often heard you yourself express, I was intending to eat only the popes' noses.'

RESTAURANT CHIT-CHAT

'Waiter! this fish is putrid!'

'Now come, sir, do try to eat it up. I've wagered the chef a pound that I'll get away with it, even though it is!'

* * *

'Excuse me, sir. When you paid for your meal, you forgot the waiter.'

'So what? I didn't eat him, did I?'

Blanquette of Rabbit

(A blanquette is a stew of white meat, especially veal, in white sauce.)

Cut the young rabbit in pieces, sauté these in butter, but do not allow them to brown. Pour white stock over them, add a bunch of parsley, cook gently; later add very small blanched onions, bind the sauce with a little flour, butter and egg yolk.

Boiled Young Rabbit

Stuff the cleaned rabbit with a mixture of fairly fat bacon, pig's and calf's liver, crustless bread soaked in milk (equal weights of bacon, liver and breadcrumbs). Season highly, sew up and truss the rabbit, cook for an hour in salted water. Serve with caper sauce.

Mustard Rabbit

Use the *rable* (back end, with back itself) of the rabbit, well seasoned with pepper, and soak in Madeira (or, failing this, red Bordeaux). Insert strips of fat bacon here and there for larding, and daub with mustard. Roast with one or two knobs of butter in the dish. Reduce the soaking liquor and mix with the cooking gravy, adding three or four ounces of cream just before serving.

Tartare Rabbit

Bone a young wild rabbit. Soak in a shallot-and-chives-flavoured *marinade*, with other herbs to your liking, oil, stock, etc. Then roll it well in salt-seasoned breadcrumbs and grill it. Serve with a Tartare sauce.

Jugged Rabbit with Noodles

('Civet' is a jugged hare or rabbit or a venison stew.)

Cut rabbit in pieces and marinate for twelve hours, with good red wine, and juniper berries in the liquor. Save the blood apart. Drain, lightly cook the pieces of meat in a pan with lard and lean bacon and a tablespoonful of flour well blended. Stir for twenty minutes. Add the spices, wine in which meat was soaked, and cook for three hours. A quarter of an hour before you serve, add the pounded liver, the blood and a little fresh cream. In another vessel cook some noodles and moisten with sauce.

N.B.—Hare may be treated likewise.

Saupiquet of Hare

In pork fat, using a saucepan, cook lightly some strips of bacon, slices of onion, garlic; add a bouquet garni and the head, liver, heart and odd scraps of your prepared rabbit. Allow to get very brown, and when it can brown no further add a half-glass of vinegar. Let sauce reduce, then blend in a tablespoonful of flour. Add a pint of red wine, spices to taste, and cook for an hour longer. Roast the hare separately, well larded. Pass all through sieve, add the hare's blood, and the gravy of the hare that has been roasted on its own, also a glass of spirits. Cut up the hare and serve in the sauce.

Amunategui Hare

Take an earthenware dish and line the bottom with basting strips of bacon and some aromatic herbs. Put whole hare on this bed and pour over a glass of *fine*. Start cooking at low heat. After half an hour's slow cooking, cover all over with thick cream, put lid on dish and cook on embers or over some other form of heat that will allow to simmer for about three hours. Serve from the cooking dish, using a spoon.

Stuffed Hare

Your stuffing is made of veal fillet, unsalted pork, ham, and the liver and heart of the hare, all chopped together. But the famous LIEVRE A LA ROYALE has the following stuffing:

The liver, lights and heart of the hare
4 oz unsalted fat bacon or pork fat
8 oz raw goose foie-gras
4 oz bread soaked in stock
6 oz truffles
(a Perigourdine forcemeat).

All the ingredients are chopped finely with parsley, some onions cooked without browning in butter; blood of hare to bind.

Jugged Hare

Jugged hare is prepared in much the same way as jugged rabbit, and may be served:

—with noodles;
—with cooked, glazed chestnuts (in such a case, 'glazed' means covered with meat jelly);
—with onions;
—with sippets (fried bread cubes);
—with mushroom purée;
—with prunes and raisins;
—with polenta (see p. 282).

N.B.—Jugged hare is just as good—some say better—reheated.

JUGGED HARE—A POET'S WAY

Take a young leveret, not a hare as yet,
One from our coastal flats will serve you best:
A 'capuchin', high-spined, of narrow breast,
Laid low at dawn, before the stars have set.

Simmer him mildly as the fire burns low,
With no harsh boiling, no unseemly stir,
And flatter him with berried juniper,
A tuft of thyme, a carrot ring or so.

As in that savoury steam your nostrils twitch,
To make the gravy satin-smooth and rich,
Add, drop by drop, the blood that's standing by,

Lard him with bacon, but with no excess,
Wash him in vintage wine—a mere caress,
And then, at table, drink the bottle dry.

HENRI CHANTAVOINE

Hind-quarters of Hare with Beets

Hind-portion, with the two legs, is well larded with bacon strips (the fascia having first been removed), then put to soak in water acidulated with vinegar and aromatized with herbs. Leave it for several days.

Then wipe, attach one or two fresh pieces of bacon for basting it as it cooks, and place in earthenware dish. Sprinkle with salt, add a little butter. Place in a very hot oven. Cook for 35 to 40 minutes, basting with cream and the marinating liquid alternately. The cream will take on a buttery consistency, mingle with the liquid and melted bacon fat, and provide a sauce which you will thicken, when it leaves the oven, with some cream and white flour worked into a smooth paste.

In a frying pan cook in butter some chopped, cooked beetroot acidulated with a tablespoonful of vinegar. Add salt. Arrange on a narrow serving dish the pieces of hare (cut up as soon as cooked) and surround with a wall of beetroot. Put sauce on the hare only, not the beets, and serve most of the sauce separately in sauce-boat.

Hare Rolls

These offer a means of using up left-over hare meat. Chop it as finely as you can, add salt, pepper, grated nutmeg. In a saucepan make a very thick Béchamel with plenty of butter. When this has got quite cold, mix with the chopped meat, two raw whole eggs and a tablespoonful of cream. Work these together very thoroughly. Grease some small moulds, patty-pans or similar, and fill with the paste. Bake them, or cook them in a bain-marie, or even poach in a little liquid.

These 'rolls' may be

(*a*) served with spinach or other vegetable purées, peas or sauté beans;

(*b*) made of rabbit meat instead of hare: in which case a little pork and more seasoning will be called for, to add to the flavour.

Potted Hare

Use the Potted Poultry recipe (see p. 142).

Venison (Chevreuil)

When the deer or buck is young the flesh is delicate, but if the animal is old, long immersion in a *marinade* is unavoidable. The usual venison treatments are:

(1) Cutlets, or collops—trimmed, flattened, dotted with the indispensable lardons of fat, then sauté in oil or butter. They are then:

- (*a*) flavoured with juniper berries;
- (*b*) served with a very sweet apple sauce;
- (*c*) served with a pepper sauce;
- (*d*) served with grapes or mushrooms, or chestnuts, or lentil purée.

(2) Haunch (*cuisse* or *gigue*); oven-roasted.

(3) Saddle: soused, or larded and roasted.

(4) Jugged or potted.

Wild Boar (Sanglier)

In most recipes called 'marcassin' rather than 'sanglier', even if more than six months old. (Strictly speaking, *marcassin*=*young* wild boar.)

Whatever the preparation envisaged, the boar's meat must be left to marinate for quite a long time. It is served in collops, haunches, jugged, or potted. All venison recipes will do for wild boar.

Boar Haunch with Juniper

Wipe the joint as it leaves the liquid in which it has been immersed. Roast it, but the meat must still be red. Strain off the fat from the cooking liquor, add a glassful of gin, and ignite. Add some juniper berries and fresh cream, and reduce sauce.

May be served with a not very sweet apple sauce.

Meat Dishes

Cooks are made, meat-roasting experts born.

BRILLAT-SAVARIN

A mutton-chop is soon absorbed, like a letter in the mails.

DR. BESANÇON

Meat broths boiled gently, quivering now and then,
Stews that have simmered slowly to perfection,
Are thick, and velvet-smooth, tawny, and spiced with herbs.

JEAN RICHEPIN

Meats are prepared for table in many ways, roasting being one of the most favoured. Roasting is brought about by the direct action of radiant heat on the meat, and the process is as old as the discovery of fire itself, the ancestor of all cooking processes.

But for a few years now, thanks principally to the efforts of the *Chaîne des Rotisseurs*, restaurants are installing roasting spits (electrically heated) in the sight of customers and therefore the use of the venerable roasting 'jack', turning the meat this way and that in front of a wood fire, is more and more restricted. There are several different approaches to the creating of a 'roast':

ROASTING ON THE SPIT: for large items. The meat must either have plenty of natural fat or be larded with bacon or pork fat, for the fat alone saves it from charring.

OVEN-ROASTING: a far more commonly used practice. The meat is cooked without close contact with an actual flame (radiant thermal heat remote from contact). Here, too, the meat needs to have its own fat or to be basted with fat. If necessary the surface may be protected from the danger of burning by the application of greased paper.

CASSEROLE ROASTING (sometimes involving BRAISING): the meat is put into smoking fat and turned as soon as the surface is browned.

PAN-FRYING: the easiest but the least satisfactory method.

A fifth procedure is really in this group (part of old 'rôtisserie' or 'grill-room' practice), and that is grilling. In theory the flame is replaced by the intense glow of incandescent embers. But the grilling process of our time is usually done by gas-grill or electric-grill.

N.B.—For grilling it is necessary (the converse of 'roasting' practice) to remove the fat from the meat.

But one final word of advice on these matters; whether you are roasting or grilling, NEVER SALT THE MEAT BEFORE SERVING. Salt draws out the juices from the interior of the meat, and thus dries it unduly.

OTHER COOKING METHODS

BOILED MEAT: boiled meats lose much of their substance to the boiling stock—as was pointed out in the Soup chapter (*see* 'Pot-au-feu' or 'Meat Broth' on p. 18).

Braising, Saute process, Frying, deep or shallow: usually combinations of 'oil' and 'water' cooking.

Steam-braising or 'Dry-stewing': cooked by steam heat in an enclosed vessel (e.g. beef à la mode). Most of the flavour and nourishment escape into the gravy, but by way of compensation the meat is tender, completely free of fibres, and partly 'digested' in advance.

N.B.—This last method dictates serving with all the gravy.

BEEF

'A sirloin has two recognized portions—the "attorney's bit" and the "lawyer's clerk's bit". The latter is the less tender. This provides a good illustration of the law of contrasts, for there's nothing tougher than an old attorney.'

Grimod de la Reyniere

Aloyau (Sirloin)

The part of the animal that begins at the 'hook' point and ends at the first ribs, bringing in the tenderloin and 'false fillet'. If it is to deserve its full name it should be roasted, or braised, whole. Roasted, it requires an accompaniment of watercress, sauté potatoes, stuffed mushrooms, etc.

Braised Sirloin

Insert and attach several good sized lardons for basting (previously soaked for an hour in Cognac). Use a piece of the sirloin for this dish (cut along the grain of the meat). Tie it with string and put in oven dish or casserole with small onions, a bouquet garni, salt and pepper. Cover the bottom and part-way up the meat with water and a glass of dry white wine. Or stock will do.

N.B.—It is often a good idea to soak the meat for a short time before cooking, and then to add the marinating liquor to the cooking vessel.

Braised sirloin may be served with various garnishes: potatoes cooked in several ways: endives; sauerkraut; Brussels sprouts; a risotto; spring vegetables; even with tomato-flavoured noodles, etc.

Bavette (Top of the Sirloin)

Is really the lateral belly portion, on sirloin level, and often attached to the sirloin. It is good for meat broths, hot-pots, and as beefsteaks (firm but quite juicy).

Bouilli (Boiling Beef or Stewing Beef)

This is the meat that makes the beef-teas, rich broths, etc., and has then to be used up in various ways, such as:

HUNGARIAN STYLE: cut into cubes and browned in butter with chopped onions. Paprika is sprinkled over, and a cream sauce is served with it.

INDIAN STYLE: curry instead of paprika, and served with rice.

PROVENCE STYLE: same method, but use pimento and garlic and serve with tomato sauce.

PARISIAN STYLE: in salad with hard-boiled eggs, potatoes (or other vegetable), and parsley.

PARMENTIER: sauté some medium-sized cubes of potato in butter (or pork fat) and when they are golden brown, add cubes of the boiled beef. Serve with chervil.

GOODWIFE STYLE: diced beef reheated with garlic and parsley (both chopped up) in butter. Mash separately some steam-boiled potatoes. Mix all together with a wooden spoon and work them well to blend, then bind with an egg and add salt and pepper. Grease a mould and put the 'paste' in it, cover with a buttered paper and cook in a moderate oven for half an hour. Serve with tomato sauce.

N.B.—A variation of this recipe. Pieces of previously cooked beef may be served as meat-balls, or croquettes—chopped fairly small, mixed with potato purée, grated gruyère or parmesan may be added. Nutmeg too.

DEVILLED: cut in slices and spread made mustard over these, then a spot or two of oil and some breadcrumbs on both sides. Grill gently and serve with a white wine and shallot sauce.

These boiled-beef preparations may be served with the following sauces, Piquante, Horseradish, Tomato, Robert. And several others.

Miroton Beef

'Miroton', not 'mironton', is correct. Contrary to the general opinion, this is not stewed fresh beef but a rehash of yesterday's boiled beef. 'Melt' some sliced onions in butter and line an oven dish with them. Put the beef on top in overlapping slices and cover with Lyonnaise sauce (made by melting thin onions slices in butter with a tablespoonful of flour and diluting with a glassful of stock mixed with white wine). Scatter breadcrumbs over and brown in the oven. Add parsley.

VARIATION

PARMENTIER BEEF: A 'miroton' as above with a ring of potato purée encircling it. May, if you like, be sprinkled with grated cheese.

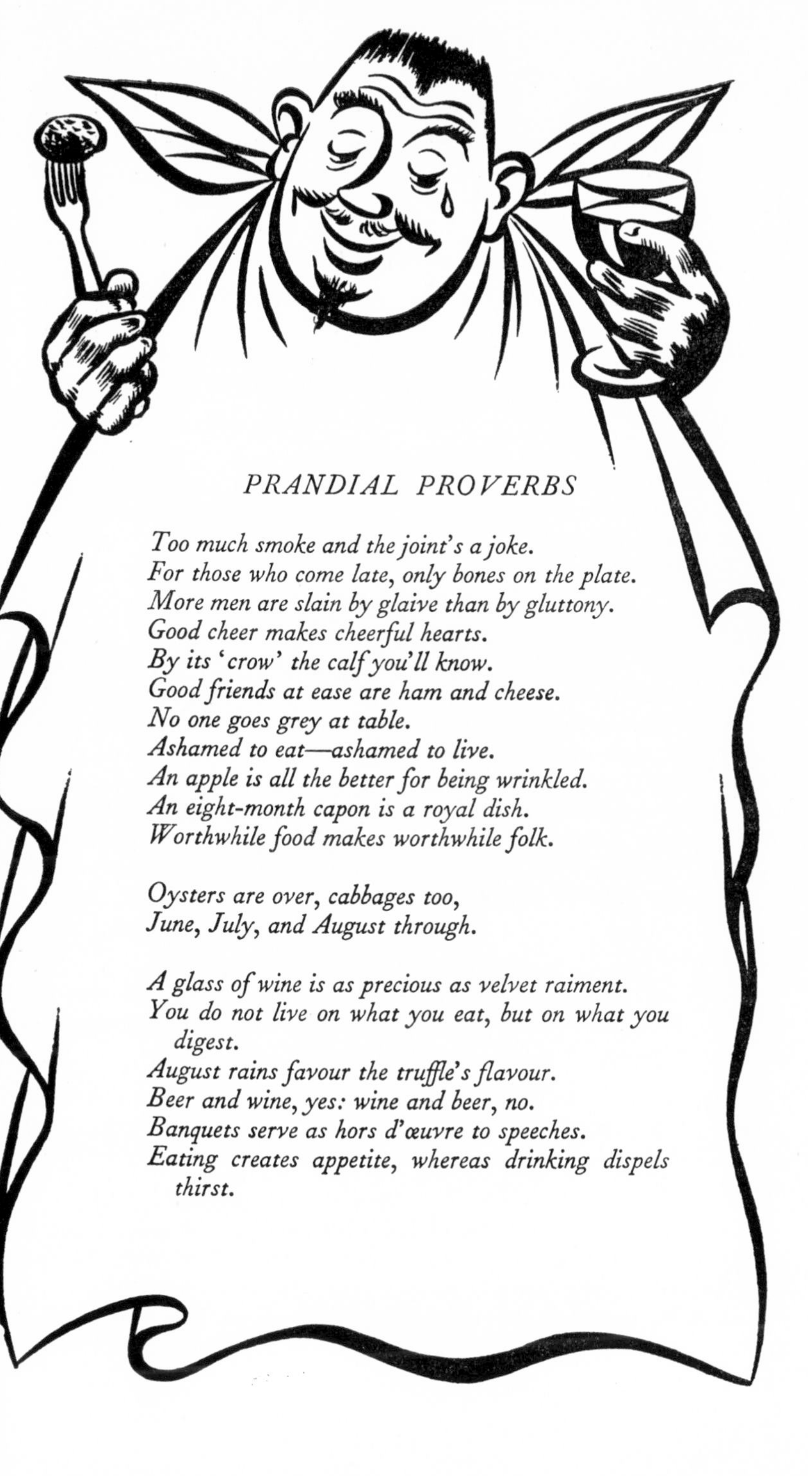

PRANDIAL PROVERBS

Too much smoke and the joint's a joke.
For those who come late, only bones on the plate.
More men are slain by glaive than by gluttony.
Good cheer makes cheerful hearts.
By its 'crow' the calf you'll know.
Good friends at ease are ham and cheese.
No one goes grey at table.
Ashamed to eat—ashamed to live.
An apple is all the better for being wrinkled.
An eight-month capon is a royal dish.
Worthwhile food makes worthwhile folk.

Oysters are over, cabbages too,
June, July, and August through.

A glass of wine is as precious as velvet raiment.
You do not live on what you eat, but on what you digest.
August rains favour the truffle's flavour.
Beer and wine, yes: wine and beer, no.
Banquets serve as hors d'œuvre to speeches.
Eating creates appetite, whereas drinking dispels thirst.

Chateaubriand

This is a thick fillet steak, a 'porterhouse'. It may be grilled or sauté. When cut smaller it is usually called 'Tournedos' (fillet-steak, or just beefsteak). They are cooked in the same ways.

Cote (Rib) of Beef

The meat covering the ribs, beginning at the dorsal vertebrae. The bones are taken out and the 'entrecôte', strictly speaking, is this meat cut from between the ribs—rib-steaks; as a joint it is of some culinary importance, and is served entire, braised or roasted, with the same accompaniments as braised beef (above).

Culotte (Rump)

The rest of the hindquarters when the sirloin has been cut away. Used in stews—and old classic family dishes called 'Daubes'.

Provençal 'Daube'

Cut the meat in inch-cubes and cover with fat bacon scraps that have been rolled in a mixture of chopped garlic and parsley. Put these to soak for a few hours in white wine with Cognac and olive oil. Season. Line a casserole with blanched rinds of unsmoked bacon or pork. Add two sliced carrots. Put the beef in alternate layers with uncooked onion rings and chopped mushrooms. Add some crushed tomatoes, 5 or 6 oz fat bacon or pork, diced and blanched, and the same quantity of stoned black olives. also a bouquet garni. Pour in the marinating liquor and three-quarters of a pint of meat gravy. Cover and seal lid on with a band of flour-and-water dough. Bake in oven for six hours.

VARIATIONS

BEARN STEWED BEEF: When the pieces leave the *marinade* they are rolled in flour, and alternate layers in the casserole are of Bayonne ham previously soaked (in cubes) in red wine.

CHAROLAIS (BURGUNDY) STEWED BEEF: Soak the beef pieces in red wine, with bay leaves, cloves, parsley. Warm the casserole containing narrow bacon strips and cook the beef lightly in their fat before adding the *marinade*.

GOODWIFE'S STEWED BEEF: Keep the beef in one piece. Cook it slightly in the fat of bacon pieces and then put it to soak in strong-bodied red wine with a tablespoonful of spirits and one of vinegar added to it. Put all in the casserole with chopped carrots and raw ham, onions, and garlic.

Of course other cuts of beef than this one are suitable for stewing (for instance, the 'chuck'). You will come across other recipes, for CARBONADE or ESTOUFFADE (occasionally used for grilled or braised meat) which are generally pretty much the same as these fresh beef stews. Here are two examples:

Flemish Carbonade

Cut the beef (chuck for preference) in small collops and brown them in butter over a brisk flame, seasoning with salt and pepper. Put the browned pieces in a sauté pan with alternating layers of sliced onions lightly cooked in butter in a separate pan. Add a bouquet garni. Add to the liquid in the first pan (the one in which you browned the meat) a little vinegar, a quart of beer and some thick veal stock, and pour this over the meat and onions. Cover, cook for two hours, serve with steam-cooked potatoes.

N.B.—A tablespoonful of moist brown sugar may be added.

Provençal Estouffade

Again use chuck for preference. Soak in the white *marinade* described in 'Provençal Daube', and if you like continue this for three days.

Drain the pieces of beef and par-cook them in smoking bacon fat. Put lid over pan and simmer for half an hour. Take out meat and put in oven dish (if possible, an earthenware casserole) with some lean bacon and a pig's trotter. Strain the marinading liquor, mix with the fat, etc., in the pan used for par-cooking the beef, and pour it, when hot and well blended, over the casserole contents. Seal hermetically and cook in oven for at least three hours.

Before taking to table, discard the bacon and the trotter bones, but chop up the trotter meat in cubes and add to main dish, together with some tomato purée and stoned olives.

Entrecôtes (Rib Steaks)

As mentioned above, the 'entrecôte' is the meat cut from between two bones in the ribs. But butchers quite often serve as 'entrecôte' various other cuts, for example the loin, of inferior taste and not as juicy. The entrecôte should be trimmed, sauté in butter, or grilled after a light application of oil. It may be covered with any of these sauces: Béarn, Bercy, Bordeaux, Burgundy, Maître d'hôtel, Marchand de Vin, etc.

Suitable garnishes are onion rings, chopped peppers, beef marrow, anchovy fillets with leaf tarragon, tomato purée, etc. Serve with potatoes, all the spring vegetables, onion purée, watercress, mushrooms.

Breton Entrecôte

Season and dress with oil a nice piece of rib-steak and leave for half an hour on a dish. Then grill it, but it must still be underdone. Blend a bare two ounces of butter with a chopped shallot and parsley, also a little pepper. Spread this creamy paste over the bottom of an oven dish, put your meat on it, cover with a plate, and put over a saucepan of boiling water. Leave for five minutes or thereabouts on this 'bain-marie'. Serve with potato purée.

Wine-Merchant's Entrecôte

Salt and pepper, cook in butter in a sauté pan. Put on a dish, and in the sauté pan liquor cook an ounce of chopped shallot, then pour in half a pint of red Burgundy and one tablespoonful of fresh cream. Add a dash of vinegar and reduce sauce. Pour reduced sauce over meat and sprinkle with chopped parsley.

Viennese Entrecôte

Beat the meat to tenderize it, sprinkle paprika and salt on it, rub with flour and sauté very briskly in pork fat or butter. Serve with fried onions and boiled potatoes.

Fillet (Fillets, Undercut, Tenderloins)

As we have seen, the sirloin embraces fillets in the same sense that fillets and undercut lie below the bone. The fillet as culinary speciality is a long narrow muscular mass lying under the loin, and the 'false fillet' or *contre filet* adjoins it, being somewhat closer to the head of the animal, and above the loin. Fillets may be known as undercut, tenderloin, as 'Chateaubriands', 'Tournedos' or 'Filets Mignons'. They supply the best roasting portions, beefsteaks, rump-steaks in their French form of 'romstecks' (the English rumpsteak being a thick slice cut from the sirloin end or the best part of the rump).

Fillet of Beef

Is roast or quick-grilled (well daubed with butter) or sauté in a sauté pan. It may be larded or stuck over with truffles (Perigord recipe). Almost any vegetables may be served with it, and it may even appear cold, or jellied. Here is a recipe for fillet of beef served cold:

Put lardons to baste its surfaces, tie it securely into shape, roast it, then leave it to get cold.

Put the cooking gravy in a small pan and stir constantly with a spatula, as you add one or two tablespoonsful of jelly. Reduce this and then strain

GRILLERS, LEARN TO GRILL

(by Mre Adrien Peytel, barrister (Paris). Chancellor of Gastronomes' Academy.)

Grilling (also called broiling) is a procedure often most seriously misunderstood. It is not a question of roasting pieces of meat as though they were coffee beans. It is not a question of drying them out in order to toughen their texture . . . as one might well suppose, when attempting, with aching and extended jaws, to swallow with a fair degree of impunity those extra-strong boot-soles often, and unaccountably, found on dinner-plates.

The specialist in the delicate art of grilling has not the patience of your simmerers, who think nothing of leaving their handiwork over gentle heat for a couple of hours. The griller works with a good red flame, and as soon as it shows signs of dying down he revives it with a powerful bellows-blast. For your pleasure he amasses quantities of dry branches, or, more democratically, supplies of charcoal: and he requires these to be incandescent, red-hot, white-hot, ready to burst into flame for the sake of his grill only when the middle portion of his subject has lost its viscous nature, its violet tinge. The griller knows, thanks to some intuitive genius, the exact moment when the meat is just right, provided it is eaten forthwith.

It is one of the essential properties of a grilled portion that it should retain inside itself, like a secret which can be divulged only to the palate, the blood that gives it flavour. And it is perhaps the difficulty of this retention that should be the griller's principal challenge.

The late Fernand Payen, Leader of the French Bar, whose love of good things we remember with affectionate respect, had his own method which recommended itself by virtue of its simplicity. Before she grilled anything, his wife would leave the item in boiling water for about fifteen or twenty seconds. In this way she ensured the formation on its surface, thanks to the solidification of the albumen, of an impermeable layer which kept the juices from escaping. The drawback is that there is a tendency to leave the meat overlong in the boiling water and, moreover, that a slight insipidity is sometimes brought about by this method.

Speaking for myself, I like the following treatment. You take a good, thick slice of beef—and you won't lose much by choosing one of the inferior cuts, say topside or skirt, so long as it's in good shape—then cover the palms of your hands with a good, not heavily perfumed, cooking oil. Shake pepper all over the meat, then knead it with masseur's gestures in order to saturate it with the peppery oil. The whole surface of the meat must be copiously oiled in this way, and not until you are satisfied with the thoroughness of your 'working' do you cook it over glowing embers, under the ordinary grill, or by brick-clamp—this last having the advantage that the heat of wood, charcoal, etc., which is placed on a metal sheet, strikes down from above, so that there is no risk of the meat's having a smoky taste.

You have now completed the manual labours which might ensure a good grill, but from this point onward advice is superfluous. If the griller is versed in all the scientific profundities of his art, he will rely on the inspiration of the moment. This will be all he needs to inform him, without the trouble of calculating times and temperatures, without the use of watch or hour-glass, that the moment has come to withdraw his grill from the heat, sprinkle it with coarse salt, and transport it at once to his guests.

Depending on the cut selected, its quality, on whether it swells or shrinks, on whether you cook long or briefly, the variables are numerous. No definite cooking time can be given, and the decision that the meat is ready to serve must be instantaneous: for if the moment comes when the core of the meat is just about done, the very next moment brings over-browning and loss of flavour.

Perhaps this is why good grillers are rarer than poets. These latter can at least sit back and wait for a benevolent Muse to come and kiss their brows, but the heat of the fire permits the former no leisure for dreaming dreams.

THE PERFECT STEAK

An American, or does this go without saying?—a Mrs. Dreser, of New York, has drawn up the 'canon of the perfect steak' after prolonged and costly experiments.

First, the steak must weigh 1 lb 12 oz. And it must come from an animal —preferably a bull—four years old. The meat must have been allowed to 'cool off' for six months, sometimes in fresh air, sometimes in the refrigerator. The thickness of the steak should be from 2½ to 3 inches. It must be taken out of the ice-box two or three hours before it is to be cooked, and as it warms up, the two main surfaces should take turns in being exposed to the air, a minute and a half at a time. The air must be warmed.

Cooking time is eight minutes. Each side must be subjected to the heat-glow—five inches distant—for four minutes. But that's not the end of it. The interior temperature of the steak, at the moment of serving, must be 120° F.

However, the perfect steak has one more quality—or defect, if you care to look at it that way. It is practically unattainable.

it, adding afterwards some chopped truffle scraps and a small glass of Madeira.

Cut fillet into thick slices and when sauce is cold but still liquid soak them in it. Arrange on a metal dish and put in the refrigerator.

Farmer's Wife Method (for beef fillet)

Prick it, trim it, roast it (surrounded with its trimmed-off portions) and baste it with its own fat.

Cook separately carrots, turnips, new potatoes, a few kidney beans or French beans, some green peas, all in a casserole lined with lean basting strips. Serve with the vegetables all round the fillet which must have its cooking juices poured over it.

Spanish-style Beef Fillet

Cover with basting lardons, tie up the fillet, put in braising pan. Cover with a fifty-fifty mixture of stock and Malaga wine, adding salt, pepper, nutmeg, cinnamon, a bay leaf. Let it simmer for an hour and a half. Then add 9 oz currants and cook for half an hour longer. Remove fat from cooking liquor before pouring latter over the beef.

(Recipe by X. M. BOULESTIN)

N.B.—The names 'Lucullus Fillet', 'Prince of Wales Fillet' and 'London House Fillet' are applied to a fillet split open and stuffed with foie-gras and truffles before being cooked in port wine.

(Contra-indicated for livery subjects and the hard-up.)

'Filets Mignons'

Individual portions are taken, as already indicated, from the fillet end. Cooked like beefsteaks, but also may be:

Breadcrumbed Filets Mignons

Flatten fillets slightly, season with salt and pepper, soak in melted butter, roll in breadcrumbs. Grill at *gentle* heat (gentle because of the size).

Curnonsky Filets Mignons

Oil them generously, and season. Put on a really hot griddle (they should if possible, be charcoal-cooked), and turn them half-way through cooking. Serve with a nut of butter and some chopped parsley. Garnishes: Dauphiné potatoes, grilled mushrooms, halves of tomatoes cooked in butter and accompanied by watercress very slightly salted and sprinkled with vinegar. Also the fillets may have a layer of fried onion rings (these are soaked in milk, flavoured, then fried in deep fat).

(Recipe by M. R. BODET of the Société des Cuisiniers de Paris.)

Filets Mignons 'Roebuck'

Leave for forty-eight hours in a *marinade* (or even longer in winter), the liquor being a venison *marinade*. See p. 166. Dry them, sauté over a good flame. Then dress with a Chasseur (Huntsman's) Sauce (see Venison, p. 181) made with the marinating liquor that you will have reduced to thicken it. Serve with noodles, rice or a purée of chestnuts (or lentils, or haricot beans, or mushrooms).

N.B.—The various 'false fillets' or 'contre filets' (pieces next to the fillet) may be cooked according to the preceding recipes, and also as:

Charente Fillet

Soak it overnight in a mixture of vinegar and olive oil, with onions stuck with cloves, nutmeg, and a bouquet garni. Add to it, next day, a few lardons, and put in a very hot oven. Pour some of the marinade over it at frequent intervals, to keep it moist and red (rare).

In a separate pan add to the cooking juices some chopped shallot, a glass of dry white wine, salt and pepper. Reduce for ten minutes. Then add a quarter of its volume in fresh cream, also a knob of butter. Sprinkle fresh chopped tarragon on the sauce and pour it over the fillet.

May be served with a dish of meadow mushrooms cooked in butter.

Beefsteaks

Appearing as 'biftecks' on French menus. Slices of good quality beef, to be sauté or grilled. They may be cut (governing factors are price paid and workings of butcher's conscience) from almost any meaty portion of the animal—e.g. top of sirloin, then flank, pin-bone.

'Bifteck' occasionally means raw or cooked minced beef.

AMERICAN BIFTECK: raw beef mixed with egg, onions, capers (and perhaps Worcester Sauce).

ANDALUSIAN BIFTECK: raw beef with onions, sauté in oil. Accompanied by rice pilaf.

BIFTECK ON HORSEBACK: with two eggs (fried in butter) on top of the beef.

Peppered Steak

Roll the beefsteak in white peppercorns that have just been crushed, and cook it to the degree that suits you in very hot butter. Add red or white wine, or *fine champagne* to the gravy to make the sauce, and thicken this with unsalted butter. Ignite the sauce and cover the steak with it.

N.B.—Some cooks add a pinch of shallot to the cooking butter.

VARIATIONS:

It is permissible to soak the crushed peppercorns overnight in the wine which you propose to use in the sauce. The advantages are that the steak will be less heavily flavoured with pepper, and that the peppercorns will not be present to crackle as you grit them between your teeth.

Tournedos (Fillet Steaks)

The TOURNEDOS are sauté in butter or in a mixture of butter and oil, and are variously named as follows:

BEARN: with Béarn sauce served separately.

BORDEAUX: with one or two slices of beef marrow on top and a masking of Bordeaux sauce.

CLAMART: with fresh garden peas in artichoke bottoms (braised) and a white wine (light) used to glaze the cooking juices.

PERIGORD: on fried bread with truffle flakes on the steak and some Madeira in the sauce.

ROSSINI: same principle as previous entry, but a slice of foie-gras sauté in butter is laid between the steak and the truffle flakes.

ALGERIAN: seasoned with paprika before being sauté in butter. Accompaniment of sweet-potato croquettes and cooked tomatoes. The sauce is made with half white wine and half tomato flavoured veal stock.

NORMANDY: sauté in butter and ignited with Calvados. Sauce made with veal stock, cider and reduced shallots. Served on fried bread with buttered apple purée.

PARISIAN: steak is served on a bed of potato croquettes, well fried and golden-brown, of same 'area' as steak. Covered with a large head of mushroom, parsley-besprinkled. A reduced sauce with Nouilly and stock.

CREAMED: sauce made with port wine and the cooking liquid, then increased by its own volume of thickened stock and a tablespoonful of double cream. Steak covered with truffle flakes, then sauce poured over.

CHORON: with 'straw' potatoes, asparagus tips and artichoke bottoms accompanied by a Choron sauce (Béarn with tomato).

Beef Ragoûts

The beef generally used for these beef stews is chump, the less useful rump cuts, the upper (and less meaty) ribs, the chuck.

The meat is boned and cut into medium-sized pieces. It is lightly cooked in beef dripping, butter or lard, with slices of carrot and onions, salt and pepper. When just beginning to crisp on the outside, powder with flour and cook until brown. Add stock or water, a bouquet garni, garlic to your taste. Boil for an hour and a half quite gently, then put the meat in a casserole with potatoes or haricot beans. Skim the fat from the top of the sauce and strain it. Pour over. Cook on with lid on for a further hour.

Burgundian Beef

This is a stew in which red wine largely replaces the stock or water. Here is one way of preparing it:

Cook separately 10–12 oz mushrooms in water acidulated with lemon. This stock, with an equal bulk of red wine, is the meat-cooking stock. Cut some fat bacon or belly of pork into cubes—about 6 oz—and cook in frying pan with some small onions until crisp and golden. Add to the beef stew and cook all together for at least three hours. Remove the fat, add the mushrooms, serve very hot.

N.B.—Some tomato concentrate may be added. M. F. Wernert recommends, moreover, the addition of a little burnt sugar (caramel) to make the gravy really dark rather than purplish.

Goulash

A 'goulash' is a stew, but a Hungarian version. The Hungarian word from which it comes is 'Gulyas', meaning 'shepherd'—so that a *goulash*, or *gulyas*, is a shepherd's meal of (oddly enough) stewed beef, pork, poultry and so on. Dr. Pomiane's notion is that it is better to call it

Paprikache of Beef

Cut the beef into small pieces, both fat and lean, adding, if you like, some pieces of bullock's heart. Place in pan with a pound of finely-chopped onions, also salt and 3 tablespoonsful of paprika. Pour over one glassful of water, then put lid on, bring to boiling point and boil over gentle heat for about two hours.

Before serving add some thick cream.

Eaten with steam-cooked potatoes.

Beef à la Mode

Lay some good-sized lardons along the 'grain' of the meat, using a piece of the meaty end of rump or a thick slice of the round. Brown in a saucepan in lard, poultry dripping, butter or olive oil. Add three glasses of water to every one of white wine, also a tablespoonful of brandy. Season with salt and pepper. Put in a bouquet garni, some sliced carrots and some onions stuck with cloves. A scrap of pork crackling and a small slice from a calf's trotter go in too, and the mixture is cooked very gently for six hours. Do not cover. Before serving get rid of the fat.

N.B.—This is nicer still re-heated or eaten cold.

Minced Beef Cutlets

Chop up one pound of rump steak without gristle and fat. Chop an onion together with a good handful of parsley, and mix this with the meat. Add a whole raw egg and a fair-sized piece of stale bread soaked well in beef broth but well squeezed afterwards in order to eject the unwanted extra liquid. Season noticeably with salt and pepper. Knead the mixture with your hands and when you think it is thoroughly well blended, form into little cutlet shapes. This quantity of meat, etc., should give six or seven. Roll them in flour and cook until golden in butter. When not quite sufficiently done, put on serving dish and keep hot. Make a roux and moisten with some beef tea and meat gravy. Now put cutlets back in the sauce to finish cooking, simmering for twenty minutes at least, keeping lid on pan. Then serve on the hot dish.

(Recipe supplied by the actor JEAN COQUELIN.)

Stuffed Beef

Cut into very thin slices three pounds of fillet beef. Rub one side of each slice with a little pimento and on the other side put strips of truffle cut very thin, and on top again a piece of lean bacon of the same size as the slice of meat. Spread on top of these superimposed slices a good layer of this mixture:

Two cloves of garlic, two shallots, three medium onions, a handful of parsley, another of chives, two bay leaves or laurel leaves (what price glory?), a pinch of cinnamon, another of ginger, a suspicion only of grated nutmeg, a crushed clove, pepper and salt, all well mixed and chopped.

This condiments layer is now to be covered by a layer of 'double slices' exactly like the first. And so you go on until all your meat, etc., is used up. The top stratum must be a beef one. Tie your block securely.

Cover the bottom of an earthenware casserole with a walnut of butter, a thin layer of chopped bacon, and put your meat block in, together with a calf's trotter and a few fresh bones. Pour in a sauce, without cooking the meat even slightly first, made of a white roux (butter, tangerine-orange size and a tablespoonful of flour) with three glasses of water, followed by a glass and a half of good-quality white wine, a tablespoonful of old brandy, spices, half a sugar lump, thyme, bay leaf, celery leaf, a branch of chervil, a large sliced tomato, two stems of parsley, two whole carrots, a whole turnip, a chopped onion, a dessertspoonful of curry.

This sauce should cook gently for two hours before it comes in contact with the meat. If you are really careful with the proportions no one taste will swamp the others.

Once the sauce is in the casserole the cooking will take a further four hours, and it must be gentle cooking. The casserole must be hermetically sealed.

When done to a turn, cut the carrots and the turnip into rings and put in the bottom of a china receptacle that is not too wide but has tall sides. Next put in the meat with its strings removed, and then the strained sauce. Twenty-four hours later you may slide it out of the container and it is ready to be eaten cold.

BEEF OFFALS

Ox-tongue

Wash the tongue and scrape it well, then cook for three hours in the oven. Then remove the tough outer skin and cut the tongue in two lengthways. Serve it either with a piquant or a tomato sauce, or

AU GRATIN: When cooked as before, cut in thin slices and put them in an oven-dish with a few dots of butter, a half-glass of stock (or white wine), some chopped gherkins, shallots, chives and parsley. You may not need salt and pepper. Sprinkle with breadcrumbs and brown in the oven.

Beef Brains

Less delicate in texture and flavour than those of calf or lamb. They may, however, be prepared in the same ways, or

EN MATELOTE: That is, in a kind of wine and herb stew. Clean the brains thoroughly, skin, cook with a bouquet garni for three-quarters of an hour in water flavoured with vinegar. Remove from liquor. In a separate pan make a roux with a walnut of butter and a tablespoonful of flour and add a glass of red wine. Thicken, add salt, pepper, a fresh bouquet garni, some small onions and mushrooms. When the onions are tender put the brains into the sauce and boil for a quarter of an hour. Serve with sippets.

Beef Chaps

Soak for six to eight hours in salted water, then cook very slowly and serve cold in salad.

Tripe

Usually purchased ready-cooked, but the job may be done at home. The ox tripes are very carefully cleaned and soaked in fresh cold water

ON TRIPE

Jean le Hir, versifier and restaurant proprietor of Caen, founder of the Confrérie de la Triperie d'Or, and French delegate of the Académie Internationale des Chefs de Cuisine de Grande-Bretagne, wrote this rhymed recipe:

You ask me, Jenny, if I'll write,
Describing in my letter,
Tripes à la mode, *and set you right*
On all that's rare and recondite,
So I could do no better
Than list ingredients: cattle feet,
Both stomachs (plain and wrinkled),
All washed in water, cool and sweet,
Then cut in cubes, precise and neat,
And plenteously besprinkled
With carrots, onions, leeks (in rings),
With celery and cloves,
Bouquet of herbal seasonings,
And in your pot the various things
Will smell of fields and groves.
Add dabs of butter, then, dear lass,
With conscious pleasure, pour
On these, our own earth's yield, a glass
Of calva, that will soak the mass.
A pinch of salt—no more.
But pepper with a lavish hand,
Fresh-ground. Now in the heat
For twelve full hours your pot must stand
(You'd better have at your command
That baker down the street!)

* * *

Now velvet-smooth, and rich, and rare,
Gold liquid bathes the meat,
A lusty dish! No mild affair!
On plates as hot as hand can bear
Dish up your evening treat.
I've sent, my dear, the recipe
My grandad's dad bequeathed to me
For 'Tripes de Caen'—the archetype
Of every recipe for tripe.

for one or two hours then cooked in water with onion rings and a bouquet garni. They are now ready for one of the following preparations:

Lyon: Cut the cooked tripe in squares. Gild five or six onions in the frying-pan with oil or butter. Then put in the tripe squares with salt, pepper, spices, and cook for twenty minutes. Before serving, add a tablespoonful of vinegar.

English: Also cut in squares, breadcrumbed, fried in oil and served with tomato sauce.

In White Sauce (Blanquette): Put pieces of cooked tripe in a white sauce with egg liaison and lemon flavouring.

Nice (Nicoise): Melt some strips of fat bacon in frying-pan and cook tripe pieces in it to golden brown. Pour in a glass of Armagnac, and ignite. Add a very thick tomato sauce.

Tripe Specialities

Tripes as used in such specialities as Tripes à la Mode de Caen are culled from more varied but reliable offal sources, including second and third stomachs, paunch, rennet stomach. And one ox-foot to four and a half pounds of other offals is the usual proportion. If you cook them at home, use a bain-marie and serve with plain boiled potatoes. Put a bed of carrot and onion rings, a bouquet garni and some parsley in a stewpot, then a layer of offals, then one of diced foot, then one of onions and bay leaves. The top one of tripe. Pour over stock, cider and a glass of Calvados. Seal hermetically and cook in slow oven for about twelve hours.

Heart, Liver and Kidneys

Of only mediocre flavour. May be cooked as Veal portions, see later, pp. 210. Remove the kidney fat, as it tastes unpleasant.

Oxtail

Steep it in cold water for at least four to five hours, and if you can manage it, let it be running water.

Cut it in pieces and put in cold water. Bring to the boil and boil for ten minutes, then take out and drain and dry. Put in casserole on a bed of carrots and onions cut in slices, with celery and a bouquet garni. Cover with stock and a little white wine and cook in the oven for three or four hours.

VARIATION:

Burgundian Oxtail: Use red wine and add tomato purée and

blanched pork crackling. Served with celery, chestnuts and as many other vegetables as you wish; also with chipolata sausages.

VEAL

Come on, the veal stew's waiting
A-sizzling in the pot,
It's nause-ause-ating
Unless it's good and hot.
Music-hall chorus

The cow's baby is at its best at the moment of separation from its mother's milk supply—when it is two-and-a-half to three months old and has tasted no other food. Its flesh should then be white and mother-of-pearlish. If it is pink, this shows that the calf has already eaten solids. It is served:

ROAST: Leg of veal (a fillet cut from the leg, or the leg itself without the bones, giving the 'noix de veau' (gravy bit), the 'sous-noix' (round) and the 'noix pâtissière'). Roast also the 'quasi' (chump end of the loin), the 'longe' (loin)—the last also called 'rognonnade'; the breast, which may be divided into ribs and either roasted entire or boned.

BRAISED: Shoulder (rolled or not).

STEWED: Brisket, top ribs, knuckle.

Blanquette of Veal (Veal in White Sauce)

Cut breast of veal in pieces and cover (in earthenware jar) with boiling salted water. Leave for twenty minutes. Take out and drain. In a saucepan melt an egg-sized lump of butter and blend in two tablespoonsful of flour. This must not be allowed to brown. Add two glasses of water, then salt, pepper, bay, thyme and parsley. When the sauce is thick and smooth add the veal and some tiny onions. Cook for an hour and a half in a slow oven. When half done add some mushrooms. Strain the sauce before serving.

N.B.—The sauce may be thickened with an egg yolk. The juice of half a lemon may be added. Sippets may be served with it. A few carrot rings may be added. It may be served with boiled potatoes, braised celery, turnips, celeriac, whole blanched cucumbers.

Ribs of Veal

Sauté in butter and served with no further treatment. The dripping and gravy may be diluted with water, stock, Madeira, white wine, spirits, etc. They may also be accompanied by such garnishes as:

(*a*) Small onions, bacon strips, mushrooms, olives, added to the cooking juices.

(*b*) Add to the sauce, some basil, curry, paprika, tomato sauce, fresh cream.

(*c*) They may be breadcrumbed.

(*d*) They may be eaten cold, jellied.

Veal Cutlets in Papillotes

Flatten some small rib portions and sauté in butter in the frying-pan. Keep hot. Chop up some mushrooms and add lemon juice. Chop up separately some onions; separately again, some shallots.

Cook the shallots gently in frying-pan without browning; then add the onions to cook lightly, next mushrooms. Add a gill of white wine, two tablespoonsful tomato purée, some salt and pepper, and garlic if you wish. Add two tablespoonsful of grated breadcrumbs and let the mixture boil up three times. Now add chopped parsley to what should be a soft paste.

Take some white paper sheets and oil them. Put in the middle of each half a slice of ham. Coat this with the paste you have just made, and add a cutlet of veal. Repeat the paste layer and top with the second half slice of ham. The cutlet bone should be across the centre of the paper. Fold the paper over and make the edges follow the cutlet shape as you turn them in very firmly. Arrange these *papillotes* on an oven dish and put in a very hot oven. The paper will swell up like a balloon at completion point. Serve.

Shoulder of Veal

The shoulder is braised, whether or not it is stuffed. Stuff either with savoury herbs and sausage meat or with an 'English stuffing' (one-third bread soaked in milk, one-third kidney, one-third veal fat; or any other stuffing combining chopped meat, fat bacon and savoury herbs. Served with all kinds of vegetables.

Escalopes of Veal

A kind of 'veal beefsteak' which needs to be flattened. Usually cut from the half-round and round, or even brisket.

They may be prepared in various ways:

ENGLISH ESCALOPES: breadcrumbed and cooked in butter.

A HEALTHY APPETITE

A captain in the Swiss Guards had in his company a drummer who often boasted that he could eat a whole calf. He backed the man's prowess in a bet with a fellow-officer. The drummer drew up his chair and began to swallow all the veal portions they brought him, each dressed with a different sauce to sharpen the rub-a-dub-dub's appetite. After some time had elapsed, and when half the calf had disappeared, the man turned to his captain and said, 'Look, sir, I think they should bring in the calf now. All these little things are quite filling, and I don't want to lose your bet for you.'

A PROPER CHOP

Cabaner, gipsy musician of the late nineteenth century, went into a restaurant and ordered a chop.

'What kind of chop, please?'

No reply.

'A mutton chop, perhaps?' the waiter suggested.

'Yes. No.'

'A pork chop?'

'Yes.' The waiter was off to order it, but Cabaner called him back. 'Everything considered,' he said, 'I think you'd better make it a beef chop.'

ANVERS ESCALOPES: sauté in butter, served with crisped golden potatoes and hop shoots (creamed).

VIENNESE ESCALOPES: floured then coated with beaten egg. Finally covered with soft white breadcrumbs, spread over with knife blade, and left in a cool place for an hour. Cooked with oil or butter in frying-pan. Served with slices of lemon.

N.B.—Anchovy fillets may be added.

NORMANDY ESCALOPES: Cooked light-brown in butter. Chopped shallots, also flour added to half a pint of milk, blended with whisk, and escalopes put in this to simmer for ten minutes. It is usual to add stock, white wine, fresh cream, or even a dash of spirits, to the cooking liquor when the escalopes are cooked, and use this as a sauce.

May be served with all vegetables (marrows, aubergines, green beans, *jardinière*, potatoes, etc.) but braised endives are a superlative vegetable accompaniment for veal in general and escalopes in particular.

Veal Paupiettes

These are escalopes rolled and tied, having been stuffed either with a slice of ham or chopped meat left-overs or trimmings with breadcrumbs soaked in milk. Cooked in a casserole with bacon strips to provide fat, and some mushrooms. Also called 'Headless Birds'. And here are

Headless Birds, Author's Style (i.e., with heads)

Choose very flat and wide escalopes. Spread over them a thin slice of ham and on the ham a paste made by pounding together hard-boiled eggs, a few olives, some anchovy butter.

Roll the paupiettes and tie firmly. Inject them (I myself use a hypodermic syringe) with *fine* champagne. On one side of each paupiette put a bay leaf; on the other side, half a sage leaf. Put a bacon strip over and fix ties round these too.

Fry a few bacon strips golden-brown in a saucepan and put the paupiettes in with them and their fat. When they are just beginning to colour, add a glass of white Macon and one of stock. Add some small onions and a sliced carrot, also a clove of garlic. Cook separately in clarified butter some mushrooms or Chanterelles (if you have only ordinary flat mushrooms, cook the heads and use the stems with the paupiettes).

A quarter of an hour before cooking is complete, add to the pan a few stoned green olives and a whole truffle. Turn out the paupiettes when done, unfasten their strings. On one end stick in an olive (with the help of a matchstick), on the other a fan-shaped paring of the truffle, to look like a tail. Put each paupiette on a nest of mushrooms and keep in the hot oven as soon as treated. Strain all the cooking liquors to obtain a smooth sauce, and add fresh cream and a tablespoonful of *fine*. Cover your birds with this.

Fricandeau (Veal Stew)

Meat taken from the round. The piece must be covered with fine bacon strips and must not be more than two inches thick. Braise it, using bacon rinds for the fat and cooking very gently. The meat must be so tender that one could cut it with a spoon. Served with endives, a jardinière, green peas, sorrel, rice, tomatoes mixed with marrow and aubergine . . . and so on.

N.B.—Despite the message of the music-hall ditty at the head of this chapter, fricandeau may well be eaten cold, the cooking extracts being jellified.

Knuckle of Veal

The knuckle is usually one ingredient of a lavish hot-pot which is eaten with hot or cold beef. But it may also be casserole-cooked. However, the classic treatment is *à l'italienne*, the preparation known as OSSO BUCCO.

Osso Bucco

Cut in slices the round end of the knuckle and dip these in beaten egg and flour. Start their cooking in olive oil in a sauté pan, adding salt and pepper. When half-cooked take out the meat and in its place put a large sliced onion and four tomatoes freed of seeds. Cover with white wine and stock. Add a bouquet garni, a bruised garlic clove, then put back the slices of meat and cook (with lid on pan) for a further ninety minutes. Reduce the cooking liquor and add to it the juice of one lemon.

Osso Bucco is served with Italian 'pastes' more often than not.

Sometimes a handful of thin strips of orange peel is added half-way through the cooking.

(One of Amy Flore's favourites.)

Breast of Veal

Ask the butcher to take out the bones. Season the inner side with salt and pepper and spread over it the following stuffing:

4 oz milk-or-stock-soaked bread, 4 oz uncooked mushrooms, chopped together with an onion cooked in butter. A whole egg to bind when you have added chopped shallots, parsley, tarragon and chervil.

When stuffed, sew it along the 'open' side firmly. Grease a braising pan, make a bed of onions and bacon or pork rinds. Put the meat on top with a bouquet garni and the bones surrounding it. 'Sweat' it for a quarter of an hour, at low heat, then add a glass of dry white wine. Let it go on reducing until the onions are brown, then cover with stock and cook at gentle heat for three hours.

During the last hour you could put endives or lettuce or chicory to braise with the meat, but it is better to braise them separately.

N.B.—You could, of course, use a meat stuffing instead of the one specified, depending on what you have by you.

VARIATIONS:

ENGLISH STYLE: the stuffing to be one-third bread, one-third kidney, one-third fat bacon.

ALSACE STYLE: when the braising is half-way towards completion, finish the cooking with a white choucroûte added (sauerkraut).

GERMAN STYLE: having a horseradish sauce served with it.

Fillet of Veal

A piece of the thick end of the loin or of the leg (rolled middle). Usually 'steam-stewed' or braised, or cooked in butter. May be stuffed or not.

Fillets in Gravy

Grate some fat bacon as cooking fat and brown the fillets in it. Add a carrot cut in rounds and an onion in quarters, also a bouquet garni. Pour over these a half-pint of dry white wine, or stock, or water. Put lid on pan and cook for an hour and a half either in the oven or over a low flame.

Grilled Fillet

Oil the meat and spread made mustard over it. The fillet should be about two inches thick, a little under if anything. Season with salt and pepper. Each side to be grilled for fifteen minutes. Pepper meat lavishly before serving.

Sauté Veal

Shoulder, breast or neck of veal required. These are the less esteemed portions on the whole, destined for the stew-pot. Veal sauté is prepared as beef ragoût (p. 195) or sauté mutton and is served with

—aubergines;
—flap mushrooms, morels, creamed mushrooms;
—garden peas;
—rice flavoured with tomato or paprika;
—macaroni;
—small savoury herbs;
—potatoes. And so on.

N.B.—If red wine is used, the sauté is named 'matelote'.

Veal Tendons (Tendrons)

Are braised without much liquid and served with almost any accompanying vegetable. But sorrel is really the outstanding garnish.

Veal Mince

Mince veal left-overs with their weight of uncooked pork (lean). Add salt, pepper, parsley, chives, a few breadcrumbs, one egg for binding. Form into small cakes to be egged, breadcrumbed, fried.

Veal Forcemeat Balls

Another way of using up veal left overs. Mince or chop very finely. Make a Béchamel and while heating very gently mix the meat, the sauce and a whole egg. When you have a dough-like consistency, form the mixture into little cakes and fry them golden-brown in boiling fat. Serve with fried parsley.

Veal Fricandelle

This is yet another 'left-overs' recipe. Mince the veal and mix with finely chopped herbs, butter, bread soaked in milk, one egg. Fry gently a large onion, also chopped, and add to the mixture. Form into round 'quoits', flour them, sauté them in butter. Bake in the oven with a ring of lightly cooked noodles surrounding them, sprinkled with parmesan.

N.B.—Potato purée may replace the bread soaked in milk.

VEAL OFFALS

Amourettes (Calf's Marrow)

Soak the pieces of spinal marrow in cold water, then trim them (this involves picking off all the bits of sinewy membrane surrounding them). Poach them for twelve to fifteen minutes in a stock of water, vinegar, salt and pepper. Then drain and wipe and cut in slices all of the same size. Let them stew for a few minutes in a Béchamel sauce with half their weight of mushrooms previously cooked and sliced in rounds. Put finally in oven-proof tableware 'shells' (of china or metal) and sprinkle grated cheese over them. Brown under grill or in the oven.

Fried Marrow of Veal

Cut in even-sized pieces poached and well-drained calf's marrow. Soak for a quarter of an hour in a little oil, a few drops of lemon juice, some salt, pepper, chopped parsley. When you are about to serve them dip them in batter and fry in boiling oil.

Calves' Brains

Blanch in stock, discard the red threads, drain and cut into slices. Prepare them in one of these ways:

WITH BLACK BUTTER (and a thread of vinegar):

NOISETTE BUTTERED (browned in butter, dash of lemon juice added): 'noisette butter' always means 'brown butter'.

BURGUNDY: with wine sauce;

FRIED: flavoured, same amount of parsley fried with it; if necessary, tomato sauce;

AU GRATIN: with mushrooms in Duxelles, breadcrumbed, browned in oven;

POULETTE: with Poulette sauce;

Or with rice, paprika, leaf spinach, anchovy paste, etc.

Cadichonne Brains

Soak in cold water, draw out and throw away the red threads, then cook for forty minutes in salted water or in stock to which the zest of one lemon has been added. Leave to get cold in the liquid used.

Hard-boil some eggs and allow them to get cold. In large lettuce leaves place some of the brains, cut in cubes, with half a hard-boiled egg. Decorate with a leaf of tarragon. Mask with mayonnaise.

Calf's Heart

Calf's heart is superior to bullock's heart. Wash carefully. Add salt and pepper to surface, put in casserole with hot melted butter and cook in oven for about forty minutes, basting with veal stock. Sauce thickened with a little butter. Serve with vegetables in season. Another possibility is to slice it, roll in breadcrumbs, and grill with slices of raw ham and boiled potatoes.

Calves' Liver

The most usual method is the English one. Sauté in very hot melted butter some large slices of calves' liver and some rashers of bacon. Serve with boiled potatoes, chopped parsley, and a slice of lemon. Other preparations:

SKEWERED: pieces of liver alternating with lean bacon and bay leaf. Or mushrooms (no stems) may be added. Grill when skewered.

LYON-SAUTE: slices flavoured and fried with onion (parboiled). Cover with plate while they cook for five minutes. Add chopped parsley and one teardrop of vinegar.

SPANISH: slices of liver flavoured and sauté in oil, served with a purée of tomatoes, onions and garlic.

IN PAPILLOTES: (see Veal Cutlets in Papillotes, p. 202). But instead of ham use a thin rasher of bacon.

Calf Crow

Proceed as for Calf's Head, p. 213.

Calf's Tongue

All ox-tongue recipes are applicable. There is also:

Calf's Tongue, Duchess Style

Blanch the tongue by plunging it for ten minutes in boiling water, then put to cool in cold water. Remove the white skin. Start cooking in butter, in a casserole, adding onions and sliced carrots. Cook for ten minutes then sprinkle with flour, put over heat and stir from time to time as it browns. Add water (or better, stock) half-way up. Season with salt and pepper. Add two tablespoonsful of tomato purée. Put lid on and return to oven for an hour and a half.

Make a thick potato purée. Add a whole egg and whip the mixture. Use this as a ring around the edge of an oven dish, gild with egg yolk. Cut the cooked tongue in slices and put them in the middle. Keep hot in the oven.

Serve separately the strained sauce, with chopped gherkins added.

Calves' Ears

Blanch some small, cleaned ears in boiling salted water. Chop some left-overs of veal and some ham and mushrooms, spread on ears (one for each person) and tie them securely with stuffing well packed inside. Begin their cooking in butter then take out of pan. Put some finely chopped onion and a tablespoonful of flour to brown in the butter, replace the ears, cover with stock; cook very slowly for three hours. Before serving cut away the ties and remove unwanted fat flakes that have formed.

Calves' Feet

These must be soaked for some time in cold water and then be boned and boiled in stock. They may be served:

FRIED: in cubes, having soaked for an hour at least in oil, and then been dipped in thin batter before frying in deep fat.

Curried: served with rice and masked with curry sauce.

With a vinegar dressing; With a Poulette sauce; or

Grilled (first cooked with melted butter, or with egg and bread-crumbs).

English fashion: may be served with Tartare sauce.

Calves' Sweetbreads

Soak out impurities by leaving them in cold water for about two hours. Then put in cold salted water and bring to boil. As soon as the water boils, remove sweetbreads and put under cold running water. Drain and wrap in a cloth, then put a weight on cloth (say a clean board and a kitchen weight on top). Remove before further preparation any fatty or hard bits. If necessary in any of the following processes, add some narrow lardons:

Grilled Sweetbreads: first daub with melted butter.

Poached: in stock, half an hour's gentle boiling.

Roast: on spit or skewer, 35 minutes.

Fried: sauté in butter, with lid on pan.

Braised: brown or white thick stock and a glass of white wine. With lardons, small onions and bouquet garni.

Sweetbreads are usually served with green peas, all kinds of vegetable purées (carrot, mushroom, lentil, artichoke, asparagus, butter beans, split pea, onion, etc.), also asparagus tips and chipolatas.

May be masked with a cream sauce, or with their cooking liquor thinned with Armagnac. Or with sippets spread with anchovy or crayfish butter.

Veal Kidneys

These must be freed of their fat and muscle, etc., before use, especially if not served whole. Either cooked whole (casserole) or sliced for grilling, sauté; or cut in cubes for impaling on skewers.

Veal Kidneys, Pan-cooked

Cook some small white onions in butter, without browning them (use fat bacon or pork cubes as fat). Add the kidneys with a little of their own fat adhering. Season with pepper and salt. Cook for twenty-five minutes, turning several times. Ignite with cognac. Take out the cooked kidneys and keep them hot while you thicken the sauce in which they cooked with a little herbal mustard. Serve with this sauce.

A CALF'S HEAD FOR SARDOU

On Christmas Day 1870, a day of bitter cold, I left the Moulin-Joli gun-battery, on the left bank of the Seine, and headed for home, in Paris, wishing to make myself clean and respectable before going to dine at Brébant's restaurant, very popular at the time in the fashionable world. As I was leaving my house again a stranger, who had watched me go in, came up to me, and with a great air of mystery showed me a basket covered with a linen napkin. 'Monsieur Sardou,' he said, 'I've something good here for you if you're prepared to dub up.'

'What sort of thing? A work of art?'

'Something better than that . . . something for your Christmas dinner.' And, lowering his voice, he added: 'A calf's head.'

Only if you had lived in Paris at that moment of history would you be able to imagine how attractive, how remarkable, was the offer he made. He lifted the cloth and showed me, decently presented on a bed of parsley, a fresh . . . an enchanting . . . a mouth-watering calf's head, the eyes closed, the ears erect. Its smell was good, too. I hesitated no longer. 'How much?' I asked.

'To you, Monsieur Sardou, hardly anything. Sixty francs, basket and all.' And really, in those hard times it was an extremely modest demand. Without haggling I requested him to carry it for me as far as Brébant's, where I gave it into the keeping of our usual waiter and asked him not to speak of it to anybody. The calf's head, he was instructed, must not be mentioned on the menu but was to be served as a middle course. 'What a surprise for the others,' I was thinking.

An hour later we were at table, struggling with horse steaks as hard as timber. And I announced my surprise item. 'A surprise?' they chorused. 'Yes, guess what.' One suggested, 'A ham,' another, 'Stewed beef,' another 'Soused eels.' Then I made my pronouncement. 'Better still,' I said. 'A calf's head.'

They applauded. Whereupon the head-waiter came in, smiling, and carefully deposited a large dish on the table. All leant forward eagerly for a closer look. But—horrid sight—the dish contained nothing but a thick, greasy yellowish liquid.

Furious, I yelled, 'And my calf's head! You rascal, where's my calf's head?' 'That's it, sir,' the waiter replied.

'What on earth do you mean?'

'Well, it melted.'

It liquefied. The fact is that I'd been sold a head made of gelatine. But the imitation was so perfect that the wily artist, I learned later, had succeeded in selling at least thirty to other greenhorns like me.'

(*From the* Memoirs *of* VICTORIEN SARDOU)

SCRAP OF SCHOLLIANA

Aurélien Scholl, most Parisian man ever to come from Bordeaux, had a truly satanic wit. He was the creator of Guibollard, son (in spirit) of Joseph Prudhomme or Calino: one of those characters whose observations, half-asinine and half-lunatic, become legendary. This little tale concerning him fits very neatly into a chapter concerned with hunting and shooting.

Guibollard and a companion were out after partridge. One flew very close to him, and his friend cried 'Shoot! Shoot it, can't you!'

'No. Flying too slowly.'

'All the more reason to bag it! You can't miss!'

'No. I don't like that weakly flight. Makes me suspect he's not as fresh as he might be.'

VARIATION:

LIEGE KIDNEYS: ignite with gin and thicken the sauce with veal gravy, adding a few juniper berries.

Sauté Kidneys

Cut in oval slices and sauté in butter. Add salt and pepper. When cooked, drain the kidneys. Lightly cook some mushrooms in the same pan, take them out, too, and drain them. Dilute the cooking fat, etc., with white or red wine, or Madeira, or champagne, then add a pint of stock.

Reduce until this sauce loses one-third of its volume. When it is of good texture replace in it the kidneys and mushrooms, and add a knob of butter as big as a walnut.

Calf's Head

It is utterly essential to soak away impurities by leaving the head in plenty of cold water for twenty-four hours in winter, six in summer, changing the water at frequent intervals. Next all bones must be removed. It is then cooked in the following white stock: 4 oz flour to 10 pints water, 5 tablespoonsful vinegar, salt, pepper, bouquet garni, onion cut in rings, all boiled together. Then cut the head in four and cook in the stock for two hours. It is sometimes wrapped in a fine cloth (fine of texture, that is) and so that it shall not cook to a dark colour some beef dripping is added to form a layer on top of the broth.

It is usually served warm with a vinaigrette, Poulette or Gribiche sauce.

LYON STYLE: it is put on a bed of onions, covered with melted butter, sprinkled with breadcrumbs and put in oven for crumbs to crisp.

PORTUGUESE: reheated in a tomato purée with onions and marrow also 'melted' to purée.

PIEDMONT: soaked in oil and lemon and then dipped in batter, cooked, served with rice.

Tripes of Calf

Are prepared in the same way as beef tripes. They are also the basis of the speciality known as 'Tripous' of Espalion (Espalion is in the department of Aveyron), and sheep tripes are a second ingredient thereof. This recipe is therefore given among the Lamb and Mutton recipes, on p. 231.

LAMB AND MUTTON

I guess a good navarin
Might be signed SAVARIN,
Loyally unctuous . . .

ROMAIN COOLUS

Mutton broth, and mutton cutlets too,
need to be shown a bit of garlic.

DUGLERE

Fulbert-Dumonteil, who used to write for the review *L'Art Culinaire* about fifty years ago, was the author of the following charming fantasy concerning mutton, which we reproduce here in the hope of pleasing the housewife in a rare moment of leisure:

'Granted, the sheep is no pioneer. He goes only along the beaten tracks which his timid race has trodden with its little hooves for five thousand years. His pace is unchanging and slow and he follows antique practice in all things as his resigned baa-ings echo down through and back through the centuries.

Maybe he was born to be shorn. But also he was certainly born to be roasted, grilled, braised, boiled, baked, spitted. His jaunty headpiece, which the stewpot so freely decorates with a scrap of Perigord bacon, is etched against a background of popular history. He is the patriarch of the pens, he is one of cookery's first begetters.

Mutton, lamb, is the most succulent meat of the whole range the butcher can offer. It is revivifying, wholesome, strengthening; an aid to digestion and even slightly aphrodisiac. There are very few stomachs that are not all the happier, all the healthier, for having engulfed it.

Unless I am badly mistaken, the very sheep which bring their cutlets to Paris are those of Beauvais, Cotentin and Normandy: of the Ardennes, of Cabourg. There is nothing so tasty yet subtle as a fine-quality leg of 'salt-meadow mutton', *pré-salé*, with a tiny shred of garlic for piquancy, and a proud accompaniment of rich 'Soissons'. And we must not overlook the small Berry sheep with its particularly delicate flesh.

As everybody knows, the best portions are saddle, cutlets, chops, breast, leg (worthy of its own separate panegyric) and the shoulder which, artistically stuffed and rolled, does not disdain a crown and garland of odorous Perigord truffles.

And who could resist the attractions of a loin of mutton on a beautifully hot couch of choice vegetables? Sweet as a nut and just right for the delicate digestion of the convalescent, is the unadorned chop, merely breadcrumbed and grilled, in the very pink of perfection. Normandy style makes it even more appetizing; à la Jardinière, it is gaiety itself; à la Soubise, a provocative dainty.

As for breast of mutton or lamb, I like it cooked in country style, either in the stewpot or after braising in well-flavoured liquor, garnished, seasoned, grilled carefully, then served with a Joyeuse Sauce.

I like, too, the well-known Haricot of Mutton of heady odours, a dish which one usually pictures as steaming invitingly from its place on the snowy cloth of some cottage table, a pitcher full of flowers on either side—a culinary eclogue.

And (with varied sauces, or as superb grilled morsel, in Liège, or Breton, or gratinated, or peasant styles; or with tomatoes or cucumbers; or in buttered-paper papillotes) it is tempting to observe that a sheep's or lamb's tongue speaks all the dialects known to cookery.

Then there's the tail—what a treat! It calls for a sorrel accompaniment, for hot-pot immersion, but is at its best with a Sunshine sauce—that is to say, soaked in well-beaten egg, fried lightheartedly, set coquettishly on a small bunch of parsley, the heavy end downwards, the point sticking up; good to look at, good to eat, a titbit and a tableau.

As for sheep's kidneys cooked on a skewer, don't mention them to me. At the mere thought of them my mouth fills with—sauternes. What could be nicer, what more touching than a fine kidney opened up into a heart-shape to accommodate a little ball, ambered, Isignytized, melting like a dream.

Then, finally, the tender, tender feet. I think they must have walked a glory road through the heart of culinary history. Poulette sauce enlivened with capers is, maybe, a little ordinary, having been cheapened by low-class chop houses. Never mind. One even meets so-called statesmen whose life-work seems to be the denigration of their own government. And there are plenty of other sauces to do honour to sheep's trotters. I like them with a Lyonnaise, I go out of my way to find them served with a Robert, I adore them with a Ravigote. But on the whole I prefer them fried, first dipped in a thin batter of clever composition, knowledgeably fried to a good colour, and served at the psychological moment with some quick-fried parsley. It's no exaggeration to call this a golden dish, a magic dish.

And now, should you ask the sonorous echoes of our southern regions to send you back the exalted name of an unrivalled dish, old in fame, lingering in family tradition, their Carcassonne, in ringing tones, will answer: 'Cassoulet!'

And so you see how good it is, from tongue to tail, the sheep; this Proteus of the gastronomic world. Its meat is generally a little fatter, a little deeper in colour, than beef. It is said to be more easily assimilated. The redder the lean, the whiter the fat, the better is the quality of the mutton.

Lamb is, of course, younger—the lamb is still the ewe's lamb until it is a year old. The sucking lamb is still unweaned and its meat is white. It is sold—and cooked, quite often—whole. The older lamb has pink flesh. Both need to be eaten 'mint fresh'. This is one of the meats that taint very rapidly. (The same recipes, generally speaking, may be used for lamb and mutton. In most of the notable restaurants 'Lamb' is the word on the menu, but 'Mutton' may sometimes be indicated.)

Stuffed Sucking-lamb

It may be stuffed with half-cooked rice mixed with the lamb's liver, heart and kidneys cooked partially in butter; or with a mixture of bread-crumbs and white pudding; or any ordinary forcemeat; or chestnut purée mixed with sausage meat.

Whichever one you choose, season it strongly, as the meat is somewhat insipid. Sew up the animal, put plenty of lardons on it, skewer it securely and cook at brisk heat, allowing 10–15 minutes to the pound.

Baron of Lamb

The 'Baron of lamb' has just been brought up-to-date by an academic dispute. Maître Maurice Garçon, a fine lawyer but an inconsiderable gastronome, maintained that it should be written not 'Baron' but 'Bas-rond' of lamb (or 'rounded lower portion'). And for a time he was judged to have said the last word thereupon. The details of his contention were: the joint represents the two hind legs and the saddle, that is to say the rounded-off rear quarters—or 'bas-rond', as the name was often written.

It was Henry the Eighth of England who once, on being confronted with this particular joint, was so impressed by its splendour that he announced: 'I declare you a baron.'

True or untrue, this account of the ennobling of a mighty dish deserved to be poetically authenticated by gastronomes. And thus the academic decision provoked a great outcry, a protest sufficiently clamorous to compel the academicians to reconsider their ruling.

Maître Maurice Garçon didn't plead guilty, but for once in a way he didn't secure complete vindication of his own case. And in future the dictionary will give both spellings.

Here is the recipe promised by the title (which may also, of course, be BARON OF MUTTON).

Roast the meat (oven or spit) and slightly thicken the contents of the dripping-pan. Serve with a garnish of assorted vegetables, braised endives, potatoes, haricot beans, butter beans, etc.

Blanquette of Lamb

See Blanquette of Veal (Veal in White Sauce), on p. 201. Use shoulder, breast and ribs.

Lamb on Skewers

Called Chachlick in Russia, Souvlakia in Greece, and by various regional names, the dish consists of inch-long pieces of lean lamb threaded on skewers with pieces of bacon, liver, potato, or onions, the choice as you please. A bay leaf is added and the skewer-loads are well-seasoned with salt and pepper. Served with watercress and a braised tomato.

Loin of Lamb (Mutton)

Consists of unseparated chops, from seven to ten ribs being included. Cooked in one piece (roast or braised) with any vegetables you choose. Excellent served cold and jellied.

Mutton Chops

First let us learn from Madeleine Decure, director of the review *Cuisine et Vins de France*, who supplies this brief guide to chop-shopping.

(1) HOW TO CHOOSE. Don't ask your butcher for 'a mutton chop', or he'll give you the first he lays hands on. Choose, yourself, the one you want. The first requirement is meat of good quality—a good bright red or pink and not a brown-red. Sniff to make sure there is no smell of wool grease. Properly hung meat is better than over-fresh, but on this matter you can only trust your butcher.

There are four kinds of chop to choose from:

(*a*) THE 'FIRST' OR 'BEST END OF NECK' CHOP, with its 'knuckle' bit cut in with it. The meat is very lean and forms a nice round mass called the 'noix'—the nut, kernel, 'pope's eye'. The fat over the bone is quite thick.

(*b*) THE 'SECOND' OR 'SPARE-RIB' CHOP. With its 'handle', too. There is more of a streaky effect and no 'pope's eye' of lean. The meat 'lines' the length of the bone, as it were.

(*c*) THE LOIN CHOP, with no 'flap'. It has lean meat that does not form an 'eye'. The long extension of the other chops is replaced by a thick fat skin portion, which the butcher rolls in on itself. This bit is generally uneatable.

(*d*) THE CHUMP CHOP. No flap. It is a kind of mutton escalope cut from the chump end of the leg.

I recommend (*a*), the best-end chops, the best-textured and the most presentable. A good one should weigh about four or five ounces when ready to cook. So ask for chops of this weight. There will be two bones —three, even, if the meat is young. They should be cut parallel with the bone, not diagonally.

Have them trimmed at the butcher's. He will remove skin and surplus fat, and get rid of small bones, leaving you only one. Also, he will scrape it thoroughly. You will be left with a good clean-looking 'handle' to your chop.

(2) HOW TO COOK. Now your work begins and is not the *least* exacting.

There are no two ways about it; the chop must be grilled. Above all, no frying-pans for chops, as is often a line-of-least-resistance practice. Grill by gas or electricity, whichever is installed in your house, but if you are in the country I do recommend a good wood fire and direct cooking for a really delicious chop (cooked on glowing embers).

The meat should be well browned quickly on the outside to retain the juices, so light up before you submit the chop to heat. It might well wait for a quarter of an hour while the grill gets really hot. Keep your grill frame under the bars—you want the 'rods' very hot, too.[1] When all is red and very hot put chop on the hot grill stand, and move this as close as possible to the source of heat. Cook for five or six minutes (according to thickness). Then take away from heat and turn chop over.[2] The second side should take four or five minutes. Put on a hot dish. Sprinkle salt on both sides.[3] Serve at once on a very hot plate. The chops should look and be crisp and brown on the outer surfaces, and still pink and juicy inside.

MADELEINE DECURE

If You Do Not Grill Your Chops

You can egg-and-breadcrumb them and then sauté in butter.

Chops sauté in butter may be served with: haricot or butter beans; flageolets; Brussels sprouts (in which case add, if you like, some white wine to sauce); a *duxelle* of mushrooms; potatoes; green peas (sauce thickened with fresh cream blended with the gravy); a *jardinière* (garnish of mixed vegetables cut up small); onion purée.

Chops sauté in oil may be served with: braised tomatoes; small onions and olives (with stones taken out); in this case blend with the gravy some white wine and some tomato sauce with a trace of garlic; tomato, aubergine and marrow purée, with garlic; polenta (with a sauce made with the gravy, a light wine and some bacon scraps); rice mixed with cubes of ham and sweet peppers; golden crisped potatoes sprinkled with paprika; mushrooms (flap).

Chops and Chick-Peas

Make a chick-pea purée. Pan-cook some lamb chops, and when half-done add the purée of peas and some Greek wine. Failing this, use sherry or Cognac. Add a trace of paprika. Sprinkling of chopped parsley. Serve very hot.

(The 'Rabelaisian', Hervé de Peslouan, assures us that neither Xenophon nor Aristophanes would have turned a cold eye on this Greek concoction.)

Mutton Chops

The English-grilled cutlet. It is to the mutton group what the Châteaubriand is to the beef group. A chop of double thickness is used (a loin

[1] So that the meat does not stick and tear as you try to turn it.

[2] Avoid pricking with fork as the gravy might then escape. Turn with your hand, holding on to the bone, or use two forks.

[3] Never salt before cooking. The salt causes exudation of moisture which prevents crisping of the outside, and from soft surfaces juices run out.

METCHOUI

Their religion forbids pork-eating to Muslims, and beef-cattle are not easily acclimatized in their homelands. (I am speaking of the Muslim populations of North Africa, not of their brethren in religion in India and Egypt.) So mutton naturally became their staple food and meat ingredient of the principal dishes of Morocco, Algeria and Tunisia.

Here is a recipe for Metchoui that appears over the signature of Georges Clarétie. It is not easy to put into practice of course, in the average home circle, but you may still appreciate it as a yarn.

Take a fat lamb, not more than a year old, and skin it without separating the head from the body. Make a twelve-inch gash longitudinally at loin level in such a way that you will be able to insert your hand. You will 'draw' the lamb through this aperture, extracting all the innards excepting the kidneys.

Now the inside must be thoroughly washed out. Place inside the cavity a handful of fine-grained salt, half a pound of butter, a little pepper and some onion chopped very small. Close the opening, using a piece of wood sharpened off to form a stake, thrusting it crosswise through the gash at a slight angle, securing it with a segment of well-cleaned and washed intestine. A metal clamp or steel skewer would taint the meat, and sewing-thread would burn.

Impale the lamb from head to tail on pointed poles. The spit must emerge from the head and be longer, both ways, than the carcase. Attach the forefeet to the neck, again using a length of intestine for tying. Stretch out the hind legs parallel with the pole and tie them in the same fashion. The two ends of the spit must rest in stones or Y-*shaped irons which allow the body to rotate.*

To one side of the spitted lamb dig out a trench as long as the roasting carcase. The pit that is to hold the fire will be laterally dug, and twenty inches below the meat immensely hot, glowing embers must be piled in.

The lamb on its stake must be turned slowly, and in such a way that the whole of its surface is exposed to the heat. It should be basted with melted salt butter or, better still, daubed (with a small brush dipped in melted butter) wherever some portion of the meat seems to be in danger of burning.

The Metchoui is sufficiently cooked when it yields no more trickles of thin juice when pricked with the point of a knife.

It is a first-rate dish. But I am afraid that a proper appreciation of it is possible only when it is eaten in the desert, in the company of unloquacious Arabs, while the wind sifts and tosses the sand of the dunes. Or where tales are told within the sheltering tent, or stories unfolded under the stars.

GEORGES CLARETIE

SUBTLE SHADES

Talleyrand was a courteous man, but not above making subtle distinctions. One day, when he was acting host to several personages, a piece of roast beef, a joint which he liked to carve himself, was set before him. He invited the various guests to partake in the following terms:

'Your Grace, may I perhaps have the honour of offering you a little beef?'

'Your Ladyship, will you do me the honour of accepting a little beef?'

'Baron, will you have the goodness to take a little beef?'

'Sir Charles, permit me to offer you a little beef.'

And having thus served the principal diners he indicated the dish and said to all the others: 'Gentlemen, help yourselves to a little beef.'

DIGESTION? WHY ALL THE FUSS?

Desbarreaux and Delbens were having dinner together, one evening. 'I shan't risk any foie-gras,' Delbens observed. 'I don't think my stomach could cope with it.' 'Good Lord!' Desbarreaux replied. 'Don't tell me you're one of those nincompoops who waste time digesting things!'

chop). It is grilled at a brisk heat, basted with butter, and seasoned only when half cooked. Served with boiled potatoes, or potato purée, and a green vegetable.

Easter Lamb

My friend and abettor, the gastronomadic Henry Clos-Jouve, gives in his well-informed article published in the magazine *L'Hôtellerie* the recipe for Martyr's Cutlet:

It is by no happy accident that the slender little lamb is the liturgical symbol of Easter rejoicing. These offspring of wool-cloaked ewes, doing their best to harmonize their bleatings with the sounds of young buds bursting into leaf, are an embodiment of spring; and they are, too, hallowed symbols of the Resurrection feast, itself symbolic.

But the coming of these clumsy and unmannerly Sons of the Ram means, to the gourmet, not a series of pretty pictures in a Sunday School prize, but a series of delicacies which cooks will fashion, for the greedy, from the various portions of the sucking lamb—connoisseurs' dishes; from leg of friable bone to haphazardly jointed shoulder, by way of melting loin chops that will deserve the gaudy garnish of the young season's first tender and bright-hued vegetables.

Do you remember Marcel Ayme's 'Long Tag' (The Cat in the Tree) Tales—the one in which two little girls met the wolf?—happily, a kind wolf, who only wanted to join in their games. But the two little blue-eyed babies discount his good intentions and issue a round indictment of this wild animal's sad reputation.

'You eat sheep, for one thing!' they accuse him—or the bolder one does, 'Yes, you do! That's a nice way to go on, I must say!'

'So I do, of course, why not?' the wolf calmly replies. 'Plenty of sheep. Where's the harm in that? You yourself do the same.'

And it is true that the race of sheep has far more cause to fear the controlled appetites of the human tribe than the fabled flesh eaters' illicit greed.

For millennia the sheep was the domestic beast most often sacrificed to glorify the love-feasts of mortal men. The quality of its flesh incited them in remotest times to invent the roasting spit. Not to please the sheep, as we all know. One might even go so far as to wonder whether this innocent beast was not specially created to satisfy the gustative propensities of men, so exquisitely fitted is it, at every stage of life, to supply a delectable variety of dishes.

We were expatiating on the toothsomeness of a leg of sucking lamb, but the nether portions of an adult *pré-salé*, roasted according to prescribed rules, are of more definite flavour, after all. They provide one of the classical items in the gastronomic repertoire, whether served in Breton fashion on a bed of beans, or enshrined in a potato gratin, as is the Dauphiné practice. And starch comes again to the service of those pieces of meat which are not of the highest quality, to give us one of the most savoury successes of the most genuine form of cookery (that is, the homeliest)—a mutton 'haricot'.

Here, now, is the whole range of mutton chops: the best neck ones, the ribs, the loin, the chump. The first are the tenderest, the next the most charming, and our forefathers would appreciate them only in half-dozens. King Louis XVI used to eat six every morning for breakfast, with a chicken and all its trimmings. I must say it sounds a more heartening breakfast than our routine drop of white coffee.

This hapless monarch had a predilection for grilled steaks, etc., in the robust tradition of the gargantuan spreads which his great-great-grandfather Louis XIV was wont to swallow; as also for the sweet things extolled by his ancestor Louis XV . . . brioche . . . champagne. At Varennes Louis XVI ordered from the innkeeper, at this fatal halt, a mutton cutlet which he ecstatically enjoyed, while irremediable disaster closed in. At the moment when he was due to mount the scaffold on that regicide 21st of January 1793, this courageous and philosophical prince chose as his final sustenance an ample chop and a glass of Médoc to go with it.

Less tragically, but no less spectacularly, the banished Louis XVIII announced, during his exile, his further discoveries concerning the sheep's thoracic anatomy. This king, with a melancholy reputation for excruciating gout (evidence of his boundless gluttony) endowed posterity with a 'Recipe for Chops' designated 'À LA MARTYRE' (Martyrdom Cutlets) and I give here the brief but far from economical formula:

'Sacrificing two or three chops for the sake of one, fix them together, sandwiching the largest and best among the others. Then put these chops to grill, turning them carefully so that the gravy from all is directed toward the favoured chop in the middle.

When the top-chops are over-done, remove them carefully, as you will be serving, of course, only the middle one—regal, all gravy and dewiness.'

The royal master-cook insisted on a Château-Margaux of his own distinguished cellars as accompaniment. We can assure you, from our own experience, that a good honest red burgundy of repute is just what is wanted to honour and collaborate with the Easter lamb in an appropriate fashion.

HENRY CLOS-JOUVE (Académie Rabelais)

Shoulder of Mutton

It is usual to ask the butcher to bone and roll this (there is also a 'balloon roll', not quite so simple to carry out but very helpful if you are planning to stuff the shoulder. Braised or roasted.

Remember that these large joints of lamb and mutton such as the shoulder will be all the better for generous 'pricking' with garlic. Or if you prefer, sprinkle on garlic powder which is now on the market in a very acceptable form.

GOODWIFE SHOULDER OF MUTTON: Roll with a central space ('balloon roll') and apply garlic. In a pan melt an ounce and a half of lard and fry it in some bacon basting strips previously blanched in boiling water. Take out, drain, put in the same fat two dozen small onions. Fry these golden brown on all sides then surround with the bones, add lardons, onions, 4 oz carrot rings, a bouquet garni. Pour on half a pint of white wine and the same of water. Cover and boil, allowing at least 1½ hours for lamb and 2 hours for mutton. When half-way through this cooking time, add one or two tomatoes. Remove fat before serving (the fat in the sauce, that is).

FLEMISH SHOULDER OF MUTTON: Braise it and half-cook, then put in a large oven dish half-full of red Flemish cabbage (*see* Vegetables, p. 255). This too, should be half-cooked. Now put on top enough cabbage to fill the pan. Cook in a very slow oven.

N.B.—The shoulder may be accompanied by potatoes (mashed, purée, etc.), dry beans or flageolets (whole or in purée), young turnips, rice, and so forth.

Mutton Epigrams

Comus alone can tell us why the Greek 'epigram'—a word meaning, the dictionaries tell us, a phrase tossed negligently into the thick of the conversation to express shrewd criticism or mordant banter—should also signify a portion of breast of mutton.

Whatever the explanation, here is the recipe for grilled breast of mutton, or 'Epigrams':

The breast will have been boiled first—perhaps to make a mutton soup, with cream of barley or rice (as is done in Lorraine). Allow the boiled meat to get cold. Cut it into heart or triangle shapes (more or less the same shape, when so many love stories end in triangles). Beat a whole egg in a plate with a tablespoonful of oil, some salt, and Cayenne pepper. Soak the meat in the egg. Oil a griddle, heat it up for ten minutes, then grill the epigrams for ten to twelve minutes at fairly moderate heat. Serve with a piquant sauce.

Leg of Mutton

BOILED LEG OF MUTTON, ENGLISH METHOD: First boil in a capacious stewpot 5 oz carrots, two clove-stuck onions, half a pound of young turnips, a bouquet garni. Add salt (one-third of an ounce to a quart), pepper and garlic. Put in the leg of mutton and bring to boil again. From that point, allow a quarter of an hour per pound. Serve it in a ring of carrots; make a purée of the turnips to serve in a separate dish. Caper sauce also separately served.

LEG OF MUTTON, GOODWIFE'S RECIPE: as shoulder.

BORDEAUX LEG OF MUTTON: Take out the bone in the thick part, leaving 'handle' bone. Stuff, using the larding-pin, with baconer's tongue and anchovy fillets rolled in parsley. Add garlic and blanched shallots. Tie up the gigot in good shape and braise with onions, carrot rings, bacon strips cut next to the rind and including the rind, and half a veal trotter, also a bouquet garni. Pour in a bottle of Bordeaux. Cover the pan and cook gently for an hour and a half. Cut away the ties and serve. Hand separately the cooking sauce, having skimmed off the fat and then strained it.

JUNIPER GIGOT: Take out bones of, and trim, a very fresh leg of sheep (killed the same day) and stick it with juniper berries. Cover with a damp cloth and hang in a draught for two to five days (be guided by the season of the year). Put on spit, cover with good-quality fat, and roast, if possible at a wood fire, basting with the contents of the dripping pan (gravy, fat) to which you have added a glass of salted water in which juniper berries are soaking. Ignite with bacon fat before serving.

(Recipe compiled by the COMTE AUSTIN DE CROZE)

SOUSED GIGOT: Beat it to tenderize, then remove skin and attach fat bacon lardons. Put in earthenware dish full of sousing liquid (glass of red wine, glass of vinegar, bouquet garni, salt and pepper, onions cut in rings, and four tablespoonsful of oil). For four days wash it over with its sousing liquor three times a day. Then cook on spit, still basting with the sousing liquor.

Serve with a piquant or a tomato sauce.

MIRABEAU FASHION: Line an earthenware casserole of large size with strips of fat bacon rind. Also place lardons here and there on the leg of mutton, as well as scraps of ham and garlic. Put the meat in, add salt and pepper, bay leaves, two large onions, three glasses of water, one of white wine. Put a plate over top as lid, and stick paper around plate, then put a glassful of wine in the plate. Simmer for seven hours.

SEVEN O'CLOCK GIGOT: Spit the leg of mutton. While it is cooking skin 30 to 40 garlic cloves and cook them in a pint of water. When done, take them from their pan and crush them, together with some of their cooking water, until they form a paste. Carefully skim off the fat from the mutton gravy in the dripping-pan. Serve meat, gravy and garlic paste, seasoning with salt, pepper and a pinch of curry powder.

(The two preceding recipes were by ALEXANDRE DUMAS the Elder.)

N.B.—The leg of mutton cooked as a straightforward roast takes a lot of beating. It must, however, remain pink and juicy at the heart of the joint and not be allowed to char on the outside. If need be, protect the surface with a greased or oiled paper. Serve with potato purée, flageolet beans, a vegetable jardinière, etc.

If you like, inject it (see p. 204) with *fine champagne* the night before you want to cook it (anyhow, a day's 'standing' is practically indispensable). Strain fat away from gravy, and dilute gravy with a tablespoonful of Madeira.

THE GIGOT

The gigot's here (on table neatly spread)
Fragrant with garlic, couched on seemly bed
Of many a blessed bean.

There's magic in the air, and hearts are light
As we recover waning appetite,
Now sharp and keen.

So far, so good. We'd tried, with moderate zest,
Hors d'oeuvre-ish snacks. But now each anxious guest
Wonders 'Which roast?'

Joy! It's a gigot; borne by serving-maid
Sturdy of build, yet ceremonially staid.
Ah, precious load! Our host,

Father of all the flock, with critic's gaze,
Inspects it. Is it worthy of his praise?
Well browned, well done?

Pink of perfection, as we all agree,
When his proud blade cleaves irresistibly,
And streamlets run,

Rose-red, from a pierced gold pourpoint, to disclose
The flesh, as sweet and wholesome as a rose.
The dreariest guest

But lately wordless, blossoms at the sight,
And scatters telling phrases left and right,
Becomes, indeed, a pest.

Often a sad, spoiled soup will, from the start,
Ruin a meal, and nullify the art
Of many a wit.

Then comes the 'leg'. Tongues wag. In highest glee,
'Knuckle!' claims one. 'Pope's eye!' cries one, 'for me,'
(or other dainty bit).

'Some underdone', for him. For her 'Cooked through'.
No problem here. A third, between the two
Can't quite decide.

*(A leg of mutton, when correctly done,
Ensures that every whim, of everyone,
Is gratified.)*

*Sometimes the talk . . . art, science, politics,
Gets out of hand, emphatic, or prolix,
Reaches some peril-point.*

*The gigot comes, and turgid speeches die.
'Quite right!' says one. And then, 'Shall you and I
Discuss this joint?'*

*Unrivalled creatures! In the springing green
You lived on flowers. On flowers alone, I mean,
And never a weed.*

*Tender you are as any youthful bride,
O, generous gigots! Dewy-fresh beside,
Lovely indeed.*

*When in the daisied vales you danced quadrilles,
Cropped the salt pastures, gambolled on the hills,
Butchers unheeded,*

*Sweet babes you seemed, gracious in infancy,
But more affecting still, at least to me,
On bean-layer bedded.*

*We munch you, then, in frankest, purest greed,
Slice after slice, and far beyond our need,
Sated, replete.*

*Still, as the Sorbonne doctor said: 'Good mutton
Never yet harmed the most outrageous glutton.'
Hungry or not—let's eat!*

RAOUL PONCHON

Mutton Hash

A means of using leftovers, trimmed-off bits, etc., and all recipes for meat hash, or minced cooked meat, are suitable. This one, however, applies particularly to *gigot* minced meat:

Remove from the leg-bone all the meat left on it, scraping right down to the bone. In a cast-iron pot melt some butter or good quality fat (goose or pork dripping) and blend with a tablespoonful of flour. When you have a warm light brown roux, pour in half a pint of stock (or of water browned with meat extract). Boil up, whisking as it thickens. Season with salt and pepper, add first a bouquet garni and then a dozen cloves of garlic, chopped up small. The total boiling time should be half an hour. Put this sauce over the most presentable slices and over the less presentable ones reduced to a hash.

Haricot of Mutton

This expression, very commonly found on restaurant menus, is a corruption of HALICOT de Mouton (from an old word, 'halicoter'), meaning 'to cut into little bits'. There are no beans, haricot or other, in Haricot de Mouton, which is a ragoût or navarin, that is, a mutton stew.

Mutton Stew

Mutton stews are made from shoulder, breast, neck or even ribs. They may be 'brown stews' or 'white stews'. The 'white stew' is nothing but the well-known Irish Stew on its travels:

In a sauté pan or small casserole (the classical recipes speak of an earthenware casserole) put the mutton pieces, of even size and shape as far as possible, each weighing some two ounces. Alternate with onion slices and potato slices. Sprinkle lavishly with garlic, shallots, parsley. Add a bouquet garni. Repeat the meat-potato-onion layers. Cover completely with water and cook slowly for at least two hours.

N.B.—Some use half waxy potatoes and half floury, so as to have a purée-thickened gravy.

The advantage of this dish is that it is made without fat.

The Irish Stew is the classic white stew. Its opposite number is the 'brown stew' such as, for instance:

Springtide Navarin

Put a little fat in pan and slightly cook some salted and peppered pieces of breast of mutton. Drain away the fat. Add chopped garlic cloves and a little flour and stir constantly while these brown together in the pan. Cover with water and two tablespoonsful of tomato concentrate. Put in a bouquet garni. Cover and cook for one hour. Then take out the pieces of meat and put in a saucepan with ten small onions, previously fried brown in mutton dripping, some quarters of young spring carrots and turnips, and a score or so of young new potatoes. Strain the sauce through a large gravy strainer and pour over the pan contents. Put pan over heat again to boil for twenty minutes. Add 3 oz of fresh green peas and complete the cooking. Skim off fat and serve with chopped parsley.

Any ordinary brown-roux-based mutton stew may be served with:

—celery-beet and celeriac;
—haricot beans, butter beans, red beans;
—curried rice;
—macaroni with parmesan and tomato, and so on.

Saddle of Mutton

This may be roasted or braised. It is treated in the same way as loin (joint) or leg of mutton. It makes fine eating served cold. The Prosper Montagné contest for 1952 set the preparation of a saddle of mutton as the test of competing cooks' skills. Among the many recipes was the following which, although it was not placed among the prize-winners, seems to have interesting features and to be easy to carry out:

ORLEANS SADDLE OF MUTTON: For eight people, take a saddle weighing about 3½ lb. Gash the upper surface, season with salt and fresh-ground pepper, then daub all over with freshly made mustard (Orleans mustard). Put it to roast in a sauté dish, in a brisk oven, and place a walnut of butter on top. Roast for about three-quarters of an hour.

To find out whether the saddle is done, pierce it with a fine, long trussing needle, plunging it right into the core of the meat then quickly testing with your lips to see if it is warm. If perceptibly warm, the meat is done. Take it from the oven and thin the gravy with a dash of vinegar and a glass of medium-dry white wine. Boil this gravy for five minutes with a few dots of butter added.

Serving: garnish with little potato 'baskets' filled with Provençal mushrooms (boletus) and Mornay cauliflower balls. And serve a water-cress salad, too.

(Recipe by M. NOEL GERMAIN, of Orleans)

Warache Malfouffe

Take:

(1) Four pounds of fillet of mutton, cut up into some fat. Put with it eight tablespoonsful of well-washed rice, a good quarter of butter, salt and pepper (the pepper especially) and a little Cayenne pepper. Mix these ingredients thoroughly.

(2) Select some tender cabbage leaves in good shape (untorn) and blanch in one or two changes of boiling water. Trim them all round.

A GLARING EXAMPLE OF GREED

Baron Brisse was one of the most outstanding trenchermen of the Second Empire: according to his own description, 'hag-ridden by an insatiable appetite'. On one occasion, he arrived rather early for a luncheon party, and an unsuspecting lackey invited him to wait in the dining-room, giving him a bottle of port wine to beguile the waiting-time.

Baron Brisse tossed off a glass of wine, and then a second, which sharpened his appetite. Then he spotted, on a handsome side-table, a large Lyon sausage, some sliced York ham, a jar of foie-gras and some Bologna sausage —a great favourite of his.

When his friend bustled in, full of excuses, three-quarters of an hour later, the baron said: 'I'm afraid I've emptied the bottle, old fellow.' 'And rightly,' his host replied. 'I'd have done the same in the circumstances.' 'And there were, on a tray over there, a few eatables I trifled with, while I was at it,' Baron Brisse went on, pointing to a few scraps of sausage-skin, all that remained.

BURGUNDIAN HOT-POT

(A rhymed recipe by an author so far untraced.)

Take a nice piece of pickled pork, red as a rose, and tender;
Add to it ham, a larger joint, some bacon, a smallish slice.
Each of them has its special worth, no-one can be precise,
'This weight', 'that size': all depends on the secret art of the blender.
One cabbage, two, three, best you can get, chop and shred them through,
Fill your pot till it holds no more, and let it stand on the hob,
Half the day, let it simmer away, shrink and seethe and throb;
And there's your Potée (round, simple name), a succulent, savoury stew.
Into your pot, volcano hot, and steaming away like a crater,
Put fresh green beans, potatoes too, adding, a moment later,
Carrots, as new as you can find, turnips whiter than paper.
Bring it to table as hot as you're able, then the delectable vapour
Sets all agog, whets appetites, before they have even tried
Their first small sip; and with such a scent the whole room's glorified.

(3) In each half cabbage leaf, rolled into a tube, put some of the mixture. Arrange the filled rolls in a casserole containing the mutton bones; and in the midst of the rolls set a few garlic bulbs, each the size of a large walnut.

(4) Pour over tomato sauce, enough to cover the contents and submerge them.

(5) Put a dish *inside* casserole to serve as an 'inside' lid. No further lid required.

(6) Cook for three hours (in a hot oven for the first half-hour, with much reduced heat for the last two and a half hours).

(7) Serve: having turned the casserole upside down on the dish in one quick movement.

(Arab recipe brought back by FREDERIC MASSON of the Académie Française).

SHEEP OFFALS

Sheep's Brains

See Calves' Brains. All recipes valid.

Liver, Heart and Spleen

These are usually referred to collectively as 'pluck', and served as a ragoût. The following recipe is for the liver only:

Sheep's Liver, Old Crock's Spleen

We owe this recipe to Alexandre Dumas who, not content with being the Three Musketeers' father, was also the creator of many a succulent dish.

'Put some thin slices of sheep's liver in very hot olive oil. Cook on both sides for five minutes, then take out of frying pan and add to the hot oil the juice of two lemons or the equivalent in vinegar. Then add chopped garlic and some breadcrumbs. Let this sauce thicken for two minutes, then put back the liver slices and some chopped parsley. Sauté all these until liver is quite cooked, and serve very hot.'

Sheep's Tongues

Same recipes as calf's and ox-tongue. But may also be skewer-cooked or done *au gratin*, or with a Poulette sauce.

Sheep's Trotters

A LA POULETTE: Singe them, wipe over thoroughly, and cut in two, removing the tuft of hair that sprouts between the two halves. In a large saucepan, blend together a little salt, 2 oz flour, 3 tablespoonsful of vinegar, then thin with three quarts of water. Boil with a bouquet garni. Put in the trotters. The boiling time must depend on the age of the sheep. When done strain the trotters, take out the principal bone, put the rest in a sauté pan. Fill it three-quarters full with the cooking liquor from which the fat has been skimmed, and add some sliced mushrooms.

In a bowl whisk together an ounce and a half of butter, the same of flour and one egg yolk. Add some of the cooking liquor, whisking all the time. Pour this into the other receptacle and boil for five minutes, stirring continuously. Add the juice of a lemon, and serve with chopped parsley.

Sheep's Kidneys

Be sure to cut away the little membraneous bits; soak them in cold water very briefly indeed. Cut them open, making the knife incision in the rounded side, but do not cut completely in two. Push a wooden skewer through to keep them open. They may then be:

QUICK GRILLED: seven or eight minutes, with salt, pepper, nut of butter, chopped parsley.

AU GRATIN: first sauté in butter, then laid on veal and mushroom forcemeat, with fat bacon. Lemon, chopped parsley.

Or they may be cut in cubes, SAUTE IN BUTTER, saûce diluted with Madeira or Champagne.

Finally, they may be STUFFED, closed up again, larded with bacon strips, cooked in oven for about twelve minutes. Ignite with the local marc-brandy. Use fresh cream as sauce liaison.

Sheep's Tripes

Generally called, in Auvergne, where the dish is frequently served, *Les Tripoux*. The mixed tripes are used, first boiled and then cut in large square pieces. A stuffing is made of chopped smoked bacon, ham, chitterlings, parsley and garlic, and seasoned with salt, pepper and appropriate spices. The squares are stuffed with this, then refolded and roughly sewn up with thread. These 'parcels' of tripe and stuffing are packed in an earthenware dish with onions, rings of carrots, and as many herbs and spices as individual taste dictates. Dry white wine and water are poured over, then a sheet of buttered paper is put over all and held in place by the casserole lid. Then the local baker gives the dish eight hours in his oven.

At Marseille this dish becomes PIEDS PAQUETS, and here is their recipe:

Clean sheep's tripes, cut in four-inch squares, and gash one corner of each (turning it into a little 'purse'). Stuff with forcemeat made of 4 oz pickled pork, 4 oz chitterlings, some chopped garlic and parsley. Roll up and push opposite corner into gash. If you find that this won't work, sew up the 'parcels'.

'Melt' some chopped bacon in an earthenware vessel. Add some sliced leeks and carrot (sliced longways) and a clove-stuck onion. Pour in half a bottle of white wine and four pints of stock. Add a few sheep's trotters, cleaned, singed and blanched, the stuffed tripe, a bouquet garni, garlic, pepper and salt. Put lid on tightly and cook gently for seven hours.

PORK

'My Lord Bishop, I have the most profound respect for the hams of your diocese.'
(Letter from PIRON *to Bishop of Bayonne)*

'Animal-king, beloved angel . . .
(MONSELET)

'The pig, that encyclopaedic creature'
(GRIMOD DE LA REYNIERE)

The gentleman is called 'hog', the lady 'sow', the children (according to age) 'sucking pig', 'piglet', 'young pig'. Gelded pigs are the 'cochons', dead ones of all ages (unless baconers) are pork. Whatever its designation the creature is, from the gastronomic standpoint, the flower of them all.

We have mentioned already, in the section on Delicatessen (p. 35), the superb variety of dishes having a pork basis. Here again is a brief list, this time including methods and garnishes preferred:

SMALL PORK SAUSAGES: grilled. Served with chip potatoes or vegetable purées.

HOG'S PUDDING: grilled or oven cooked, or sauté in butter or fat. Served with potato purée or steamed potatoes lightly cooked again in butter. Or they may be eaten cold, in salad; left-overs, with skin removed, may be mixed with the egg-mixture for omelettes.

CREPINETTES: small flat sausages made of chopped pork and herbs, with a little Cognac. They should be grilled slowly and basted with butter, having had a light breadcrumb coating to begin with. Go well with potato purée.

PIGS' TROTTERS: usually also served with potato purée.

SAUSAGES: used as a Potée (hot-pot) ingredient and in sauerkraut, but generally grilled and dished up with potato purée, or a purée of split peas, or lentils, or haricot beans. Or served with rice (more often a chipolata accompaniment), or red or green cabbage.

N.B.—Sausages and 'puddings' should be pricked with the knife-point before being fried or grilled, to prevent splitting and bursting.

Loin of Pork

Like a loin of mutton, it consists of a row of chops. These must be roasted (without detaching) or pan-cooked, and served with any chosen vegetables. Use the good cooking juices thickened with stock as gravy.

Fresh pork is often a little dry, often flavourless. It may therefore be syringe-injected with Cognac and rubbed hard, two hours before cooking, with salt blended with such aromatic herbs as thyme, bay, tarragon.

Ribs of Pork

These are first sauté in oil, dripping or butter, then:

(1) ALSACE-COOKED: that is, with sauerkraut and stock-thickened gravy.

(2) ARDENNES-COOKED: with sauté potatoes, bacon or ham cubes, browned onions. Cooking liquor thinned with white wine, and juniper berries strewn in it.

(3) PROVENCE-COOKED: lightly pricked with garlic. Accompaniment of flap-mushrooms and tomatoes sauté in butter.

(4) MILANESE: first egged-and-breadcrumbed, then dished up with macaroni, noodles, or similar, in tomato sauce.

(5) NORMANDY-COOKED: when you turn to cook the second side of meat, add a mixture of grated cheese and cream. Thin sauce with cider-vinegar and add cream.

(6) FLEMISH: when brown, put in earthenware dish with sliced dessert apples, and complete cooking in oven.

(7) VOSGES-COOKED: complete cooking with accompaniment of onions lightly cooked in butter. Thin sauce with white wine. Serve with mirabelle plums cooked without sugar.

(8) PARISIAN: with Robert sauce (*see* p. 57) and potatoes in chips.

(9) COURLAND-COOKED: breadcrumbed and grill-cooked, then garnished with a mixture of red cabbage and twenty or so chestnuts boiled together. Serve separately a clear light brown sauce with lemon juice and chopped parsley.

Chine, Other Roast Joints of Pork

All loin recipes are suitable. These may also be cooked on the spit, but constant basting is more than usually necessary.

Hams

'Ham' and 'Jambon' seem almost everywhere to have two distinct meanings. It is a question of 'baconer' or 'porker' origin as often as not. The rolled and specially treated shoulder joint, salted and otherwise preserved, is the ham of the cooked meat shops, or the farmhouse chimney. But the name is also given, and incorrectly, to fresh legs of pork—a 'jambon' being made to correspond with 'gigot'.

These pork legs, however, salted and smoked according to varying formulae of great regional importance, form an interesting catalogue in most pig-eating countries. I give a 'short list' from France:

Bayonne Ham: eaten raw; Toulouse ham; and the Brittany, Auvergne, Morvan hams. Some are salted only, some smoked, some also eaten either cooked or uncooked.

England has, among others, Wiltshire and other 'county' hams and the esteemed York ham, eaten as a breakfast ham or served as 'Smoked Ham with Leeks' or with several sauces.

Parma Ham is the best-known Italian version. It is a first-class hors d'œuvre ham, and one of good texture for dicing into risottos, 'Italian pastes', etc. Prague Ham, like York, is poached and served in various culinary specialities. Mayence gives another ham most often eaten uncooked.

FRESH HAM (or GAMMON): braised and served with the cooking fat as sauce basis. Different vegetables as garnish. It may also be baked and the sauce is then diluted with Madeira or white wine, and a good accompaniment is a *macédoine* of fresh vegetables with some of the same sauce added, but with cream as well.

HAM IN MADEIRA SAUCE: you begin with a brine-pickled ham which you must de-salt by steeping it in water for two days and nights. Then wrap it very tightly in a linen cloth and put in large stewpan, covering with water and adding savoury herbs. Cook for three hours. Then take off the linen cloth and remove the rind of the ham on the

HAREL'S PET PORKER

In 1850 Harel, who was director of the Odéon, kept in his house in the rue Madame a handsome little piglet which he loved so dearly that it was allowed to sleep in his bedroom. Oddly enough, the writer Jules Janin (who had a pet goat) lived in the same house: so did the actress Mademoiselle Georges, with her tom-cat; so did J. de la Salle, with his pug. These last three were constantly complaining of the noisy grunting of Harel's pig and one day, when he was out of town, they got together and slaughtered it.

Two days later, Harel returned; and he and the rest found themselves at Janin's table confronted by an endless variety of pork confections. 'Smells good,' said Harel, as they took their places. But as sausages succeeded hog's pudding, and so on, and when a superb piece of roast pork came to table, he began to wonder. The crime could be concealed no longer. Harel, hearing their confession, shook his head slowly, nodded approval. 'Poor creature,' he said. 'I loved him, true enough. But never so much, I think, as today. He was never more attractive, I must say.'

PUDDINGS FOR CHRISTMAS

Now mince your onions finely—finer yet!
Then fry them gently with their weight of bacon;
They must not brown, but mildly seethe and sweat
To primrose yellow, tossed and turned and shaken.
And when their piquant odour floats away
In fragrant wafts, the pig's blood joins the pan
With salt and pepper, nutmeg, spices, bay,
Add, last, a glass of Cognac, if you can.
In the cleaned casings, one end stitched and sealed,
Enclose (and ram it down), your sausage meat.
Tie them; and next, to simmering water yield
For twenty minutes, over moderate heat.
Then drain, and place them in the hearth, hard by
The flaming, crackling Yule log, where they will,
If supervised by your paternal eye,
Gently, so gently, grill.

ACHILLE OZANNE

convex part, leaving a deep collar of rind surrounding the bone. Transfer ham to a braising pan and pour in half a bottle of Madeira. Cook for half an hour in the oven, quite often basting with the wine. This is served separately as sauce.

N.B.—Madeira Ham needs some such 'green' accompaniment as braised lettuce, leaf spinach or endives.

Chambertin Ham: same as previous recipe, but any good burgundy replaces the Madeira. Surround with small glazed onions and mushrooms.

Creamed Ham: this, too, is similar to Ham in Madeira Sauce, but the braising is done with half Madeira and half Mirepoix sauce (*see* p. 60). When the ham is done and taken out of the cooking liquor, this is reinforced with half its bulk of fresh cream. The new sauce is then reduced to two thirds of its volume.

N.B.—Saupiquet: A *Saupiquet* is a creamed-ham variation of Nevers (so it usually appears as a 'Nivernaise', as does the Nivernaise speciality carrot dressing). The amiable chef, M. Lhoste, supplied this Saupiquet recipe: De-salt a household ham, remove a good deal of the fat, sauté it in butter in the frying-pan, having cut it into really thick slices. Make in another pan a brown roux, moisten with meat gravy and a little smooth tomato sauce. Add this to a 'reduction' of: a glassful of vinegar with crushed peppercorns, shallot, juniper berries, tarragon leaves. Boil the sauce mixture for half an hour, then sieve it, bind with butter, add fresh cream. Pour on ham slices.

Alsatian Ham: Braise it (*see* Fresh Ham) using as braising liquor half Madeira and half white Alsatian wine. Serve on a bed of braised sauerkraut, with plain-boiled whole potatoes.

Parsleyed Ham: An excellent dish to serve cold. Typical of Burgundy, and a favourite Burgundian hors d'œuvre at Eastertide. From many possible versions, I have chosen that of M. Rachouchot, who for many years was chef as well as proprietor of 'The Three Pheasants' at Dijon, and thoroughly well earned his years of retirement. 'De-salt a piece of Burgundy-cured ham. Blanch it for an hour, then put in cold water. Next, put it to cook in a stock made from a piece of veal knuckle, some veal bones, all the aromatic herbs you have handy, not forgetting chervil and tarragon, six shallots, and two bottles of a local white wine. When ham is done, take out and mash the meat with a fork, combining fat and lean, and pack tightly into a salad dish. Clarify the cooking liquor so that your jelly shall be of good clear appearance. When you see that it is beginning to congeal, add to it plenty of chopped parsley (a tablespoonful of good vinegar and a glassful of white wine with it). Pour thickened and congealing sauce over the ham and when set, serve in the same bowl.

Potée

A potée is a kind of hot-pot, but the word should not be applied, say, to a beef-and-vegetables mixture. It is strictly a 'pork hot-pot'. There are very many regional versions—it is a sorry hamlet that does not name its own Potée—but the base is invariable.

LIMOUSIN POTEE: A piece of pickled pork (in recipes and bills of fare, look for the name 'petit-salé') and a Milan cabbage. Put the meat in plenty of unsalted water. Boil and remove scum. Put in the cabbage, with a piece of lean smoked bacon, salt and pepper, garlic, bouquet garni, turnips, leeks, and sufficient carrots. Cook all together for about two hours, adding potatoes after 1¾ hours.

Serve with a dish-garnish of small grilled chipolatas.

SAVOY POTEE: Instead of the 'piece of lean, smoked bacon' of Limousin, use sausages and a savaloy, but add with potatoes, not before, the latter item.

AUVERGNE POTEE: Cut a pig's head (cleaned) in four to cook with 2 lb lean bacon and a piece of local-cured ham. When half an hour has elapsed, add some beans. A savaloy and potatoes fifteen minutes before dishing-up.

LORRAINE POTEE: In bottom of stewpan put plenty of pork cracklings or rinds, a white cabbage, some carrots, turnips, green beans and peas, a few haricot beans, a piece of lean smoked bacon, a smoked 'blade', a Lorraine sausage, a half-cooked pork fillet (roast). Cover all these with stock and cover with lid, cook for three hours. As usual put in the potatoes only fifteen minutes before end of cooking-time.

ALSACE POTEE: A hot-pot of various vegetables, including celery, and a smoked ham, cooked for an hour and a half. Add garlic sausage, potatoes.

N.B.—Some people, especially those of poor digestion, will find it advantageous to blanch the cabbage separately, not adding it to the potée until it is well advanced.

An Economical Choucroute

Proportions: Two pounds of choucroute, ½ lb garlic sausage, 10 oz lean bacon, 4 oz lard, 4 slices cooked ham, 12 juniper berries, 2 carrots, 1 onion, a bouquet garni, ¼ pint white wine, salt and pepper.

Wash the choucroute (sauerkraut, pickled cabbage) in two waters, drain it, squeeze in your hands to remove more water, then spread it on a table napkin and disentangle some of the knots and complications. Prick the sausage and put it in clean cold water with the bacon (this may be smoked or unsmoked). Boil, keep on the boil for three minutes only, then strain away the liquor.

Grease well a cast-iron pan or an earthenware dish, using all the lard (or goose-dripping could replace it). If you have one or two scraps of pork crackling, put them in the bottom. Now make a layer of one-third of the choucroute. Top it with the garlic sausage and the bouquet (tied with the juniper berries in a little muslin bag). Moisten with a small glass of white wine or with stock.

The next layer consists of another third of your cabbage. Spread over it slices of bacon (smoked or white, but this time really salt). Add the carrots, cut into fours lengthways, and the onions cut in rings. Cover with the rest of the cabbage and fill the vessel three-quarters full with white wine or water. Boil over fire or gas-flame, then cook in oven for four hours.

Pork Offals

A list of the principal ones with their uses, and their names as they appear on Bills of Fare:

LIVER (LE FOIE): its principal use is as a forcemeat ingredient, but it may also be prepared in the same ways as calves' liver.

BRAINS (LA CERVELLE): is dressed in the same way as lambs' or calves' brains.

HEART (LE CŒUR): as sheep's heart.

HEAD (LA HURE): used for potted head, brawn, or 'head-cheese' as it is called in the U.S.A.

TONGUE (LA LANGUE): prepared like calves' tongues.

LUNGS, LIGHTS (LE MOU): may be used in 'jugged' dishes, stews, ragoûts, but there's not much to be said for the practice.

EARS (LES OREILLES): when not made part of the various 'pig's head' dishes, may be grilled, broiled as trotters are broiled, or even stuffed in the same way as, oddly enough—the

TAIL (LA QUEUE)!

TRIPE (LES TRIPES): stomach, etc. Used in the making of 'Andouilles' and 'Andouillettes' (large and small chitterlings-sausages).

And last, KIDNEYS (LES ROGNONS): which are usually treated as veal kidneys. However, here is a different possibility, an invention of Gustave Pignot. It is named

Dijon Kidneys

The pig's kidneys are sliced so that the veins, etc., may be removed. They are then very lightly tossed in melted butter over a low flame for two or three minutes to sweat out the superficial but unpleasant odour. This will taint the butter, which must be thrown away. Use enough butter, this second time, to cook the kidneys through, but they should still be red. The only way to achieve this is to turn them constantly and cook for no more than five minutes. Pour champagne over them, set it alight, then put them on a plate to keep warm.

Now add to the butter in which they were fried some skinned tomatoes (or tomato purée if tomatoes are hard to get), a little more butter, and a glass of port wine, some chopped parsley, salt, pepper, some fennel-flower. Allow all these to reduce. Add a tablespoonful of white mustard and two of aromatized mustard. Cook on for ten minutes and you will have a smooth, thick sauce in which you put the kidneys to simmer—but they must not boil. (Remember that they must still be rose-pink when they come to table, not overdone and rubbery.)

In the serving dish make a liaison of two well-beaten eggs and pour the sauce over this drop by drop, stirring all the time, vigorously, too. Put in the kidney pieces and sprinkle with freshly chopped parsley.

THE ART OF USING UP LEFT-OVERS

This *is* an art, madam. For if you simply serve them as undisguisedly-that-which-they-are, you will hear that 'it's always the same old thing in this house'. A little imaginative treatment makes all the difference and enables you to show your husband yesterday's meats in an entirely new dress, thus keeping him happy without much outlay.

You may prefer them that way, too.

Generally speaking, left-over meat shows up well in a salad, either with a vinaigrette sauce and plenty of parsley, or with ordinary mayonnaise. Moreover, you could mince this meat, or make a meat pie, croquettes, meat balls or rissoles, meat-and-potato cake. Be sure, though, if you find it rather dry, to add some sausage meat or even fat bacon. Several kinds of meat may quite well be minced together. Season generously, add an egg-yolk if you like, as well as a hint of garlic. Or milk-soaked bread.

Baked in a buttered or greased tin or mould, a fairly rich 'forcemeat' of this nature also makes quite a good meat loaf to serve with salad or potato salad. Either deep- or shallow-fried meat-balls, croquettes, rissoles, etc., are all the better for a home-made tomato sauce accompaniment.

A final notion—Parmentier Mince (or meat-and-potato cake) is made by sandwiching your mince between two layers of potato purée in an oven dish, sprinkling with grated gruyère cheese, dotting with butter, baking gently. This may be eaten hot or cold.

In Savoy, the remains of a leg of mutton are used for making 'Agnelotti'—local name. This recipe for them is supplied by M. Henri Bordeaux, of the Académie Française:

Savoy Agnelotti

Make a pastry crust with flour, salt, a little water and two eggs. Prepare also a plateful of minced meat, using for choice (and traditionally) the meat left on a leg of mutton earlier enjoyed. Cook this for a few minutes with some fresh butter, a little clear meat broth (consommé), a pinch or two of flour. Let it get cold. Roll out dough, and using a teaspoon, cover its surface at regular intervals, and leaving a dough surround each time, with little piles of meat mixture. Put your second piece of pastry on top, and use a liqueur glass to cut out the Agnelotti (or little round pastry and meat sandwiches).

These must now be poached for twenty minutes in boiling consommé, then taken out of liquid, drained, and put on a presentable oven-dish, with butter. As each batch is added to dish, sprinkle with grated gruyère cheese mixed with pepper. Mix consommé and meat gravy (two-thirds of former, one-third of latter) and cover dish with this. Brown in the oven for three-quarters of an hour.

It is most important that the pastry should be rolled out extremely thin.

Vegetables

FRESH VEGETABLES

Vegetables are indispensable to good health on account of their unique constituents, which does not mean that you are called upon to become vegetarian. There are three groups to be considered: fresh vegetables being taken to include: (*a*) dried vegetables, (*b*) green vegetables, (*c*) cereals and such derivatives as 'pastes', semolina, etc. Roots, tubers and the potato, a most important item in the dietary of many, stand apart from this classification.

Cooking methods are essentially the same as for meats: grilling, stewing or boiling, steaming, braising, baking. Boiling is probably the commonest method of cooking vegetables, even though the least desirable, for unless the cooking water is utilized as stock or soup, it carries away for ever some of the most valuable elements.

N.B.—Moreover, water that is too hard or limy is a bad medium for vegetable-cooking, and it is usual to improve it with a pinch of bicarbonate of soda.

Naturally enough, vegetables are most often thought of as a meat accompaniment or a fish-dish garnish, but they are capable of serving as dishes in their own right. But as few of them are of sufficiently pronounced flavour not to need a little assistance, it is usual to take extra trouble with their presentation and seasoning.

If financial considerations, or matters of regime, dictate entirely vegetarian meals, it is clear that more time, more thought and even more imagination must be devoted to the preparation of such meals than to others embracing a wider range of ingredients.

Potatoes

It is only reasonable to begin with this staple vegetable, for one is really hard put to it to imagine how we ever got on without them. The general impression is that they were brought back from America by Christopher Columbus. In his report to his sovereign, written at the conclusion of his third voyage, he is said to have observed: 'Moreover, I have brought back a kind of batata with flesh not unlike that of a carrot, but not as sweet.' From Spain, potatoes went on to Italy (there was a Pyrenean barrier in those days) and then northward into Germany. But, oddly enough, they just rubbed shoulders with Savoy on the way through, for potatoes appeared in Savoy a hundred years before they were found elsewhere in France. They were known there as 'Cartoufle' (compare the German 'Kartoffel').

It was Parmentier, veterinary surgeon to the armies, who studied the potato while a prisoner in Germany. He was, at the time, working voluntarily for a doctor. He grew some experimentally, and we know the rest of the story—culminating in the potato-field anecdote. It was actually in Paris that Louis XVI fenced in his potatoes and set a guard over them, his sole object being to induce the public to steal and taste a vegetable at which they had been turning up their noses for so long.

POTATOES IN 'FIELD DRESS' (not in their 'Dressing-gowns', 'baked potatoes'): These are firm, waxy kinds, not the floury, bursting ones. Put in boiling water and cover with lid. Serve with butter, or with double cream, or anchovy purée, or herring fillets.

POTATO PUREE: This time chose floury, thinner-skinned potatoes that will disintegrate in the cooking.

(*a*) Do not attempt to make purée with the 'field dress' potato.

(*b*) Do not use much water for boiling them.

(*c*) If possible, steam the potatoes.

(*d*) Some actually *cook* the potatoes in milk.

When potatoes are cooked through, put them through potato-masher. Thin them with

(1) their cooking water (not recommended);

(2) milk;

(3) meat gravy. When, of course, the flavour will be utterly changed.

The more vigorously, the longer the purée is beaten, the better it will be. Add butter, salt, pepper, a little grated nutmeg. Other helpful supplements are fresh cream and egg-yolks.

P.S.—Never waste any purée not used for its original purpose. You might sprinkle with grated cheese (in oven dish) and serve very hot with a salad of lamb's lettuce.

Or you could proceed in the same way, but 'stuff' the purée by separating it into two layers and sandwiching (*a*) some cooked salad left-overs, (*b*) some minced meat, (*c*) onion purée.

Or, finally, you could form it into croquettes, very highly spiced, with garlic added. Roll in dry flour and sauté in oil. Serve also with a salad.

SAUTE POTATOES: Cook potatoes in their skins and leave them overnight to dry out. Then skin, cut in rounds and ovals, and sauté in frying-pan with lard, butter, or even olive oil.

N.B.—Swiss Reuchtis: potatoes first cooked in their skins, mashed with fork after skinning, then sauté in the form of a cake fried golden-brown on both sides (like the English breakfast fried-potato cake, excepting that the potatoes for this were probably peeled and boiled). The Swiss Reuchti is also a breakfast dish, to be served with café au lait.

FRIED POTATOES: Peel, wash and dry the potatoes. Slice and plunge into smoking-hot fat (lard, beef dripping, oil, but use the dripping only as a last resource). Lower the flame, and when cooked and put aside, reheat the fat to smoking-point to receive not the next batch, but the same batch for a further few seconds' quick frying. Drain.

Chips: may be cut across the potato or in long strips half-a-finger through. They may also be long and matchstick narrow (*Pommes allumettes*). In a julienne of slender little rods they become *Potato Straws.* Or the whole potato may be cut spirally into a narrow ribbon: *Chatouillard potatoes*. 'Chips' of the French menu are usually thin rounds.

SOUFFLE POTATOES: see the account of their origin on p. 247. Are cut in slices about one-fifth of an inch through. When, on their first frying, they rise to the surface of the fat, drain them and allow them to get cold. Then plunge them into a second pan of frying fat—for this purpose beef kidney fat is excellent—shaking the container constantly. Take them out as soon as they are puffed-up and browned, and put on a cloth that will absorb the fat. If you wish to, or have to, they may be put into a third pan of fat.

MAITRE D'HOTEL POTATOES: Firm potatoes not inclined to cook to bits are peeled and boiled (in milk, or, more usually, water). Served with butter and chopped parsley. But the best way is to use

STEAMED POTATOES (sometimes called 'English-cooked'): A steamer is used, and the potatoes lose part of their seventy-eight per cent. water content. They are more digestible and more nourishing.

POTATOES AU GRATIN: Rub oven dish with cut garlic and butter it. Put in raw, sliced potatoes. Add salt, pepper, grated nutmeg, grated gruyère cheese (plenty of this). Moisten with boiled milk (to which a beaten egg may be added). Sprinkle top of dish with parmesan, dot with butter, cook in a gentle oven for three-quarters of an hour.

POTATO SALAD: Season while the sliced cooked potatoes are still hot. Use white wine, not vinegar, which has a drying effect. Serve with plenty of parsley and any accompaniment you like (beef chops, meat left-overs, herring fillets, beetroot, celery, etc.).

ROAST POTATOES: A form of sauté *raw* potatoes. Put butter, oil, or (better), small lardons of bacon in a casserole. New potatoes should be small ones left whole. Old potatoes should be cut into small cubes.

For the reason given under 'Steamed Potatoes', this is a good method, as much of the water evaporates as they bake in the oven.

Goncourt Potatoes

Pork dripping in frying-pan, potatoes cut in rounds are par-cooked, then seasoned with salt, pepper, basil, laurel. Two seed-free tomatoes added. Cover with water and cook at lively heat.

Serve with these a young cucumber (raw, naturally) cut in chunks (peeled first).

(Recipe from LEO LARGUIER of the Académie Goncourt.)

Potatoes with Bacon

Use bacon fat or fat bacon or lard to brown some cubes of very *lean* bacon. Take out the cubes and brown some onions in the fat. Place with the bacon cubes. Use the fat and a little flour to make a thin roux, and dilute with stock (or water, if you have no stock) and add either tomato concentrate or two fresh tomatoes. To this sauce add potatoes cut in quarters, salt and pepper, a bouquet garni, the onions and bacon. Cover and cook at moderate heat.

Marcel Grancher Potatoes

Fry potato quarters in plenty of butter, and when these are tender and golden brown set them in a dish with salt and pepper and ample quantities of *fines herbes* (parsley, chervil, tarragon, chives, chopped shallots). In the little butter left in the frying-pan cook very briskly a mixture of fresh cream and egg-yolks. Stir as it thickens (cooked, it would curdle). So remove from heat before it curdles, and pour over potatoes.

Duchess Croquettes

Choose steam-cooked, floury potatoes. Make into a purée, with butter and salt added. Add also some thick cream and egg yolks (in the proportion of 4 oz cream and 4 egg yolks to two pounds of potatoes). Make the purée-paste up into small, short 'sausages' about two-thirds of an inch in diameter, flouring your hands first. Fry light brown, preferably in butter.

N.B.—Two ounces of parmesan cheese may be added to the paste.

Sweet Croquettes

Bake or boil in their skins some floury potatoes. Cut in two lengthways and spoon out the interiors, then pass these through sieve. Butter a sauté pan with plenty of butter, and put the sieved potato in it, and stir constantly as some of the water content evaporates. Keep it in motion with spatula. Add caster sugar.

When smoothly blended, pour in a very little orange-flower water. Spread the potato 'dough' on a floured board. Form into 'bottle-corks'. Mix a beaten egg with a tablespoonful of oil, season with salt, dip the 'corks' in this and roll in breadcrumbs. Drop into boiling frying fat. Serve hot, sprinkled with sugar, vanilla-flavoured previously.

Stuffed Potatoes

Peel some large, uncooked potatoes. Cut out a hollow in the middle of each, butter the inside surfaces, fill with stuffing, arrange side by side in oven dish or pie dish, cook in slow oven for three-quarters of an hour.

The stuffing to consist of the potato removed from the hollows, chopped with meat scraps and sausage meat. Or of chopped raw ham. Or meat with milk-soaked soft breadcrumbs. Or a *duxelle* of vegetables. Or a mushroom forcemeat.

Whichever stuffing you choose, it must be highly seasoned, and each one needs onion, if not a little garlic. Grated cheese is an improving final addition.

Further ways of serving potatoes: IN VARIOUS STEWS;

HUNGARIAN FASHION (i.e. with paprika); CREAMED; with a Béchamel sauce or tomato sauce.

* * *

SWEET POTATOES (PATATES) and JERUSALEM ARTICHOKES (TOPINAMBOURS)—the former with a pronouncedly sweet taste—may be treated as potatoes. But it is a useful plan to take advantage of their semi-sweetness and make them into fritters.

Artichauts (Globe or Leaf Artichokes)

'. . . *This is, perhaps, more subtle of flavour, more delicate of texture, than any other green vegetable. Besides, it's fun to eat!*'

CURNONSKY

' . . . *Apricots you must buy,*
Cool melons, summer's artichokes in plenty,
Cream, strawberries, that all my fare be dainty
Under this blazing sky.'

PIERRE RONSARD

' . . . *These glorified thistles!*'

(The elder PLINY)

Rabelais mentions these vegetables, alleged to have an aphrodisiac quality, but for which healthful and nourishing qualities can certainly be

THE TRAIN WAS LATE—POMMES SOUFFLÉES WERE INVENTED

Soufflé potatoes . . . and there's nothing quite like a soufflé potato . . . were an accidental discovery, dating from the inauguration of the very first railway in France—the line from Paris to Saint-Germain.

There was a banquet to celebrate the occasion, of course, and fillets of steak with fried potatoes comprised one of the dishes to be served. But the 'official train' was held up and the unhappy cook had to remove his fried potatoes from their boiling fat and set them aside to drain—and, alas, cool.

When Louis-Philippe and Amélie his queen at last took their places at table, the cook could only replace his cooked potatoes in the re-heated fat, prepared for any kind of ghastly outcome. But the result was spectacular. The 'chips' at once puffed and swelled like fritters . . . delicate, digestible, light as air. . . .

'Pommes Soufflées' *had been invented.*

GASTON DERYS

COUP DE GRACE . . . OR INGENUOUS LASS?

The other day a friend of ours was telling us about his great-uncle. The old fellow had just been informed by his doctor that he had probably only a few hours longer to live, so he at once ordered for himself some foie-gras and a cauliflower in cheese sauce. A young woman who happened to be present was quite outraged. 'I never heard of such a thing!' she protested.

'Indeed, yes!' agreed the Vicar, also at hand. 'At so solemn a moment, when he was about to be called into the presence of the Supreme Judge of us all, to be thinking of stuffing himself with food!'

'That's not what I meant,' said the critic in her gentle voice. 'It's just that I can't bear *cauliflower in cheese sauce.'*

claimed. When presentation is important, it is usual to serve the hearts only, usually styled 'artichoke bottoms'. The leaves may be used at another meal or, if kept on during the cooking process, spooned off, puréed, and used in any stuffing you may be making. Young artichokes may be eaten raw, in a VINEGAR DRESSING, or

Artichoke Remoulade

Chop and pound sorrel, chervil, parsley. Blend, in mortar, with raw yolk of one egg, bread soaked in milk, a few tablespoonsful of olive oil, salt and pepper. Juice of a lemon. Stir, bind thoroughly.

This *remoulade* for raw artichoke dressing may also be used with cooked ones. (Another Remoulade recipe appears in the Sauces chapter, on p. 56.)

Barigoule Artichokes

Partly cook in water, take out at about three-quarters-done stage. Separate leaves, pull out the 'choke' and replace with a stuffing made from grated bacon, chopped mushrooms, parsley, shallot, and so on. Bard and tie up each artichoke and complete cooking in oven-dish (covered casserole) with a bouquet garni and some carrot rings. Moisten with white wine. Leave in oven about three-quarters of an hour. Unfasten ties, serve in some of the cooking liquid.

N.B.—Either a meatless stuffing or one made with left-over meats will serve.

Greek Artichokes

Cut leaves of young artichokes at 'choke' level. Discard 'choke' or 'hay' portions. Soak leaves in lemon juice and garnish with an onion purée. Put in casserole with diminutive onions and some very young white beans. Season with salt, pepper. Just barely cover with water. Cook for twenty minutes. Then add six or seven tablespoonsful olive oil. Complete evaporation of the water in very hot oven, with lid off. Served cold.

Lyons Artichokes

Quarter the artichokes. Clip off the tops of the leaves and discard the 'choke'. Put butter, salt, pepper in pan and gently cook artichoke quarters therein.

Toulon Artichokes

Trim leaf edges, remove 'choke', season them raw with salt, pepper, grated nutmeg, powdered bay. Melt some lardons in olive oil in earthenware casserole, with chopped onions, a clove of garlic; then add artichokes and submerge in a liquor which is two-thirds meat stock and one-third white wine (e.g. Cassis). Add two tablespoonsful tarragon vinegar.

Cover with soup-plate or hollow-arched lid and cook in very slow heat for five to six hours.

(Recipe from the writer HENRY KISTEMAECKERS)

Artichoke Bottoms

These may be served either with melted butter and parsley or in the various garnishes mentioned incidentally. They are also good with tomato sauce, a Béchamel, meat juices and gravies. They may be variously stuffed, with or without meat. Typical stuffings: spinach; chestnut purée; risotto; onion purée; asparagus tips; tomatoes.

Purée of Artichoke Bottoms

Crush them and beat olive oil into them with a fork. Add a flavouring of garlic and the juice of a lemon, with salt and pepper.

Asperges (Asparagus)

'. . . *And if anyone had eaten asparagus, people would have pointed him out as a curiosity; but nowadays young maidens are as shameless as court pages . . .*'

FURETIERE: *Le Roman Bourgeois*

But those were the old days. It is usual now to serve only the 'tips', served at the ends of their stems. It is best to peel, not scrape, then cook for about twenty minutes in salted boiling water. They may then be eaten very hot, fairly hot, or cold, with these sauces: vinaigrette; melted butter; white; mayonnaise; rémoulade; mustard; Tartare; and so on.

N.B.—Asparagus comes in 'white', 'violet' and 'green'. To each his own, as they say, but I prefer the green, 'Lauris asparagus'.

Aubergines (Egg-plants)

This plant (we eat its fruits) was originally Indian. Various kinds are now fairly commonly grown throughout the Mediterranean basin. This explains why so many recipes for it mention the use of oil. Aubergines may be braised, fried, sauté, cooked with stuffing.

Egyptian Aubergines

Slit lengthways and fry in oil until half-cooked. Take out the pulp without spoiling the shiny purple skins. Chop the pulp and an oil-fried onion and replace in the skin. Put in an oven-dish, cover with dashes of oil, complete cooking. Before taking to table put on each half-aubergine a ring of fried tomato. Sprinkle with parsley.

Oriental Aubergines

Cut in six pieces one aubergine for each person. Fry. Reshape each aubergine but between all the adjoining slices insert a forcemeat of chopped mutton, garlic, parsley, onion, soaked breadcrumbs. Cook in dish just wide enough to take them, steeping in oil, for half an hour.

Turkish Aubergines

Same formula, but serve with a dish of rice, plain-boiled, and a sauce with red pimento.

Brazilian Aubergines

Slit in four lengthways. Gash them, rub in pepper and salt. Leave for three or four hours. Throw away the water that has run out, roll them in dry flour, sprinkle with Cayenne pepper, fry until outsides are crisp in a little oil. Then take from pan and in same oil put some seed-free tomatoes, a little garlic, parsley. Mash with fork as they cook, adding Cayenne pepper, and turn this thick sauce on to the aubergines, which will have been kept hot. Reheat all together in oven.

Chilean Aubergines

Fry very young ones whole. Cook separately, until about half-done, some rice (boiled in water). Drain this, and fry in butter until tender. Mix with aubergines. Season heavily with allspice.

Peruvian Aubergines

Halve them, leave in salt to exude some of their water. Cook on griddle plate. Pimento to be added generously. Sauce to be made with olive oil, parsley, lemon juice.

Freebooters' Aubergines

Blanch in boiling water several whole aubergines, then submerge in a sauce of Cayenne peppers and sweet peppers, with oil and aromatic herbs.

(The seven preceding recipes are given in M. R. DE. NOTER's book mentioned on p. 274.)

Creamed Aubergines

Cut longways in two, without skinning. Take out flesh and chop it. Mix with a thick white sauce and grated gruyère cheese, adding pepper, salt. Fill the aubergine skins and set in buttered oven dish. Cook for a quarter of an hour.

The aubergines may also be stuffed with ham, bacon, sausage-meat, meat left-overs, mushroom purée.

COURGETTES (small, compact-fleshed marrows): are very much like aubergines and may be similarly treated. They combine in the

RATATOUILLE OF NICE: a famous southern dish. The following items are sauté, but *separately*, in olive oil (different cooking for each vegetable): sliced aubergines; sliced marrows; sweet peppers; tomatoes freed of seeds; onions. Say about half a pound of each. In a deep oven dish pile one on another as cooked. Add salt and pepper, a few blanched basil leaves, a tablespoonful of olive oil, a mere dash of lemon juice. Bake for a quarter of an hour.

Betteraves (Beetroots)

These are generally bought ready-cooked for use in salads as hors d'œuvre or to be combined with larger green salads (especially of corn-salad or lamb's lettuce). It is a good idea to sprinkle them first with grated horseradish. Other ways:

—English-cooked: boiled, dished-up with butter.
—In Béchamel: baked (enclosed vessel) after boiling and masking with sauce and buttering dish.
—Creamed: as before, cream replacing Béchamel.
—Lyons: with slices of onion.

Another CREAMED BEETROOT recipe: Cut into rounds of even size raw beetroots and potatoes. Cook in very little water, with a few large onions, some salt and pepper. When done, set them in 'succession' in a hot dish and thicken cooking water with a flour liaison, adding fresh cream. Add sauce and serve.

Bettes (Chard, Spinach-Beet)

Sometimes written 'blettes'. Leaves may be used as a cooked salad, or with spinach, or (only a few at a time) in soup. The ribs may be blanched in boiling salted water for about ten minutes, then served with butter; or gratinated; or with a Béchamel; or with tomato sauce, or cream, or meat gravy.

Carottes (Carrots)

Usually boiled, then served:
—English-style: with fresh butter handed separately.
—With melted butter poured over, sprinkling of parsley.
—In Béchamel.
—Creamed.

But, like so many vegetables, carrots are better cooked without water if young and tender enough.

Carrots and Savoury Herbs

Blanch for five minutes. Cut longways and cook the carrot-sticks in butter in a sauté pan. When quite done, add chervil, parsley, chives and a little tarragon (all finely chopped).

N.B.—Some even add a little sugar, but carrots have plenty of natural sweetness.

It is also possible to make *Carrot Jam.* A Hindu recipe for this suggests ten pounds of carrots cut in cubes, two pounds of sugar, cooked for five hours in nine pints of milk. Eaten frozen. You might care to try it, some time. . .

Cardons (Cardoons)

'*Artichokes, but only the stems are eatable.*' (CURNONSKY)

Quite good eating, though, once they have been rigorously cleaned and prepared. Cut in pieces, wash and scald these, then pull out all stringy parts. Rub with lemon juice to prevent blackening. Boil in water into which a little flour has been smoothly blended. Bring to boil, stirring until they are bubbling. Then cover with lid and leave to simmer for two hours.

Cardoons are served: with butter; in cream; with savoury herbs; fried in batter (after the previous lengthy cooking, of course); Greek style (*see* Greek Artichokes); au Gratin; in gravy; with marrow. And so on.

Celeri (Celery)

Sticks of celery. The tender young shoots are useful as a salad. The rest is washed, stripped of the coarser fibres, blanched, then prepared in same ways as Chard, Cardoons, Carrots. Celery is like cardoons but of less delicate flavour.

Celeri-Rave (Celeriac) Purée

Also called turnip-rooted celery. Use the celeriac with yellow-fleshed potatoes in the proportion of 2 lb celeriac to 12 oz potatoes. Blanch celery only for ten minutes. Put a little butter in the bottom of a saucepan, with onion quarters. When just showing transparency, add the blanched celery and the raw potatoes cut in fours. Cover with salted water. Add a bouquet garni. Bring to boil and remove scum that rises. Put lid on, cook gently for half an hour. Drain, pass through sieve, make into purée with a little boiling milk and some butter.

Served with fried bread cubes.

Concombres (Cucumbers)

'*Taylers' Holiday, when they have leave to Play, and Cucumbers are in season.*' (CANTING CREW).

Usually eaten raw (often after lying under a weight and with a rubbing

FONTENELLE WAS FOND OF HIS FOOD

. . . and most of all, he loved asparagus in oil.

One day, the Abbot of V. came to see him and stayed to dinner. The abbot, too, was an asparagus-worshipper, but he liked his in a prepared sauce. Fontenelle went down to his kitchen and asked his cook to serve half of the bunch of asparagus in oil, and half in sauce. Then he went back to resume his literary discussions with the old man.

All at once the latter, seized with a sudden illness, fell to the floor. Straightway Fontenelle bolted toward the kitchen, yelling, 'The lot in oil! The lot in oil!' Then he came back to render aid.

This is an oft-repeated tale. But it doesn't explain why Fontenelle Asparagus is a melted-butter preparation:

ASPERGES A LA FONTENELLE: *Dip each of your cooked asparagus tips into melted butter and then into a soft-boiled egg (using the asparagus, as it were, as a bread sippet).*

'GRATIN' OF DAUPHINE

The 'Dauphinois' of Paris have taken their native dish, the 'Gratin', as aegis and device, their poets write verses to praise its virtues; and in days gone by, one of them went so far as to enshrine its recipe in a sonnet:

Gratins, fresh-cooked, are regal nourishment
And, in our lands, a dish of high esteem,
Eaten by all, day in, day out, supreme
Winter and summer through, and even in Lent.

No complications, no perplexing theme
For this. In flattish pan your complement
Of sliced potatoes. Then embellishment
Of eggs, salt, garlic, butter, milk and cream.

And that's enough to make a handsome dish,
But if the perfect cook is what you wish
As well, deft-fingered, mistress of her art,

Look for some carefree girl with grace, finesse,
And beauty—and a true-born 'Dauphinesse'
And, if you can, contrive to win her heart.

MAURICE CHAMPAVIER

of salt to extract some of the water). May also be cooked and served: with butter; with cream; stuffed; fried.

Parsleyed Cucumbers

Slice coarsely several green cucumbers into a saucepan with salt, pepper, 2 oz butter, 4 lumps sugar. Cover with water. Bring quickly to the boil, then with lid on pan cook more gently for half an hour. Then remove lid and reduce liquor to the consistency of a thick syrup. Serve with plenty of chopped parsley.

Crosnes (Chinese Artichokes)

Or, it is said, of Japanese origin, and first grown in France at Crosnes, in the Seine-et-Oise department, whence the name.

Excellent when very fresh (as shown by whiteness). To clean it, shake it vigorously in a piece of heavy linen, with plenty of coarse salt. Then wash and blanch in salted water. May be served in salad, with butter, with herbs, meat or poultry gravy, etc.

Velouté-Sauced Crosnes

Make an 'ivory roux' (which means that the flour must not have time to brown as it cooks gently with the butter). Add stock and let this sauce cook on, uncovered, for twenty minutes, with a clove and a pinch of nutmeg. Add a walnut of butter to the reduced sauce, put in the Chinese artichokes, add salt, pepper and chopped parsley.

Choux (Cabbages, Sprouts)

'Cabbages! Cabbages, frozen through!
Melt in your mouth like morning dew!'
Old Paris street cry.

'If you intend to drink copiously at a banquet
and to attack all that offers with keen appetite
first eat some raw cabbage pickled in vinegar,
as much as you think will do the trick.'
CATO

Preliminary Observation: It usually pays (unless you are short-cooking, and unless you are dealing with a young spring cabbage) to cook it in two waters. There are many varieties, and we are concerned mainly with the white (sauerkraut cabbage), the green (hot-pots, minestrones, soups), the red.

Braised Green Cabbage

Line bottom of stewpan with larding scraps of bacon, add quarters of cabbage, salt, pepper, grated nutmeg, an onion stuck with cloves, a large carrot, a bouquet garni. Pour some meat stock over, add a few more lardons, and bring to boil. Put lid on pan, then put it in oven for an hour or two to cook slowly.

Creamed Green Cabbage

Cook and drain a green cabbage and cover it with Béchamel, sprinkle grated parmesan over it, leave in oven for five or ten minutes.

Chestnut Cabbage

Blanch a cabbage.

Skin, and boil in salted water, a dozen large chestnuts with the same number of small sausages about as long and as wide as the chestnuts (the prescription takes for granted the sympathetic co-operation of your sausage-seller).

Cut out the cabbage heart and put in its place the cooked chestnuts and sausages. Tie up the cabbage and cook in meat gravy or thick stock —briskly for the first quarter of an hour, then at gentle heat. Serve (with fat skimmed away from sauce). Drink white Mâcon with this.

(Recipe from the actress LUCIENNE REAL)

Stuffed Green Cabbage

Wash the cabbage and blanch it (whole) for fifteen minutes. Then put it in cold water. Pull off the leaves one by one and drain. Reconstruct the cabbage, lining the inside of each leaf with a layer of stuffing (any one you like, remembering that this is an excellent way of using up meat). Tie up the re-made cabbage and braise in the same way as the 'Braised Cabbage' of three recipes ago. May be served hot, with a sauce of the reduced braising liquor, or cold.

Cabbage Salad

Cut into a fine julienne, blanch for ten minutes, drain, dry in a cloth, season with vinegar.

Flemish Red Cabbage

Cut the red cabbage into strips and the strips into small pieces. Put into saucepan containing a tumblerful of red wine, add a tablespoonful of vinegar, half a pound of raw potatoes cut into small cubes, a large sliced onion, some bay, a good lump of butter.

Cook for at least three hours, sweeten with brown sugar. The amount of sugar varies according to family tastes.

Palm Cabbage

Cut into a julienne of thin strips and left in salt for twelve hours to 'scour' it. Eaten in salad with mustard. Or with a Béchamel, lemon juice and Cayenne pepper.

Brussels Sprouts

Cooked soft or nut-crisp (to your taste) in salted water. Served:

—English-style: with separate fresh butter.

—sauté: finished in melted butter after careful draining.

—creamed: butter-braised after semi-cooking and covered afterwards with fresh cream.

—au gratin: butter-braised after semi-cooking, covered with parmesan, browned in oven.

—in gravy.

—cold, as salad ingredient (fully cooked first).

—with bacon: semi-cooked, then browned with lean bacon strips; sprinkled with parsley.

Choux-Fleurs (Cauliflowers)

Same principles apply as for Brussels sprouts. Cauliflower is first cooked in salted water, then served: English style; or butter-sauté, then masked with Béchamel; with Mornay Cream, Hollandaise, Tomato sauce; black butter; au gratin; or in salad with a vinaigrette dressing, a Tartare, Rémoulade or Mayonnaise sauce.

N.B.—The stump, thick ribs, coarse leaves detached from ribs, should be cooked at the same time and used later in soups, even if you require only the 'flower' for the dish in hand.

Soused Cauliflower

Detach the separate 'flower' clusters and cook them in salted water for ten minutes. Take out and drain. Aromatize some vinegar, add an equal amount of white wine, and complete the cooking in this. Put into an earthenware dish, cover with olive oil, and wait 24 hours before serving.

Champignons (Mushrooms)

'. . . *Voluptuaries who, with amber knives and silver plates, prepare their mushrooms with their own hands.*'

PLINY

' . . . *There are two kinds of mushroom, the poisonous ones and the others. The difference is generally perceived too late.*'

ROBERT DE GICEY

Mushroom hunters without the true instinct or the fungologist's expert knowledge should refer all doubtful specimens in their 'bag' to the experts before cooking. The alternative is to buy cultivated mushrooms, called 'of Paris' in France, and 'forced' in England.

Mushrooms (Field or Forced)

Remove the rubbery skin and boil for five minutes in a little salted water containing the juice of a lemon and a little butter. (This liquor should not be thrown away, as it is a useful basis of several sauces.) Drain. The mushrooms may then be:

—Stuffed (incorporating their stems in the filling).

—Used in salad (with vinegar or mayonnaise dressing).

—In omelettes.

—In patties, or vol-au-vent cases, with Béchamel.

—In Poulette sauce ('German sauce', i.e. with chopped parsley).

—Creamed. Of course they enter into many garnishes as well.

They may also be sliced raw (rubbing cut edges with lemon juice to prevent blackening) then grilled, or shallow fried in butter. Other possibilities are:

Madeleine Decure Mushrooms

Cook as described above. In a separate pan have some breadcrusts soaking in a fifty-fifty mixture of stock and white-wine. Season with salt and pepper. Cook, then strain liquor, adding some butter and an egg so as to obtain a really thick sauce. Rectify seasoning. Add sauce to the mushrooms and sprinkle with a 'mimosa' of hard-boiled egg yolk.

Catalan Mushrooms

Make a court-bouillon with an onion coloured in olive oil, four cloves of garlic (crushed), a bouquet garni, salt, pepper, a gill of white wine. Add the washed and dried mushrooms. Boil for five minutes and leave to get cold. Drain and serve. (The cooking liquor will serve as a good soup stock, adding meat stock and some form of Italian paste.)

Viennese Mushrooms

Blanch some mushroom caps in stock, then soak them in a thick fritter batter. Fry and serve with a mayonnaise containing chopped herbs, or a similar sauce.

Mushroom Matelote

Boil for half an hour some red wine and aromatic herbs. Cook for five minutes in this stock some whole mushrooms. Add one glass of *fine champagne* and boil up again. Thicken sauce with 'worked' butter. Let it boil again all together for a minute. If possible, serve with eggs poached in red wine.

(Another DR. POMIANE recipe)

ALL THE ABOVE RECIPES ARE FOR MUSHROOMS IN GENERAL, BUT CEPES (FLAP-MUSHROOMS), GIROLLES (CHANTERELLES) AND MORILLES (MORELS) HAVE, AND DESERVE, THEIR OWN PARTICULAR RECIPES, SOME OF WHICH ARE:

Flap-Mushrooms, Cèpes

These may well be called 'vegetable meat', their country name. They are fine, round-bellied mushrooms which need to be eaten very fresh, and they must be carefully inspected for mushroom worms. They are cooked: BORDEAUX fashion, PROVENCE fashion.

Bordeaux Flap-Mushrooms

Peel, wipe dry. Chop up stems and if heads are very large cut into 'bias' slices. Warm a small glassful of olive oil in a sauté pan. Cook the heads in it at a brisk heat, then lower flame for ten minutes, cooking on until they are nicely browned. Put into a vegetable dish.

In a frying pan with some fresh oil, smoking hot, put the stems (chopped) and some chopped shallots, salt and pepper, to sauté for five minutes. Add to vegetable-dish contents and sprinkle with chopped parsley.

Provence Flap-Mushrooms

The preparation is similar but instead of shallots, chopped onions and garlic are used.

Other methods: grilled at low heat (previously daubed with olive-oil); Béarn-cooked (i.e. with bits of garlic inserted in their flesh, like a leg of lamb).

Chanterelles

Appear as both 'Chanterelles' and 'Girolles' on French banquet menus. Cook as 'Flaps' but the most delicious way of using them is inside an omelette.

Morels

These should be washed in several waters, slightly acidulated with vinegar, for they seem to collect grit. On the other hand, too many washings spoil the aroma. Is there any way out of the dilemma?

If you are using dried morels or morils (those with rounded, instead of pointed, ends) soak in water for several hours. But they, too, need careful washing, and it's obviously impossible that they should have the same aroma as freshly-gathered specimens.

A preliminary to all other preparations is slow, 'enclosed' cooking in butter (heads halved if over-large).

Creamed Morels

Put into saucepan or, better still, an earthenware casserole, a piece of butter and your morels. Add a half-glass of stock and the juice of a lemon. Mix flour and butter smoothly in a small basin, add fresh cream. Blend thoroughly. Put this in with the mushrooms and cook without letting the contents boil.

Morel Pastry

Cook as before (enclosed) in butter, with salt and pepper, adding the juice of a lemon. Cook at good heat, then draw to side of hot plate to simmer. Make a white roux, allow it to get cold. Bring to boil a pint of fresh cream (whisking it all the time, or it will curdle) and pour over the cold roux. Then allow this cream sauce to thicken over gentle heat for half an hour, diluting it finally with the mushroom-cooking liquor. Put in the morels. If you think it necessary, first strain the sauce through muslin.

With the mixture fill pie-crust flan or vol-au-vent case.

Truffles

The truffle is the diamond of *cuisine*: a black diamond, certainly, but of what pure ray! And Brillat-Savarin, psychologist of food lore, was not over-lyrical when he wrote that 'The truffle is an indispensable element of cookery on the grand scale, which is a luxury and an art, simultaneously.'

These precious jewels 'mined' from the soil of France (there are, indeed, a few white ones in Piedmont and Morocco) seem to be, as it were, the fragrant heart of Périgord. Is it mushroom? or fruit? or vegetable? Even the botanists cannot agree as to definition. It lies concealed under the roots of certain 'green oaks' (called variously 'holm oak', 'holly oak', 'ilex') and we are only just beginning to understand the mysterious laws of nature that dictate its appearance in the heart of the wasteland, under grey and purplish stones, where clumps of these oaks are established. These truffle beds—whether of Drôme, Ardèche, the Cevennes, or, of course, Périgord—are smelt out by pigs or by dogs, according to locality.

Robert-Robert, poet and gourmand too, has written: 'The truffle smells of the earth, it smells of the rugged holm-oak; it has the bay-laurel's heady odour, the scents of mastic-tree and creeping thyme. I believe that I prize this fragrance more highly than the truffle itself . . . when truffles lend their bouquet to a fine, fat Dauphiné turkey, or a Languedocian guinea-fowl; or mottle a block of golden brawn, or speckle a brandade's cream!'

A diamond, yes. And at almost as prohibitive a price.

Endives (Endive, Broad-Leaved Chicory)

> *Endive, named also escarole or scarole, or 'bitter lettuce', is valued more for its medicinal qualities than any others. It is not much grown in gardens, because it is always bitter. However, if it is tied and covered with fine sand during the winter, it will become tender and white.*
>
> CHARLES ESTIENNE

A salad ingredient, of course, but it is also a very palatable vegetable, though all too often cooked in water, or braised, whereas the following method is much to be preferred.

Put endive, or chicory, in casserole with butter and the juice of a lemon. Cook (with lid on) for 45 minutes. They may be more bitter this way, but with a wholesome, acceptable bitterness, and none of their value washed away. They may be served: with black butter; cut into quarters (once cooked as described), dipped into batter, and fried; au gratin (and, if you like, put a slice of ham over the endives before adding the grated cheese).

Epinards (Spinach)

First wash. Then re-wash. Then wash again.

Then blanch rapidly in a great deal of boiling, salted water. Next, refresh in cold water. Drain, and squeeze out the water. Cook in covered vessel with butter. It is a very frequently used accompaniment or garnish, purée form being preferred, but it should be served more often than it is

TELL ME WHAT YOU EAT . . .

A few years ago, the Gallup Institute tried to discover which foods and drinks the average American, Frenchman, Englishman, Swede, and Dutchman would choose if given unfettered choice of the 'ideal meal'. Here are the results of this enquiry:

AMERICAN MENU

Fruit and shrimp cocktail
Vegetable soup or chicken broth
Steak with potato purée
(or chipped potatoes)
Green peas
A green salad
Bread, butter
Apple tart
Coffee

FRENCH MENU

Assorted pork-meat hors d'œuvre (sausage, ham, tartlets, etc.)
Roast chicken
Green peas, runner beans
(or Brussels sprouts)
Cheese
Fine pastries
Wine, Coffee.

ENGLISH MENU

Sherry
Tomato soup
Plaice or sole fillets
Stuffed chicken with sauté potatoes
Green peas, Brussels sprouts
Fruit jelly and cream
Coffee, white wine
Cheese and biscuits

SWEDISH MENU

Smorgasbord
Broth
Veal cutlets
Vegetables
Fresh fruits
Coffee
Beer or Schnapps

DUTCH MENU

Hors d'œuvre
Vegetable soup
Roast beef
Potatoes baked in the oven
Vegetables
Chocolate pudding

as a leaf vegetable, when its full flavour is more pronounced. It may then be served with butter handed in a separate dish. Or with meat gravy. Or cream.

If you want it as a separate course, spinach au gratin is a good answer. Or pancakes, the basis being half pancake-batter and half chopped spinach. Or croquettes (two-thirds spinach purée, one-third potato purée).

N.B.—All such recipes will serve equally well for cooking 'New Zealand spinach', and with very slight modifications, for Sorrel.

Oseille (Sorrel) Purée

Half-fill a capacious stewpan with water and in it soften some sorrel, then drain it thoroughly. Make a blond roux and thin it with stock. Put the sorrel into this, with as much sugar as you yourself need to temper its sharp flavour. Cover, leave at low oven heat for two hours. Pass through sieve, and use as sauce liaison butter, or cream, or egg yolks, as convenient.

Fèves (Beans)

These podded beans, when fresh, may be eaten, with no other addition than salt, as hors d'œuvre. If they are broad beans, or butter beans of a certain age, remove tough skins. They are cooked in boiling water and eaten: with separate butter; creamed, or with cream; in salad; as purée; in stews. And a few may always be added to soup. Or juliennes.

Fenouil (Fennel)

This is harvested as a bulb in the Midi and it often grows wild in France and England. If you are using the bulb as a vegetable, blanch for five minutes before braising or cooking in casserole in butter. Served creamed, au gratin, or with meat gravy.

Haricots Verts (Green, French, Kidney, Runner Beans)

All cookery books, and all cooks, will tell you that the various types of green bean must be cooked in boiling salted water then served: with butter (English fashion); maître d'hôtel (i.e. with parsleyed butter); au gratin; in gravy; sauté in oil or butter, with garlic added; in salad, with tomato sauce.

But believe me, if you get hold of any that are newly gathered and very tender, wipe them without washing, put them in a casserole with two tomatoes, an onion, a bouquet garni, salt and pepper. And, it should be needless to remind you, some good butter. Put on the lid and cook thus, with no water, in a slow oven. The flavour will be vastly superior.

All kinds of beans removed from their pods (red, green, or white) and dried for future use are dealt with later, under the heading 'Dried Vegetables'. But such beans, unpodded but still fresh, are cooked without the soaking prescribed for dried ones.

Navets (Turnips)

Usually a hot-pot or stew vegetable, but the young and tender spring turnips should be cooked in the same ways as young carrots, and served with butter, or creamed, or with herbs. They are braised to accompany roast duck. Young turnip greens cooked as spinach are an English discovery.

Large turnips may be stuffed (after ten minutes' blanching) either with a mixture of the turnip pulp and potatoes or with a mushroom *duxelle* (*see* p. 60); or a forcemeat of any suitable kind would do nicely.

Oignons (Onions)
(a note from Dr. Pomiane)

The onion began by being a god. In Egypt's antiquity it had the same hierarchic status as Isis and Osiris. It later occupied an intermediate position between mortal man and eternity. Onions were sealed into sarcophagi to enable deceased to pay for their journeyings in the devious byways of the underworld.

But the Egyptians did not invent the onion. They had to go out and look for it, and they found it somewhere in the region of Baluchistan, Afghanistan and Kurdestan. It is still to be found there, growing wild.

So the Egyptians, then, worshipped it. The ancient Hebrews, more realistic, ate it as though they were gods themselves. And when they left Egypt somewhat hurriedly, they bitterly deplored their loss of the aromatic bulb. In later epochs the Greeks rejoiced in it, so did the Romans. Garlic had a similar history. However, certain guests at Xenophon's feast complained that every single dish had garlic in it. One Nicitas contrived to eat so much of it that Charmide made a jest of it, saying that he did so merely in order to prove to his wife, by the unpleasantness of his aura, that he had not so much as dreamed of kissing any other woman while separated from her.[1]

Whatever its drawbacks, the onion is an indispensable food and a remedy for many ills. Apart from its culinary uses, it has its medical history. To begin at the end of this, onion has, in the course of centuries,

[1] Compare the reply made by Marguerite of Navarre (Queen Margot) to Catherine de Medici, when her mother was urging her to divorce Henry IV: 'How then could I act like that woman of ancient Rome who, when her husband reproached her for not having warned him that his breath was bad, told him that she had imagined it to be the same with all men, since he was the only one she ever came near to.' (*Author's note*).

been credited with curing hepatic ascites, cirrhosis of the liver, alcoholism, diabetes, cancer of the liver.

I think that in all such claims of marvellous therapeutic powers, one must accept partially and reject partially. But we ought to ask ourselves how solid is the basis on which such claims rest. And, obviously, this basis is the chemical composition of onion-juice and its peculiar curative qualities.

The onion contains a little fat, much sugar, and a variety of nitrogenous elements. It contains a glucoside which, when acted upon by a soluble ferment, found in the bulb, is transformed into strongly aromatic onion essence, more or less acceptable to various noses. This essence contains allylic sulphur. None of these substances accounts satisfactorily for the onion's curative properties. But the presence of such sugars as glucose, laevulose, accounts for its usefulness in the creation of 'caramel' for roux and brown sauces.

But we almost always forget, in this matter, to go back and consult Pasteur's pioneer findings. By 1858 that brilliant investigator had established that onion juice checked completely the growth of yeasts and lactic ferments. But once boiled, it lost its destructive power over microbes' development. This bacteria-inhibiting property of onion juice might well be the first-discovered item in the so recently developed story of bacteria-inhibiting substances such as the sulphonamides, penicillin and streptomycin.

So it seems that there's nothing new under the sun, in culinary art or in medicine. And it is a fact that in our history of humanity, brief as it is, the onion is the oldest known vegetable.

Parmentier Onions

Cook in plenty of salted water two pounds of onions, reducing to a purée. Make separately a potato purée (same quantity). Thirdly, make a thick Béchamel. Mix all together and serve.

Stuffed Onions

Stuff them raw, removing centres, with a left-overs stuffing. Put lardons of bacon or pork in a casserole and gild onions on all sides, then cover with lid and cook for about an hour. Dilute cooking liquor with water or stock, add fresh cream to it, pour over onions and serve.

Fried Onions

Cut large onions into thin slices that will fall into rings. Let these soak in milk, flour them, fry in deep, hot fat. Fry parsley to go with them.

Glazed Onions

Choose small, even-sized onions. Put in pan with a little butter and cook to a light brown over gentle heat. Then add some good stock, and leave to reduce. If you like, add a little sugar.

Queenly Onion

Take a really mighty onion, stick many cloves into it, and cook gently in water with a bouquet garni. When reduced, add a glass of Madeira. Serve with a white sauce with capers in it. If any cooking liquor remains, use in making the white sauce. But it is better that none should remain.

Onions with Garlic

Blanch some Spanish onions and some cloves of garlic. Core the onions. Pound the onion middles in mortar with garlic, salt, pepper, olive oil. Stuff onions with this and put in oven in a buttered plate or dish.

Greek Onions

Follow 'Greek Artichokes' recipe (p. 248).

Cream of Onions

Gild some pieces of onion in oil. Cover with stock, cook gently, for at least half an hour, with lid on. Sieve. Add two tablespoonsful of cream of rice dissolved in milk (one glassful). Whisk. Put this 'cream' in a casserole, sprinkle with parmesan cheese, add dabs of butter and gratinate for a quarter of an hour.

This 'onion cream' may be served with chipolatas, slices of beef left over from earlier meal reheated by shallow frying, and so on.

Panais (Parsnips)

This mediocre vegetable is used for feeding cattle, and occasionally human beings.

ROBERT-ROBERT

Carrot and turnip procedures will do for parsnips. And there is:

Parsnips in Sauce

Wash some large but tender parsnips and blanch them for half an hour in boiling water. Cut in 'fillets' and place in stewpan with some good butter, a bunch of parsley, chives, some garlic, shallots, cloves, basil. Add salt, pepper and a pinch of flour, and some good strong stock.

Leave to cook in the reducing stock. Take out bouquet of herbs.

Thicken sauce with egg yolks and milk and add a dash of white vinegar before pouring it over parsnips and serving.

This recipe is an invention of the court chef, La Varenne, and was much appreciated at the royal table, according to our learned friend, the gastronome Hervé de Peslouen.

Green Peas

Green peas, green peas, green peas,
As tender as you please . . .

Song of DRANEM

FRENCH GREEN PEAS: Put a little butter in saucepan, add the peas, a few small onions, two young lettuces. Salt, pepper. A bouquet garni. Melt butter without browning. Add water.

HALT! We now come to a difference of opinion. Some say cover with water and boil hard to evaporate it. Others say, a few tablespoonsful only. And I am with the latter group.

But in either case, cook with the lid on. As soon as the peas are done, take out the bouquet and add, away from heat, some nice fresh butter.

POLISH GREEN PEAS: Equal quantities of carrot rings and peas cooked in water in covered vessel. When this has evaporated add butter and fresh cream. Mix all together and reheat, but mixture must not come again to boil.

ENGLISH GREEN PEAS: Put peas in boiling water, with a sprig of mint if possible. Strain cooked peas in colander and serve with shells of butter.

TURKISH GREEN PEAS: Cook in casserole for a long, long time at gentle heat. Put onions, peas, cubes of mutton, a clove of garlic, a glass of water in the covered casserole. Cook some rice separately and do not mix in until just before eating. Add a tablespoonful of olive oil over the top, unless the mutton was on the fat side.

BASQUE GREEN PEAS: Cook in saucepan in lard (better still, goose dripping), adding seed-free tomatoes, sweet peppers and cubes of raw ham.

NORMANDY GREEN PEAS: These are 'French Green Peas' to which you add, just before serving, cream combined with egg yolk.

FLEMISH GREEN PEAS: Spread over wide pan base 4 oz carrots (new ones) and cover with cold water. Season with a little salt. Add a generous tablespoonful of butter. Cook, covered with plate or lid, until almost all the moisture is gone. Add 8 oz green peas and cook on until they are tender.

N.B.—The sweetness of peas cooked in these ways will be augmented if a few of the pods are tied into a little bunch and added while they cook. Sugar-peas or string-peas, that are not stripped of the pod, may be cooked in the above ways.

Leeks

'. . . *Poor man's asparagus* . . .'
La Sagesse des Nations

The green part of leeks is usually left for soup. The white is thoroughly washed (cut fairly deep as the grit and earth are surprisingly deeply embedded) and boiled in water. Seasoned to taste:
—With a vinegar dressing (hot or cold); in Béchamel; au gratin (in which case, mix grated gruyère cheese with the Béchamel, and sprinkle the same on top before putting in the oven; Indian style (with onions in the white sauce and, especially, curry. Also a few drops of lemon juice; in tomato sauce (garlic included); or creamed.

Flamiche

A kind of savoury cake that is a favourite in Picardy. Put sliced leeks in pan with some melted butter (use the white of leeks only). Add salt and pepper. Cook slowly. Make a pastry with flour, two eggs, salt, melted butter. Knead it well and roll it out, but not thinly. Butter a pie-dish and line bottom and sides with the pastry. Mix a raw egg yolk with the cooked leeks. Spread over the pastry. Cover top of leek pie and seal edges with water. Bake golden-brown.

Salsifis (Salsify, Scorzonera)

There is just one drawback to salsify: they are hard to clean. Not many people can tell you offhand that the true salsify is white and that black salsify should be called 'Scorzonera'.

The young stems are fine in salad. They smell like hazelnuts. As for the roots . . . scrape them, wash them, cook in salted water, with lemon or vinegar to acidulate it, for at least two hours. Serve them: in Béchamel; fried; with butter; with gravy; creamed; in salad; sauté, with herbs; as purée; in fritters; in Provence fashion (i.e., with tomatoes and garlic).

Salad Vegetables

We deal later with salads in general. But most salad vegetables may also be presented as a vegetable dish, cooked in water, or braised, or

CLOSE, A HARBINGER

Contades, Marshal of France, was given a command in Alsace, and there he stayed from 1762 to 1788. He had brought with him his chef, named Close, a native of Normandy. It is Close who had the idea of giving his employer a treat, and enclosing some foie gras in a little warm overcoat of chopped veal before encasing it in a cuirass of golden pastry—thus creating the pâté de foie gras. And, as Charles Gérard said, he also gave it a soul by inserting a few Perigord truffles.

Contades left Close behind when he said farewell to Strasbourg in 1788, and the chef married a pastrycook's widow and settled down, now supplying on a commercial scale the famous pasties previously reserved for the Marshal.

TRIPLE ALLIANCE STRAWBERRIES

A great gourmet was the Marquis de Cussy, whose recipe this is. He used to blend strawberries with vanilla-flavoured cream and champagne. But he always ate copiously of this confection, and the 'triple alliance' of flavours was a formidable challenge to delicate digestions. Therefore it was his practice, when he had ordered this dessert at home, to content himself with a comparatively meagre meal: soup, sole fillets, a quail, and some asparagus of distinguished quality. This consumed, he was given his strawberry mousse—I'd forgotten to mention that fruit, cream, vanilla and champagne were beaten and pounded together.

A FINE ESTABLISHMENT

'Does Mrs. X keep a good table? Did you dine well?'

'Does she what? If the soup had been as warm as the wine, if the wine had been as old as the goose, if the goose had been as plump as the hostess . . . well, it wouldn't have been too bad.'

ARMORIAL BEARINGS

Alexandre Dumas senior was a very discriminating eater, but often, alas, his pecuniary embarrassments dictated scanty fare.

On one of these days of embarrassment his son suggested that an appropriate heraldic device for him would be 'Beaucoup de gueule sur peu d'argent.' (It sounds like respectable 'gules' and 'argent', but possible (and obviously proposed) renderings are 'large appetites supported by very little money', or 'wide mouths, narrow purses'.)

'steam-baked', the method depending on relative tenderness. They may be chopped small or served as whole leaves; it is a matter of taste.

Cooked salad is usually an accompaniment, even a sustainer, of poached eggs, small grilled sausages (sippets added), meatless stuffings. Those who find unadulterated spinach or sorrel too acid in flavour might combine cooked salad with these.

Beet leaves or turnip tops may also be so used.

Tomatoes

Used as a vegetable, tomatoes are usually stuffed:

(*a*) with a blend of sausage-meat, hard-boiled eggs, chopped garlic and parsley.

(*b*) with cooked rice (done in meat stock) mixed with aubergine pulp and garlic.

(*c*) with a mixture of risotto and ham dice.

(*d*) with a mixture of minced meat scraps and milk-soaked bread.

(*e*) with a mixture of sliced mushrooms and truffles.

Or, indeed, with a mixture of these mixtures.

The raw tomato is emptied and light pressure is applied to get rid of excess juice. The interior is seasoned with salt and pepper, stuffing added, tomatoes are set on oiled oven-sheet, a drop of oil is put over them, and they roast for about fifteen minutes.

Fried Tomatoes

Scald them first to loosen skin, then remove skins, cut in slices, add pepper and salt. Dip in batter and drop in boiling fat. Drain and serve with fried parsley.

Tomato Ragoût

Cut small tomatoes in fours, sprinkle with salt, put in colander to drain. Put butter, lard or olive oil in pan, fry a few onions golden in it, together with some strips of lean bacon. Cook the tomato quarters gently next (with no lid on pan) and add a tablespoonful of flour, another of spirits, another of white wine, and some stoned black olives. Thicken sauce with butter.

Tomato Sauce

This may be purchased ready for use, but whenever possible the good housewife does without the preserved item and prepares something fresh at home. It takes time, but it is not wasted time. To make tomato sauce cook gently in butter in a closed vessel some very finely chopped carrots and onions, in equal amounts, totalling about 4 oz. Add 4½ lb quartered tomatoes—'pressed' to reduce juice content and relieved of their seeds. Put in salt, pepper, bouquet garni, two tablespoonsful of caster sugar. Bring to boil, stirring constantly, then put in covered pan to finish cooking in the oven (a slow oven) for about two hours.

Sieve the sauce. Reduce in saucepan (no lid) over a good heat. Stir all the time with a wooden spoon.

Tomato Gratin

Oil an oven dish. Put half-tomatoes (squeezed and drained) on it, seasoning them with salt and pepper. Put all around them finely chopped parsley, garlic, chives, and on top golden bread raspings and grated parmesan. Brown in the oven.

Tomato Conserve

You need really to be a country dweller if you are to make this. In a great cauldron put 22 lb tomatoes without seeds, 2 bundles of celery cut up small, 20 onions, 20 bay leaves, 3 cloves of garlic, 10 cloves, peppercorns, a pound of butter. Fill to half-way up this accumulation with water or white stock, and boil for four hours. Pound and sieve. To the liquor obtained add a basin of flour, half the quantity of caster sugar, some salt. Cook this reinforced liquor for a further two hours, then pot it and seal hermetically.

One Last Word on Fresh Vegetables

Let me repeat once more that for fresh, tender vegetables, newly gathered, there is nothing to beat waterless cooking. And the best garnish in summer for almost all meat dishes, even those in sauce, is a VEGETABLE JARDINIERE (mixed garnish of vegetables in season). A good *jardinière* will contain as great a variety as possible, cooked in casserole (enclosed) in butter. Begin with those that need longest cooking time—carrots, young turnips, stick of celery, green beans and peas, fresh 'seed' beans, onions, new potatoes, tomato quarters, a few lettuce leaves. The variations are infinite. Add some lardons, a hint of garlic, cream, brown butter, meat gravy, to your whim.

In summer, add a vinegar or mayonnaise dressing. If any left-overs are on your hands, add to water and stock (or even tinned soup if you have no fresh stock) and your soup will be excellent.

DRIED VEGETABLES

Haricot beans excepted, these are almost as old as time. Lentils were known to the Egyptians, chick peas were part of the ancient Roman's daily dietary, and the later dried beans (butter beans, etc.) were, as age succeeded age, now the staple food of the poor, now the special preserve of the wealthy.

These are the cheapest of all the nitrogenous, or leguminous, foods. They are, moreover, very rich in albumin, and consequently the highest in calories.

Haricot Beans

The older, the harder, with these beans. Whatever your plans for them, you must soak them overnight in cold water in a cool place. Then wash them in several waters before boiling (in cold water to start with. Add a small amount of bicarbonate of soda to the water, then salt, bouquet garni, garlic. When tender, drain and use as you please. You may be using ordinary white beans or green 'flageolets' (small, unpodded kidney beans) or red haricots. Each has its special uses as a garnish, but all may be served in these ways:

—in salad (with herbs and onion).
—plain-boiled, with butter served separately.
—au gratin (blended with veal gravy, sprinkled with breadcrumbs, browned in the oven.
—Breton style (reheated in their original cooking water, served with salt butter and parsley).
—purée (with a little cream and some grated nutmeg).
—with tomato sauce (also garlic or onion).
—with bacon (three-quarters cooked and finished off in casserole with bacon strips).

Ardeche Haricots

Three-quarters cook in water (as described above). Cook in a saucepan in olive oil, quite gently, some unchopped onion and garlic, then add beans. Pour in a glassful of stock and white (dry) wine (half-and-half mixture). Put on a lid and cook slowly until beans are tender.

Take out beans with pierced spoon. If sauce is thin, reduce it. If too thick add stock. Skin some hogs' pudding and stir it into the sauce with a wooden spoon, adding a tablespoonful of vinegar. Pour this over beans and sprinkle with parsley before serving.

Red Beans in Wine

Cook in half-and-half mixture of water and red wine, adding some blanched fairly lean bacon. Remove and drain beans. Put them with the diced bacon and some butter into a sauté pan. Reduce the cooking liquor and add to it a glass of red wine. Blend butter and flour and use these to bind the wine sauce. Pour over beans.

N.B.—Don't waste the bean water—at least, not all of it. For if you have any beans left over you can put them through a sieve, add to bean water, add cream, butter, or tomato purée and serve this soup with fried bread dice.

Lentils

'*These X-word puzzle lentils.* Ervum Lens
(Shortened, of course, to Ers)
—These specimens
Cost Esau's birthright, sana *though his* mens.'
(ABELUT, local poet)

The very tiny brownish ones are best. Pick over, soak in cold water, as with haricot beans, and put them in cold water with a little bicarbonate of soda. Boil until tender. All the above preparations are suitable, but better still are:

Lentils with Bacon

Cook them in the minimum of water, with a piece of smoked bacon. Then make a roux with an addition of bacon scraps and small onions, and add to the cooking water. Put with the lentils.

Roman Lentils

Cook them in rain water with pepper and cumin, and when three-quarters cooked, braise them in water with a little vinegar in it, also sage, mint, parsley, saffron.

(Recipe from *Ten Books of Praiseworthy Luxury*, 1567)

Peas

Dried peas are usually found in the form of 'split-peas', and are as often as not served as split-pea purée. They are soaked only long enough to soften them, then boiled (in cold water to start with) for a good hour and a half, with a bouquet garni. (And a pork bone or two, if you think necessary). Pass through sieve, add butter, serve with sippets.

Chick Peas

Provide an excellent basis for bacon soups. Must be soaked for the whole of the day before cooking, then put in cold water with a little bicarbonate of soda and cooked for twenty minutes. Change the water, putting them this time into boiling water with spices and bouquet garni. Seasoned with tomato, garlic and parsley. Or if they are to go in a salad, with olive oil.

Rice

As an energy creator, rice takes some beating, as it has a rating of about 1,600 calories to the pound. But it has several deficiencies (e.g. of protein, fat) and it would be sheer stupidity to base a family's dietary on rice for the simple reason that it is a staple food for some races.

There are several kinds of rice but all of them are of oriental origin. Within the last few decades rice has been grown in Italy (Piedmont) and even in France (Camargue).

It is no exaggeration to say that most French and English housewives are failures as rice cooks and as macaroni, etc., cooks too. Rice dishes have all too often the appearance and consistency of the geologist's magma or the kennelman's mixture for feeding his hounds.

This is why:

Rice grains are surrounded with a thick surface layer of starch. When cooked in water this turns into glue. This glue sticks the grains together.

How can this be avoided?

There are two methods:

(*a*) Cook the rice in so much water that its volume diminishes the strength of the starch.

(*b*) Cook the rice in so little water that when the rice grains have absorbed it, none is left over to dilute the starch.

The second method appeals to the author more strongly than the first. For the reader's interest, here is an extract from a little book by M. R. de Noter, *Good Colonial Cookery*. The subject is Annam rice.

'The rice is cooked in steam from boiling water, after careful preliminary washing. It is put into very little water indeed, just enough to keep the rice from sticking to the bottom of the pan.

Then the heat is increased and the cooking time should not exceed twenty minutes from the moment when more heat was applied. This cooking period is so precise that the Annamite peasant treats as a unit of time the number of minutes required for the cooking of a pot of rice. He also says, here and now, "To get to such-and-such a place you need the time it takes to cook one—two—three—four—pans of rice." He is speaking invariably in multiples of twenty minutes.

The water must be salted. The rice grains, when done, must be whole.

Rice cooked thus tastes better than rice cooked by our usual methods. It may be eaten with any dish you choose. The Annamites make it more savoury by adding a fish sauce—which we can replace by a meat sauce or curry sauce.

The method does, of course, demand a certain amount of practice, for it is easy to put too much or too little water. Either mistake is practically

PILAU

Because of the beard that encircles his face
The Turk spurns all soups and has put in their place
The PILAU *that's solid, and not to be feared*
As it's decently swallowed in spite of a beard,
Since broth's oily traces, he rightly protests,
Are apt to disgust the more mannerly guests.
So it's broth for the beardless, it's soup if you shave,
It's none for the man whom his whiskers enslave.

But listen, you shaggies, you're easily able
With pilau's pure gold to illumine your table:
Get a pound of good rice at the shop of Chevet
(It's north of the Louvre and hard by the Palais.)
—Levantine for choice, if his stocks will permit
For rice grown in Egypt is sullied with grit;
On hot, glowing cinders seethe gently a dram
Of water, some beef, not much veal, and some ham,
A fowl in her prime, that has fed at her ease
On wind-wafted seeds in the blossoming leas.
Six hours of slow cooking will mellow the lot
To a savoury stew. Add your rice to the pot,
To cook for an hour. Then shake in as a relish,
Some delicate saffron to gild and embellish,
And thus, such a pilau our art will devise
As the Prophet himself might consume in the skies.

(This Rice Pilau recipe furnished by the poet-gastronome MERY)

fatal. But once your period of trial and error is over, you will quite confidently assess the amount of water which your rice of the moment requires for its cooking.'

Rice Pilaf

Melt some butter or fat in your saucepan, add a few onions cut in rings (they must not brown) and your rice (unwashed). Mix and stir around for a bit with your wooden spoon, then add one and a half times the bulk (of pan contents) of salted water or boiling stock. Bring to boil, put lid on and go on cooking for ten minutes. Then take off lid and cook until liquid has completely evaporated.

White Rice and Rich Rice

This is the Annamite rice exactly. When drained, season with butter. The rich rice, or rice with a meat sauce, is white rice as before with an equal bulk of good beef broth, reheated in the oven.

Creole Rice

Put the rice in a capacious pan with a good deal of boiling water in it. Boil, with the lid on, for twenty minutes. Taste for tenderness, and as soon as the rice is soft pour contents of pan through a large strainer, rinse the rice in warm water, and dress with a sauce flavoured with saffron and pimento.

Risotto

Cook an onion, without browning it, in butter. Add rice and toss and shake well so that every grain is well soaked in butter. Add one and a half times bulk of hot stock, in several instalments, waiting each time for the rice to absorb what has already gone in. Cook with lid on, for fifteen minutes. When ready, add butter and grated parmesan.

N.B.—These 'mother-recipes' have, if one dare say so, one or two variants. It is possible to add to the risotto pieces of bacon, diced ham, tomato sauce, chopped garlic, saffron, a few green peas, mussels, mushrooms, and so on.

To Creole rice, pieces of crab meat (or similar) might be added.

Here is a recipe given by the dramatist DENYS AMIEL:

Valenciennes Rice

In a casserole (preferably earthenware) bring to the boil some olive oil—and it must be olive oil—and cook in it some salt breast (bacon). In my part of the world, the Midi, they use ham (cambazzon), neither too fat nor too lean, cut into small cubes. Chop some onions and a clove of garlic, a red pimento, a ripe tomato, salt and pepper, and cook all this in the same oil. When you have a kind of smooth, thick sauce put in some unwashed but well cleaned rice (rubbed in a cloth). Sauté for a few seconds only. Then three-quarters fill the pan with boiling water slightly flavoured with any good meat extract.

Before this you have done several things: cooked a chicken; boiled some mussels; cooked a crawfish. This last, and the chicken, are chopped into pieces and the mussels are mixed with these. Add to the first affair just described. Sprinkle some saffron or curry powder over the dish—I prefer saffron, as it's more characteristic of the South—and leave all to cook together for half an hour.

And that is Valenciennes rice. I advise you to drink with it a bottle of Vouvray; or, better still, a Johannisberg, a Rhine wine.

Here are three variations of this concoction supplied by Buffet managers as follows:

CERBERE (Monsieur Deleon): Make a sauce with a mixture of rabbit and poultry offals, put in a sauté pan, add green peas, artichoke hearts, and one cupful of rice per person. Mix all well together and add boiling water to equal three times the volume of rice. Cook for about twenty minutes.

MONTPELLIER (Monsieur Ribes): Cook half a pound of rice in boiling water (salted) for eighteen minutes. Drain and dry in gentle heat. Cook two pints of mussels in their own water, remove from shells, season with vinegar, olive oil and mustard dressing (using plenty of mustard). Add two coarsely chopped tomatoes and a tin of tunny fish crumbled into small bits. Put the rice in a ring with the mussel salad in the middle. Serve cold.

HENDAYE (Madame Courrèges): Make a court-bouillon with onions, bay-leaf, bouquet garni, pimento. Add to it a gurnard, six (Dublin Bay) prawns, a few slices of crawfish, a score or so of mussels. Take them out when done and strain the court-bouillon. In the frying pan cook gently some diced ham and a few slices of chorizo (a very highly seasoned Basque-country sausage), the wings and legs of a chicken and some nice lean bits of veal. When almost cooked take out of pan.

Put 10 oz rice in the frying pan, stir into the cooking medium in pan, then cover with the stock. Cook for a few minutes then add to the meat and fish and complete cooking in the oven.

Rice of the Eight Wonders
(Chinese recipe)

Wash rice thoroughly and put it to cook in quantities of boiling, salted water for twenty minutes. Take out of the water and sauté in frying-pan for five minutes with two tablespoonsful of olive oil or groundnut oil to every half-pound of rice. Also a bare ounce of very finely chopped onion,

2 oz each of the following five ingredients: smoked ham, pork fillet, soya-ham, soya-sauce, mushrooms. An egg. Simmer gently for a quarter of an hour, then serve.

Rice and Fish
(Japanese recipe)

If the fish is very fresh, it must be cooked in court-bouillon, then placed on a long dish, on a bed of plain boiled rice (already cooked). If you are using dried or salted fish (cod, tunny, herring, sardine, anchovy, etc.) take out the bones, pound fish to a smooth paste, and blend with the boiled rice. This dish is both appetizing and nourishing.

Rice Purée
(Malay recipe)

Wash the rice thoroughly and grind it in a coffee-mill, but one kept for rice only. Take a volume of water equal to the volume of rice before grinding (about 4 oz water to 3½ oz rice).

Salt the water to your liking, boil it, throw in the ground rice when it is boiling steadily, then cook over gentle heat for 30 or 40 minutes. You will obtain in this way a rice purée which will form, as it gets cold, a solid block that can be used as though it were bread.

P.S.—If salt is replaced by sugar an inexpensive cake results. It may be served with, for example, gooseberry jam.

(The three preceding recipes are M. DE NOTER'S)

Fried Rice

Take plain boiled rice, add butter and egg yolks, also a little parmesan. Form into croquettes and fry them in boiling fat. Serve with tomato sauce.

Other rice dishes useful as sweet course or dessert dainty will be found in Chapter XVI.

ITALIAN PASTES AND KINDRED PRODUCTS

'*A melodious dish of macaroni, golden as a guinea, aromatic as the Orient, copious in its flow as the ambrosia of Olympus; a macaroni all compact of drinkable sunbeams gave the dinner an illustrious opening, like the Semiramis overture.*

MERY

FRESH PASTES: Break three eggs into an earthenware dish. Add a little salt, beat the eggs and pour in flour, stirring at first and, as soon as it is possible, kneading with the fingertips to obtain a homogeneous paste.

Roll out several times with the rolling-pin, then leave it to harden somewhat for an hour (having rolled it out as thinly as possible and covered it with a cloth).

Now divide the paste into several portions and roll each very thinly indeed (½ cm at the most) and cut into thin strips. Once again leave to dry for an hour. Now put the strips into salted boiling water and let them just bubble (no fierce boiling) for a quarter of an hour. Drain away the water and dry off the rest by placing the strips in a buttered and seasoned sauté pan over low heat.

N.B.—The three eggs may be replaced by six yolks (or even eight).

DRY PASTES: The cooking is of primary importance. The paste pieces must be firm and slightly brittle, not in the least soft. To achieve this, throw into plenty of salted boiling water (they would stick together in too little) and keep them on the boil for just under fifteen minutes. Then drain and wash in hot water to get rid of every trace of starch (but if you are preparing them in advance, better to wash them in cold water which will arrest the cooking process) and proceed according to the recipe you are following.

The different treatments of cooked 'paste' are:

—simple addition of melted butter.
—browned in butter.
—with grated gruyère or parmesan.
—with meat gravy.
—with tomato sauce.
—au gratin.
—with cream. And so on.

They may be combined with:
—button mushrooms (sliced) in butter.
—ham cubes (or bacon, pork).
—truffle flakes.
—stoned olives.
—pickled shrimps, mussels, etc.

Some paste-products may be stuffed (e.g. rectangular ravioli and tubular canelloni). Some delicatessen shops have them for sale ready-stuffed. Or you can make your own stuffing from meat left-overs or, failing these, from spinach (and the result's excellent). They may be covered with tomato sauce, or with a Béchamel, and sprinkled with grated cheese or breadcrumbs before finishing in the oven.

Here are a few more 'paste' recipes.

Creamed Noodles

Cook and drain noodles, mask with a sauce made with butter and cream (half-and-half) and then cover with breadcrumbs and brown in the oven.

Alsatian Noodles

Use freshly-made noodles. Keep back a couple of ounces and cook the rest in a great deal of water. Drain, then replace in hot saucepan on a gentle heat to 'evaporate' the rest of the water.

In a frying pan melt some butter, and in it brown the uncooked noodles you kept apart (having previously chopped them into small squares). This needs a fair amount of butter, do not stint it. Pour all your boiled noodles into a casserole and put the fried ones on top. Season with salt and pepper and serve very hot.

Macaroni Timbale

Choose large-bored macaroni and cook it only lightly. Cut in very short lengths (an inch). Butter an oven dish and put into it your macaroni mixed with a thick tomato sauce, a little powdered saffron, some diced raw ham, some broken olives, some mushroom slices done in butter. Sprinkle with grated parmesan and finish cooking in the oven.

N.B.—The top may be gilded with an egg yolk.

Paste-shell Salad

Use 'coquillettes' or shell shapes of Italian paste in salad (or for that matter, any other form of paste) in summer. To improve the colourless look, use a little saffron. Dress with a vinegar and mustard dressing and chopped herbs.

Paste Loaf

Macaroni is the best choice for this (and for once it may be very well cooked rather than underdone). When cooked, mix with beaten eggs, six to a pound of macaroni, turn mixture into a buttered mould, cook for half an hour in bain-marie.

N.B.—This 'loaf' may also be sweetened with sugar and 'stuffed' with cooked apples.

Macaroni Croquettes

Use fine macaroni, cook in salted water, drain, chop into small pieces.

Make a Béchamel sauce with a knob of butter, a tablespoonful of flour, nearly half a pint of milk. Add the macaroni, a little grated gruyère, salt, pepper, nutmeg. Cook for five minutes, add two egg yolks.

Pour this mixture into a dish and set aside to cool for several hours.

Roll it into little balls, coat these with white of egg (beaten to a snow)

ON CHEESE

. . . And may I, every time I think
Of cheese, be moved to take a drink!
Kneel, sinners all, and on your knees,
Sharers of my discrepancies,
Loudly and boldly yell with me:
'Heaven bless the soil that gives us Brie!
May its green pastures, fertile plains,
Never be vexed with lashing rains!
May Flora, with her jewels, her smiles,
Her half-a-million amorous wiles,
On lawns and meadows never old,
(In spite of winter's cruel cold,
His visage glacial and unkind)
Detain for ever, intertwined
In arms of alabaster white,
Sweet Spring, her loving satellite.'

* * *

Get far behind me, Pont l'Evêque!
Cheese of Auvergne . . . Milan . . . betake
Those charms elsewhere, for only Brie
Deserves my matchless minstrelsy.
Golden its glory! Golden, too,
Pure yellow is my cheese's hue,
Yet not from spleen! The moment after
You press its skin, it splits with laughter,
And richest cream, no stay, no stint,
Oozes beneath your fingerprint.

* * *

Hold hard, you guzzlers! Wait for me!
A cheese that's fit for royalty
Consumed at such unseemly speed—
The devil take you. And your greed!
Each single bite is worth a crown,
And muscatel to wash it down.
Your very teeth for shame should chatter
For making Brie a trivial matter!
. . . So, may I, every time I think
Of cheese, be moved to take a drink!

Lackey, more wine!

SAINT-AMANT

then with breadcrumbs, and let them stand for a while before being fried in deep fat.

Niokis

These are made by taking some *unsweetened* choux pastry (see p. 309), and letting small balls of it, about half the size of an egg, fall into gently boiling water seasoned with salt.

The nioki will gradually swell and puff up, and after a quarter of an hour's cooking may be lifted out, drained, and served with either meat gravy or parmesan. Or perhaps with tomato sauce.

Polenta

This consists of air-dried maize flour (or cornflour) (or Indian meal) and is much used in North Italy. It is dropped shower-like into salted boiling water and cooked for half an hour. A little butter is added to the cooked polenta, and sometimes grated cheese. The boiled meal is spread on a wetted dish and left to get cold.

Then pieces of the required size are cut from it and cooked in butter, gratinated in the oven (with grated breadcrumbs or cheese) and served with tomato sauce.

N.B.—Milk may be used instead of water, and in this case sugar replaces cheese. But if the idea is to obtain a nourishing and inexpensive sweet dish, a better effect is achieved by using semolina rather than polenta.

In some places (notably Corsica) a chestnut polenta is made. In Franche-Comté they use dried maize-meal that is oven-dried, not air-dried, and from it they make their GAUDES which Pasteur enjoyed so much. Here are two old recipes for

Gaudes (Hasty-Puddings)

Gaudes, so well thought of in Franche-Comté, are simply maize flour. Two forms are possible. You may want the recipe for the gaudes that will do nicely for the family breakfast; or you may be thinking of the other gaudes, which may take the place of soup at dinner time.

First boil 3½ pints of water in a large saucepan. Blend nearly a pound of maize flour with cold water and pour the smooth paste into the boiling water. Stir well to avoid lumps and curdling. The slow cooking must continue for an hour and a half. Twenty minutes before this time has elapsed, clarify with a little milk, add a few pinches of salt, and, at the last moment, a nut of butter.

The gaudes look a little on the heavy side, but are easily digested. They are, in fact, like the Franche-Comté folk: slow of speed but subtle of wit.

The second gaude recipe provides for a thick brew that gives a dish of unusual consistency ('catons' as it is called). The 3½ pints of water are brought to the boil in a big iron pot, the pound (an ounce more than a pound) of meal is added, and the stirring (with a wooden spoon) of this redoubtable mixture is vigorously sustained for at least a quarter of an hour. A little salt is added and sometimes some butter, if one wishes to do one's guests really well.

As this brew is very hard to manage it is a useful idea (once the 'catons' are served) if on plunging the spoon into the mixture you find it clogged and plastered, to soak it in a bowl of milk so that that particular spoonful shall not be too dense.

In days gone by, in very large families, each child took his spoon and his bowl of milk and they all stood round the big pot and attacked the 'catons'. This was the one and only meal on winter nights!

SALADS

'Salad makes the stomach glad'
LOUIS-PHILIPPE I

Salads have one drawback—for those who are fond of wine—they destroy the aroma and the bouquet of the said wine. The moral is: *Eat your salad without drinking any wine and wait for the cheese before you empty your glass.*

That, at all events, is the opinion of most gastronomes. At the risk of being brought to book I shall now give my own. It is even more rigid.

(1) It is perfectly legitimate to drink with salad—to drink a glass of water. And I would add that a glass of water (Vichy, perhaps, in France) halfway through a meal is indispensable, or almost. It cleanses the mouth, and it washes the taste-buds so that they are all set to do justice to the dishes yet to come. Moreover, it quenches the thirst. For wine is not a satisfier of thirst—and so much the better for that, in a sense, for one would in the end desist from drinking it; the alternative being to go on drinking without being thirsty, thereby committing the sin of gluttony.

This being so, it is good practice to take at least one tumblerful of water in the course of a meal. If we choose the salad course for this duty, all will be well.

(2) But why does salad (with artichokes, asparagus, the eggs that some even more exclusive compilers add) do such violence to wine? First, through its very nature. Second, because of the vinegar which is one ingredient of its seasoning and dressing.

Then why in heaven's name put vinegar into a salad? Here, to my mind, is the best . . . even the only . . . salad dressing:

Mix well in a bowl an egg yolk, some tarragon mustard, salt and pepper. Add oil (olive, if you like it) drop by drop, stirring without pause. One drop of hot water, then straight it all goes on to the salad, to be followed by a sprinkling of fine herbs. Then toss the salad round and round for as long as you can.

In some salads the addition of a drop of lemon juice would not be out of place, but a dressing of *nothing but* lemon juice is to be condemned.

All salads have something to recommend them, and the choice is a matter of taste. But do not waste outside leaves of salad plants, nor yet the stumps and cores, for they will make quite a difference to your soups. The following alliances are good:

—Corn salad: beetroot.
—Lettuce: hard-boiled eggs.
—Dandelions: bacon or ham scraps.
—Chicory: Sippets rubbed with garlic.
—Cos lettuce: anchovies.
—Endive: potatoes.
—Escarole: fennel.

A salad of chopped leaves, etc., may be served with mayonnaise; or long and cos lettuce with fresh cream and a dash of lemon. Left-over meat or vegetables (with a few exceptions) may, as has been pointed out earlier, make most useful additions to salads.

Cheese Salad

Diced Gruyère or Dutch cheese, with salt, pepper and tablespoonful of cream, a small pepper (chopped), some sliced black olives, all left to blend together for an hour or so, then put with a watercress salad and served.

Chrysanthemum Salad

The white or yellow petals for choice. Wipe them (do not wash as this would obliterate the scent) and dress with a tablespoonful of lemon juice, another of sugar, two of olive oil, and a little salt.

Beaucaire Salad

Cut some leafy celery into short 'pencils' and cut up some endives. Cut (as for a julienne) a small celeriac, a nice tender one. Chop up small a few dessert apples and a slice of cooked ham.

Mix all in an earthenware dish with some table salt, white pepper, Cayenne pepper and the juice of a lemon. Leave to combine for two hours. Season with a mustard-based mayonnaise. Sprinkle with chopped savoury herbs and add a garland of cooked beetroot.

Lettuce Cream

Mix two egg yolks with 4 oz fresh cream in a small pan and warm gradually, whisking all the time. Add salt, and let the mixture thicken. When it is thick and smooth set it somewhere to cool. Add the juice of one lemon and pour over salad of lettuce.

C. B. C. Salad

Made of corn salad, beetroot (red) and celery. Shallots in the dressing, finely chopped. If possible, use walnut oil.

Cheeses

Dessert?—well, since you mention it—
A pickled herring, if you please!
And then, to clean our tongues a bit,
Some chunks of Roqu'fort cheese.

Café-concert ditty of 1900

Between Aristotle's and Curnonsky's Day Cheese has won its Stripes in the Literary Field

First, the word itself (*fromage*). It is, as it were, a deformation of the word 'formage'. It is, in a few words, the result of shaping the curds of milk, coagulation usually being achieved by submitting it to pressure. As early as the year 200 B.C. Aristotle was describing, in his works, the making of the cheese which Homer and Vergil celebrated with such transports, Lyric transports, naturally.

Brillat-Savarin used to say that a meal without cheese was like a beautiful woman with one eye missing; and Curnonsky, Prince of Gastronomes, adds: 'Of all cheeses, only those of France are so numerous, so varied, and offer such a wide range of flavours, that there is something for every palate, even the most palatial. They supply the apotheosis of a good meal, like the grand finale of a fireworks display.'

François Villon, in his will, bequeathed to his friend Jehan Ragnier a 'talmouze' (cheese-cake), that is to say a kind of cheese soufflé, while Charles d'Orléans is sending cheeses, in 1407, as New Year gifts to the ladies of his heart.

Talleyrand, gourmand that he was, esteemed it the finest of entremets, and he persuaded Metternich to ordain that French cheeses should always be available for his table. Whenever Balzac's path lay through Orléans he made a point of ordering, at his inn, three or four Olivet cheeses to be served with walnuts and wine. Zola, in the 'Ventre de Paris', has written what amounts to a Cheese Symphony.

And for such reasons the poets . . . from Semiramis, who liked only cheeses from the milk of white cows (doubtless through eclecticism), to Marie Harel, who invented Camembert, by way of Ninon de Lenclos (at whose table wines and cheeses were united in courtly matrimony), for such reasons, I say, poets have praised in the same breath women (of taste), and this delectable food, even as V. Meusy, for example, has done:

Anacreontic cheese,
Our every meal's bouquet!
Life has no pungencies
On a cheeseless day.

The Doctors tell You: Cheese is a Medicine

Cheese will supply you with calcium, protein, fat, and important nutritive elements—and that's why doctors recommend it. The Romans, early manufacturers of 'caseus', knew of its digestibility and had recourse to it as an antidote for certain poisons.

In his work on 'The Growth of the Child', Dr. Levesque advises giving cheese from the age of eight months. 'Many kinds of cheese', he said, 'will be tolerated at this age, not only the mild cream cheeses but also a "cooked" cheese, which must be pounded, and later on fermented cheeses.'

Cheese should not be regarded as a dessert item but as an ingredient of main dishes that is too useful to despise. It would be better to serve rather fewer vegetables and flour-based dishes and more cheese.

The Three Phases of the Biological action of Cheese Ferments

There are three cheese 'families':

(1) 'FRESH', UNFERMENTED CHEESES: the product of spontaneous coagulation (cream cheeses, 'white' cheeses), or of curdling with rennet (petit suisse, double cream and similar cheeses).

(2) SOFT-BODIED FERMENTED CHEESES: (such as Camembert, Livarot) and hard-bodied fermented cheeses (e.g. Dutch, Roquefort, Cantal).

(3) CHEESE OF 'COOKED' BODY: (such as Gruyère, Port-Salut). The milk (cow's, goat's, ewe's or even mare's as used in the Italian Caccio Cavallo) undergoes various processes: coagulation, curdling with rennet, then shaping; and it is in the course of these procedures that biological transformations occur. The technicalities which control these have been greatly modified by the discoveries of Pasteur and Duclaux. Three stages which are not quite clear-cut, since overlapping occurs, are these:

(*a*) the phase during which lactic ferments work on the lactose and change it into lactic acid;

(*b*) the 'fungoid' phase, when fungus-growths spread over the surface and form a thick film that is known as 'cheesemakers' white'. These growths consume the lactic acid as soon as it is produced, and contribute towards the ripening of the cheese;

(*c*) the period during which the secondary microbes are active—moulds, usually of an orange colour ('cheesemakers' red') that serve to keep in check the pullulation of the aforementioned fungoid growths.

How the Housewife should buy her Cheeses—in France

It is usual in France to inform the purchaser of the proportions which have gone to the making of cheese by stating percentages in a somewhat oracular fashion.

So if you see on a thousand-gramme cheese the following indications: 47% e.s. and 40% m.g., they mean that this particular piece of cheese represents 470 grammes of 'extrait sec' (dry extract)—that is to say, that if all moisture were somehow withdrawn from the cheese, 470 grammes of dry matter would be left behind.

And, of these 470 grammes, 40%, otherwise 188 grammes, would be fat content.

The housewife would therefore be well advised to take note of these figures rather than of the superficial appearance of the cheese she is buying. She should also look for the 'guarantees of quality' which will assure uniform standard of texture and taste.

Calendar of Cheeses

Broadly speaking, autumn and winter are the 'cheese seasons'. Many cheeses, however, may be eaten all the year round. Others are at their peak of perfection in the summer months, generously interpreted as May to November.

Here is a short list or 'calendar':

CHEESE TO BE EATEN THROUGHOUT THE YEAR

Autun, Aurore, Normand, Beaufort, Brie de Melun, Brillat-Savarin, Comté, Excelsior, Roquefort, Port-Salut.

CHEESES TO BE EATEN FROM SEPTEMBER–OCTOBER, TO JUNE–JULY

Cancoillotte, Riceys Cendré, Epoisses, Gournay, Livarot, Marcilles, Olivet, Pont-l'Evêque, Reblochon, Saint-Nectaire, Saint-Agathon, Soumaintrain, Tomme de Savoie, Vendôme.

CHEESES TO BE EATEN FROM NOVEMBER TO MAY

Bleu d'Auvergne, Brie de Coulommiers, Camembert, Cantal, Chaumont, Fourme, Gex, Laguiole, Pithiviers au foin, Rocamadour, Sassenage, Septmoncel, Vacherin.

CHEESES TO BE EATEN FROM DECEMBER TO APRIL

Recollet, Mont-d'Or, Munster, Chevret, Bossons, Beaupré de Roybon.

CHEESES TO BE EATEN FROM MAY TO NOVEMBER, IN THEIR PRIME

Broccio Corse, Chabichou, Chevrotin, Crottin de Chavignol, Levroux, Rigotte de Condrieu, Saint-Marcellin, Sainte-Maure, Valençay, Persillé de Savoie.

This is a résumé of advice which the cheese specialist Androuët will give you if you go to consult him. And he'll give you a great deal of further information into the bargain.

THE CANCOILLOTTE

I

They've sung you songs a-plenty
All about some local dainty
From the pot,
But Franche-Comté, more's the pity,
Never had a single ditty
For Cancoillotte.

II

To make good this sad omission
I shall sing, with your permission,
One that's not
Too darn silly or incredible
For to show how richly edible
Is Cancoillotte.

III

To concoct this special showdish
One sole mode is strictly modish,
On the dot.
There are rules there's no neglecting
If you're thinking of confecting
A Cancoillotte.

IV

Allow your milk to curdle
And the curd, unless it's stirred'll
Form a clot.
Wrap in duster which you'll squeeze . . . it's
Now the basis of your cheese . . . it's
Your Cancoillotte.

V

Under quilt, hot-water-bottle,
In your bed, your cheese, kept hot'll
Gently rot.
Let it rest there . . . be not hasty . . .
Melt it down, and there's your tasty,
Prime Cancoillotte.

VI

There are folk of slender learning
Who condemn it, undiscerning,
As 'God knows what'.
But these means they so disfavour
Give its unambiguous flavour
To Cancoillotte.

VII

It beats Gruyère, Roquefort, hollow,
Makes all rivals hard to swallow,
Tops the lot.
Whacks your goat-cheese to a frazzle,
And your Brie we quite out-dazzle
With Cancoillotte.

VIII

Well, Franche-Comté, here's a native
Both devoted and creative,
Sound patriot,
Whose song of acclamation
Must ensure proliferation
Of your Cancoillotte.

Doggerel song sent to author by M. MYARD, of the Auberge d'Arbois, rue Lesueur, Paris

FOOTNOTE FROM THE PRINCE DE LIGNE

'Witty people, these French,' M. de Poelnitz said with enthusiasm as he and the Prince de Ligne were on their way home from a Du Barry dinner remarkable for the abundance and excellence of its wines. 'Witty?' the Prince replied. 'What on earth is the point of being witty when you can offer wines of that class?'

Madame Harel has her Monument

Whereas so many statues perpetuate the memory of men even the names of whom have vanished from recollection, and that for many a long year; of men whose acts have proved even less memorable; there is a statue erected on the little market-place of the village of Vimoutiers (Orne) which bears witness to public gratitude to that worthy farmer's wife who, round about 1790, 'invented' Camembert.[1]

Her name is Madame Harel. High-quality Camembert is made with whole milk, unskimmed, in winter. The process is not unlike that for Brie. The difference is due to the bacteria which give to Camembert a slight bitterness, a special feature said to be due to the oat-straw stands used for the drainage of the cheeses.

The cheese should be pale yellow, of smooth texture, unholed, and not runny.

A Few Cheese Details . . . or Cheese Lore Without Tears

ROQUEFORT is made with ewes' milk into which crumbs of a special bread, previously dried and pulverized, have been scattered; the bread has been made to develop a certain variety of mould.

BROCCIO is a Corsican cheese of goats' milk base, much employed for fritters, in ravioli, and in the creation of a special cake known as 'Fiadene'.

GRUYERE, if the real thing, takes its name from a Swiss valley. It is both pungent and salty-flavoured, and should be without holes. It must not be confused with Emmenthaler (another Swiss cheese) or with Comté-Français.

FROMAGE-FORT (Strong cheese) is a Lyon and Beaujolais cheese. It consists of skim-milk cheese grated into stoneware pots with salt, spices, leek juice and enough white wine laced with brandy to cover. It is hermetically sealed and left to ferment for a fortnight in gentle heat. Eaten with a spoon.

LE MAROILLES, as soon as dry, is put in cellar and turned often, washed over with beer. Good maroilles, that is.

MONT D'OR was formerly made in the Lyon region with indoor-bred goats' milk. There is none nowadays.

PARMESAN is made in Lombardy and Romagna and needs four years for ripening. After this it will keep for twenty years. It sometimes happens

[1] If truth must be told, Camembert in a very similar form had already been in existence for quite a time.

that as the paste ripens harmful bacteria cause it to liquefy in patches. When this occurs a kind of surgical operation has to be carried out: the cavity is opened up, curettage is performed, and cicatrization with a red-hot iron completes the process.

SASSENAGE is a cheese of Roquefort type made from a mixture of ewes', goats' and cows' milk.

Cheese is Never out of Place at Table

The expression 'between pear and cheese', meaning simply 'at dessert', or 'over the walnuts and wine', seems to indicate that at one time, in France, cheese was served as a sort of side-dish after the fruit. This is an inadmissible practice. The truly fastidious deplore the custom of serving cheese already grated. Gastronomes never take butter with cheese.

But it is allowable to serve cumin with Munster. (For Cumin, *see* p. 66).

Cheese is a marvellous complement to wine . . . Bordeaux, Côtes du Rhône and Burgundy, those of fullest body and finest bouquet, make a splendid accompaniment; and even a simple, familiar, loyal Beaujolais is not to be despised.

CHEESE DISHES (ENTREMETS)

Cheese Soufflé

The substance of a soufflé is, in general, a thick Béchamel sauce to which are added, away from heat, egg yolks and the whites whipped to a snow. To this mixture very finely grated Gruyère is added and the mixture is poured into a deep oven dish well buttered. Minimum cooking time: twenty minutes in a quick oven.

Cheese Tart

Use short pastry (*see* p. 308). The tart is only partially cooked (if necessary fill with haricot beans to keep shape while baking), then the soufflé mixture described in the previous recipe is piled into pastry cases and the cooking is completed in a slow oven.

Cheese Ramekins

Using the same pastry in individual moulds, half cook the pastry cases. Now add to each a thick layer of grated Gruyère. You will have prepared separately a mixture of one or two egg yolks with fresh cream, thinned down with milk. Pour this liquid mixture into the pastry cases and complete cooking in slow oven.

Burgundian Gougère

Bring to the boil in a thick pan three-quarters of a pint of milk to which you have added a good quarter pound of butter and a pinch of salt. Add, all at once, half a pound of flour, mixing it in rapidly and stirring constantly with a wooden spoon. Allow mixture to thicken over a gentle heat. Now add, one at a time, half a dozen eggs, followed by six ounces of Gruyère cut into small cubes. The mixture must now be transferred to a well-buttered pie-dish, gilded with some extra egg yolk and sprinkled with grated cheese, then baked for half an hour in a hot oven. The Gougère may be eaten hot, cold, or re-heated.

Cevennes Gougnette

Prepare, on the day before it is wanted, a pancake batter (half wheat flour, half buckwheat). Make some very thin and very well-buttered pancakes, pour on to each a thin layer of melted Cantal cheese, and fold each over before serving.

(Recipe supplied by dramatist JACQUES DEVAL)

Neufchatel Fondue

Set two and a quarter pounds of Gruyère, cut into thin slices, to melt in one and three quarter pints of white wine in a copper pan. Stir constantly to avoid a lumpy mixture; bind with a small quantity of flour thickening. Pour a wineglassful of Kirsch over it and set this alight as dish comes to table. The diners will take turns in dipping their bread into the Fondue.

Welsh Rarebit

Melt small pieces of Cheshire cheese with half their weight of butter, and knead the resultant mixture. When it is runny add two egg yolks, salt, Cayenne pepper and a glass of beer. Stir all together in the pan without allowing mixture to boil. Spread on toasted bread and allow ten minutes in the oven for browning.

Goat's Cheese Pie

Make a dough with a pound of flour, half a pound of caster sugar, a half pound each of lard and butter, four egg yolks, a pinch of salt.

Prepare an ordinary white sauce, thin this down with the best part of a pint of milk, then boil for ten minutes, stirring continually, until sauce is really thick, binding it further with two egg yolks; drop into it four or five very fresh little goat-cheeses cut into slices. Add a handful of grated Parmesan, some tiny strips of cooked ham, and mix all well together.

Line a pie-dish with the pastry and fill with the sauce mixture. Gild with egg yolk, sprinkle with sugar, and bake in a fairly warm oven for three quarters of an hour.

Dessert

Desserts were developed to a fine art for the purpose of keeping girls and young women and children at table to join in family colloquies.

CAREME

Gourmands of the finest sort have invariably completed their dinner before dessert is served. The fact that they go right ahead and take dessert is mere politeness . . . but they are usually extremely polite.

GRIMOD DE LA REYNIERE

FRUITS

Add to Pomona's riches Flora's treasure,
Then rose and jasmine, lily and carnation
Change staid desserts to gardens plann'd for pleasure;
And nature-lovers shout for joy to see
Your blossom jam and candied picotee.

BERCHOUX (*Gastronomy*, Canto IV)

Fruits are, of course, as old as the universe. Otiose to refer yet again to Eve's apple which led to so much trouble. She has to be forgiven. Someone had to discover that fruit is an aliment in some respects peerless. In their season they may—and should—be eaten raw. If you have plenty of variety available, serve a *macédoine* of fruits, prepared some time before eating with sugar and some spirit of exquisite bouquet; or champagne; or even wine (red wine only if red fruit predominates). Generally speaking, fruit's alcoholic accompaniment should be, if I may go so far as to dogmatize about this, a *compatriot*. This cuts out pineapple in kirsch, but pineapple with rum is a logical blend.

Cooked fruit appears as compôte, fruit purée, in syrup, in jams and jellies. But apples and even pears are excellent when oven-baked, and peaches may be boiled like so many boiled eggs.

Baked Apple Dumplings

Peel and core (with corer or, if you haven't one, a sharp-pointed knife). They need to be very ripe. Make some short pastry and for each apple cut a large round of rolled-out paste. These must be as thin as you can make them. Fill apple middles with caster sugar and top with a little 'cork' of butter. Place apple on dough and lift the edges all round it to enclose the apple, sealing with water. Put the dressed fruit on a greased oven-sheet, gild with beaten egg-yolk, and bake in a hot oven for half an hour. When done—pierce with a knife, which should encounter no resistance—sprinkle with sugar, and if the idea appeals to you, inject a little rum.

Goodwife's Baked Apples

To every land its own version. In France we usually core without peeling, then score the skin all round about halfway down to prevent bursting-through of the pulp. Centres are filled with a blend of caster sugar and butter in equal bulk, and the apples are put in an oven dish with a few tablespoonsful of water and baked for 20 to 30 minutes. When the soft pulp is about to ooze through the slit skin, the apple should be ready. Put a good spoonful of gooseberry jelly into each hole and keep hot, with the oven door open and themselves well to the front, until the moment of serving.

Apple Cake

Take a pound of peeled and sliced apples and twelve ounces of sugar. Cook in cold water and when the mass is well done, pass it through a sieve and add five sheets of gelatine previously dissolved in a little water. Beat the mixture with a whisk for forty full minutes. Then pour into an oiled mould already lined with a cooked sponge cake. Leave in the cold for at least six hours. Then take out of mould and surround with kirsch-flavoured cream. The apple compôte will be snow-white (thanks to the air you have beaten into it) and of very firm consistency. And it is delicious.

(Recipe from M. THEODORE DUBOIS, of the Institute)

Compôtes and Fruit Stews Generally

Often called 'marmelades' but are not marmalades in the English sense as they are eaten almost as soon as made. They are, indeed, a quickly-made sweet for busy days, consisting of fruit cooked with sugar and only just enough water to prevent burning. The 'compôte' must be eaten that same day. If it is cooked longer, with more sugar, it is indeed a marmalade, or conserve, and may be potted and kept stored for several months. All fruits, or almost all, may be used in compôtes.

Pear Compôte in Red Wine

Boil some red wine with 4 oz sugar to the quart, or as much as 5 oz if you like, and lemon slices with rind but no pips. Flavour with cinnamon. Put in the pears (small ones may be left whole) and cook at a slow simmer. Take pears out when tender. Reduce the liquor to a half or less and pour over the fruits in a serving fruit-dish.

Green Gooseberry Compôte

Choose very green, barely ripe gooseberries. Boil water and sugar (half a pound of sugar to 1¾ pints water, and a little vanilla. Skim and put in 2 lb gooseberries, boil gently for ten minutes. Take out fruits, reduce syrup, pour over gooseberries, set aside to cool. Before serving mix some vanilla-flavoured sugar with cream, and top with this. Use clotted cream.

Fruits in Syrup

The syrup is made by boiling 18 oz sugar with 1¾ pints water, or proportionally. Skim off impurities, leave over flame until a syrupy consistency is suddenly perceptible—a kind of oiliness supervenes. There are then two possible ways of proceeding:

(1) Put the fruits into a glass jar. They must be cleaned, topped and tailed, stoned if necessary. Cram the jar as full as you can without crushing, pour syrup over, allow to get cold, then cover jars.

(2) Put fruits in the syrup to simmer for about five minutes. When cool, turn into jars.

Certain fruits without much natural sugar (e.g. apricots) need a little gelatine with them: one or two sheets should be added to the syrup.

JAMS

A Brief History of Jams

The following information was given by M. Roger Parisot, speaking for a national concern allying the great fruit preservers and jam-makers of France: The procedures whereby fruit is preserved in the form of jam are almost universally the same, and are of great antiquity. The essence of all processes is that fruit and sugar must cook together for periods discovered by trial and error to be the best. At one time the words 'jam', 'preserves' covered all kinds of sugar-conserved items, the only real distinction being those between 'solid' and 'liquid' products. The name is now reserved for liquid, or at least 'pourable', preserves.

It is in the Middle East, centre of an old and highly developed civilization (or successions thereof) that the abundant variety of fruits and the presence of cane-sugar, of Bengalese origin, first inspired the inhabitants to improve and finally perfect the art of fruit-preserving. So it is not to be wondered at that a taste for jam, in those days a costly luxury, should have come to France and England as did cane sugar and many hitherto unknown fruits, with the returning Crusaders. It is thanks to them that Europe, by the end of the Middle Ages, was producing, to rival the rose, citrous-fruit, musk-scented jellies of the Caliphs' Araby, such delicacies as quince marmalade, robs, jellies of varied fruits, barbary-plum (or barberry) jams—even angelica and violet conserves.

As time passed, families evolved their own recipes and kept the secrets jealously to hand on from mother to daughter. And in very many instances the products were also part of the family pharmacopœia, since many jams and similar preserves were deemed to be medicines as well as tit-bits. Angelica, for instance, was 'good for the lungs' and myrtleberry jam was said to be the repository of all the virtues essential to a cure for what our ancestors termed 'stomach flux' and we, diarrhœa.

Nearer to our own times is the period which came at the close of the seventeenth century, when jam-making and fruit-preservation were at the height of perfection. This was a moment in history when men were living a kind of life which (their lack of science apart) was not so very different from ours. And the same applies to their jam-making. The culinary literature of the time includes an amazingly large number of works devoted almost exclusively to jam-making. One, chosen from many, was entitled 'The Royal and Bourgeois Jam Maker', with over eight-hundred different recipes for jams, syrups, robs, etc., in one volume. However, the good housewife in stillroom and kitchen gradually lost the habit of making all her own preserves, fruit pastes, etc., and it was considered quite praiseworthy to buy these from the confectioners, organized into a corporation since the thirteenth century.

It is indisputable that properly made jams of sound ingredients are a wholesome food, easily digestible, and of proved nourishing, sustaining and energizing qualities. The medical faculties have only a few cases to quote in which their use is contra-indicated, and on the whole admit them among prescribed foods for all sorts and conditions of people.

When to Make your Jam

The following table was published in *Cuisine et Vins de France*:

JAN. TO MARCH	Seville oranges, for marmalade.
MAY	Rhubarb.
JUNE	Strawberries.
JULY	Strawberries, raspberries, cherries, gooseberries.
AUGUST	Gooseberries, blackcurrants, apricots.
SEPTEMBER	Peaches, mirabelles, mulberries, tomatoes, Victoria plums, greengages, quetsche plums, myrtles.
OCTOBER	Pears, figs, apples, grapes, fruits preserved in grape juice.
NOVEMBER	Quinces, oranges, apples, pumpkins, chestnuts.
DECEMBER	Oranges.

And here is a list of practical counsels:

(1) See that all jars, etc., which are to contain jam are entirely grease-free. One may wash in vinegar as well as water, to be sure.

(2) Use no iron or tin-plated iron cooking vessels, as these will blacken the fruit.

(3) Choose very ripe (but not over-ripe) fruit, to save sugar.

(4) Granulated sugar is best, but choose the whitest.

(5) The general rule is to use equal weights of sugar and fruit. But cooking times are based on the assumption that the rule is being observed, and the less is the sugar, the more prolonged must be the cooking.

(6) Too much sugar gives a crystallized jam. Too little, a fermented jam. To avoid fermentation add as little as one-thirtieth of an ounce of salicylic acid to two pounds of fruit.

(7) If you wish to use honey instead of sugar, use it at the rate of one of honey to two of fruit (in pounds). It is better than sugar for gooseberries and raspberries, among others.

(8) Cooking heat needs to be both brisk and even.

(9) A saccharimeter whose use is well understood is a boon.

(10) Skim the cooked jam and do not tie down until cold. The different methods of covering are:

(*a*) if you cover while jam is still hot use a cellophane cover, moistened outside.

(*b*) if you leave standing for one day, before you put on the top cover put a circle of paper soaked in spirits on the jam surface itself.

(*c*) as (*b*), but use glycerine rather than spirits if you think there is any danger of crystallization.

(*d*) cover when cold with melted paraffin wax.

Orange Marmalade

Take good sound oranges and prick with a fork to release the bitterness of the zest. Soak in cold water for 36 hours, changing the water fairly often, and pricking the oranges again three or four times. Set them (still whole) in cold water to boil, and cook for half an hour after boiling point is reached. Then take them out and cool in several changes of cold water. Cut each into six or eight sections, take out pips, remove skin and pith. Pile the pieces together and chop very finely into detached shreds, with a sharp knife. Cut the skins likewise.

Put the cut pulp and skins with their weight of sugar, and the escaped juice (or merest drop of water, as their own juice suffices), to cook together for about 70 minutes, stirring constantly.

Fig Jam

Choose very ripe figs, keep whole, prick with knitting needle, blanch for five minutes in boiling water, then drain. In the same water dissolve and then cook for fifteen minutes a weight of sugar equal to weight of

CHATTERBOXES

Such folk are the bane of a dinner-table. Perhaps the moment has come to re-tell an oft-told story. At a dinner given by Madame Aubernon, a well-known blue-stocking, Victorien Sardou was well launched on an endless dissertation. Renan indicated that he'd like to put in a word, but the hostess silenced him with a gesture. She was a highly capable manager in such circumstances. At long last, Sardou rounded off his discourse, and Madame Aubernon turned her attention to the author of the Life of Jesus.

'*What were you about to remark a few minutes ago,* cher maître?'

'*Oh, my goodness . . . I only wanted a few more green peas,' said Renan.*

ARTLESS YOUTH

In the course of a sumptuous banquet a little boy, his appetite more than satisfied, burst into tears. When asked what ailed him, he complained: 'I can't eat any more!' 'Never mind,' advised the person sitting next to him, 'you can put some food in your pockets.' 'But I've stuffed them full to the brim already!' lamented this fond darling.

FATHER FRANCIS DINES IN TOWN

Exquisite roasts—and he consumes them with obvious appreciation. And as each new dish is carried to the table, our good Father Francis exclaims with fervour: 'Ah! my dear soul! Now that's a dish that simply cries out for a good draught of wine to go with it!'

And so it continues with every single course. As dessert is being placed before the diners, one of these makes bold to ask: 'Father, I'd rather like to know . . . with what do you not *drink wine?'*

'*Water, my friend; not with water.*'

'*And when, Father, do you drink water?*'

'*Never, my son, never. It's an invention of the devil.*'

cooked figs. Add a vanilla pod and the zest of a lemon. Then put in figs and cook for twenty minutes. Skim and pot.

The next recipe is a Turkestan speciality:

Black Radish Jam

Peel the black radishes and cut in fine strips. Cook in water until all has evaporated. Melt separately a tumblerful of honey. When it is about to boil, add the radish and go on cooking until the jam is of a tawny-russet colour. Put in pots and sprinkle with ginger.

Jellies

The pectin of fruits is transformed into pectic acid, and jelly is the result. Certain fruits, such as apples, quinces, gooseberries, black-currants, raspberries, have far more pectin in them than others, so that they jellify almost automatically in the right conditions. But others with less pectin need to be combined with apples or quinces, or you can use a natural product such as agar-agar to ensure jellying of the fruits.

APPLE JELLY: Cover quarters of unpeeled apples with cold water. Boil and cook thoroughly. Put apples in strainer with muslin lining and squeeze out all the liquid. Add an equal quantity of sugar, to the liquid of course, and boil for forty minutes.

N.B.—Do not waste the apple débris. Use in a tart or to go with a milk pudding.

QUINCE JELLY: same procedure.

GOOSEBERRY JELLY: Put gooseberries in a bowl in a gentle oven with no water, or very little, having topped and tailed them first. Either red or green ones will do. Strain the juice that is yielded and boil for half an hour at least with its weight of sugar.

RASPBERRY, MULBERRY, BLACKCURRANT JELLIES are similarly made. The English style is to use only the juice that drips without forcing. This means a clearer, more brilliant jelly. The French actually squeeze the juice through the strainer, which means a more flavoursome jelly.

PINEAPPLE JELLY: As with apples. When the juice is ready, double its bulk with apple juice. Sugar must equal their combined weight.

ORANGE JELLY: First make an apple jelly then add the liquid obtained by boiling orange zest in water (3 oranges to 1¾ pints apple juice).

Marrons Glacés
(Crystallized Chestnuts)

These are so costly to buy that it is a wonder more families do not have their home-made supply. They may be less beautifully finished, especially your first attempts, but persevere. It is a long job, but at least it is not a hard one.

First peel the chestnuts. Don't waste time with the little pointed sweet chestnuts—you need the large, edible chestnuts of Turin, Lyons, Ardèche. The first skin is removable by hand, with the aid of a knife. The second is tougher. Put nuts in boiling water for two minutes, then shake and rub them all together in a bag or coarse cloth, so that the skins are rubbed off. Pick off the rest, also the fibrous threads, by hand.

Now for the cooking:

Wrap them in pairs in scraps of muslin and place them in a copper pan (above all, no iron to blacken them). Cover with cold water and bring almost—but not quite—to boiling point. *They must not boil at any stage, not even for a second.* The cooking must, however, go on for two hours. The nuts are done when a pin or needle pierces them easily.

Now for the 'crystallizing':

Keeping them in pairs in their muslin, plunge them into boiling syrup (25 oz sugar to 1¾ pints water). A vanilla pod is added to syrup. The syrup thermometer should, at moment of putting in the nuts, read 25°. Cook gently away from direct heat until thermometer reading is 32 (you are measuring, of course, syrup density).

The actual 'glazing' is the last process. Remove on a strainer and unfasten the muslin. Meanwhile raise sugar concentration to 37, and it must be boiling. Put into it all the chestnuts which are still whole, and leave for half an hour.

Soak a spatula in syrup and rub the inner surface of one part only of the pan. At this contact the syrup will whiten. Push back the white and recommence the scratching action. When you have done this four or five times, the adjacent surface of the syrup will be frothing. Into this part of the syrup put the chestnuts one by one, take out with spatula, put on wire tray to dry in a warm place. Two hours should be enough.

The syrup and broken chestnuts could make a jam.

Chestnut Pudding

Add demerara sugar to a marron purée, dissolved and stirred over gentle heat. Blend them, stirring with a wooden spoon, and then, having removed pan from heat, drop in three egg-yolks, one at a time, then four egg whites whipped into a snow. Butter a mould and fill with this mixture. Cook (bain-marie or double cooker) for about fifty minutes.

When cold, serve with English Cream, *see* p. 324.

Fruit Juice Cup

In a fruit-juice presser put cherries and strawberries in a two-to-one ratio (raw or cooked). To this juice add two small glasses of kirsch, also 8 oz sugar to 2¼ lb fruit. Serve in a fruit cup with a tablespoonful of Chantilly Cream, *see* p. 324.

Cakes and Confections

Fine Arts . . . there are five, namely: painting, sculpture, poetry, music and architecture; and the principal branch of this last is pastry-and-cake-making. ANATOLE FRANCE

Men become passionately attached to women who know how to cosset them with delicate titbits. H. DE BALZAC

When it rounds off a good meal, a sweet confection is like the crowning piece of a splendid fireworks display.

TALLEYRAND

PASTRY MIXTURES AND FANCY PASTRIES

(1) Short Pastry for Pies, Tarts, etc. Put your flour on the pastry board—half a pound for a decent-sized tart or flan—and work into it half as much butter, with a pinch of salt. (It is better to mix with a silver fork than with the fingertips, which soften the fat too much.) When the blend is satisfactory, pour on a little cold water, stirring with a spatula. As soon as you have a homogeneous mass, roll it out with a rolling-pin. Leave it to 'settle' for a short while before lining the greased tart- or pie-dish with it. Prick here and there with a fork, to prevent puffing-up.

If appropriate to its subsequent use, an egg may be added and the water sweetened with sugar. The type of pastry made with or without these additions is suitable for tarts, flans, 'quiches', certain pies (with vegetables, etc.).

(2) Flaky Pastry. On pastry-board put salted flour and mix gradually with about half its weight of cold water, using the fingertips and working it to a smooth and even-textured dough. This is the softening or 'annealing' process. Weigh your lump of dough, then flatten and roll out. Weigh up its weight in butter (you now see the point of the earlier weighing) and spread this butter over the centre of the rolled-out dough. Fold over the edges to conceal it completely. Using the rolling-pin, form a rectangle of pastry, three times as long as it is wide. Then fold this oblong in three, width advanced toward width, and you have a podgy square. Roll this out again, changing what was width to length, what was length to width. Do not press hard. *Whatever else happens, the butter must not be pressed beyond the edges. If you see a scrap of it oozing out through a crack in the pastry, seal it in at once.*

Refold into threes. Leave the pastry for about twenty minutes (if possible, in refrigerator), then renew the operations, rolling dough, however, in opposite directions, and as before making length into width and width into length. Once again, rest pastry, then resume. In all you will give it six such total transformations, and mathematicians will tell you that that represents 729 layers of butter between, or rather among, 730 layers of pastry.

Cooking calls for a really hot oven. Flaky pastry is used for tarts (and must be pricked with a fork to avoid undue swelling); it is used for girdle-cakes, Twelfth-cakes, vol-au-vent cases, turnovers, croissants (crescent-shaped milk rolls) used as garnishes for spinach purées, lentil purées, etc.; for various 'named' pastries (e.g. Genoese pastry slices, also called 'mille-feuilles')—and, finally, for meat-pie crusts. When used for this last purpose, the butter may be replaced by kidney-fat and refined beef dripping.

(3) Shortbread Dough. This is not unlike the first pastry described, a typical general-purpose short pastry, but it must contain an egg-yolk (not the white) and some brown sugar in generous amount. The proportions are: sugar, 1; butter, 2; flour, 3. It is usually a biscuit or cake dough, but may be used for rich tarts.

(4) Yeast Doughs. These are flour, butter, sugar and egg mixtures leavened with baker's yeast (buy it from your baker at the rate of half an ounce to a pound of flour). Let your pastry stand overnight.

N.B.—Use baker's yeast, not barm. The latter could serve for a bread dough, but its flavour is too strong for delicacies.

This pastry is used for Savarin, Kugelhopf, Brioche-based confections.

(5) Choux or Bun Pastry. In a small pan put water, salt, sugar, a little orange-flower water, and half the quantity of their total weight in butter. It works out at about 18 oz butter to a bare quart of liquid. Melt together. Take same amount of flour as of butter and put in when the other ingredients are boiling. Stir briskly with a spatula. Dry off to some extent over gentle heat.

Remove from heat. Add to the dough, two at a time, as many as a dozen eggs and more if you so wish. This pastry must be used as soon as made. It serves for all kinds of pastries, for nioki, for beignets soufflés (soufflé fritters).

AND HERE ARE RECIPES...

Grape Tart

Use No. 1 Pastry. Bake the tart case in a flan mould for 25 minutes in a moderate oven. The case may be either empty or filled with dry haricot beans or cherry stones—the last being the best choice. Take from tin and set aside to cool. Sieve some apricot conserve and spread a layer over the bottom of the tart. Cover it as closely as possible, and in symmetrical arrangement with white and black seeded grapes, alternating the colours. The rest of the apricot conserve is spread over the top.

Sweet-Gruel Tart

Pastry as before, pricked ready for baking. The day before, you will have mixed 4 oz flour and a pint of boiling milk, whisking thoroughly, then cooked the mixture in a bain-marie, or double saucepan, for about a quarter of an hour; next you will have set it to get cold in an earthenware vessel with a ball of butter on top.

We are back in today. Turn your sweet gruel into a bowl, beat into it, with a wooden spoon, some caster sugar and two eggs. Whisk again and pour into flan case. Bake in a moderate oven for about forty minutes.

Fruit Tarts

The fruit is usually cooked first, or perhaps tinned fruit or fruits preserved in syrup are used. But a strawberry tart is at its best when uncooked strawberries are spread on a bed of vanilla cream (*see* Creams, p. 324) or on a layer of gooseberry purée.

Auvergne Tart

Again Pastry No. 1. A bowl of cream, fresh cheese curds, four egg yolks, four tablespoonsful of caster sugar, all mixed and blended by hand, with the four egg-whites beaten to a snow. Work up a really creamy mixture. Line the flan case with pastry, fill with the mix, and cook in a hot oven.

(Recipe from M. JEAN BONNEFON)

Alsace Tart

Pastry No. 1, but this time well sweetened. Deck it with apple slices and bake in a hot oven. When apples are done, add two whole eggs beaten with milk and flavoured with cinnamon. Sprinkle with sugar and put back in oven until eggs are done.

Chestnut Tart

Mix equal quantities of chestnut meal and caster sugar with six egg yolks, the zest and juice of a lemon. Beat the whites to a snow, add to the well-blended mixture of other ingredients. Grease mould or tart-tin and spread this chestnut paste over it evenly. Cook in a hot oven for forty-five minutes.

This tart will keep, in a cool place, for well over a week.

Tatin Tart

Pastry No. 1. Butter the mould with exceptional lavishness. Cover with layers of apple slices, with dots of butter and a fair amount of sugar. Put

THE HIGH COST OF LIVING?

Charles Asselineau mentioned in a letter to Monselet that in reading François Colletet's Tracas de Paris *he had come upon a list of prices charged at the Cabaret de la Pomme de Pin. In the following rhyme, the poet reconstituted the author's menu and the details of his bill at this famous old tavern near the Pont Notre-Dame:*

'Come here then, you idlers, d'you hear me down
there?
Look at my money, I've eaten your fare!
One-fifty for capon, say six sous for bread,
And two for the cheese. Wine was eighty, we said
(Centimes, of course!) Ham ten sous. Five to
spare.
Yours, man. And thanks for a wonderful spread.
Lastly—two sous. When I've gone from the place
They'll help you, perhaps, to remember my face.'

And that's the kind of meal one got for three francs fifty-five in 1670.

Monselet, for his part, found a bill of fare of the well known Véry restaurant, dated 1803. Let's have a look at it.

Etretat oysters	0.60
Calf's sweetbread with sorrel	2.00
Boned and broiled pigeon	2.50
Fillet steak	1.25
Cheeses	0.30

and the wines offered were:

Chablis	2.00
Beaune	3.50
Richebourg	5.00
Champagne	7.00

Again, take for comparison this list from Maxim's in 1900 ('La Belle Epoque') to be found in the memoirs of Hugo who spent Twenty Years as Maxim's Maître d'Hôtel *(book published by Amiot-Dumont):*

Marennes oysters	3.00
Broiled kidneys	3.00
Grilled rib steak	2.75
Asparagus	1.50
Cheeses	2.00

and the wines:

Chablis	3.00
Rhine wines	3.00
Champagne	18.00

a pastry lid over. Cook in a very hot oven for half an hour. To serve, turn it over on a dish so that top becomes base.

N.B.—Be very careful to press down very firmly the edges of the pastry lid, as apple juice must not run out.

Sponge Cake (Savoy Biscuits)

Break six fresh eggs, separate yolks from whites, and beat yolks with a fork, adding 8 oz caster sugar and the grated rind of a lemon. Whip the whites to a snow, pour in the yolks-and-sugar mixture, and add 4 oz potato flour. Beat all together for fifteen minutes. Butter a deep dish, put in the cake mixture so that it does not come higher than the half-way mark, and bake for half an hour in a moderate oven.

German Flan

Use either No. 1 Pastry or No. 4 (Yeast or Brioche). Make your flan in the ordinary way and garnish with the following:

Cut up some apples into small pieces, line flan with them. Put one or two eggs into a basin (the size of the tart dictating the number of eggs) and beat well, adding as you whisk a pinch of cinnamon and enough caster sugar to thicken the eggs without making them 'unpourable'. Turn eggs on to the apples, making certain that the fruit is only half-submerged. Cook in a fairly hot oven.

Clafoutis

An admirable cherry flan—the cherries black and juicy. The recipe? Take 8 oz flour, 4 whole eggs, 2 tablespoonsful caster sugar, 2 liqueur glasses Cognac, a pinch of salt, 2½ pints milk. Sift flour through sieve into an earthenware dish. Mix salt, eggs, sugar. Knead all the ingredients (excepting, of course, the milk) until you have a smooth dough entirely free from lumps. Then add the milk and the cherries (I repeat, *black* cherries) from which the stems have been removed. Mix again, then pour in the Cognac.

The mould or baking tin must be very lavishly buttered or the Clafoutis will stick. Leave in the oven for about half an hour. Powder with icing sugar after taking out of oven tin.

How delectable they were, those Clafoutis of my childhood days! Even now I occasionally bring off a good one.

(Recipe from JULES CLARETIE, of the Académie Française)

Batter Fritters

Also called *Pets de Nonne*. These are soufflé fritters (choux pastry) and here is a recipe from M. MAURICE DEKOBRA called *Pets de Nonne Damnée*, or, in prosaic English,

Doughnuts (Almond)

First cook the classic batter fritter according to customary rites. These will be fried choux pastry pieces. Let them get cold, then with your finger (or a large nail) make a hole in each and fill with ground almonds and semolina soaked in coffee. Reheat the filled beignets and when piping hot inject each, using syringe, with a few shots of curaçao.

And any gourmet not caring for my speciality will be reviled by the shades of the venerable Vatel.

Fritters

The fritter mixture is a simple combination of flour, eggs, water, blended with a little butter. Every province has its own recipe and its own collection of odd fritter names (Roussettes, Oreillettes, Bugnes, etc.). Here are a few examples:

Easy Fritters

In an earthenware bowl mix 8 oz flour with two whole eggs and a walnut of butter, a little salt and about 3 tablespoonsful of sugar. When evenly blended, flatten the paste and cut into strips or circles. Leave for a time before frying. Other possibilities:

Use egg yolks only for a better result.
Add fresh cream.
Add grated lemon zest, rum, orange-flower water.
Make fritters containing acacia flowers, apple, pineapple, etc.

Strawberry Fritters: Combine the flour, two eggs, two tablespoonsful of kirsch, four of water. Soak your strawberries in sugar to start the juice running. Cloak each in the fritter paste and drop in boiling-hot oil.

Apricot-stuffed Fritters: Put half-apricots to soak in kirsch and sugar. Make the batter with flour, egg, a tablespoonful of oil, a gill of beer and another of water. Allow to ferment. Prepare the following cream: half pint of boiling milk stirred into two egg yolks beaten together with 2 oz sugar and 1 oz flour. Whisk the cream, then move from heat and add to it the kirsch in which the apricots soaked. Put the halves of apricots together again to make whole ones, putting a ball of the cream in place of the stone. Put them at once into the batter and then straight into boiling fat.

Lyon Bugnes: Blend 4 oz butter with sugar, lemon zest, a pinch of salt. Add two egg yolks (or even three) one at a time, and a gill of rum. When your paste is smooth add at one 'dose' 9 oz flour and work all together with your hands. If you need to, add a little milk. Form into a ball and leave it for a couple of hours. Then roll the ball into a long sausage and cut this into portions. You need long, thickish bands which you gash in two places, then bring over the ends and tuck them into the gashes to make 8-shaped knots. These are fried in very hot oil.

ALSACE SCHWOBE-BROEDEL: 1 lb flour, 1 lb sugar, ¾ lb butter, 8–12 oz peeled and well-pounded almonds, a little rose essence, the zest of one lemon, a trace of cinnamon. Make all this into a dough, roll it out to a quarter-inch thickness, cut with pastry cutters, gild with egg yolk and put into a fairly brisk oven.

(Recipe from M. PAUL ACKER)

DAMPFNUDELN: Take 2¼ lb flour, a piece of butter of egg size; melt butter in a scant pint of warm milk. Add flour, work the dough thoroughly, then add four whole eggs, a few currants, a pinch of salt, some brewer's yeast (as big as an egg again) mixed with a little warm milk, a tablespoonful of rum or brandy.

Leave dough to rise in a warm spot. When well risen, have a panful of boiling fat ready. Into this you will drop, large spoonful by large spoonful, your dampfnudeln. When one side is golden, turn them. When cooked on all sides, pile in a pyramid and sprinkle with sugar. You will be delighted, I promise you that.

(Recipe from ANDRE LICHTENBERGER)

Pancakes

'Everyone knows how to make pancakes,' wrote Dr. Pomiane in his agreeable fashion. 'Two eggs, flour, water, salt, sugar, a frying-pan, butter, something to cook over . . . and the job's done.'

Well, that is it, more or less. But you are at liberty to set about it differently, if you will. To add various alcoholic flavourings, for instance. To add jam; to ignite your pancakes; to stuff them with different cream fillings. But you have often heard about Crêpes Suzette and are not quite clear about their creation:

Crêpes Suzette

(1) Make your batter in the usual way but instead of water use chilled milk and allow six whole eggs to 8 oz flour. Your sugar should be vanilla-flavoured. You need Cognac or rum in the batter.

(2) While the batter is standing put in a warmed earthenware dish 5–6 oz butter, beat and soften it with a wooden spoon, adding 4 oz caster sugar, the juice and grated zest of two mandarine oranges, and a glass of curaçao.

VERSES FOR THE VERY GREEDY

Theodore Botrel (of *La Paimpolaise*) wrote this narrative verse about buckwheat (Saracen corn) pancakes, as made in Brittany. His Breton words are retained and explained.

BUCKWHEAT PANCAKES

Evening has faded, now it's night
And time to ride the jolting cart
Toward the farm, and get our bite
Of supper. Drop your work, we'll start
The homeward jaunt. A kitchen smell
Steals out to cheer us, drifting round . . .
That's good hot soup . . . I know it well . . .
And buckwheat pancakes, I'll be bound!
And now, my Marivonne . . . I seem
To see her toss the sifted wheat

In milk that's topped with crusted cream.
The fourch-tân[1] *darts. With ready heat,*
Fanned by her flirted pinafore,
The furze twigs crackle, hiss and burst,
To redden hearth and kitchen floor.
She takes the pillig-du,[2] *but first*
Must grease it with some bacon fat.
Trim Marivonne, of slender waist,
Sprightly but deft, now rolls out flat,

[1] Fourch-tân = small fork for pushing fuel in brazier.
[2] Pillig-du = pan.

With firm rozel,[3] *her airy paste.*
The bass[4] *goes in, more furze is burned,*
The cake swells up, and in its pride
Grows golden. Quivers. Then is turned
With twist of Sklisen[5] *(short and wide*
Like Grecian glaive in wars of old).
The first for Tad-coz.[6] *Look, it's done!*
And then their fill for young and old.
And, if they choose to leave him one,
The Klasker-bara[7] *gets the last,*
Tomorrow. Charming Marivonne,
We thank you for our rich repast:
Now someone broach a cask. Bring on
Some mugs of cider, cool and sweet.
Mug . . . pancake . . . mug. Mug . . . pancake . . . I
(And you, and ours) thus drink and eat,
Until, full-fed, our smaller fry,
Grouped round the threshold, by and by
Will eye the moon, and jerk a thumb
To show the wonder there on high—
A buckwheat pancake in the sky!

FRUMENTY AT NOHANT

Snow-white, in the hollow of a violet plate,
Frumenty, made from Berry-ripened corn,
Glinted among the gaudy blossoms, borne
Towards us, ceremonially, in state.

We saw its paunch, enriched with wheat, dilate,
Speckled with cream, to sweeten and adorn,
Snow-white, in the hollow of a violet plate,
Frumenty, made from Berry-ripened corn.

Flaubert was served three times, the tales relate.
Brillat, had he been with us, would not scorn
The pride of Berry, great among the great,
Since Sand herself extolled it, native-born . . .
Snow-white, in the hollow of a violet plate.

GABRIEL NIGOND

[3] Rozel = rolling-pin.
[4] Bass = dough.
[5] Sklisen = palette-knife.
[6] Tad-coz = grandfather.
[7] Klasker-bara = one begging his bread.

(3) Make your pancakes in the usual way in a small frying-pan of very thick base. As you are serving, put a layer of the orange butter on each pancake, and fold in fours and eights.

Flemish Waffles

Warm some milk, crumble yeast into it, whisk. Add sugar, salt, cinnamon; the proportions are 3½ oz sugar, 1 pint milk, 1 oz yeast. Add by degrees 8 oz flour and four egg yolks when flour is all worked in. Work up a uniform, smooth paste and if it is hard to work, but not otherwise, add a little butter. Cover with a porous cloth and leave to stand. Three hours later whisk again (this time the volume will be greater) and beat in the egg whites, which you will, in the interval, have whipped into a snowy froth.

Cook in hot buttered waffle irons. Cook 45 minutes on each side.

Brittany Far

Half a pound each of flour and sugar, a tablespoonful of brandy, a tablespoonful of orange-flower water, 1¾ pints milk, 4 eggs. Blend the flour with a little of the milk, add yolks, then whites lightly beaten, then sugar, rest of milk, orange-flower water, brandy.

Pour mixture into a thinly buttered tart tin, put into a brisk oven for a minute or two, then lower heat and cook for half an hour to an hour, according to heat of oven. Some people (outside Brittany, for we have come to the end of the 'Far' recipe) add raisins and serve with a vanilla flavoured *crème anglaise* (*see* p. 324).

Bigoudens

Proportions: 1 lb 6 oz flour, 8 oz good butter, 4 egg yolks, 10 oz sugar, 4 tablespoonsful double cream, ¼ teaspoonful table salt, a small glass of brandy, 8 oz almonds.

Put flour in a ring on a scrubbed table. Draw a little of it to the middle, add sugar, butter, eggs, cream, salt, brandy, and mix and work all together. When well mixed, work in the rest of the flour. Knead it, break up into pieces for that purpose, then assemble into one big ball. Put the almonds in very hot water for ten minutes, then rub off the brown skins. Chop them, but not into very small pieces. Put the almond pieces in the oven for 8–10 minutes to dry. When cold, stir into the dough. Roll this out a quarter of an inch thick, first flouring the table to prevent sticking. Cut little rounds with a pastry stamper and put them on a greased tin or oven sheet. Gild with egg yolk. Put them in the baker's oven (or your own) for 15–18 minutes. Take out and allow to get completely cold before storing in tins with well-fitting lids.

(Breton recipe)

Wasser Schestribe

Break four eggs into nine tablespoonsful of flour and work for some time, making sure that the dough is neither too heavy nor too wet. Add salt, then a little milk to the flour *before* you put in the eggs, however. Put pan with very hot oil or fat ready to fry them, then drop the paste through a funnel in such a way that it drops in circles into the fat.

(Alsace recipe)

Burgundian 'Millet'

Not to be confused with bird-seed. You take four tablespoonsful of flour, two eggs, a little unsalted butter. Mix into a soft dough. Grease an oven dish, pour in the prepared dough, then cover it with a cupful of milk in which six lumps of sugar and a little salt have been dissolved. Put in oven and at first stir a little, then leave for 25 minutes.

(The flour may be replaced by semolina cooked in either milk or water.)

Surprise Cake

Mix in saucepan six egg yolks, 2 oz sugar, ½ pint milk. Put in bain-marie (or use double saucepan) and stir until you have a soft, smooth mixture. Take away from heat. Now make a butter-cream with 8 oz chocolate and 8 oz butter in bain-marie, and mix with the first composition. Line a cake mould with sponge fingers, soaked in rum and water. Pour in your cream, cover with biscuits, put in a cool place. Next day turn out of mould and serve with English cream (*see* p. 324).

Quick Cake

Beat two eggs and 5 oz flour and 1½ oz sugar in a bowl. Thin mixture with a bare pint of milk and a glass of rum. Melt a walnut of butter in frying-pan[1] and drop in a tablespoonful of the mixture. It will spread and brown. Then pour in the rest and transfer to oven for ten minutes. Eat hot, with gooseberry jam, etc.

'Pain Perdu'

You really need your hard, dry old crusts of bread for this. Soak them in sweetened milk until they have absorbed plenty of it. Beat two eggs and mix with the soaked bread, adding cubes of dried figs, and of dates, also a few currants. Butter a mould and fill with the mixture. Bake and serve with a caramel cream.

N.B.—There is another well-known 'Pain Perdu' recipe, with fewer ingredients for the crusts to lose themselves among. The bread is not, however, crusty this time—but slices of bread with crusts removed.

[1] Use pan without a long handle.

They are soaked in milk, then dipped in beaten egg and fried golden-brown in butter. Powdered with vanilla-flavoured sugar.

Gannat Brioche

Four teacups flour, 4 eggs, 2½ cups of milk-top cream, boiled; 3½ oz Gruyère cheese, 2 packets Alsace yeast, pinch of salt. The mixture is cooked in a buttered mould for at least an hour in a hot oven, the top gilded with egg yolk before it is put in. To test for cooking time, insert a knife blade—cake is done if it comes out clean.

Gargouillau

Put in a bowl a glassful and a half of flour, salt to taste, two eggs beaten into milk. Make a kind of batter with this. Cut one pound of pears into rings, mix in a glassful of caster sugar, now mix the sweetened fruit with the batter. Put on to well-buttered oven sheet with confining edges, dot with butter, bake for half an hour.

The Gargouillau is a speciality of the Creuse department.

Strudels

Noodle paste mixed with butter, rolled out as thinly as possible and cut in squares. These are covered with cubes of apple, small knobs of butter, cleaned currants, chopped almonds, and a good sprinkling of cinnamon. The edges are moistened, the squares rolled into a kind of fat tube, daubed with melted butter, gilded with egg yolk. Put them in a sauté pan with a little milk and poach gently until all the liquid has evaporated. Then sprinkle with sugar.

Jewish recipes add poppy seeds as well, and make the cakes in triangular form, naming them Haman's Pouches. The black soul of Haman is represented by the poppy seeds and is thus ingested in a two-thousand-years-old traditional act of vengeance.

Siberian Kacha

Boil gently with 5 pints of milk and a walnut of butter 8 oz blanched pearl barley, stirring all the time. When done, remove from heat and add 8 oz butter, 6 beaten eggs, half a glassful of sour cream. Bake in a mould.

Terrinée ('A Panful')

A bare quarter pound of rice, 3 oz sugar, a dessertspoonful of cinnamon, a pinch of salt, 3½ pints milk. Take a glazed earthenware dish and put in the rice, sugar, salt, cinnamon, mix well, then add the milk. Bake in a fairly brisk oven for three hours. Serve in the same dish, hot or cold.

Menchikof

Eight ounces of peeled almonds, filberts or hazelnuts, pounded to a milky cream, half a pound of caster sugar, half a pound of unsalted butter. Cream the butter first until it is really soft and smooth. Then add the sugar and nut-paste and a small bowlful of 'made' (i.e. cooked) cream, strongly flavoured with vanilla. Line a mould with sponge fingers, pour in your mixture, lay biscuits over the top, put the mould under a heavy weight and keep in a cold place until the following day.

(Recipe from M. PAUL ACKER.)

Hazel and Almond Balls

Beat three egg whites to a firm snow; add 10 oz caster sugar, 4 oz hazelnuts, 4 oz almonds. The nuts must be pounded, but with their thin brown skins still on them. Roll the mixture into small balls and powder them with sugar. Leave overnight to harden on a lightly-buttered oven sheet. After this 'resting' cook them in a very slow oven, so that the middles remain a little liquid when the outer surfaces have dried.

Pumpkin Cake

Mix two glassfuls of flour with cold milk to the consistency of a fritter batter. Cook separately 1 lb pumpkin, salt it when tender, drain away all surplus liquid. Put pumpkin in pan with a walnut of butter, add a glassful of caster sugar, a quarter ounce of yeast, vanilla flavouring, 2 or 3 egg yolks, and mix well. Finally fold in the egg whites beaten to a snow and bake in a greased tin in a hot oven.

Doughnuts

Take a glassful of caster sugar, half its bulk of melted butter, three eggs, one glass of milk, four tablespoonsful brewer's yeast, one dessertspoonful of grated nutmeg. Mix all these ingredients, then add enough flour to make a dough that will not stick to the fingers. Knead and roll out for a good spell, and finally roll out to one-third-inch thickness, cut into rounds (with a glass or pastry-cutter), and make a hole in the middle of each. Drop into boiling fat and leave for five to ten minutes.

(Canadian version)

El Baklavas

Work together half a pound of flour and two eggs. Add a little salt when the dough is smoothly blended, cut into three portions, and roll out each piece until you cannot roll it any thinner. Pound in the mortar 10 oz blanched and peeled almonds and, in a separate mortar, 10 oz pistachio nuts. Spread an almond layer on your first piece of pastry, cover

VERSES FOR THE VERY GREEDY
(continued)

'FRIVOLES' (OR 'FLIGHTY CAKES')

Among the local dainties of Champagne,
Of old tradition, and remembered well,
One, above all, our village wives retain,
Though mentioned by no latter-day Vatel.

First roll some biscuit dough—some bagatelle
Not over-short, or fancy: good, but plain,
Sliced into diamonds. If you can, attain
Exact proportions. Let them fry, pell-mell,

In boiling fat. Then, presto! Drain, and eat
All sizzling hot: but modify their heat
With good, young wine. Then watch them disappear!

One festive day, in Bacchus' honour, stroll
To some hotel, and ask them for 'Frivoles'.
Then tell me if you've ever found their peer.

ARSENE THEVENOT

Our last verse concerns the classic ALMOND TARTLETS of the worthy pastrycook Ragueneau who figures in *Cyrano de Bergerac*:

Beat some eggs to froth, with brisk
Lively whisk,
Then with lemon juice dilute
(Choose, of course, a perfect fruit).
Now pour in
Sweetest almonds, soft as silk,
Pounded to a creamy milk.
Many a tin
Fit for tartlets you must find.
When with pastry these are lined,
Lightly press
Here and there, in favoured spots,
Soft and juicy apricots.
These you dress,
Drop by drop, with flavoured foam.
Bake them golden, out they come,
Counterparts,
Merry flocklets, frolicsome
Almond tarts.

EDMOND ROSTAND

this with the second piece, spread on this a pistachio layer. Cover your confection with the top third of pastry. The whole thickness is now cut into diamond shapes, quite small so long as shape is maintained, and baked in a moderate oven, on an oiled dish, for about twenty minutes.

Now blend in a frying pan some honey, orange-flower water and sugar. When golden and melted, put the cooked cakes in, withdraw them, pop them back again several times to get crisp but not honey-drenched. Let them get cold before eating.

(A Turkish recipe)

El Mistouf

Sweet Version of Couscous

Work some medium semolina (1¾ lb) with a little water in a deep dish to aid granulation. Then spread muslin inside a wide strainer, put the semolina on the muslin, and then fix the strainer firmly over a large pan of boiling water. As cooking proceeds, this mass must be moistened from above, three times.

Chop up in small pieces 1¾ lb stoned dates and put them with your couscous over the pan, where they will soften further. Put into a mortar some skinned almonds, currants, pistachios, caster sugar, grated chocolate, powdered cinnamon, orange peels, orange-flower water. Blend all together, crushing vigorously. When the couscous is done, stir in this mixture, pile in pyramid on serving dish, decorate with dates, almonds (whole) and pistachios (also whole).

(Arabic recipe)

Josephine Baker Flan

Beat three tablespoonsful of sugar into three fresh eggs. Separately, blend two tablespoonsful of flour and nearly a pint of milk. Mix the two sets of ingredients and strain to remove any lumps or threads. Add two teaspoonsful of kirsch and two of green Chartreuse. Then stir in three bananas cut up in rings and some zest of lemon. Pour into oven dish and bake for twenty minutes.

(Supplied by GASTON DERYS)

Filbert Pudding

Four ounces each of caster sugar, butter, and filberts from which skin has been removed, are pounded together. Make separately a good ¾ pint of English cream of fairly solid consistency. Spread several sponge fingers with the nut-butter-sugar paste, put them in layers in a mould, and pour some of the cream (warm) over each layer until mould is full. Leave overnight in a cool place, then serve with a vanilla-flavoured cream.

(Recipe from M. LUCIEN TIBIER, chef at the Elysée)

Walnut Loaves

Three ounces sugar, 7 oz ground walnuts, 13 oz flour, just under 3 oz butter. Mix well and form into a dough with warm water. Form into small loaves and bake for three-quarters of an hour in a moderate oven.

Rigollots

Mix 8 oz caster sugar and 3 whole eggs. Add by degrees, to avoid lumps, 8 oz flour. The result will be a rather liquid dough that is not quite a batter, however. Butter an oven pan or large cake tin and spoon on to it very small pats of the mixture, allowing plenty of space between. They spread into thin biscuits that will keep for months in suitable containers. Five minutes' cooking time will be ample.

Toulouse Cake

Six coffee-cupsful powdered sugar, the same of wheat-flour, and six eggs. Put flour in deep mixing bowl, form a well in the middle of it. Beat eggs in another bowl, add sugar, flavour to your liking (e.g., with lemon, vanilla, essence of bergamot-orange), stir well to distribute flavouring. Pour into the flour, and it is a good idea to add peeled almonds chopped into very small scraps. A shallow mould (not more than an inch high) is oiled or buttered, cake mixture poured in, a few peeled almonds set on the top, and cake baked in a medium-hot oven.

Caramel Rice

Cook rice in milk, allow to get cold. Then mix in a glassful of English cream (p. 324) and two egg whites beaten to a snow. Put in a mould around the insides of which a caramel syrup has been run, and bake for three-quarters of an hour. Serve with a caramel-flavoured English cream.

Milk Rice

Wash rice, cook for five minutes in boiling water. Strain away liquid and toss rice into sweetened and vanilla-flavoured boiling milk. Simmer gently. (You need 4 oz rice and 4 oz sugar for two pints of milk.) Serve cold.

N.B.—Cinnamon may replace vanilla. An even better substitute is grated chocolate.

Empress Rice

Cook rice in milk and stir into it assorted preserved fruits (the candied kind). Dissolve two sheets of gelatine in some English cream and blend into the rice. Put in a mould to get cold, and serve with Chantilly cream.

Madeleine Decure's Cake

Half a pound of fine quality chocolate

Four oz sweet almonds (with skin) pounded in mortar to a cream

Four oz good unsalted butter

Four new-laid egg yolks, and four whites beaten to a snow

8 oz finest caster sugar

Three tablespoonsful sifted flour.

Melt chocolate in very little water over gentle heat, in saucepan. When it is a thick, smooth paste, add all the other ingredients, excepting egg whites, and beat the mixture for ten minutes. You will find it very stiff, but persevere.

Butter a charlotte mould—but a nice saucepan of good contours will serve just as well—and then fold into your mixture, without actually stirring, the egg whites snow. Put into mould or pan and bake very slowly (in a slow oven). When it is only just pale brown stand it on a sheet of white paper and ice it. To make the icing, melt two tablets of chocolate, a little butter; the icing must be glossy and thick.

(To test whether or not the cake is done, prick it with a cocktail-stick, or some little stick of similar kind. It should be just a little creamy when withdrawn.)

Various Creams

CHANTILLY CREAM: Fresh cream is well whisked, and as you are about to lay the whisk by, add a 'shower' of caster sugar, at the rate of 5 oz sugar to 1 lb cream. May be flavoured with vanilla (powder form) and used with Savarins, Saint-Honorés, Meringues, various kinds of Choux pastry.

A mixture of Crême Chantilly and Chestnut Purée makes the famous NEGRE EN CHEMISE.

ENGLISH CREAM: Is a rich egg custard. Beat together egg yolks and sugar, then thin with boiling milk. Proportions: 1¾ pints milk, 8 oz sugar, 8 egg yolks. Once mixed, do not allow to come to boil again, but cook while stirring with a wooden spoon. Flavour with vanilla, praline, chocolate, coffee, lemon, or a liqueur.

CUSTARD CREAM MOULD (Crème Renversée): Five oz sugar, 1¾ pints milk, desired flavouring. Boil these ingredients. Five egg yolks are whisked in a bowl, boiling milk is poured over drop by drop, with constant stirring. Transfer to buttered mould (or, better still, one lined with caramel syrup) and cook in bain-marie or oven for three-quarters of an hour.

RECIPE FOR A FIRST-CLASS DINNER PARTY

When you have censored the list of people to whom you owe a dinner, have gone through it with a small tooth-comb, eliminating with delicate touch all the idiots, all the snobs, all with irritating affectations, all scandalmongers: then choose from among the number of your cronies a few of the wittiest, men who have also receptive stomachs and sole rights (if this be possible) to charming wives.

Then arrange your guests with discrimination to encircle a round table (a square one is a discouragement to general conversation). As soon as soup has disappeared, acquaint your guests with the details of the menu you have so lovingly concocted for their enjoyment. This will enable them to plan, in advance, how much room to leave for their own favourite.

From this moment onward the sole preoccupation of host and hostess alike must be to put into practice Brillat-Savarin's delightful prescription: 'The entertainment of friends involves ensuring their well-being for as long as you have the privilege of sheltering them.'

It is quite unnecessary for you to serve up, in your anxiety to give your friends a real feast, any highly complicated dishes, or any of the roasts of macabre darkness yielded by exotic beasts.

Those reindeer collops! . . .

Those bear chops! . . .

And what donkeys!

For the sound traditional dishes of France, properly prepared with butter of farmhouse quality, cooked with devotion, simmered with respect, roasted with fine judgment, and served piping hot, will always earn you the congratulations of even the goutiest gourmets.

With the exception of one or two delicatessen specialities imported from outside, such a dinner as this should be of home cooking. For we can agree, surely, that ready-dressed, and ill-dressed, victuals supplied at so much per head by firms none too highly remunerated for their pains, are a joke in doubtful taste, and in some cases fall little short of being gruesome outrages directed against the digestive system.

Yes, indeed. We in France could hardly protest too energetically against these suspect mixtures, these dark, anonymous sauces, these lukewarm chickens, these re-heated fillets, basic constituents of such foul junketings: of these menus which feature, also, 'mousses de foie-gras' that appear to be nothing but last night's scraps pounded to a paste: not to mention those appalling 'chauds-froids', all a-bristle with black-beaked heads of little birds, the weakly,

shrivelled bodies of which are engulfed in jellies with disquieting depths . . . or encrusted in a whitish compound whose solid and resistant texture places it in regions which my culinary knowledgeableness has so far ignored.

And as for wines, your friends will appreciate a good, wholesome table wine of pleasing bouquet (unless, of course, you can rout out a vintage bottle or two). But whatever you do, you must beware of imitating those establishments, bold as brass but of dreadful omen, where wines of 'Borgia' type, cynically decked out in lying labels, are mournfully announced by hired undertakers' men wearing lisle-thread gloves.

HENRI CAIN

WOMEN AT TABLE

One Joseph Despaze composed a song advocating 'men-only' dinners. Its concluding message was:

'Friends, aren't we happier men with men?
Our instincts point the proper way!
At dinner, men, just men, I say,
Women at supper. Wait till then.'

M. A. J. de Coupigny wrote two verses as rejoinder:

'Often your darling, disinclined
For dalliance in the day's cold light
Has melted, softened, as she dined,
When love put all her doubts to flight.

The struggle's hopeless, fellow-men,
Their charms defeat us, they are stronger.
Let's dine and sup with beauty—then,
If we are clever . . . keep them longer.'

A LESSON IN MANNERS

Alexander II, Emperor of Russia, had invited to his table an elderly officer, a man of high courage, who had lived for many years in army camps and knew nothing of society. After dessert, finger-bowls full of perfumed water for finger-rinsing were placed before the diners. The old soldier, having no idea of their purpose, swallowed the contents of his bowl, and the young people at table were ready to laugh when Alexander, checking them with a withering stare, picked up his bowl and drank the water at one draught.

PASTRYCOOK'S CREAM: Four egg yolks, 5 oz sugar are beaten into a froth, then an ounce of flour is blended in, with a pinch of salt and vanilla-flavoured caster sugar. Half a pint of boiling milk is added, while whisking vigorously. If you add to this mixture 3 to 4 oz ground almonds, you have a frangipane cream, useful as garnishing cream for flaky pastries and tarts.

BUTTER CREAM: This kind of cream is the one used in Mocha cakes and 'Yule Logs'. It is a mixture of butter and 'sandy' sugar in equal quantities. Coffee (or chocolate) flavouring and two egg yolks are added. Leave in a cool place. The flavouring should be either very strong coffee or melted grated chocolate.

And here are a few miscellaneous confections:

Beauvoir Cream

Use so many eggs, so many tablespoonsful of rum, so many tablespoonsful of sugar (the 'so many' being any one number). For one portion: beat one egg yolk, one tablespoonful each of rum and sugar together. Beat one egg white separately, and when very stiff, add to mixture.

Virgin Snow Cream

Beat 4 egg whites to a snow and pour over them just under one pint of vanilla-flavoured and sweetened milk, warm but not hot. Strain through fine strainer. Put in pan and beat gently, stirring until the mixture is of creamy consistency. Add one glassful of kirsch and set aside to get cold.

Very good with a chestnut cake.

Sabayon Cream

Beat whites of three eggs with caster sugar and put over gentle heat. As you whisk add Marsala or some liqueur-natured white wine. When it has thickened, remove from heat, add a glass of rum, and serve at once.

Chocolate Mousse

Grated chocolate is mixed (over a very low flame) with egg-yolks. When mixture is smooth, add the egg whites, beaten stiffly. Set in a cool place.

Ice Creams

English cream (*see* above) may be flavoured to your liking and put in the little freezing (ice-cube) sections of your refrigerator. These are agreeable little individual ice-creams. The same method may be applied to Sabayon cream, or coffee or chocolate mousse.

Soufflés

Soufflés are egg whites beaten to a snow, mixed with a cream or purée and the egg yolks. In the oven the yolks coagulate and imprison the inflated bubbles of egg white, so that the soufflé swells to airy lightness. The soufflé mixture goes into a buttered dish and is sprinkled with sugar, then put into a hot oven for 15 or 20 minutes, according to its size. Sweet dessert soufflés usually have a pastrycook's cream base (flavoured with vanilla, coffee, chocolate, etc.) and may also contain spirits, fruit jellies, crushed pralines, diced preserved fruits, fruit purées.

Mireille Soufflé

Three separate creams are made first: a chocolate-flavoured, a filbert cream, a vanilla cream. Beat egg whites separately (double the number of yolks used in the creams), and add to each cream one-third of the egg-whites mixture. Butter soufflé mould, sprinkle with 'sandy' sugar, and put in the creams, each in its own third of the dish. Bake for 18 to 20 minutes.

(Recipe supplied by M. JOURDAN of Marseille (Buffet gastronomique)

Normandy Soufflé

Make a pastrycook's cream, adding one raw egg yolk, a spot or two of Calvados, the same of Grand Marnier. Cook three peeled apples in the oven. Mash two Duchess (or similar) sweet pears.

Mix the whites of a few eggs with the cream. Put half the mixture in a mould, add the apples and the pear purée, then put in the other half of the mixture. Bake in the oven.

(Recipe supplied by M. MARCEL DORIN)

Wine

WINE

It is a useful general rule to put water in wash-basins, good wine in tumblers meant for water, and spirits in glasses meant for good wine.
CURNONSKY

Pure water?—a myth!
DR. BESANÇON

You say it's delicious? Unthinkable!
A duck would, no doubt, quack 'Hosannah!'
But water has never been drinkable,
Except by a miracle, at Cana.
X. DE LA PERRAUDIERE

The vineyard's siesta is summer's poetic highlight.
RAMO GOMEZ DE LA SERNA

Ah, if only the Seine were of good Beaune wine,
And I had a paunch of giant strength,
Yards wide!
Under a bridge I'd lie full-length
And drink and drink till the Seine was mine,
And safe inside!
EMILE GOUDEAU

'Tis wisdom to love wine.
THEODORE DE BANVILLE

But these are poets' frivolities, and pure, fresh water is perfectly acceptable to the knowledgeable gastronome, even if only to separate one wine from another, by giving the drinker a 'new mouth'; also with salad, artichokes—and, some say, eggs—which are not suitably accompanied by wine.

Moreover, water is a thirst quencher; and Brillat-Savarin, acknowledging the fact, added that for that very reason it must be drunk only sparingly.

But to get back to wine. That is, wines.

Is there any rule regulating their marriage with various dishes? To quote Brillat-Savarin again (*Aphorisms*, XII): 'The order in which they should be taken is from the mildest to the headiest and those with the most pronounced bouquet'. But it is best to be guided by one's own personal tastes so long as the following axiom is observed.

Never associate the sweet, liqueur-like white wines of distinction with game or brown meats.

Never associate distinguished red wines with shellfish or other fish.

And, having declared that there are no rules, let us make haste to set out in full this directive given by Dr. Paul Ramain who called himself 'Countryman and unattached gourmet'—a homely and modest disguise for one of our most eminent connoisseurs:

LOCAL WHITE WINES: with delicatessen (pork dishes) of the same locality; fish, crayfish (with or without sauce); such regional dishes as contain neither game nor meat; vegetables, plain meat cuts, cheeses.

DRY WHITE WINES: Eggs, sea-fish (or river and lake fish not highly seasoned)—poached or grilled; creamed crayfish; shellfish soups; shellfish generally, including oysters, lobsters of various kinds; salted provisions; pork confections; raw and smoked ham; minor meat entrées; cardoons, beans, roast veal (or veal in sauce); truffles, mushrooms, creamed morels; soups and hors d'œuvre; many kinds of cheeses, including unfermented cheeses.

MELLOW WHITE WINES: Melons; highly-flavoured fish; Marennes oysters; fish stews; lobsters; spiced shellfish dishes; certain soups and hors d'œuvre; creamed chicken, etc.; rice; entrées with Madeira added; foie-gras (yes!).

LIQUEUR-NATURED WHITE WINES: main dishes, certain fruits, ices, some cheeses; green or dry almonds; char; trout in meunière style (no flour); biscuits; melon; foie-gras without truffles but glazed and of high quality. Or else—all alone.

LIQUEUR WINES: As 'five o'clock drink'; at dessert; or when 'fasting', as a tonic for the digestion.

EXTRA-DRY CHAMPAGNE: All by itself on an empty stomach; or, as an end-of-the-evening drink, try it iced. Never as 'five o'clock drink'; never as a dessert wine. Sometimes with truffles, often with soups, occasionally with crayfish, prawns, or other highly-flavoured crustacean. May also be drunk from start to finish of a meal.

DRY CHAMPAGNE: As aperitif or to round off an evening, in this case unaccompanied by any kind of food. Drink also with crayfish, highly-seasoned dishes, dried fruits. Not objectionable with foie-gras and truffles.

MEDIUM-DRY OR SWEET CHAMPAGNE: The truly characteristic French wine. To be used only as a 'tea-time' wine, a dessert wine, replacing liqueur-type white wines—but not after or before these.

VIN GRIS (PINKISH, not often GREY), PALE-REDS (ROSES) of LOCAL TYPE): As, for instance, of Touraine or Les Riceys.

Drink with pork *charcuterie*, cold pork, hors d'œuvre, caviare, roast joints, quail, thrushes, lamb, mushrooms, poultry, ducklings, cooked cheeses (e.g. Septmoncel, Morbier, Gruyère), veal, sea-fish grilled or poached, bouillabaisse, brandade (salt cod pounded with garlic and cream), oysters (I can vouch for this myself). These wines must be cool.

RED LOCAL WINES: Use as a transitional wine at family meals, as a cooking wine (except in speciality recipes), and to accompany snacks.

LIGHT RED WINES: may be a Bordeaux of vast distinction, or an eminent Burgundy that hasn't quite come off, or of a poor year; or maybe . . . a really aged wine.

There are also to be found some light red wines resulting from bad seasons in the Rhône vineyards. But as a general rule, the uninitiated think of a light red wine as being a Beaujolais, Chinon, Bourgueil, Saint-Julien, or one or two Médocs. These wines, of excellent flavour and easy of digestion, should be served before heavier-bodied wines (even of the very same vintage). They call for the following dishes: poultry, white meats, lamb, ducklings, thrushes, quail, ham, cold meats, partridge, mushrooms, pheasant, goose, turkey-poult, foie-gras, meat entrées, cheeses, dried fruits, meat pies.

FULL-BODIED RED WINES: Might be the same as those of the previous section, but either younger or of a more favoured year. The fullest-bodied, and somewhat 'heavy', are the Châteauneuf-du-Pape and Ermitage reds. The latter are very harsh in their earlier days and must remain longer in bottle than the former. A full-bodied red wine is not always 'a drop of the real stuff'. It *may* be thus, but is capable of transforming itself rapidly into a light-bodied wine. This goes for quite a number of Burgundies.

These full-bodied wines must be complemented by: red meat, beef cuts, wild duck, duck, grouse, venison, kid, boar, hare, woodcock, snipe,

ON WINE

Full long, in deep-arched cellars, dank and cold,
Beneath a vault encased in nitrous crust,
Among the spiders' webs, and thick with dust,
In this year's bottles youthful wines grow old.

In still and shadowy tombs, for months untold,
The splendid liquor stays, as stay it must
Until at last, to honour a noble trust,
It makes us briefly wise and briefly bold.

Even thus, some alchemy, secret and slow
(Friend Chaze), transforms man's musings which, at need
Yield to the sweet restraint of metric lines.

A rippling sonnet, like a suave bordeaux,
Mellows. And, cellar born, you rightly read
Fine lyrics, as you sip your seasoned wines.

FRANÇOIS COPPEE

FROM THE HEART

While on a vist to Cognac vaults a few cronies (including the prince of gastronomes, Curnonsky) were invited to sample each of the magnificent brandies stored away in innumerable casks.

As a precaution against intoxication the hosts advised, as each glass was filled, that their own procedure therewith should be followed. 'Spit it out again! Spit it out!' they suggested repeatedly.

And, with death in their hearts, the guests SPAT IT OUT.

But then they reached a 'Fine Champagne', even more admirable than its predecessors. And from somewhere in the gloom came Curnonsky's rebellious roar of: 'Be damned to that! I'm swallowing!'

NAPOLEON AT TABLE

'To dine like a soldier,' Napoleon used to say, 'come and have dinner at my place. If you wish to dine like an emperor, go and eat at Cambacérès' house.'

pheasant, partridge, *Perdrix aux Choux* (*see* p. 169), mutton, poulet Marengo (i.e. fowl fricasseed with mushrooms), foie-gras, poultry generally, Souvarof, cheese, dried fruits.

So there it is. Try to follow these rules—and then do violence to them!

Our male readers may perhaps appreciate (women, for the most part, are less ardently attentive to such things) this little

TABULATION: COMPARISON OF QUALITY FOR THE PRE-EMINENT FRENCH WINES

covering the years 1933 to 1949:

compiled by PROFESSOR ROGER (Wine Academy of France)

	Bordeaux		Burgundy		Cham-		Côtes		
Year	Red	White	Red	White	pagne	Centre	du Rhône	Jura	Alsace
1933	2	2	2	3	4	4	5	3	2
1934	4	4	4	4	3	4	4	4	5
1935	1	1	2	3	2	3	2	3	3
1936	2	2	2	1	2	2	4	2	2
1937	3	5	3	4	4	4	5	4	4
1938	2	1	3	3	3	2	2	4	2
1939	2	2	2	1	1	2	3	2	2
1940	2	2	2	2	0	2	3	1	2
1941	1	1	1	1	2	1	3	1	2
1942	3	4	3	3	4	3	3	5	4
1943	3	4	3	3 or 4	4	3	4	4	4
1944	1	2	1	2	2	1	3	1	2
1945	5	5	5	4	4	5	4	5	5
1946	2	2	2	2	2	2	4	3	3
1947	5	5	5	5	5	5	5	5	5
1948	2	2	2	2	2	3	2	3	3
1949	4	4	4	3	3	4	4	3	2

0=very bad year
1=mediocre year
2=average year
3=good year
4=outstanding year
5=exceptional year

TOUR OF FRANCE (FROM WINE TO WINE)

Wines of the Loire

The Loire, the gentle-voiced Loire with its peaceful valleys, the heart of France, where the wines are subtle, pleasant, of infinite variety. First comes the trinity, Anjou, Vouvray, Saumur. Then come the wines known as Pouilly, Sancerre, Chavignol, Muscadet, Chinon, Bourgueil. . . .

It is important not to confuse Pouilly and Pouilly. One Pouilly is Burgundian, not far from Mâcon . . . a wine flourishing on a chalk soil. It is named Pouilly-Fuisé. The other one sees the light at Pouilly-sur-Loire, at Tracy, or at Saint-Andelain, also on chalk-soiled hillsides. Its aroma of gunflint reminds one of Rhine wines or of Muscadet, and it is called Pouilly-Fumé.

Muscadet itself comes from the lower reaches of the Loire (Loire-Inférieure). It is a clear white wine, never acid, a good companion to hors d'œuvre, to pike done in butter. A minor muscatel-Anjou wine of the region is Gros-Plant.

Vouvray wines are of several types: full-bodied, of heavy bouquet, liqueur-like, light, fruit-tasting. It is produced in seven districts of Vouvray, and is a very palatable, comforting drink.

Orleans wines are elegant reds or fruity whites, perfect table wines: for example, Gris-Meunier, really sturdy; or Auvergnat (red or white); or a Rosé Gris-Meunier.

King of the vine-clad slopes of Layon, growing on a crumbly shale in the Touraine-Anjou region, is the 'vin-pineau' (the black grape wine)—to quote Rabelais; the 'black burgundy' or marvellous Quart de Chaume, to be drunk cold but not icy-cold as a dessert wine.

Banyuls, Muscat, Frontignan

Four places—Cerbère, Banyuls, Port-Vendres and Collioure share the glory of this naturally sweet wine, a wine that smiles in your glass, banyuls-apéritif and dessert wine. It should be served at room temperature and drunk just as it is.

When Rabelais was first student and late professor at the Faculty of Medicine of the University of Montpellier, he made the acquaintance of Muscat wine and fell in love with it. The soil in which it grows is of chalk and gravel warmed by the Mediterranean sun, and it makes a soft, sweet, still wine like nectar.

Lunel and Rivesaltes formerly yielded excellent wines; Maraussan, and above all, Frontignan, are the outstanding names nowadays. But quite a long time ago Voltaire was writing from Ferney: 'I do ask you one favour, and that is that you will be so kind as to save my life by sending me a nice little quarter-cask of Frontignan.'

Wines of Savoy

Red wines are few and far between but two white wines have been found worthy of a registered name: Seyssel and Crépy.

Seyssel has an aroma of violets and is very good in its fifth year.

Crépy, dry and light, matures in bottle and sometimes ferments.

Other wines of the region are the Marestel, Abymes (red and white).

the generous and dark-red Montmeillan wines; also Thonon, Féternes (near Evian) and Ayse (near Bonneville).

But it is noteworthy that only really hot seasons have yielded good vintages in Savoy—1934, 1937, 1947.

Corsican Wines

Powerful wines, of which the Cap Corse is the most flavoursome. But a Patrimonio and the Sartène wines too are worthy of notice.

Champagne Wines

Three districts (and three types of wine-growing soil) multiply and at the same time unify entitlements to this resounding appellation: the white-wine slopes and terraces, the Marne valley and the Reims 'mountain' region. Trained on vine supports, with an occasional square of pole-trained vines, the vineyards stretch over the flanks of the hills—the high quality black grape, the Chardonnay white.

A red champagne: Bouzy

It may not be generally known that at one time the stock laid down in the Champagne cellars was as much as 180 million bottles! All vintage years were represented: those of the past, 1893, 1906, 1911, 1920, 1921, 1926 (no longer available). But 1928 was the finest year of the century; 1929 and 1933 were good years; 1934 a remarkable year; 1937 gave a distinguished wine, 1941 and 1942, one of splendid aroma. Before any year's worth may be assessed, five years' maturation in the cellar must elapse.

Good champagne should be drunk dry, very cool (but not iced) in a balloon glass. The wide-mouthed 'cup' shapes and tall champagne glasses are, rightly, outdated.

Alsatian Wines

The Alsace wine-growing district extends from Thann to Marienheim over a soil partly granite, partly chalk, and with some crystalline silica, or occasionally slate and gypsum. The climate, but above all the aspect, and the protection of the mountains, give Alsatian wines a nectar and bouquet peculiarly their own. The most abundantly produced red wines are the Trottinger and Meunier. Choice wines (white) are Traminer, Gewurtz-Traminer (both full-flavoured), the Muscats, Tokay (nothing to do with Hungarian, a wine of a pale red grape), Sylvaner and, above all, Riesling.

The word 'Zwicker'—and I give this information to benefit those who may perhaps let themselves be beguiled by its strangeness—means a blend of a quality-wine with a sound everyday one. Good years are

TOPER'S LOGIC

The Comte de Mirabeau (brother of the Mirabeau who declared 'We are here by will of the people and shall not depart except at bayonet-point!'), known as 'Mirabeau-Tonneau', an illuminating name, indeed, said one day to his valet: 'You're loyal, hardworking, in fact your services are eminently satisfactory, but you'll have to go.'

'But why, Monsieur le Comte?'

'Because, in spite of the arrangement we came to, you get drunk on the same days as I myself get drunk.'

'And is that my fault, sir? You get drunk every day!'

TOPER'S VIEW

The comic actor Lepeintre, who had a great reputation in his day, had been invited to dine with the son of King Louis-Philippe: and, some time afterwards, at the Court itself.

'Which establishment offered the best dinner?' a friend enquired:

'Well, it's like this. At the King's place, two glasses are set in front of guests: at the Duke of Orleans' place, three glasses. I needn't say more?'

Briffaut tells this story in his Paris at Table.

ADVERTISEMENT

This advertisement was published by a tripe-seller of renown in Napoleon's day:

Monsieur Cauchois
Deserves something akin to worship for his calves' heads,
which often make his own spin,
So numerous are the orders therefor with which he is inundated.

few and far between: 1893, 1904, 1921, 1929, 1934, 1935. The wines of Alsace are at their peak of drinkability when between five and eight years old. They are to be drunk very cool with hors d'œuvre, fish, and, it goes without insistence, foie-gras.

Perigord Wines

The white wines: Monbazillac, Haut Montravel, Côtes de Montravel, Rosette, Bergerac, Montravel.

The red wines: Pécharmant, Bergerac.

Monbazillac is a sweet wine assaying an easy 15–16 degrees and, in exceptional cases, 20 degrees. Five districts on the left bank of the Dordogne produce about 165,000 bushels of it. It is mainly a dessert wine.

Fifteen districts on the western boundaries of the Department furnish various Montravels—high-quality wines of good bouquet, usually very mellow. To the north of Bergerac are silico-argillaceous soils producing the full-flavoured white Rosettes. Sometimes they are very sweet and still and liqueur-natured, for example, Pécharmant (also called Pech-Charmant, 'pech' meaning summit)—a red wine of good body and rapid ageing, with 1940, 1946 and 1948 as good years. Especially right with cheese.

Navarre Wines

A clove of garlic rubbed over his lips and a drop of Jurançon to follow were the baptismal rite for Good King Henry. This Jurançon, a heart-warming and noble wine, enjoys universal prestige. But other notabilities are: in Béarn, Gan and Haut Gan (of a small-scale yield, red and white, Monein and Vicq Bielh). In the Basque country hard by, the celebrated Irouleguy (splendid for use in the preparation of a 'coq au vin', in no way inferior to the same dish prepared in Burgundy) shares its glory with the wines of Louhassos and Itrassou.

Burgundy Wines

The great 'burgundy' class must be subdivided. The Côte d'Or, heart of Burgundy, is of course *The* region, but three other important sub-divisions are:

(a) Beaujolais

This vast wine district includes the slopes of the right bank of the Saône, from Lyon to Mâconnais. The 'Bas-Beaujolais' begins at the very borders of the town of Lyon and yields that well-flavoured and simple wine which is used as a cooking wine in that capital of table-treasure, Lyon.

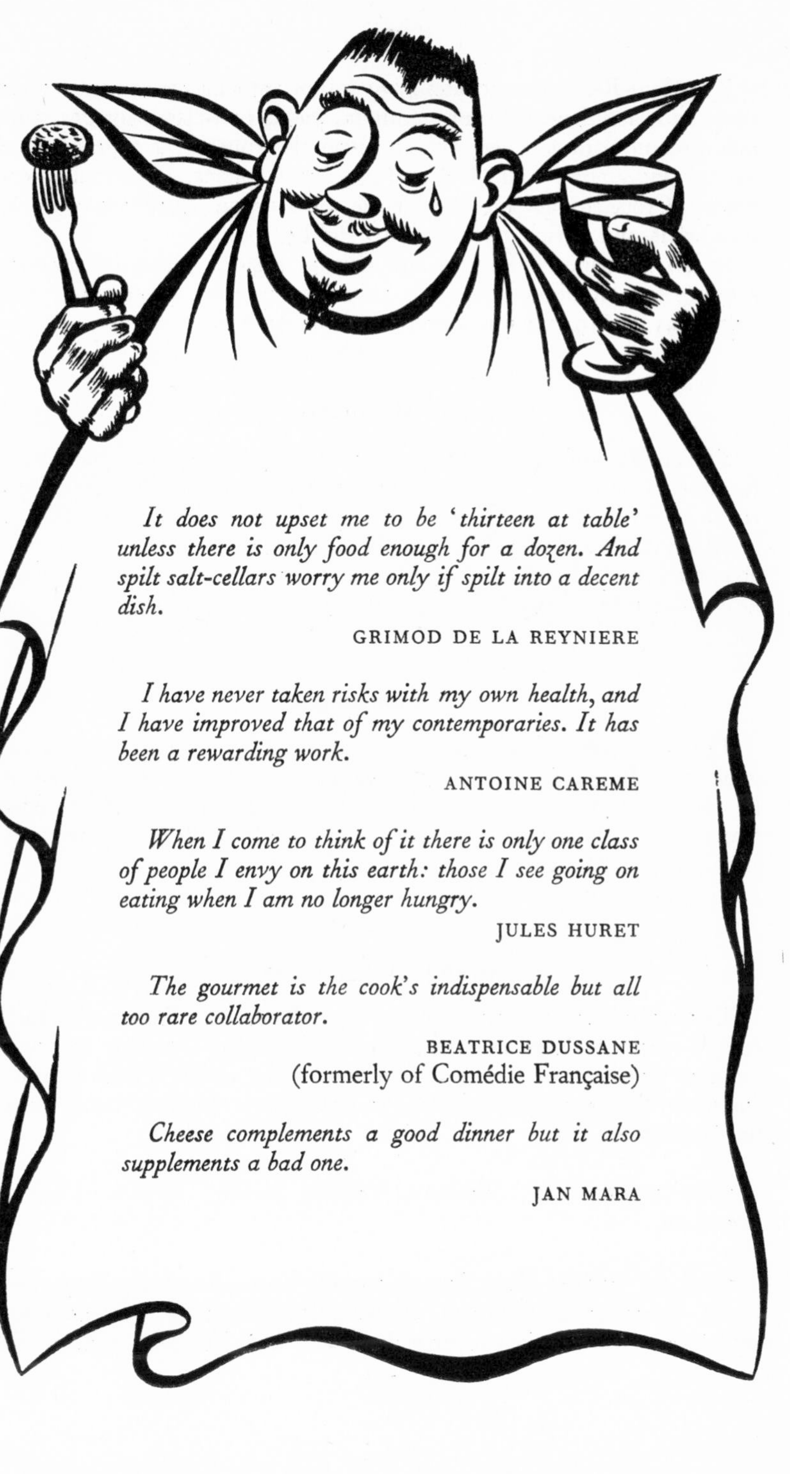

It does not upset me to be 'thirteen at table' unless there is only food enough for a dozen. And spilt salt-cellars worry me only if spilt into a decent dish.

GRIMOD DE LA REYNIERE

I have never taken risks with my own health, and I have improved that of my contemporaries. It has been a rewarding work.

ANTOINE CAREME

When I come to think of it there is only one class of people I envy on this earth: those I see going on eating when I am no longer hungry.

JULES HURET

The gourmet is the cook's indispensable but all too rare collaborator.

BEATRICE DUSSANE
(formerly of Comédie Française)

Cheese complements a good dinner but it also supplements a bad one.

JAN MARA

The Haut-Beaujolais includes many important wine centres and a good year, with a sufficiently sunny autumn, yields first-class vintages, with reds predominating. There are, for example, Juliénas, a wine of good flavour and ageing well. The best are Les Capitans, Les Mouilles-en-Bessey, Croix-Rouge. Also Le Fleurie, Le Morgon (of substance rather than spirit, and of rich garnet-colour) and Lebrouilly.

In the Romanèche-Thorins and Chenas regions, climatic variations produce the Moulin-à-Vent. It is either red or rosé; exceptional years were 1945 and 1947. I was forgetting Saint-Amour.

(b) Mâconnais

The chalky soil gives these wines (coming from the same vines as the Beaujolais) perhaps a greater firmness and generosity. They are white, red, even rosé: Mâcon, Aligoté, Milly-Lamartine, Pouilly (various). Best of all are the Pouilly-Vinzelles and Pouilly-Loche and, especially estimable, the Pouilly-Fuisé, a white wine of a beautiful greeny-gold colour, heady and exhilarating, combining dryness with suppleness.

(c) Châlonnais

The same type of soil more or less as the Mâconnais. A good white wine is the Rully (there is also a sparkling Rully). A red wine of class is Le Mercurey (Clos des Montaigus, Clos du Roi, Clos Voyen, Clos Marcilly, Clos Fourneaux, etc). And joyous rivals of Rully and Mercurey are Givry and Montagny.

And now to the

Grands Bourgognes

Two wondrous successions of wine-clad slopes, with Beaune and Nuits Saint-Georges as 'capitals', are responsible for such a variety of noble vintages that it is not possible to do much more than list them without comment. But never mind, they are so well known that their names speak for themselves.

COTE DE BEAUNE: Santenay, Volney, Savigny, Beaune, Corton, Pommard.

COTE DE NUITS: Nuits Saint-Georges, Vosne-Romanée, Romanée-Conti, Romanée Saint-Vivant, Richebourg, Echezeaux, Clos-de-Vougeot (not as it is so often incorrectly styled, Clos Vougeot), Chambolle and Musigny, Bonnes-Mares; Gevrey-Chambertin, Clos du Tart. All these are red. For the whites: Meursault, Chassagne-Montrachet, the various Chablis (superb with oysters).

Saint-Pourçain Wine

Better known in other days, rather regrettably forgotten, these are the product of some of France's most ancient vineyards. For the Phoenicians planted the first vines ever to grow on the hills overhanging the Sioule and the Bouble (its tributary). The Saint-Pourçains are produced over six thousand acres of a plantation stretching from Moulins to Saint-Bonnet de Rochefort, taking in forty-six parishes.

The red is a full-blooded wine, the white is crystalline and of delicate bouquet.

Wines of Provence

Are red, white or rosé, light and pleasant wines of which the best known, perhaps, is Porquerolles rosé.

Rhône Valley Wines

Roussette grape vines (of the same excellent stock as the Haute-Savoie ones) clothe the Côtes du Rhône, a highly notable product of which is a very sound white wine, Hermitage or Ermitage. But the king of them all, from Orange to Avignon, is the result of blending a veritable motley of grape varieties (but all flourishing on the same clay-and-chalk soils that the vine enjoys)—the Châteauneuf-du-Pape. It is ruby-red, rich in alcoholic content, and improves with age. Over on the other side of the Rhône on the right bank, that is on the slopes of gravelly hills, grows the Tavel, a somewhat pungent rosé which becomes more even and velvety as it ages, and may be appreciated at two stages of existence: when young (and cool) with hors d'œuvre; when older (and at room temperature) with the roast.

Farther south, towards the sea-coast, is the renowned Cassis (white wine), incomparable accompaniment of Bouillabaisse.

Languedoc Light Wines

In the Hérault there are vineyards covering about 2,500 acres between Montpellier and Béziers and producing the splendid white wine known as Clairette[1] de Languedoc—white verging on golden, and used in the manufacture of really good vermouths. This is just right with the heavily-seasoned dishes of the region, and is drunk at cellar temperature.

[1] Clairette is not claret—it originally meant light-red sparkling wines, but not claret as known in this country.

Bordeaux Wines

Here (as with the rival Burgundies) we must subdivide. The Gironde produces wines of all possible colours and varieties—red, white, dry, sweet, mellow, syrupy, foaming, etc. The Bordeaux vineyards are, indeed, without their like on the face of the globe. The Bordeaux may be set into five groups:

(a) Medoc

A triangle bounded by the sea and the Garonne encloses the territory of the major red wines. Haut Médoc beats Médoc. There is Château-Margaux and fifty or more satellite vintages. There is Saint-Julien and its accompanying Châteaux—Léoville-las-Cases, Léoville-Poyferré, Léoville-Barton, Gloria, Gruaud-Larose, Talbot. There are the Pauliac: Château Latour, Château Mouton-Rothschild, Château Lafite-Rothschild. Saint Estèphe has less body but often more richness than the Pauliacs that are such near neighbours. Examples: Clos d'Estournel and Château Montrose.

(b) Graves

The Graves district is spread all along the left bank of the Garonne, from the river's edge to the Landes forests. The red Graves (the best) are robust and powerful, the best known of these being Haut-Brion. Others are: Château Pape-Clément, Château la Mission, Haut Brion, Chateau Haut-Bailly, and Domaine du Chevalier.

White Graves, more usually encountered, offer among others, Haut-Brion and Château-Virelade.

(c) Saint-Emilion

Grown on the calcareous soils of the Dordogne's right bank. One of the finest wines of France, and thirty-two districts share the honour of producing it. It is the only Bordeaux that might (from afar) be taken for a Burgundy. From many justly famous names, we select: Château Ausone and Château Cheval Blanc.

(d) Sauternes

South of Langon, left bank of the Garonne. Velvety white wines of good bouquets. Five districts (including Barsac) produce it. The most sumptuous of all, all gold and amber, is the Château d'Yquem.

(e) Various Bordeaux

We must not overlook the Fronsac vineyards (near Libourne); Saint Croix du Mont: and, between the Garonne and the Dordogne Entre

Deux Mers—not invariably a white wine, as there are some full-bodied and well-coloured reds among them. The white wines are mellow (Saint-Macaire, Sainte-Foy) as is also the Cérons (very near to the Graves).

And as for all the Wines not mentioned . . .

There are all the little local wines, so enjoyable, so full of vivacity; and others which are not easy to fit into the broad geographical classification just made, but which are no less magnificent for that: Blanquette de Limoux, from the white grapes that turn slowly golden on the hills of Limousin; Dalou white wine and Varilhès red, both of Ariège. Then we have Cornas d'Ardèche (red) and from the same region the sparkling Saint Péray. Auvergne has its Chanturgue, used in the preparation of an exceedingly toothsome 'coq au vin'. And among so many others are the white Riceys, favoured by Louis XIV, the wines of Bar-sur-Aube, Javernant, Laines-aux-Bois; those of Saint-Pantaléon (Drôme), and of Die.

The dinner waits!

Take your places at table. Never, if you can so arrange things, more than eight or ten, and never less than four. Then the meal should be pleasant indeed.

People who indulge in private colloquies at table are heart-scalds. So are talkers of politics. The topics are provided by the food set before you, and even then there is no need to expatiate. Sparkling wit can keep to go with the coffee.

The quality of the dishes will be enhanced by attractive surroundings and appurtenances; never overlook such factors. A cloth of more than ordinary whiteness, with flowers—a few arranged on its surface are better than vases, which get in everybody's way—with fine cutlery and table china; crystal glass; good lighting; all have something to contribute to the wholesome joys of elegant self-indulgence.

Table dispositions, of course, vary from land to land. In France, the forks are on the left of the plates and their pointed ends touch the cloth. Knives, fish-knives and spoons are on the right. Above the plates the dessert spoon and fork lie horizontally. This is pretty general, but *autres pays, autres mœurs.* Allow a good amount of space between the places, for eating is not enjoyable when adjoining guests jostle one another.

The thinner the glass, the rarer the drink. But do, for goodness' sake, bear in mind that a display of six or eight glasses at each place is old-fashioned practice. All that will be required are the large glass for water and a capacious wineglass (which will naturally be changed when a new wine is brought on). For the wine, balloon-shaped glasses, of course, and for champagne too, as it is no longer *de rigueur*, I am pleased to say, to use 'cups' or extra-tall 'flute' glasses for it.

The host and hostess, when you are receiving at home, sit facing each other half-way down the table, in France, and at the two ends of the table in England. The order of precedence is then:

For women guests:

(1) Right of host.
(2) Left of host.
(3) Right of the right-hand neighbour of hostess.
(4) Left of left-hand neighbour of hostess.
And so on.

For men guests:

(1) Right of hostess.
(2) Left of hostess.
And so on.

Works of etiquette-instruction, of honest intention and hair-splitting puerility, will give you plenty of information concerning conduct at table—and precepts which you must studiously ignore. They condemn, for instance, forearms on the table; picking up food with the fingers; dipping one's bread in the gravy. But I say that there is nothing better than a fowl's drumstick or a lobster's claw, or a stick of asparagus, held in the fingers to be nibbled at and stripped. Or even chip-potatoes. And provided there is no successful politician present—provided you are in good company free of stupid snobbery and starchy formality—the hostess herself will indicate that this is a meal unspoiled by ridiculous taboos. Need I insist that it is quite possible to pick a bone in a delicate fashion without looking like a cannibal gnawing at a clergyman's tibia. Besides, finger-bowls are there for use, not to quench the dog's thirst, or yours.

I defy any man to do justice to a Homard à l'Américaine without raising his table-napkin to collar level. You need an unworried approach and a well-protected necktie if certain dishes are to be thoroughly enjoyed. If you, as hostess, are determined that all your guests shall keep their napkins on their knees (see 'Instructions for Urbane Diners') give them cold veal. It's safe.

Do not allow smoking before coffee. It is unworthy of a gourmet. And if you spot any individual adding water to one of your vintage wines, two courses are open to you. Let your temperament dictate your choice. You may merely decide then and there that he shall never darken your doors again, or you may have him ejected forthwith. Your reputation will thereby be enhanced.

Sunday
Menus

Luncheons

Fruits de mer
Mauviettes à la minute
Croquettes de pommes de terre
Salade de laitue
Fromages
Crêpes flambées au Grand Marnier

*

Cervelle d'agneau beurre noisette
Filet de bœuf rôti fermière
Fromages
Gâteau de riz aux abricots

*

Crevettes avec beurre
Choucroute Alsacienne
Fromages
Tarte aux pommes

*

Maquereaux marinés
Noix de veau braisée
Nouilles au beurre
Salade M.C.B.
Gâteau au chocolat Madeleine Decure

Dinners

Velouté Parmentier
Soufflé au fromage
Salade scarole
Fromages
Tarte à l'ananas

*

Consommé de volaille
Poule au riz
Salade d'endives
Fromages
Beignets de pommes

*

Crème de champignons
Truite Meunière
Salade russe
Fromages
Pommes Bonne-Femme

*

Crème de lentilles
Poulet sauté Marengo
Pieds de céleri au jus
Fromages
Crème anglaise vanille

Luncheons

Shellfish hors d'œuvre
Larks cooked in butter
Potato croquettes
Lettuce salad
Cheeses, various
Pancakes (ignited with Grand Marnier)

*

Lambs' brains cooked in butter, with lemon
Roast beef fillet with mixed vegetable garnish
Cheeses
Rice with apricots

*

Shrimps with butter
Alsace choucroute
Cheeses
Apple tart

*

Soused mackerel
Braised veal (pope's eye)
Noodles in butter sauce
C.B.C. Salad (corn-salad, beetroot, celery)
Madeleine Decure chocolate cake (egg almond and chocolate cake, see p. 324)

Dinners

Potato soup
Cheese soufflé
Endive salad
Cheeses
Pineapple tart

*

Chicken soup
Boiled fowl with rice
Chicory salad
Cheeses
Potato fritters

*

Cream of mushroom soup
Grilled trout
Russian salad
Cheeses
Baked apple (with gooseberry jelly)

*

Cream of lentil soup
Sauté chicken (in oil with tomato purée and mushrooms)
Celery cooked in gravy
Cheeses
Vanilla egg custard

Luncheons

Merlans au gratin
Gigot froid sauce rémoulade
Salade de cresson
Fromages
Galette feuilletée et gelée de groseilles

*

Escargots de Bourgogne
Noix de veau rôtie
Endives braisées
Fromages
Pommes en robe

*

Thon à l'huile, olives, laitue, œufs durs et tomates
Tripes à la mode de Caen
Salade
Fromages
Nègre en chemise

*

Raie au beurre noir
Côtes d'agneau grillées
Salade d'endives
Fromages
Tarte Tatin

Dinners

Lotte à la crème
Macaroni au gratin
Fromages
Gaufres

*

Consommé vermicelle
Pot-au-feu
(viande et légumes)
Salade de mâche
Fromages
Pruneaux

*

Velouté de lentilles
Omelette au lard
Salade de pissenlits aux œufs durs
Fromages
Salade d'oranges

*

Velouté Parmentier aux croûtons
Beignets de Langoustines
Laitues braisées
Fromages
Gâteau de riz au caramel

Luncheons

Whiting (breadcrumbs and grated cheese)
Watercress salad
Cheeses
Flaky pastries with jellied gooseberries

*

Snails, Burgundy fashion
Roast veal
Braised endive
Cheeses
Baked apple dumplings

*

Tunny fish in oil (with olives, lettuce, hard-boiled eggs, tomatoes)
Caen tripe
Salad
Cheeses

*

Skate with black butter sauce
Grilled lamb chops
Endive or chicory salad
Cheeses
Apple pie, pastry *base* only

Dinners

Burbot, creamed
Macaroni in cheese sauce
Cheeses
Waffles

*

Vermicelli soup
Hot-pot (meat and vegetable)
Corn salad (Lamb's lettuce)
Cheeses
Stewed prunes

*

Lentil soup (smooth)
Bacon omelette
Dandelion and hard-boiled egg salad
Orange salad

*

Potato soup, creamed, with fried bread cubes
Norway lobster fritters
Braised lettuce
Cheeses
Rice with caramel sauce

Luncheons

Salade russe
Canard à l'orange
Laitue à la crème
Fromages
Gâteau surprise

*

Sole Meunière
Steak au poivre
Pommes soufflées
Cresson
Crème renversée au chocolat

*

Friture d'éperlans
Poulet cocotte
Fonds d'artichauts
Camembert
Soufflé au Grand Marnier

*

Morue, pommes de terre et œufs durs à l'aïolî
Croûte aux champignons
Pois mange-tout au beurre
Fromages
Gâteau de riz

Dinners

Velouté de céleri
Chevreau rôti, pommes sautées
Pissenlits au lard
Fromages
Petits pots de crème au café

*

Soupe à l'oignon gratinée
Œufs Meurette
Cresson
Petits Suisses
Biscuits de Savoie

*

Consommé d'abatis
Queue de bœuf à la Bourguignonne
Fromage Epoisse
Tarte alsacienne

*

Potage crème de moules
Œufs pochés avec épinards
Oignons farcis au maigre
Salade d'endives et betteraves
Fromages
Flan allemand

Luncheons

Russian salad
Duck with orange
Creamed lettuce[1]
Cheeses
Surprise cake (a moulded cream sponge, *see* p. 318)

*

Grilled sole
Peppered steak
Soufflé potatoes
Watercress
Custard mould with chocolate sauce

*

Fried smelts
Stew-pan chicken
Artichoke bottoms
Camembert cheese
Grand Marnier soufflé

*

Cod, potato and garlic-flavoured hard-boiled eggs
Mushrooms in vol-au-vent pastry
Buttered whole peas
Cheeses
Rice cake

Dinners

Cream of celery soup
Roast Kid with sauté potatoes
Dandelions with thin bacon strips
Cheeses
Coffee cream pots

*

Onion soup with grated cheese
Eggs
Watercress
Cream cheeses
Sponge cakes

*

Giblet soup
Oxtail, Burgundy style
Epoisse cheese
Alsace tart (sweet pastry, apples, eggs, cinnamon)

*

Cream of mussel soup
Poached egg with spinach
Stuffed onions (meatless for Lent)
Chicory and beetroot salad
German flan

1 For creamed salads see page 285 (Creamed Lettuce).

Luncheons

Œufs mayonnaise et laitue au cerfeuil
Navarin printanier
Fromages
Tarte à la rhubarbe

*

Crevettes grises au beurre
Gigot d'agneau rôti
Purée mousseline
Salade de laitue à la crème
Beignets aux pommes

*

Alose rôtie
Canelloni sauce tomate
Asperges
Fromages
Moka

*

Cervelles au beurre noir
Entrecôte Béarnaise
Laitues braisées au jus
Fromages
Beignets de fleurs d'acacia

Dinners

Crème de laitue
Jambon aux èpinards sauce Madère
Fromages
Soufflé Normand

*

Potages aux herbes
Viandes froides
Salade de romaine
Fromages
Crème renversée au citron

*

Crème de champignons
Selle d'agneau Orléanaise
Cœurs de romaine
Fromages
Meringues crème Chantilly

*

Potage Parmentier aux croûtons
Truites Meunière
Cœurs de laitue à la crème
Fromages
Crème anglaise

Luncheons

Egg mayonnaise with lettuce and chervil
Spring stew (mutton, vegetables, etc.)
Cheese
Rhubarb tart

*

Shrimps and butter
Roast leg of lamb
Mashed potatoes
Creamed lettuce salad
Apple fritters

*

Baked shad
Canelloni with tomato sauce
Asparagus
Cheeses
Mocha cake

*

Brains in black butter
Ribs of beef, Béarnaise
Braised lettuce in gravy
Cheese
Acacia flower fritters (*see* p. 313)

Dinners

Cream of Lettuce
Ham and spinach with Madeira sauce
Cheeses
Normandy soufflé (pear, egg and apple cream mould, as described on p. 328)

*

Herb soup (sorrel, chervil, lettuce, purslain, etc.)
Cold meats, assorted
Cos lettuce salad
Cheeses
Lemon cream sponge

*

Cream of mushroom soup
Saddle of mutton (Orleans fashion)
Lettuce hearts
Cheeses
Meringues Chantilly, sweet cream

*

Potato soup with fried bread cubes
Trout (grilled)
Lettuce hearts (creamed)
Cheeses
Individual custards

Luncheons

Omelette au thon
Côtelette de mouton grillée
Pommes nouvelles persillées
Salade
Oranges, noix

*

Colin froid mayonnaise
Filet de bœuf rôti
Epinards en branches
Fromage Pont-l'Evêque
Fruits

*

Soles Meunière
Entrecôte Bordelaise
Pommes soufflés
Salade de laitue
Fromage de Camembert
Tarte aux fraises

*

Alose Bercy
Gigot d'agneau rôti
Pommes nouvelles sautées
Coulommiers double-crème
Baba au rhum

Dinners

Soupe Normande
Sole grillée
Pommes à l'anglaise
Salade de laitues Mimosa
Gâteau de riz au caramel

*

Potage Pélou
Poulet rôti
Salade de cresson
Mousse au chocolat

*

Potage Crécy
Carré de porc rôti pommes frites
Fromages
Crème anglaise

*

Pamplemousse
Gigot froid mayonnaise
Carottes nouvelles
Fromage de Cantal
Brioche et confitures

Luncheons

Tunny omelette
Grilled mutton cutlet
New potatoes with parsley
Salad
Oranges and walnuts

*

Cold pollack, mayonnaise
Roast fillet of beef
Leaf spinach
Pont l'Evêque cheese
Fruit

*

Sole, grilled with butter
Rib steaks, Bordelaise style
Soufflé potatoes
Lettuce salad
Camembert cheese
Strawberry tart

*

'Bercy' shad
Roast leg of lamb
Sauté new potatoes
Coulommiers double-cream cheese
Rum baba

Dinners

Turnip, leek and carrot soup
Grilled sole
Boiled potatoes
Mimosa lettuce salad
Caramel rice

*

Pelou soup (radish leaf, nutmeg, etc.)
Roast chicken
Watercress salad
Chocolate mousse

*

Crecy soup (carrot and cream of rice)
Loin of pork (roast) and chip potatoes
Cheeses
Custard moulds

*

Grapefruit
Cold mutton (leg) and mayonnaise
Young carrots
Brioches with jam

Luncheons

Cœurs d'artichauts mayonnaise
Caneton rôti
Petits pois à la Française
Fromages
Œufs à la neige

*

Langoustines
Selle d'agneau
Haricots verts
Fromages
Tarte aux fraises

*

Concombres, tomates
Sauté de veau champignons
Pommes de terre au beurre
Fromages
Fraises à la crème

*

Tête de veau fines herbes
Pigeons rôtis
Petits pois
Salade romaine
Fromages
Fruits

Dinners

Bouillon de légumes vermicelle
Colin poché beurre fondu
Asperges sauce mousseline
Fromages
Fruits

*

Soupe fermière
Cervelle d'agneau lyonnaise
Petits pois à la Française
Fromages
Crème Chantilly, Gaufrettes

*

Potage cressonnière
Coquilles Saint-Jacques sautées
Haricots verts persillés
Fromages
Fruits

*

Soupe à l'oseille
Œuf à la coque
Pommes de terre sautées
Salade de laitue à la crème
Fromages
Gâteau Toulousain

Luncheons

Artichoke hearts and mayonnaise
Roast duckling
Garden peas
Cheeses
Egg Snow

*

Norway lobsters
Saddle of lamb
Runner beans
Cheeses
Strawberry tart

*

Cucumber and tomatoes
Veal sauté with mushrooms
Potatoes with butter
Cheeses
Strawberries and cream

*

Calf's head with herbs
Roast pigeons
Green peas
Cos lettuce salad
Cheeses
Fruit

Dinners

Vegetable and vermicelli broth
Poached cod with melted butter
Asparagus with mousseline sauce
Cheeses
Fruit

*

Mixed vegetable soup
Lambs' brains, Lyon fashion
Garden peas
Cheeses
Sweetened whipped cream and wafers

*

Watercress soup
Scallops au gratin
Runner beans with parsley
Cheeses
Fruits

*

Sorrel soup
Boiled eggs
Sauté potatoes
Creamed lettuce salad
Cheeses
Toulouse cake (eggs and almonds, *see* p. 323)

Luncheons

Melon
Poule en daube
Jardinière
Fromage blanc à la crème
Tarte aux abricots

*

Carrelets au gratin
Noix de veau rôtie
Ratatouille Niçoise
Fromage de chèvre
Tarte aux cerises

*

Friture d'éperlans
Epaule de mouton braisée
Flageolets à la crème
Salade romaine
Fromage 'à la feuille'
Choux crème Chantilly
Fruits

*

Pieds de mouton poulette
Pintade rôtie
Haricots verts au beurre
Fromage de Camembert
Fraises des bois, framboises et groseilles au sirop

Dinners

Soupe aux fèves
Tronçon de colin boulangère
Salade de laitue
Fromage de Brie
Abricots au riz

*

Crème de tomates
Cuisses de grenouilles Provençales
Petits pois
Salade romaine
Fromage de Gournay
Compote de prunes

*

Soupe Garbure
Noix de veau à la gelée
Salade de légumes mayonnaise
Cœurs à la crème

*

Œufs brouillés aux tomates
Foie de veau braisé
Aubergines en beignets
Salade de cresson
Fromages
Fruits refraîchis au kirsch

Luncheons

Melon
Braised chicken
Mixed vegetables
Cream cheese
Apricot tart

*

Dabs au gratin
Roast veal
Stew, Nice fashion
Goats' milk cheese
Cherry tart

*

Fried smelts
Braised shoulder of mutton
Creamed flageolets (small kidney beans)
Cos lettuce salad
Wrapped cheeses
Chantilly cream buns
Fruit

*

Sheep's trotters with parsley sauce
Roast guinea-fowl
Green beans with butter
Camembert cheese
Wild strawberries with raspberries, and gooseberries in syrup

Dinners

Bean soup
Cod steaks (Bonne Femme) *see* p. 106.
Lettuce salad
Brie cheese
Apricots and rice

*

Cream of tomato soup
Frogs' legs Provence fashion
Green peas
Cos lettuce salad
Gournay cheese
Stewed prunes

*

Garbure soup (bacon, goose fat, cabbage)
Jellied veal
Vegetable salad, mayonnaise
Cream 'hearts'

*

Scrambled eggs and tomatoes
Braised calves' liver
Eggplant fritters
Watercress salad
Cheeses
Fruits in kirsch

Luncheons

Carpe à la Juive
Gigot d'agneau boulangère
Haricots verts
Fromage Pont-l'Evêque
Fruits variés

*

Melon
Escalope à la crème
Girolles
Salade laitue
Fromage de Cantal
Flan Joséphine Baker

*

Artichauts rémoulade
Brochet sauce câpres
Pommes sautées
Chicorée frisée
Fromages
Mille-feuilles

*

Crabes à la mayonnaise
Sauté d'agneau forestière
Fromage Gruyère
Glace et gaufrettes

Dinners

Consommé froid
Croûte aux champignons
Viande froide salade
Fromage 'à la feuille'
Glace Framboise

*

Potage Julienne au riz
Tomates farcies
Fromage blanc à la crème

*

Potage à l'oseille
Vol-au-vent
Petits pois à l'anglaise
Fromage Roquefort
Brioche mousseline au sabayon

*

Potage aux tomates
Turbot farci
Haricots verts persillés
Fromages variés
Crêpes Suzette

Luncheons

Carp (Jewish style)
Roast leg of lamb
Kidney beans
Pont l'Evêque cheese
Assorted fruits

*

Melon
Creamed veal collop
Chanterelles (mushrooms)
Lettuce salad
Kirsch, chartreuse and banana pie

*

Artichokes with rémoulade sauce
Pike with caper sauce
Sauté potatoes
Curled chicory
Cheeses
Flaky pastries

*

Mayonnaise of crab
Sauté lamb
Gruyère cheese
Ices with wafers

Dinners

Cold clear soup
Mushroom tartlets
Cold meat and salad
Wrapped cheese
Raspberry ices

*

Rice Julienne soup
(mixed vegetables)
Stuffed tomatoes
Cream cheese

*

Sorrel soup
Vol-au-vent
Green peas with mint
Roquefort cheese
Brioches with cream and egg and wine sauce

*

Tomato soup
Stuffed turbot
Green beans with parsley
Assorted cheeses
Pancakes Suzette (*see* p. 314)

Luncheons

Harengs grillés sauce moutarde
Entrecôte Bretonne
Jardinière
Fromage blanc
Fruits

*

Crevettes au beurre
Côtelettes de porc sauce piquante
Purée de pommes de terre
Salade
Camembert
Compôte de mirabelles

*

Perdreaux rôtis
Pommes paille
Cèpes à la Bordelaise
Roquefort avec beurre
Soufflé au Grand Marnier

*

Sardines grillées
Civet de lièvre
Pommes vapeur
Salade de laitue
Livarot
Fruits rafraîchis

Dinners

Bouillon haricots au vermicelle
Œufs au bacon
Aubergines farcies
Salade de laitue
Crème renversée au caramel

*

Consommé perles du Japon
Queue de bœuf sauce tomate
Artichauts à la crème vinaigrée
Munster
Pommes Bonne-Femme

*

Consommé Tapioca
Œufs brouillés aux girolles
Salade Scarole et céleri en branches
Fromage blanc à la crème
Tarte aux reines-claudes

*

Potage jardinière
Brochet beurre blanc
Cèpes à la crème
Roquefort
Cantaloup

Luncheons

Grilled herrings and mustard sauce
Beef ribs, Breton style
Mixed vegetables
Cream cheese
Fruit

*

Shrimps in butter
Pork chops with sharp sauce
Potato purée
Salad
Camembert cheese
Stewed mirabelle plums

*

Roast partridge
Potato straws
'Flap mushrooms' (Bordeaux style)
Roquefort and butter
Grand Marnier soufflé

*

Grilled sardines
Jugged hare
Steamed potatoes
Lettuce salad
Livarot cheese (of Calvados)
Fresh fruit salad

Dinners

Beans and vermicelli broth
Eggs and bacon
Stuffed egg plants
Lettuce salad
Caramel cream

*

Pearl barley soup
Oxtail and tomato sauce
Artichokes with butter
and vinegar sauce
Munster cheese
Baked apples

*

Tapioca soup
Scrambled eggs with chanterelles
Endive and celery salad
Cream cheese
Victoria plum tart

*

Mixed vegetable soup
Pike with melted butter
Creamed 'flap' mushrooms
Roquefort and cheese
Canteloupe melon

Luncheons

Matelote d'anguille
Faux-filet rôti
Pommes Duchesse
Fromages
Gâteau au potiron

*

Coques rémoulade
Perdrix aux choux
Salade de chicorée
Fromages
Baklavas

*

Œufs en gelée
Poularde Bonne-Femme
Artichauts farcis à la barigoule
Salade
Fromages
Tarte aux raisins

*

Pâte de campagne
Epaule de mouton Bretonne
Salade de laitue
Fromages
Poires glacées au Grand Marnier

Dinners

Huîtres et coquillages variés
Cèpes Bordelaise
Rôti froid, salade de laitue
Fromages
Moka au café

*

Consommé vermicelle
Langue de bœuf sauce suprême
Macédoine de légumes
Fromages
Pain perdu

*

Consommé de volailles
Coquilles Saint-Jacques au gratin
Salade de romaine
Fromages
Gelée d'ananas

*

Potage au potiron
Œufs mollets — épinards
Viandes froides
Salade
Fromages
Marrons bouillis

Luncheons

Eel stew (with herbs, onion, wine)
Roast sirloin
Egg and potato croquettes
Cheese
Pumpkin pie

*

Cockles with remoulade sauce
Partridge and cabbage
Chicory Salad
Cheeses
Honey, almond and pistachio cakes (*see* p. 320)

*

Jellied eggs
Roast fowl, country style
Stuffed artichokes (mushroom, bacon, shallot, etc.)
Salad
Cheeses
Black and white grape tart

*

Meat, sausage and shallot pie
Shoulder of mutton, Breton style
Lettuce salad
Cheeses
Glazed pears with Grand Marnier

Dinners

Oysters, and other shellfish
Bordeaux 'flap' mushrooms
Cold joint with lettuce salad
Cheeses
Mocha (coffee cake)

*

Vermicelli soup
Ox tongue and supreme sauce
Mixed vegetables
Cheese
Rich bread pudding

*

Chicken or game soup
Scallops au gratin
Cos lettuce salad
Cheeses
Pineapple jelly

*

Pumpkin soup
Poached eggs on spinach
Cold meats
Salad
Cheeses
Boiled chestnuts

Luncheons

Céleri rémoulade
Thon à l'huile
Côtelettes de mouton
Fromage de chèvre
Tarte aux marrons

*

Fruits de mer variés
Faisan rôti sur canapé
Pommes paille
Salade de cresson
Fromages
Saint-Honoré

*

Crevettes au beurre
Lapereau de garenne à la moutarde
Pommes persillées
Salade Beaucaire
Fromages
Tarte aux poires

*

Fonds d'artichauts à la macédoine de légumes
Poule au riz
Fromages
Mousse au chocolat
Langues de chat

Dinners

Consommé
Faux-filet grillé
Pommes gaufrettes
Fromages
Macédoine de fruits rafraîchis

*

Velouté de laitue
Cervelle de veau Cadichonne
Pommes persillées
Salade verte
Fromages
Pain à la noix

*

Huîtres
Filets de sole aux moules
Petits pois
Salade
Fromages
Choux à la crème

*

Consommé tapioca
Omelettes fines herbes
Salade
Fromages
Pudding aux avelines

Luncheons

Celery and remoulade sauce
Tunny in oil
Mutton cutlets
Goats' milk cheese
Chestnut tart

*

Assorted shellfish
Roast pheasant on toast
Potato straws
Watercress salad
Cheese
Saint Honoré pastries
(glazed buns, preserved fruit garnish)

*

Shrimps in butter
Young wild rabbit, mustard sauce
Potatoes with chopped parsley
Beaucaire salad
(celery, endive, apple, etc.)
Cheeses
Pear tart

*

Artichoke bottoms with mixed vegetable garnish
Fowl with rice
Cheeses
Chocolate mousse
Finger biscuits

Dinners

Clear soup
Grilled sirloin
Wafer potatoes
Cheeses
Fresh fruit salad

*

Cream of lettuce soup
Calves' brains
Potatoes with parsley
Green salad
Cheeses
Walnut cake (*see* p. 323)

*

Oysters
Fillet of sole with mussels
Green peas
Salad
Cheese
Cream buns

*

Tapioca soup
Green herb omelettes
Salad
Cheeses
Hazel-nut pudding (*see* p. 322)

Luncheons

Moules marinières
Foie de veau maître d'hôtel
Pommes chips
Cresson
Fromages
Crêpes à la confiture

*

Terrine de lièvre
Matelote d'anguille
Nouilles au beurre
Salade de laitue
Fromages
Poires au sirop

*

Filets de harengs à l'huile et au beurre
Côte de porc charcutière
Pommes purée
Fromages
Salade d'oranges

*

Champignons à la Grecque
Tournedos Béarnaise
Pommes paille
Salade de chicorée
Fromages
El Mistouf

Dinners

Potage Julienne
Dindonneau rôti
Endives braisées
Fromages
Riz au lait

*

Crème de pois cassés
Langue de veau braisée Duchesse
Salade M.C.B.
Fromages
Rigollots à la confiture

*

Velouté au céleri
Escalopes de ris de veau panées
Pommes soufflés
Salade de cresson
Fromages
Tarte à l'ananas

*

Crème de mollusques
Epaule de mouton rôtie
Salsifis en beignets
Salade de mâche
Fromages
Crème à la Vierge

Luncheons

Mussels with onion sauce
Calves' liver
Chip potatoes
Watercress
Cheeses
Pancakes with jam

*

Potted hare
Stewed eels in wine
Noodles in butter
Lettuce salad
Cheeses
Pears in syrup

*

Herring fillets in oil and butter
Spare-rib of pork
Potato purée
Cheeses
Orange salad

*

Greek-style mushrooms
Fillet steak, Béarn fashion
Potato straws
Chicory salad
Cheeses
El Mistouf (*see* p. 322)

Dinners

Vegetable soup
Roast young turkey
Braised endive
Cheeses
Rice and milk pudding

*

Cream of peas
Braised calf's tongue
C.B.C. salad (corn-salad, beetroot, celery)
Cheeses
Jam 'plasters' ('Rigollots', *see* p. 323)

*

Cream of celery soup
Sweetbread scallops (fried in egg and breadcrumbs)
Soufflé potatoes
Watercress salad
Cheeses
Pineapple tart

*

Cream of shellfish soup
Roast shoulder of mutton
Salsify fritters
Corn-salad
Cheeses
Kirsch cream

LITTLE LEXICON

This is a brief selection of words that will be useful to housewives following French recipes, and some often appear on menus to describe the cooking process or the garnish one may expect.

French Word	*English equivalent*	*Explanation*
ABAISSE	(*a*) UNDERCRUST (*b*) PASTRY rolled out thinly	Flaky, short, puff, etc., pastry rolled or 'lowered into a flat disc'.
APPAREIL	'APPARATUS' only in sense of assemblage of ingredients for one dish.	A quick way of indicating, in recipes, 'the dish so far as we have taken it'.
BARDER	to BARD	Put lardons or narrow strips or thin slices o bacon or even fat pork on meat before cooking (*see* Lardon).

French word	*English equivalent*	*Explanation*
BLANCHIR	(*a*) to BLANCH (almonds, etc.). (*b*) to SCALD (meat, leaves, etc.).	The process varies, as any English cookery book will demonstrate.
BOUILLON	(*a*) STOCK (*b*) MEAT BROTH (usually BOUILLON GRAS) As process, to cook à petits bouillons=to simmer à gros bouillons=to boil rapidly, with big bubbles.	A word to 'feel' in its context rather than to translate.
DARNE	SLICE, STEAK, SLAB	Often means a 'fish steak'. Always means a rather thick slice. A *darne* should be cut with the bone, a *suprême* not.
DEGLACER	to UNGLAZE, UNCONGEAL	No one word is satisfactory. It means to thin and dilute with wine or stock or other boiling liquid the matter in which meat, etc., has browned.
DEGORGER	to STEEP	Soak, for varying periods, to remove impurities.
DEGRAISSER	to (*a*) SKIM (*b*) TRIM	In both senses, removing unwanted fat, cooked or uncooked, solid or liquid.
EMINCER	to SLICE	Not mince, which is *hâcher*, *hâcher menu*. Yesterday's meat sliced and served in a thick sauce is called *émincé* sometimes.

French word	*English equivalent*	*Explanation*
ESCALOPER	to CUT MEAT IN THIN, EVEN SLICES (by extension, cut mushrooms, shellfish, etc., similarly).	Remote from the 'scallop-shell' meanings, only by usage.
FONCER	to LINE BOTTOM OF MOULD, CASSEROLE, etc.	Originally a technical word meaning to put in the actual cask or vessel base.
FRAISER	to KNEAD	Means also 'soften' or 'fold', but the context is all-important.
GLACER	(*a*) to ICE WITH ICING (*b*) to ENVELOP IN MEAT GLAZE (*c*) to FREEZE	A meat-glaze is the juice (gravy) extracted by long cooking and evaporation resulting in a jellifying consistency.
JULIENNE	JULIENNE is now adopted.	Mixture of vegetables, especially of small-chopped ones for soups or garnish.
LARDONS	LARDONS, LARDOONS, BASTING STRIPS	Usually of bacon. Applied to dry-natured meats, etc. and to spitted or oven-cooked ones likely to char outside before inside is done.
LIER	to THICKEN, or to MAKE a LIAISON, or BIND	Reinforce gravies, sauces, etc., by adding ingredients strongly affected by heat (such as egg yolk, certain cereals).

French word	*English equivalent*	*Explanation*
MACEDOINE	MEDLEY of FRUIT or VEGETABLES	It is in *Haute Cuisine* that fine distinctions are made when dealing with macédoine, julienne, brunoise, etc.
MANIER	to WORK, KNEAD	To 'work' dough, or butter. Not like kneading, the object of which is to distribute qualities, but a means of expelling water, whey, etc.
MARINADE	SOUSING, SOAKING, PICKLING LIQUIDS—a 'MARINADE'	'Leaving to soak' or to steep. We say 'to marinade' or 'to marinate', both are acceptable. Wine, vinegar, spices, oil are principal ingredients.
MASQUER	to MASK, or cover fairly lightly with cream, sauce, etc.	*Napper* is also (less academically) used for the process.
MATELOTE	loosely, STEW	See note at end of 'Sauté Veal' recipe on p. 206.
MIREPOIX	THICK MEAT-AND-VEGETABLE STOCK-SAUCE	Added to increase flavour. Usually a mixture of onions, carrots, celery, raw ham, cut in cubes, cooked in butter with bouquet garni. Cooked only to 'melting' or 'transparency' point.
MONDER	to HULL, BLANCH, or STONE	As case may be, almonds, raisins, etc.

French word	*English equivalent*	*Explanation*
MOUILLER	literally to 'MOISTEN'	Adding liquid in any required quantity to dish in preparation. To 'water', although any specified liquid will be named.
NAVARIN	MUTTON STEW WITH POTATOES AND TURNIPS	A ragoût, but of definitely expected contents.
PANER	to BREADCRUMB	With crisp or soft breadcrumbs. When '*à l'anglaise*' is added, it is usual to 'egg-and-breadcrumb'.
POCHER	to POACH, to COOK PARTIALLY in water without boiling.	Not strictly 'poaching' process; although water must boil first, it is usually allowed to go off the boil. A small-scale 'parboiling'.
REDUIRE	to REDUCE	Diminish bulk of sauce by evaporation—and automatically thicken its consistency.
SALMIS	SALMIS is the only accurate word.	(*a*) *Roast* game or poultry cut up and served in a sauce cooked separately. (*b*) The same, but roasting is only partial and cooking of cut pieces is completed in sauce, often at table with bain-marie (or similar).

I GENERAL

Index

Index

Index

II RECIPES

AS far as possible 'menu names' are listed here, e.g. Catalan whiting, Racouchot perch. 'Whiting', 'perch', etc., for general reference appear in the first section of Index, but this section gives regional treatments prominence.

Index